# MARVIN GAYE

## I Heard it through the Grapevine

### SHARON DAVIS

EDINBURGH AND LONDON

This book is dedicated to
Hazel Eagle

Copyright © Sharon Davis, 1991
The moral right of the author has been asserted

First published in Great Britain 1991 by
MAINSTREAM PUBLISHING COMPANY
(EDINBURGH) LTD
7 Albany Street
Edinburgh EH1 3UG

ISBN 1 84018 320 9

Reprinted 1992
This edition 2000

A catalogue record for this book is available from the British Library

Typeset in Garamond
Printed in Finland by WS Bookwell, 2000

# I HEARD IT THROUGH THE GRAPEVINE

# Contents

OK Marvin, what really happened?
Did you hurt your daddy?
Did you hurt him so much that he had to hurt you
That he didn't know what to do?

Come on, Marvin, I was your friend
Wasn't there something to tell me – before the end?

And I've tried so hard to talk to you
But you choose to ignore me, tho' you want to talk too.
I can't go any further – trying to explain
'Bout the hearts, and the love songs,
The hurt and the pain.

And my dear friend Marvin, who really cares?
Whether I really knew you – 'cos you were never theirs.

But my dear friend Marvin you will never demise
For as long as I live, you're a star in my eyes.

*Dotty Green*
*Singer/Composer*
*1989*

# Foreword

Marvin Gaye was a man of rare qualities. His work speaks for itself but away from the public glare he was complex, unpredictable yet an amusing and a charming man. He was, for the most part, an absolute gentleman in female company, an interested listener with a considerate manner and a sympathetic ear. He had few genuinely close friends and only a handful found a place in his heart. I wouldn't describe myself as one of those chosen few but he was always gracious to me during his stay in London. Sure, work had thrown us together, but when we clashed professionally we made the best of the situation, both knowing we had a job to do. Then we'd laugh about it.

When I first met Marvin I was pretty nervous because I'd been forewarned that he was a difficult man to relate to. Yep, it was initially an uphill struggle but the climb was worth every tiring step, and I hope I eventually gained his trust and respect.

This book would not have been conceived or accomplished without some invaluable assistance, but the instigator was Marvin himself who originally talked of the idea in 1981. Before we could work together our lives went separate ways so he never actually saw the project through to the end. Nonetheless, without his initial encouragement I probably never would have put pen to paper. I started work on the project in June 1982 but due to the publisher's policy the book's content was strictly confined to Marvin's professional life. Therefore much of my research, including ten years' worth of memorabilia, remained unused to collect dust, The book was published shortly after Marvin's death in 1984, and was on sale for six months before the publisher went into liquidation. My writing career really got off to a good start! Eventually the book's rights reverted to me and my original manuscript was resurrected – dust and all! – to form the basis of this book, alongside numerous newly conducted interviews and further extensive research.

The project wouldn't have been completed without two very special ladies, Martha Reeves and Kim Weston (oh! the hours we talked), who generously and freely gave me their help and time. Their dedication alone was an inspiration! For Martha to support this project is the greatest honour I could have wished for. My gratitude likewise extends to my family for organising their lives around this project during the most difficult of times; to Gill Trodd for keeping the faith and believing in me; Kay Rowley, my original editor and constant encourager; Dotty Green my loyal soulmate and Sandy Philpott for quietly being there. And to those who continually showed their love and support, Ingrid Maus, Michelle Fellows, Honor Head, Jaki Graham, Henry Sellers, Graham Canter, Dave Godin, Peter Prince, Bob Killbourn, Jeff Tarry, John Hassinger, Clive Richardson, Keith Russell, Jim Hegarty, Barry Murphy, Ian McCulley, Pete Scotney and my brothers and sisters in soul including my loyal readers – I wouldn't change you for the world! – too numerous to mention, but who know who they are.

Many thanks must also be extended to Dusty Springfield for sharing her Motown memories with me, *Blues & Soul* magazine for generously placing its entire operation at my disposal, likewise Motown's Gordon Frewin for his kind contributions and Motorcity Records' Ian Levine for sharing his organisation's assets (including his artists) with me. Finally, my utmost appreciation to the *Los Angeles Herald Examiner* and Margaret Douglas of the Los Angeles *Daily News* for allowing me access to their files, to the sources of information now unknown to me due to their names being lost through the passage of time, and to Mainstream Publishing, particularly Bill Campbell and Tim Binding, for supporting a project so dear to me.

This book was written with love.


*Sharon Davis*
*1990*

# | Introduction by Martha Reeves

I wish I could have been Marvin's help-mate, more like a Real Sister, not just a love-mate. My first encounter with Marvin Gaye was at Hitsville, USA, in 1961. As secretary, one of my jobs was to call musicians, awake them from their slumber, and get them to the Studio, to record all the wonderful Sounds of Motown. Marvin always answered the phone with a beautiful and warm voice, and called you 'Baby', like you wished to be called that again. I took special pride in calling the Musicians and even participated in the actual recordings. Marvin played drums, the way a singer wanted to hear them. Ask Smokey: he'll tell you how Marvin travelled as back-up-group-member. Marvin was occasionally prompt: if you told him 2 p.m., he might show up by 3.30. We willingly made allowances.

William Stevenson, known affectionately as 'Mickey', was a genius and first identified Marvin's talent. Harvey Fuqua and Berry Gordy sought to get a 'Hit' on Marvin. 'Hitch Hike', 'Pride And Joy' and 'Stubborn Kinda Fella', let the world know the adoration Rosalind Holmes, Annette Helton, and I felt for Marvin Gaye. In the days of Four-Track Recording Machines, we stood real close on just two microphones and *My Ears and Heart* told me I was hearing one of the finest voices I shall ever hear.

My book will tell more. I thank you, Sharon Davis, for the honour of participation here, and I appreciate and respect your opinions. You are a thoughtful and caring woman. God bless you.

*Martha Reeves*
*1991*

# 1. | Journey to the Sky

*Marvin was a rebel in a lot of ways . . . and wasn't quite as afraid of his father as the rest of us.*

(Frankie Gay)

*You have to lose the stigma of being a child of God.*

(Marvin Gaye)

*Marvin had a lot of class. He always dressed very well, even in school. He wasn't just your normal, everyday guy.*

(Sondra Lattisaw)

*It was an awful insult when you walk around and you got money and you can't eat.*

(Martha Reeves)

More than five thousand people queued in the damp cool evening on 4 April 1984 from Forest Lawn drive to the Chapel of the Hills to pay their last respects to Marvin Gaye whose body lay in an open coffin inside a white wooden chapel. Before the day ended an estimated thirty thousand people had filed past his white coffin in the flower-filled sanctuary. A further twenty thousand were turned away. Most of the mourners were fans, some were friends, others merely curious, dressed in jeans and sweatshirts, furs and jewellery. Most were black but there was no age limit as they waited patiently, many sobbing uncontrollably, as they viewed Marvin's body dressed in a military-styled uniform – an outfit he'd worn on his last American tour. The jacket was decorated in white and gold braid, the collar was white ermine. Not since the funerals of Clark Cable in 1960 and Jeannette McDonald five years earlier had so many mourners flocked to the cemetery's Church of the Hills in Hollywood Hills.

Marvin Gaye was hailed as one of the world's finest singers and composers, the prince of music; and during his reign of over twenty years his work inspired and delighted millions. Yet if he had been told this he'd have laughed and said the best was yet to come! Marvin Gaye was the epitome of sophisticated love, and he used the emotion in his music to capture the hearts of the world's lovers. He oozed an aura of sensuality which acted like a magnet to women who pined to be in his company, while men queued to shake his hand. His public believed him to be a man of the world, a hero of his race, a demi-god of all things good.

His life, however, was a contradiction. It fell short of the rags to riches story that befits so many of his ilk because his years of fame and fortune were not idyllic. Whenever he found happiness he attempted to destroy it. When he was successful, he mistrusted it. He was also unrealistic about everyday life, most aspects of his career, a bad judge of character and unreliable. However, there was one aspect of his personality that was utterly dependable – he could always be relied upon to speak his mind irrespective of the consequences. And he was always prepared to stand or fall on that premise. A middle-line attitude was definitely not one of his characteristics.

Gaye's complex life was aggravated by drug abuse, wild decisions and a destructive nature. On the other hand, the genius of the man was unquestioned by many. His intense commitment and devotion to his music was typified by his quest for perfection in everything he recorded, and no other artist has been able to imitate his voice or equal his imaginative mind. Even when Gaye's personal life was at its lowest, he was able to record some of the most sensitive music known to the modern world.

Marvin Gaye's early death brought a sudden end to a turbulent career that remained unfulfilled.

Most people accepted the fact that he would not live to a great age because of his regular drug intake but it was always presumed he would die from his own hand. He wasn't afraid of dying, he treated it in much the same way as most things in life – with caution, respect and courage.

The full extent of the tragedies and joys in his life, and the circumstances leading to his death on 1 April 1984, are only now beginning to fall into place and what follows is an attempt to present a fair and realistic account of his forty-four years, while acknowledging the darker, negative and unhappy side of his life. It is a Dr Jekyll and Mr Hyde story; the only difference being Marvin Gaye's story is true.

Marvin Pentz Gaye was the much-wanted first son of Alberta and Marvin Gay Snr, born in Washington D.C.'s Freedman's Hospital on 2 April 1939.

Washington D.C., America's capital, so named after the country's first president, George Washington, and where in 1800 the seat of American government was placed, was a prosperous city for its white population. Situated on the Potomac River, Washington D.C. was the first city in the world to be built specifically as a nation's capital, designed by Major Pierre Charles L'Enfant. The District of Columbia (D.C.) lies between Virginia and Maryland, approximately two hundred and twenty miles south-west of New York, and several hundred miles from Detroit, Michigan. Like most major American cities Washington D.C. was split into rich and poor areas, the black population confined to the latter. And it was in this environment that Marvin Gaye grew up.

He spent his first seventeen years living in a slum area which he called 'Simple City' on 1617 1st Street. His parents, Alberta, nick-named 'Babe', from North Carolina, and Marvin Snr from Kentucky, actually met in Washington D.C. and later married in 1935. The marriage began on a shaky footing when her husband insisted that her infant son, Michael, born from love but out of wedlock, be sent to live with an aunt, even though he longed for a son to carry on the family name. The Gays' first home was an apartment on 1st Street where they raised their family until their home was demolished in the mid-Fifties. They moved to another apartment at 10 Sixtieth Street in the East Capitol Dwellings. Marvin Gaye lived there with his sisters Jeanne and Zeola and younger brother Frankie. Family life differed little from others at this time although Marvin admitted he never enjoyed a 'normal' childhood due to his religious upbringing, his unhappy relationship with his father and the slum neighbourhood the family lived in. The situation was sorely aggravated because his mother harboured a secret dread of future heartache as she told author David Ritz in *Divided Soul* – 'My father was a violent man who shot my mother. Mama survived, but the fear still lives inside me. My father died in a hospital for the insane.' She then discovered her own husband's family also carried a violent streak which she believed could flare up in her husband also.

When Marvin Gaye was finally born four years into the marriage, his father's prayers had been answered and he felt his much-wanted son was destined for greatness – 'I thanked God for the blessing of his life. I thanked God for Marvin, I knew he was a special child.' Yet, Gay Snr's happiness appears to be short-lived. Alberta said – 'My husband never wanted Marvin. And he never liked him. He used to say that he didn't think he was really his child. I told him that was nonsense. He knew Marvin was his. But, for some reason, he didn't love Marvin, and, what's worse, he didn't want me to love Marvin either. Marvin wasn't very old before he understood that.' A special bond subsequently grew between mother and son – a position Marvin himself would experience in later life – which irritated his father and subconsciously could have led to the enmity between them. Nonetheless, Marvin had a high regard for his father, citing him as a major influence in his young life – 'My father is a black man. My mother is very fair. My father's hair is very kinky and my mother's hair is fair. My father is very strong and extremely independent. He has a magnificent body and a great voice. My father used to sing, just sing. He would take the guitar and sing. He was the fiery type. We're rootsy, our blackness and our spirituality is of a very real non-pretentious type. I rather like that.' All the children inherited their father's singing talent, although only Marvin and Frankie later became professional singers.

Marvin Gay Snr was a well-respected Pentecostal minister and like most church families he persuaded his children to become involved in his church's activities. Therefore Marvin entered the church at three years old when his father encouraged him to sing, and even at this tender age the Reverend recognised a talent which he felt would lead to a singing career. Marvin possessed a special quality in his vocal interpretations that enthralled his congregations. Gay Snr: 'I used to travel and do evangelical work and sometimes Marvin would come with me. When he sang I realised he could deliver a song and that he had a unique style. After a time, when I travelled with Marvin people would always want him to sing. He had a quick grasp of the Scripture, and sometimes as a small boy he almost sounded like a grown man, a minister.' Marvin, who later also duetted with his brother, Frankie, admitted he began to enjoy the attention received through his singing, and remembered when he was five his father took him to a church convention at the Church of the Living God in Kentucky. Marvin: 'I sang "Journey To The Sky" and afterwards my father came up to me with tears in his eyes and said he was proud of me.' Alberta Gay: 'He was a small child but he would sit in church where all the other children were by the preacher . . . and we would see his little head up there between the pews and he would just sit there for the whole service . . . He was a child who really loved the church.'

The Gay family religion was all-consuming and the church's rules of prayer meetings, fasting and divine healing were strictly adhered to. Sundays meant the family turned its back on everyday life to concentrate on devoted prayer and gospel readings. The origins of modern Pentecostalism appear to have been associated with a religious meeting that took place in January 1901 when a member of the Bible College in Topeka, Kansas, spoke with an unknown tongue. It was assumed this 'speaking in tongues' was evidence of a spiritual baptism and it became a regular feature in Pentecostal meetings as the Movement quickly spread across America. At one time Pentecostalism looked set to overtake Christianity as more and more people became addicted to the fiery, intense services with highly charged congregation participation. At its strictest women were forbidden to wear make-up, and like believers in Catholicism, were not allowed to wear sleeveless dresses or have uncovered heads during the services. Marvin Gaye: '[It was] apostolic, spiritual – a very social, basic, earthly spiritualism. Speaking in tongues, shouting, tambourines, tarrying. Tarrying is calling on the name of Jesus and believing in what He believed in and saying it over and over again until we reached some sort of hypnotic trance or state, and many times the tarrier isn't even aware, he's really in quite a high pitch of spiritualism. It's quite an experience to watch.' Tarrying became part of his life for seventeen years – '[It was] your classic mode of the fire-and-brimstone black preacher – I'm talking about how most people think of black ministers – in our body, most of the preachers always spoke, and the emphasis was not on the show or trying to make you feel something by becoming highly emotional with a sermon and thereby touching other people. That was part of it, of course, but that wasn't the thing that stood out in my mind. The thing that stood out in my mind was that there was a general overall spirit, a really encompassing spirit that was all around us everywhere, and at any moment you would see it affect people . . . I think it's a very ethnic thing and a thing that I love about blacks.'

Watching the power his father had over a congregation astonished and scared the young boy because once the sermon gave way to preaching, the atmosphere grew to uncontrollable emotions as a spiritual intervention became apparent. Marvin: 'The body was small but the spirit was intense and very evident to anyone who passed by or came in. It immediately encompassed them. And there were very strong people who seemed to bring the spirit forth. When they spoke in tongues, the words were foreign, but they were almost clear to me. I was frightened because of how the spirit came forth. I wondered why the spirit had such disregard for their bodies, making them bump into things and fall on sharp objects. Or when they tarried, it became evident physically that they shouldn't do it that long. And yet the spirit is there and their mouths begin to foam and that's part of it.'

Marvin overcame the terror of tarrying when he was taught the meaning behind it – the power of the mind, the strength of their faith. This led to him searching for a God he could believe in. Gaye: 'I'd like to get a link with Him. I'd like to be able to touch and feel Him, communicate quite easily with Him, which I think can be done. But in order to be a good conductor you have to have your channels free and clear of inhibitions, and free of negative prompters that cause evil, and prompters in life. I think once you do that you're well on your way to knowing what God is, what He's all about.'

Eventually, Alberta Gay's secret fear of her husband's violence became reality. The well-run, stable household was disrupted when Marvin became subjected to his father's violent temper. From an early age and into his teenage years, he was beaten regularly by him. On some occasions the beatings were warranted through misbehaviour or provocation, while other floggings were, he later admitted, attempts by him to gain his father's love and attention. He told David Ritz – 'By the time I was twelve, there wasn't an inch of my body that hadn't been bruised and beaten by him. But father did something else far worse. You see, he's a man with a subtle mind. He understood that if you're interested in inflicting pain, prolonging the process adds to the excitement. He'd say, "Boy, you're going to get a whipping." Then he'd tell me to take off my clothes and send me to the bedroom I shared with Frankie . . . It wouldn't have been so awful if he had hit me right away . . . He'd make me wait an hour, or even more, all the while jangling his belt buckle loud enough so I could hear.' Despite endeavours by the family to shield him from his father's anger and torment (knowing the psychological consequences they could bring in later life) Marvin Gaye grew up with a strong and rebellious, yet insecure and unstable nature. It was a subject he often referred to in interviews when reminiscing about his childhood and the sad relationship with his father: 'Living with father was something like living with a king, a very peculiar, changeable, cruel and all-powerful king. You were supposed to tip-toe around his moods. You were supposed to do anything to win his favour. I never did. Even though winning his love was the ultimate goal of my childhood, I defied him. I hated his attitude. I thought I could win his love through singing, so I sang my heart out. But the better I became, the greater his demands.' Frankie Gay: 'Marvin was a rebel in a lot of ways. In other words he would tend to have his own mind about things and wasn't quite as afraid of my father as the rest of us.' While Alberta Gay conceded – 'All the children were very scared of him. I tried to protect them as best I could, but I was very frightened myself. My husband was a fearful man. I was afraid he'd beat me.' She thought about divorce often but stayed because the children needed her, and she felt sorry for her husband who, she believed, would have been unable to manage the household without her.

Marvin Gaye was educated at Randall Junior High and Cardoza High schools where he was taught the regular, obligatory lessons with emphasis on his city's history. Although the youngster was fascinated by Washington D.C.'s heritage and spent much time visiting the exquisitely architectured establishments devoted to America's political pulse, he was furious and frustrated that this part of the city was white-dominated and run, while he and other blacks were expected to live at the other end of the social scale. Thus he grew up to loathe the city and the anger he felt at this time, living in a substandard environment where segregation was the law of the land, stayed with him for the remainder of his life. Particularly when he clashed with the American tax system.

At school, Marvin recalled, he was a placid and lonely child. Academically, he claimed he was a failure, although he was popular with his teachers, who believed his quest for knowledge was more of a muddled attempt to gain his father's respect, rather than to benefit his own future. The young boy was studious, well-behaved and rarely became involved in playground fights because, 'I could never get angry enough to fight back'. However, he was always conscious of being a Pentecostal minister's son and had the misguided opinion that he was different to his school friends. Marvin: 'It was quite a hardship on a child because he constantly had to prove himself to his comrades that he's as normal as they are. You have to do something rather bad or you're not accepted. You have to lose the stigma of being a child of God.'

While Marvin was at school, the Reverend Gay lost interest in his church when it was split into divisions and he wasn't offered his own congregation. Nonetheless, he continued preaching for some time before abandoning that too. After taking and leaving several nine-to-five jobs he became introverted and reclusive, traits Marvin would adopt as an adult, leaving the financing and running of the household to his wife who worked from five o'clock in the morning, seven days a week. A relative remembered Babe Gay working as a domestic with her – 'We'd cook and take care of the kids, we'd mop and clean and do whatever was needed. During the winters . . . when it was fifteen degrees with freezing sleet and snow coming down . . . we waited for the bus to take us to Maryland or Virginia. I never did know Mr Gay to work.' Marvin: 'My mother worked very hard so we could always have enough to eat.'

With the obvious upset in his homelife caused by his father's position, Marvin Gaye kept a low profile and threw himself into school work, learned to play the piano, took an interest in secular music and participated in most kinds of sport, particularly boxing. He discovered that boxing attracted girls; they admired the danger of the sport and the courageous boys with well-developed bodies. Marvin's father considered his son, being slightly built, too frail for the sport and objected to him becoming involved in any form of physical activity; this made Gaye all the more determined. He joined the school swimming, football and track teams and actually considered sport as a career, after abandoning ambitions to become an aviator. Gaye: 'I quickly changed my mind about that after growing up a bit. Had I not been an entertainer then I'd have been an athlete. Mind you, I was fascinated by nature. I used to fool around with worms, beetles and birds. It was some strange force that made me aware of nature at that time.' Unsure of his future, the youngster looked seriously at music as a possible avenue – 'I knew I could sing. My friends and I used to sing all the way home from school, do all the different parts and sing all the songs. My mother kept me singing as well. She'd say "get up and sing" and the ladies in the church would hug me and pat me on the head. Psychologically and sensually I liked that.' Although he enjoyed singing in church, at home he loathed it – 'When I was a kid, I used to have to sing a song every time there was company around at home. Then the visitors would give me a pat on the head and a kiss. I hated that.'

His interest in music grew at the Cardoza High School and after mastering the drums, piano – by now he could play the blues as prolifically as the gospel – and guitar became an in-demand addition to his school orchestra. He also spent much time playing hockey at the Howard Theatre studying artists like James Brown and Jackie Wilson. Watching them from the stage sidelines inspired him to form his first group The D.C. Tones, even though his fellow students considered singing to be effeminate. Sondra Lattisaw, lead singer with the group and mother of American soul singer, Stacy, also studied at Cardoza and told *Rolling Stone* magazine – 'Marvin had a lot of class. He always dressed very well, even in school. He wasn't just your normal, everyday guy. He played piano for our group, I never knew he could sing. All he did was sit at the piano and smile. He smiled all the time. He was quiet and shy.'

Like most school groups, The D.C. Tones petered out and Marvin, now a cigarette smoker, decided he wanted to be a solo singer. However, he lacked the confidence to pursue this goal and found solace, he said, in the local doo-wop band The Rainbows. They performed in and around the Washington area and occasionally the group members (including at any one time Don Covay, James Nolan, Billy Stewart, John Barry, Chester Simmons, Sonny Spencer) would let the young, ambitious Marvin sing lead. However Gaye never actually performed with the group and this is substantiated by Reese Palmer, his close friend, in *Divided Soul* – 'I read somewhere that Marvin began in The Rainbows. That's not true. Don Covay and James Nolan came out of The Rainbows but not Marvin.' In 1981 music historian Peter Doggett wrote in *Record Collector* magazine that Marvin was a member of The Raindrops not The Rainbows in 1955. Presumably they are one and the same group.

Nonetheless, Marvin went on record several times explaining his situation with the group by saying, music, like boxing before it, attracted young girls and, by being with The Rainbows, he was once again aware of his attraction. On stage he learned movements to excite them, while off stage he enchanted them with his retired manner and lean, attractive looks.

His love of music also helped him to blot out his unhappy home life and he felt confident he could succeed as a singer. Success was a long way off, but a positive step in the right direction was made during the early Fifties when The Rainbows (with Marvin?) went to New York to record 'Mary Lee'/'Evening', a single for Bobby Robinson's Red Robin label, reissued a year later by Pilgrim Records. This was followed by the 'Shirley'/'Stay' single several months later. Whether Marvin participated in these recordings or stayed on the periphery isn't known, but it was after these recordings that he said he knew where his ambitions lay. When he reached seventeen, he dropped out of high school to pursue the musical career he pined for. His father, now a regular drinker, had other ideas. He had hoped his son would study to become a lawyer but when Marvin dismissed the idea as ridiculous due to his academic inadequacies, he gave him two options, neither included music. Gay Snr: 'I said either get a job or go into the service. I was afraid. I'm a worrier and I thought he could get in with juvenile delinquents.' By this time the relationship between them was said to be abysmal. Marvin remembered his father often threatened to disown him, particularly if he failed to obey the household rules, one of which was he was not allowed in the house during the day for longer than necessary. Subsequently, the young boy when not at school spent most of the daylight hours roaming the neighbourhood and staying with friends.

So, once again son obeyed father and joined the Air Force although his reason for doing so had little to do with any pride or loyalty to his country. Rather, it seemed to be an egotistical move; Marvin was inspired by the fantasy images on the cinema screen of the romantic wartime heroes whom women adored. Unfortunately for him, quite the reverse happened. Gaye: 'It was a horrible experience, and the worst thing I have ever done. I hated the discipline and was always getting into trouble because I was a frustrated member of the ground staff. I was never taught to fly – I peeled potatoes!' He rebelled against the Force's regulations and refused to accept he was simply an everyday serviceman, with no special privileges – and certainly no heroic image! The regimentation eventually made him pine for the family household he had wanted to escape from, and his behaviour convinced his superiors he was on the verge of a nervous breakdown. Gaye: 'I was ready to go home and they said I couldn't because I was in the service. They would say, "OK do KP," and I would say, "Excuse me, but I can't do KP [kitchen patrol]. I'll do it tomorrow if that's alright with you." And they'd say, "Hell no, it's not alright with us. You do KP. No matter what." It is kind of frightening. So I guess I'm crazy. They said I was crazy.'

The more stubborn Marvin became the more the service was determined to break him, and as a last resort they insisted he receive psychiatric treatment. He refused – 'I figured at that point that I didn't have to do anything. It was ludicrous. I lost all perspective. If they told me to get up, I'd throw dirt on myself. If they threatened to shoot me, I was mad enough to say "I dare you". And it would have been OK dying then if I could have heard just one of them say, "He sure didn't go for none of this shit, did he?"' However, he studied for a high school diploma and was allowed to sing and entertain his colleagues at the Kansas, Texas and Wyoming bases. More importantly, he laughed years later, he lost his virginity — 'I was with a hooker and I'd just come off the saltpetre, which is something they put in your food to keep your sexuality at a low ebb. They didn't want any funny business in the barracks. I remember losing my virginity to this day. Virginity. That's a strange word for a man to deal with. I never thought of myself as a virgin. I think the word is . . . it's not eunuch because that's a man who has been castrated. But there is another word that describes a man who has never had sex with a woman.'

It took a year before the Air Force acknowledged the rebellious young man would never reach officer grade, so offered him an honourable discharge. It was a happy non-conformist who returned to Washington D.C. to face his father's wrath, and to what was left of The Rainbows.

Marvin was happy again and, he said, threw his energies into the group: 'But my father was still upset for a while about that because I suppose he thought I'd never shape up to much.' Frankie Gay: 'My father being a minister taught us all that a minister would teach his children at that time and Marvin embarked on a career that was kinda looked on by the church as not gospel music and I think my father's desire for both of us was to do spirituals.' The Rainbows, heavily inspired by the doo-wop group The Moonglows, performed locally in record shops and house parties until Bo Diddley, an innovator of black rock and roll, invited them to record with him. This prompted a name change for the group, and with the line-up comprising James Nolan, Chester Simmons, Reese Palmer and Marvin they became The Marquees. The group sang backing vocals on Billy Stewart's 'Baby, You're My Only One'/'Billy's Heartache', and as The Marquees, with Reese Palmer on lead, recorded his penned and Bo Diddley-produced 'Wyatt Earp'/'Hey Little School Girl', both singles released by OKeh Records in 1957. OKeh was a subsidiary label of Columbia Records and was the brainchild of A&R executive Carl Davis, who was responsible for discovering The Dukays. Their lead singer was Eugene Dixon, later to become Gene Chandler. Carl Davis also signed Curtis Mayfield and Major Lance to the label, both of whom were destined to become leading artists in black music. When 'Wyatt Earp' bombed, Simmons left the group. It appears that Frankie Gay was anxious to join the outfit. He had a sweet singing voice that would have easily blended in, but Marvin refused to consider the move. He was, he later admitted, afraid Frankie would prove to be the better singer. Nearly three decades later the two brothers would work together on tour, yet Marvin never recorded the promised album with Frankie. Conceivably, there was a competitive attitude between the brothers although it never reached malicious proportions. Both were fine, unique singers at this point and the music industry could have catered for both in the future. Yet Frankie had to wait for five years after Marvin's death to enjoy a serious stab at recorded success.

The Marquees moved from OKeh to the Chess/Checker label where they backed Bo Diddley on 'I'm Sorry'. Chess Records was owned by Phil and Leonard Chess and, although the company wasn't as aggressive as its competitors in signing new acts, it was responsible for signing the successful Fontella Bass on Checker and Billy Stewart on Chess. When Leonard Chess died in 1968 the company was sold without having achieved its full potential as a leading soul label. With this recording experience behind The Marquees, Marvin expected the group's career to take off. When it didn't, he was disappointed but nonetheless they were in demand on the touring circuit and the tiring, but exciting, round of one-night performances began again. Nothing deterred the handsome Marvin from being before an audience, and as his young innocence, ice-cool style and sweet-soul voice continued to attract young women, he begged The Marquees to give him more lead vocals – the star spot. However, Gaye's easy ability to appeal to women began to conflict with his strict religious upbringing. This played on his mind until he accepted that much of his sexual persona was probably inherited from his father, who had at one time or another caused concern in his local community around the East Capitol Dwellings with his transvestism.

However, Marvin's future Tamla Motown singing partner Kim Weston who had met Gay Snr socially was unaware of this – 'Our conversations were about human nature and God . . . I have no knowledge about him dressing up in women's clothes.' Nonetheless, neighbours noted that he occasionally wore fashionable clothes and a wig while out. Marvin told David Ritz – 'My father likes to wear women's clothing. As you well know, that doesn't mean he's homosexual. In fact, my father was always known as a ladies' man. He simply likes to dress up. What he does in private, I really don't know nor do I care to know.' There were times, he pointed out, when his father wore his hair long and curled, thus appearing feminine, and this was something he feared would be hereditary because he too had an interest in women's attire.

In 1957, now sure of his audience's acceptance, the ambitious young singer became frustrated with the confines of the group. He longed for solo stardom, to be the second Frank Sinatra, but, once again, was afraid to take the step. Most of The Marquees' stage songs were cover versions of hit recordings and Gaye grew tired of singing tried and tested compositions, so he began experimenting with songwriting, an art he felt would stand him in good stead should he ever have the courage to embark upon a solo career. His very first composition, titled 'Barbara', was reputedly swiped from a popular television show; it was a good initial attempt but, without anyone to guide him, he continued to blunder through his experiments without writing anything of significance but nevertheless learning the rudiments of constructing a song. When he later became a Tamla Motown artist, The Miracles' lead singer and composer William 'Smokey' Robinson taught him how to create a story line that captured the listener's imagination, and how to build a melody around that story line. Robinson's poetic phrasing would become apparent in Marvin's later work, when he was quick to credit his teacher, among others – 'One of my definite early influences was indeed Smokey, and musically I was very much into Ray Charles and James Brown. I love all aspects of music and during my early days I would listen to all forms of music and developed my taste and creativity from a broad base.'

Marvin Gaye's stagnant situation with The Marquees was to be changed, not by his own hand but by the 1928 Kentucky-born Harvey Fuqua, writer/producer and then lead singer of The Moonglows. The Moonglows, originally known as The Crazy Sounds, formed by Bobby Lester during 1951 in Louisville, comprised Fuqua, Alexander Graves, and Prentiss Barnes as vocalists, and Buddy (Billy) Johnson as guitarist. Unlike his colleagues, Fuqua (whose uncle Charlie was an original member of The Ink Spots) had had no professional experience prior to joining the outfit except singing at school and in church.

After devoting 1951 to local performances, the quartet was seen by the R&B DJ Alan Freed who, in later years, instigated the popularity of rock music in America. Freed auditioned The Moonglows and helped secure a recording contract with the Cleveland-based Champagne Records. However, as their debut single 'I Just Can't Tell No Lie' was released during 1953, the record company folded, whereupon Freed signed them to Chance Records in Chicago. The Fuqua/Freed composition 'Baby Please' was The Moonglows' first release in December 1953 and a year later their penned 'Rockin' Daddy' and 'Secret Love' became R&B semi-hits. Once again, just as the group's popularity was growing the record company closed down!

Chess Records bought out the group's contract to release 'Sincerely' which became an R&B number one and a number twenty pop hit. (The McGuire Sisters enjoyed bigger success with the song some time later.) The Moonglows' second Chess release was 'Most Of All', another hit (no 5 R&B) and during 1955 they went from strength to strength with 'In My Diary', 'Foolish Me', 'Slow Down' and 'Starlight'. Now also an established touring unit, The Moonglows' career was at its peak and a string of further hits followed including 'We Go Together' (no 9 R&B), 'See Saw' (no 6 R&B/no 25 pop) and 'Over And Over Again'. However when Chess issued two singles ('Shoo-doo-bedoo' and 'New Gal') via its Checker offshoot credited to Bobby Lester and the Moonlighters, other group members became discontent, forcing Harvey Fuqua to take over the lead vocals. The change seemed to work because in 1958 they (under the name of Harvey and The Moonglows) enjoyed the topselling single, the immortal 'Ten Commandments Of Love' (no 9 R&B/no 22 pop).

Eventually the success slacked off and the group disbanded, leaving Fuqua to record for Chess as a solo artist, until he could find a substitute group. Marvin Gaye: 'Harvey decided to form a new Moonglows. They still had a recording contract with Chess at the time and Harvey heard The Marquees do "The Ten Commandments Of Love" at a gig and asked us to become the new Moonglows.' Another group was born and nineteen-year-old Gaye, Harvey Fuqua, James Nolan, Reese Palmer, Chester Simmons and Chuck Barksdale left Washington D.C. for Chicago, Illinois, on the south shore of Lake Michigan. They stayed in accommodation owned by Leonard and Phil Chess and from this base Harvey Fuqua began moulding his fledglings into professional recording artists, while working as a talent scout for Chess Records, a prestigious position he enjoyed for some time.

However, when Marvin moved to Chicago it annoyed his father. Frankie Gay: 'Dad wasn't keen on the life he was slipping into, staying out late every night and so on. Harvey Fuqua was having some other pressures so eventually he and Marvin decided to leave home.'

One of the new Moonglows first recordings was the unreleased 'That's What Girls Are Made For', a track Fuqua later fronted and released with The Spinners in May 1961 on the Tri Phi label. It reached number twenty-seven in the pop charts (no 5 R&B). As a member of Harvey and the Moonglows Marvin sang backing vocals for Chuck Berry on his Chess single 'Almost Grown'/'Back In The USA' and on the unreleased track 'Do You Love Me'; for Etta James on 'Chained To My Rocking Chair' and lead on 'Mama Loochie'/'Unemployment' and 'Twelve Months Of The Year'/'Don't Be Afraid Of Love'. Marvin then sang on Harvey Fuqua's 'Blue Skies'/'Ooch, Ouch Stop' and The Moonglows' 'Beatnik'/'Junior'. Despite enjoying some recording success, the group's future work failed so they were forced to rely on concert dates to earn a living. Like most black groups, The Moonglows toured the Southern States of America as part of their performing itinerary, and were appalled at the treatment they were subjected to because of the colour of their skin by the white population. Blacks were not allowed to stay at certain hotels, and should a white touring manager check in for a night, he wasn't allowed black visitors. Restaurants would refuse to let blacks eat on the premises and they had to order their meals at the back of the establishment for a takeaway. Future Tamla Motown artist and backing vocalist for Marvin, Martha Reeves angrily remembers her first reaction when faced with racial discrimination – 'It was an awful insult when you walk around and you got money and you can't eat!'

Several hundred miles across America from Washington D.C., Detroit, Michigan, which faces Canada over the Detroit River situated near the Great Lakes of Erie and Huron, was a thriving industrial and commercial centre. Apart from the lucrative motor vehicle industry (General Motors, Chrysler and Ford), military tanks, aeroplanes, chemicals and steel were manufactured. However, another industry was destined to put Detroit (derived from the French word 'de'troit', meaning a strait) on the world's lips – music. And, while The Moonglows were struggling to survive, the first rumblings of a new musical sound was being created by a young, ambitious black man, Berry Gordy Jnr.

Berry Gordy Jnr was one of eight children, and his family moved from Georgia to Detroit, where he was born on 28 November 1929, in search of a better life. Once settled in the city's black-dominated West Side, the family opened a print store and grocery shop where the children worked. Thus, at a young age the Gordy children's business expertise was developed. Berry Gordy Jnr refused to work in his parents' shops, preferring to develop his passion for music. He listened to the radio all day, humming songs and making notes. His first composition was 'Berry's Boogie' which won first prize at a local talent show. However, the young Gordy was prevented by his father from taking his musical ambitions further so followed in his brothers Robert and Fuller's footsteps and joined one of Detroit's amateur boxing teams. Eventually Berry Gordy qualified as a featherweight, left school and turned professional. Boxing attracted many blacks because it was one of the rare industries where they could earn good money, and was an alternative to the car factory assembly lines. Among his numerous fights Berry met the Golden Gloves champion Jackie Wilson, who was later to become instrumental in his musical career.

Boxing was abandoned when Berry Gordy joined the Army in 1951 for the Korean War. In 1953 he was discharged and married nineteen-year-old Thelma Louise Coleman in Toledo. During the day he worked for his parents, while night times were spent in local clubs mingling with Detroit's jazz musicians. With his Army savings and a $700 family loan, Gordy turned his interest in music into reality by purchasing the 3-D Record Mart in 1953, specialising in jazz records, his prime love. However, after two years of selling jazz to a limited market the Record Mart went bankrupt, leaving Gordy no option but to seek work as a trimmer in Ford's Wayne Assembly Plant for a weekly wage of approximately $87. He was bored and discontented with the humdrum of his daily life, and pined for his music. This in turn reflected on his home life and his marriage. Gordy admitted he was musically frustrated but nevertheless determined to succeed – 'I read in a magazine that you could get your songs written up in sheet music by paying $25. I got a song of mine written up called "You Are You". I'd been inspired by seeing a film with Danny Thomas on the life of Gus Todd. Doris Day was in it and I wrote this song for her after seeing the movie. So I was inspired by her and Danny Thomas of all people.'

In 1956 Berry Gordy's marriage ended in divorce and, prior to his own recording operation, his ex-wife opened two labels, Ge Ge and Thelma, with limited success. Gordy went to live with his sister

Loucye while his other two sisters Gwen and Anna worked for The Flame Show Bar (a prestigious theatre for black entertainers) having secured the cigarette and photography franchises. As Gordy frequently visited this and other clubs he became aware of the wealth of raw, untapped talent Detroit held and concentrated more than ever on his songwriting. Gwen and Anna also helped by introducing him to everyone they met through their work who showed an interest in his compositions.

When boxer-turned-R&B singer Jackie Wilson began his recording career and was looking for songs to record Berry Gordy approached him with some he had written with Billy Davis aka Tyron Carlo. Wilson liked them sufficiently to record some – 'To Be Loved', 'Lonely Tear drops' and 'Reet Petite', which when reissued in 1986 became a British number one single. Wilson: '"Reet Petite" was a funny record. I loved it on first sight so that shows you how nutty I was. Berry wrote it in the way I sang it, so if I hadn't come along, God knows who could have recorded it.' Wilson also remembered that Berry Gordy was a little man with a big dream – 'I always said he was underrated as a songwriter . . . he was more into publishing than recording because at the time I wasn't even signed to a record company. He was far more interested in getting his songs recorded.' Gwen Gordy: 'We were all musically inclined, and Berry and I would often work as a team writing songs in the late Fifties for Jackie Wilson, among others. I always wanted to be in the record business and I knew Berry was interested, so I was constantly asking him if he was ready to venture into the business fulltime, but at that time he wasn't ready.' Detroit already had numerous singers and independent R&B labels like Jack and Devorah Brown's Fortune with subsidiaries including Hi-Q which were causing a ripple in the local market place. And artists like John Lee Hooker and Dinah Washington in the Forties, Della Reese and Lavern Baker in the Fifties, while the Franklin family was preparing to take over the Sixties when the Reverend C. L. Franklin's daughters Erma, Carolyn and Aretha began singing. Interestingly, although Berry Gordy was heavily inspired by the Reverend's recorded work (lashings of tambourines and a gospel church overtone) which can be detected in Tamla Motown's early recordings, he wasn't interested in working with the Franklin sisters, all of whom, particularly Aretha, became influential names in popular music.

After 'Reet Petite' was recorded Gordy met a young poet, Janie

Bradford. This meeting fuelled a future writing commitment together and Bradford, with others in Gordy's musical team, unwittingly conceived the raw basis of the future 'Motown Sound'. Encouraged by Jackie Wilson's success Gordy left his trimmer's job to concentrate on music full time, and in 1958 he met fellow music enthusiast and future second wife Raynoma Liles after she won an amateur singing contest in a Detroit nightclub. The emcee of that club recommended she should contact Gordy. Liles: 'I went by his place with my sister. I had about one hundred songs written, most of them lousy, but they were songs. I guess Berry thought the songs could have been better, but I went on to work with him and his talent.' She joined Gordy's musical team, now comprising Bradford, Brian Holland and Robert Bateman, and formed and fronted The Rayber Voices ('Ray' – Raynoma; 'Ber' – Berry), adding backing vocals to singers they were associated with. Herman Griffin's 'I Need You' released in 1958 on the House of Beauty label (HOB 112) was the first single to carry a Rayber Voices label credit. It was also the first song to be published by Berry Gordy's future publishing company, Jobete, opened by Raynoma, who also initially ran it during the Sixties. The publishing house was named after Gordy's three children from his first marriage – Hazel JOy, BErry and TErry.

As time passed Gordy persuaded other talents to work with him; slowly he built up a prolific working team to license his finished master recordings to large white-owned record companies. He rented a studio and hired a second-hand disc-making machine and charged singers $100 to use his facilities. He worked regularly with Detroit-born Marv Johnson, a former part-time clerk at the 3-D Record Mart, and in 1958 the Detroit-based Kudo Records released Johnson's Gordy-penned 'My Baby-O', and Brian Holland's 'Shock'. Holland's brother, Eddie, likewise recorded a Gordy song for Mercury Records. Unbeknown at this time, the young Holland brothers were destined to become major influences in Gordy's future. However, before that happened, he met William 'Smokey' Robinson.

Born on 19 February 1940, Smokey (so nicknamed by an uncle) was another Detroiter. From the age of six he began experimenting with songwriting and became an avid lyric reader of the popular song books of the time. While at school he formed his first group The Five Chimes whose membership, after several changes, later formed The Matadors. Their sister group, The Matadorettes, was fronted by Claudette Rogers who in time joined Robinson's group replacing her brother Sonny. During 1957 Robinson, Rogers and their friends Ronnie White and Pete Moore, and Claudette's brother Bobby auditioned for Jackie Wilson's manager Nat Tarnopol, his musical director Alonzo Tucker and his songwriter Berry Gordy. They failed the audition, featuring original Robinson songs, because Tarnopol believed Claudette and Smokey should perform together as duets were popular at the time. However, Gordy disagreed. He was interested in the group's repertoire and offered to manage them. He arranged a handful of local low-keyed gigs for them before collaborating with Robinson to write their first song, 'Insane', for Wade Jones. They then worked on The Matadors' first single 'Got A Job'. Gordy disliked their group name, so numerous alternatives were written on scraps of paper and thrown into a box whereupon 'The Miracles' was first out. 'Got A Job' was released and distributed by End Records, a New York company, in November 1957, followed by 'Money' (not the Barrett Strong track). Both sold reasonably well.

Berry Gordy was ambitious, he wanted to expand, to open his own record label like his sister Gwen who, encouraged by her working relationship with Billy Davis, had, at Chess Records' suggestion, opened the Anna label in 1958. The label was named after her sister, who was also a partner, and was enjoying some success despite radio airplay restrictions at the time where the number of black acts achieving any chart status was spasmodic because whites re-recorded black originals and radio airplay was given to the white cover-versions. Nonetheless the Anna label boasted talented producers, writers and singers although their full potential would not be realised until they changed record labels. Interestingly, Anna's biggest selling single was the Berry Gordy/Jamie Bradford composition 'Money (That's What I Want)' recorded by Barrett Strong and leased in 1959 to Gwen Gordy by her brother. Berry Gordy: '[That was] the first popular song I wrote. I was very broke at the time. I was embarrassed because when people asked me what I did for a living I would say, "I write songs". They would have sons and daughters that were becoming doctors and lawyers, and my mother and father were always somewhat embarrassed when I would tell their friends I wrote songs. Even though I had many hits, and there were other writers who had many hits, we just didn't have any profits. And coming from a business family, my father and mother always talked about the bottom line, and the bottom line is profit.'

Having his records scattered around different companies was not an ideal creative and working environment for Gordy and he realised that if he was going to fulfil his ambitions he needed to take drastic action. With encouragement from Smokey Robinson, he once again persuaded his family to loan him $800 from the family Ber-Berry Co-op fund to open the Tamla label in 1959, a subsidiary of his future Tamla Motown company. 'Tamla' was a spin-off from Debbie Reynolds' hit of the time 'Tammy's in Love'; Gordy intended to use 'Tammy' but it was already registered as a label. And 'Motown' was the abbreviation of Detroit's nickname 'motor city', also used by local businesses. It's thought that Gordy only registered the distinctive Motown 'M', later used on record labels, and the 'Tamla Motown' logo in full and not the word 'Motown' which, over three decades later, enabled concert promoters to use the name for touring ex-Motown acts.

The Motown label opened in 1961 when Tamla had released over twenty singles. (The company Tamla Motown will be referred to as Motown hereafter even though the official name-change did not occur until 1976.) Marv Johnson's 'Come To Me' launched Tamla in January 1959 although he wasn't a Motown artist as such. When Berry Gordy secured a licensing deal with United Artists he had to relinquish his rights to Johnson but nonetheless continued working with him on singles like 'Merry-Go-Round', 'I Love The Way You Love Me' and 'You Got What It Takes'. In time Gordy would sever his ties with white majors to press, promote and distribute his own product from his small, but expanding company on 2648 West Grand Boulevard, Detroit. Raynoma Gordy transformed the near-derelict two-storey building, slotted between a beauty store and a funeral parlour in a row of rundown houses in a once affluent neighbourhood, into a pulsating music concern. Berry and Raynoma Gordy and their young son Kerry lived in the upstairs of the house, while the record company offices were downstairs. The kitchen was gutted to become the control room, the dining-room to become the sales and distribution office, and book keeping took over the living-room. Raynoma: 'That house was unbelievable because it already had a studio – one that had been used for photography – built on the back.' And under her expert guidance (she wrote lead sheets, held weekly music classes for the artists, was Motown's first string arranger) a distinctive sound emerged from the basement studio – 'It was a completely natural sound. All we did was put up some theatre curtains and maybe a rug. There was nothing contrived about it. All of the rhythm players had this natural talent that Berry and I could relate to. That was the original, the funky Motown sound.' A sign reading 'Hitsville USA' was hung over the porch to advertise Gordy's determination to succeed and in the front window a poster proudly declared 'The Sound Of Young America'.

Competition was fierce from Detroit's record labels with artists like The Detroit Emeralds, The Reflections, The Falcons (with members including future solo stars Eddie Floyd, Joe Stubbs – brother of Four Tops' lead singer Levi – and Wilson Pickett), The Fantastic Four, J.J. Barnes and Edwin Starr. However, these and other acts were R&B through and through while Gordy wanted artists whose records would appeal to the white market and therefore generate money. As time passed and Motown became powerful, instead of competing against some of these local labels Gordy bought them out!

With Motown underway, the Gordy family businesses were dosed down so that everyone could be involved in the new venture. Gordy's father 'Pops' became company consultant and leading figure in the daily running of the operation. Berry's sister, Esther, who married local councillor George Edwards, handled the administration and later with Thomas 'Beans' Bowles headed ITM (International Talent Management), Motown's in-house management company. Esther had in fact worked with her brother prior to Motown – 'I was his secretary when he was a songwriter for Jackie Wilson, around 1957. During that time, he had many different partnerships, and when he decided to start the company it began with the personal management of Marv Johnson and Smokey Robinson and the Miracles. I was the gal Friday, secretary and co-ordinator of that management company.' As part of his job, Thomas 'Beans' Bowles, also a sax player, toured with artists like Marv Johnson from 1960 onwards as road manager, music director and driver.

Another Gordy sister, Loucye, was Motown's first head of sales and responsible for collecting money owed to the company. In July 1963, her husband, Ron Wakefield, a musician, became a copyist in the arranging department, moving to artist co-ordination a year later. Prior to working for her brother, Loucye had worked for the government with shrewd business woman Fay Hale. Once Loucye was installed she persuaded Hale to join her, saying 'You don't have to like the music, just remember the names!' Sadly, Loucye died in 1965 without seeing her struggles reap rewards. Berry's brother Robert became apprentice studio engineer for 65 cents an hour after leaving his post office job. He also enjoyed a short recording career when he released the 1958 single 'Everyone Was There' under the pseudonym Robert Kayli for Carlton Records, and in 1959 he was persuaded to record again for the Anna label.

Raynoma Singleton (who divorced Gordy after one and a half years of marriage and later married and divorced ex-Motown singer Barbara Randolph's husband, Eddie Singleton) fondly recalled those early days – 'People did whatever it was necessary to do. Everybody did something, from maintaining the exterior of the building, painting and so forth, to what we called snacktime" when someone had to cook and serve lunch.' Weekly salaries were $3 on average but nobody complained. Raynoma: 'This is how interested everyone was in just being a part of it and watching it grow. It was fun, something that was in our blood, not just a job. It was a bunch of people who really believed, working together for a specific goal.'

Berry Gordy hand-picked his early musicians, producers and writers. The musicians were mostly native Detroiters with jazz backgrounds, while the composers either wanted a permanent base to work from or respected Gordy's ambitious talents. However, like Gordy most of his creative staff couldn't read or write music, so William 'Mickey' Stevenson was placed in the trusted position of overseeing the Artist & Repertoire (A&R) Division run by writer/producer Clarence Paul. Stevenson quickly proved to be a valuable member of staff and worked very closely with Berry Gordy, who later entrusted him with deciding which artists should record what songs. When Stevenson felt Motown's records should have an edge over competitors, he encouraged Gordy to introduce string arrangements on records, although problems arose when the Detroit Symphony Orchestra grieved at the absence of sheet music. Gordy and his writers would hum the songs to the orchestra and cared little how the composition was recorded as long as the result had hit potential. These amateur, yet effective, techniques of the early Sixties dissolved when Gordy's musicians insisted his writers outline their songs on paper. They, in turn, would develop the music.

Brian Holland, whom Gordy met and worked with as a teenager and who recorded 'Shock' in 1958, began his Motown career as a recording engineer before moving into the creative area. Holland's talent for commercial sound didn't peak until he was joined by his brother Eddie and colleague Lamont Dozier. After recording for Mercury Records and United Artists, Eddie Holland sang demo recordings for Jackie Wilson. He actually joined Motown as a singer, where his debut 'Jamie', released in January 1962, was his only success. Lamont Dozier, as a member of The Romeos, recorded for the Fox label, before joining The Voicemasters and later recording as a solo artist using the pseudonym Lamont Anthony. During 1962 he recorded one single 'Fortune Teller Tell Me', then teamed up with Freddie Gorman and Brian Holland to write and produce. Gorman, previously a Ric Tic label artist, worked with Holland and Dozier until he left Motown in 1963 to front The Originals. Mickey Stevenson, by this time, had become aware of the potential of three writer/producers working together and encouraged Lamont Dozier to replace Gorman, and the famous team of Holland, Dozier, Holland was born. Working for a basic salary, plus royalties, Dozier was responsible for creating the song, Eddie Holland assisted with lyrics and melody, while Brian Holland engineered the song's structure. The trio was later responsible for some of Marvin Gaye's early work although their greatest successes were channelled through The Supremes, Martha and the Vandellas and the Four Tops.

From 1959 Motown's back-room staff, especially musicians, were more important than the artists themselves although none were afforded any public recognition or, at the very least, credited on record sleeves. This tight band of experienced perfectionists ran the studio in their own way and guided inexperienced creative staff. There were several priceless musicians who played an integral role in building Gordy's empire, like keyboardist/bandleader Earl Van Dyke, who after being drafted into the US Armed Forces worked on the New York club circuit before returning to Detroit and Motown. Apart from being a studio musician where he recorded with most artists including Marvin Gaye, Van Dyke headed his own touring group known as 'Earl Van Dyke and the Soul Brothers' or 'The Earl Van Dyke Sextet' and recorded several records including the 'That Motown Sound' album, containing backing tracks of the company's Sixties' hits, in 1965.

Joining Van Dyke were keyboardist Johnny Griffin, bassist James Jamerson (who died from a heart attack in 1983), guitarists Robert White, Joe Messina and Eddie Willis, percussionist Jack Ashford and saxophonists Eli Fountain and Choker Campbell. Like Van Dyke, all played for Marvin, and Campbell and his 16-Piece Band also recorded an album containing backing tracks of released singles. Titled 'Hits Of The Sixties' it was issued during 1965. Joining these, and other musicians, was drummer extraordinaire William 'Benny' Benjamin, probably the most famous of all using Motown's Studio A. His ability to play numerous rhythms simultaneously earned him the respect of his contemporaries and artists alike. In the studio he had no equal, yet his personal life was in turmoil with a drug and alcohol problem, and when he was unable to work two drummers trained by him – Richard 'Pistol' Allen and Uriel Jones – replaced him. Tragically, Benjamin died following a stroke in 1969. Other musicians – Paul Riser, Hank Cosby and David Van De Pitte – also later became prolific writers and arrangers, with Riser becoming a member of Motown's horn section. Once again all worked with Marvin at one time or another.

As these musicians' wages were well below existing union rates, many moonlighted for nearby Ed Wingate's labels Ric Tic and Golden World, among others. However, one of Berry Gordy's strictest rules was loyalty and when he became aware of Motown soundalike records being released by these and other labels, he increased their wages. In time Gordy bought out both Ric Tic and Golden World, reputedly for $1 million, which included the artist rosters, the labels' names and the Golden World studios which he badly needed.

Meanwhile, Motown's innate music continued to be born in the basement studio at 2648 West Grand Boulevard, known affectionately as 'the snake pit'. It was well named; it was a poky, claustrophobic room with sound-proofed walls which did little to contain the music within. A toilet, situated near the studio, acted as an echo chamber, while tin cans, bells, hand claps, foot stomps, chains and so on improvised as musical instruments. A cubicle large enough for one singer stood near the console board, where the producers would oversee the recording sessions, while the backing singers fought for spare microphones. Author Nelson George wrote: 'The control room had two Ampex 8-track machines near the wall next to the door. Engineers like Mike McClain and Lawrence Horn and some of the other producers had, through trial and error, built the original 3-track recording machine into an 8-track by the mid-Sixties. Microphone cables hung from the ceiling like branches of black licorice sticks. Looking over the main 8-track console into the studio, you'd see chairs positioned there for guitar and bass players. The piano was to their immediate left and the drums diagonally across from the piano . . . Side rooms had been built into the wall next to the piano after Berry Gordy had purchased the building next door.

There vibes, organ and percussion instruments were usually stationed. There was no room for large amplifiers in the studio, the guitar and bass were right into the console, and were heard through the room's one speaker.' In time, when money was available, intricate, expensive equipment was installed and sadly much of the 'amateur' magic was lost.

Berry Gordy kept a tight rein on all his employees; this was typified by his introduction of a general fines system for absenteeism, below standard work and so on. He introduced a punch clock and card system similar to that used at Ford when he worked on the assembly line there. He was a strict boss, a stickler for perfection and his demands were considered excessive, yet he could be generous to a fault. His determination to achieve high standards included him rejecting one hundred Smokey Robinson compositions, and numerous other songs costing thousands of dollars to produce which were canned (material recorded, unreleased and stored). Years later several of these songs were unearthed and released on collectors' compilation albums. Robinson told *Soul* magazine why Gordy had rejected his songs – 'To be honest, at first I was insulted. I thought I was kinda hot, you know. But Berry taught me some basics and we became fast friends.' He acknowledged that Gordy's policy was simple. Every tune recorded had to be a potential number one single, therefore in-house competition between writers and producers was intense, particularly as Gordy had more personnel than he really needed. Gordy: 'The people at Motown had a choice of sitting in a studio creating something that would make them feel good and proud, or they could be out robbing somebody's house or taking dope or doing some of the things that people do when they're bored.' All his creative staff worked in the cramped conditions at number 2648, a situation considered ideal by Gordy for his family of music. A song could be conceived in one of the small rooms then passed throughout the building for opinion and alteration until it was completed. Berry Gordy then had the final decision whether the song should be recorded or not. When Motown expanded and Gordy became involved in other areas the A&R director would make the final decision. Once a song was recorded it would go before Quality Control and if passed for release would be played at a local dance hall where punters would be asked for their opinion.

At this time, generally speaking, when artists signed a recording contract, Berry Gordy also secured their publishing rights via Jobete and handled their careers with ITM. These contracts were invariably incomplete and did not guarantee that the signatories' records would actually be released within a certain period of time. The Supremes' Mary Wilson wrote of her first recording contract in her autobiography *Dreamgirl: My Life As A Supreme* – '[It] was fourteen pages of double spaced type outlining my obligations to Motown as a "singer and/or musician" for the next year . . . no advance, no salary and permission for Motown to recoup monies they'd advanced to us or spent on our behalf from the royalties we would be entitled to . . . in the event one of us chose not to continue with The Supremes, her replacement would be chosen by Motown . . . if someone was to be fired from the group, only Motown could do it.' Although Wilson did not have sight of the three other Supremes contracts at this time, she assumed they were all identical to include – 'For recordings sold in the US (and not returned) I was to be paid three per cent of ninety per cent of the suggested retail price for each record, less all taxes and packaging costs. That three per cent royalty only applied when I cut solo records . . . As a solo artist I would get approximately 2 cents for every 75-cent single sold. If I or any of the other Supremes recorded a million seller as a solo, that person's net would be around $20,000 before other expenses were deducted. Recordings made as a group were subject to a different royalty formula. Instead of each of us receiving three per cent, we had to divide that three per cent four ways. The real royalty rate for each of us was ¾ per cent of one per cent or .0075. Thus my earnings per 75-cent single would drop from 2 cents to about half a penny. At this point a million seller would earn about $5,000.'

However, in essence, Motown's contracts differed little from those offered by other companies at the time although Clarence Paul thought otherwise, as he told David Ritz – 'Just about everyone got ripped off at Motown. The royalty rates were sub-standard. Motown had their own songwriting contracts which were way below the rest of the industry. Tunes were stolen all the time and often credit wasn't properly assigned.' Across the Atlantic, British record companies also paid meagre royalties. For example, when The Beatles joined EMI's Parlophone label in 1962, the one-year contract paid 1d for a double-sided single to be shared between each Beatle!

In 1965 when Smokey Robinson became vice-president of Motown he was responsible for signing new talent, therefore had sight of the recording contracts. He stressed in his *Inside My Life* autobiography – 'I can testify that much of what's been written about Motown's manipulations is unadulterated bullshit . . . I saw the contracts; I knew that the deals offered were straightforward and, for those days, standard as the twelve-bar blues.'

With ITM handling artists' tours and their financial affairs all acts had plenty of stage work and no money worries – at least that was the intention. This policy appeared to work with the first league acts, but backfired with the runners-up. Barbara Randolph, who joined Motown to replace Florence Ballard in The Supremes and who later became Marvin Gaye's duettist, was one to fall foul of the ITM system – 'Before [Motown] I'd go out as a single and work all over the United States. But once you've signed to them, you can't do that any longer. And if they don't give you work, then you're there without any income, and you're not making money off records. We were assigned to managers which we paid for, and that manager was in charge of getting you work. I had a lot of trouble with my manager [because] he wouldn't get me any work.'

Irrespective of the scepticism surrounding binding contracts, artist favouritism, rigid regulations, scanty wages and so on, young artists flocked to become part of the Motown scenario. Some were lucky, others not. This was the working environment Marvin Gaye was destined to join, and one he would later rebel against.

# 2. | Pride and Joy

*Harvey was the father figure Marvin needed, and the man
Berry Gordy couldn't be to him.*

(Graham Canter)

*I was eager to be with music and be a part of music and I'd
learn anything and do anything.*

(Marvin Gaye)

*Marvin might have dabbled with a little grass or something but
I never knew him to have the kind of drug problem he
ultimately wound up with.*

(Barbara Randolph)

*News of the marriage came as quite a shock to all of us . . . we
were all hurt and confused when he began avoiding us.*

(Mary Wilson)

Back in Chicago, Harvey Fuqua's luck with The Moonglows ran out
in 1960. He disbanded the group, keeping Marvin Gaye with him.
Fuqua, eleven years his senior, believed with continued tuition he
could perfect Gaye's amateur performances, and patiently taught him
the tricks of the trade. In turn, Marvin admired and loved his gentle-
natured, softly spoken mentor, who represented a father figure he
could easily relate to. Gaye later admitted Fuqua showed him more
attention than his own father and, of course, unlike Gay Snr,
encouraged his nagging musical ambitions. Harvey also became his
spiritual guider and close friend, and the two were devoted to each
other for the rest of Gaye's life.

London nightclub and radio DJ Graham 'Fatman' Canter, who
met Marvin during his exile in London in 1980, noted their special
relationship – 'Harvey was the father figure Marvin needed and the
man Berry Gordy couldn't be to him. Berry had such a massive
empire and so many artists to look after, particularly Diana Ross and

the Supremes, he didn't have much time for Marvin. He needed someone to tell his troubles to and to bounce off his musical ideas. Harvey was always there. The father and son situation was obvious . . . When working together Harvey would put his arm around Marvin when he couldn't hit the right note he was straining for. He'd say, "Take a break, you can do it." He'd tell Marvin he was a million dollars, the most brilliant thing since sliced bread, and generally build up his ego. He pampered him, if you like, but at the same time tried to keep that rod of iron between them.'

With The Moonglows disbanded Fuqua became unhappy with his talent scouting position at Chess Records as he told author Nelson George: 'I started feeling closed in. I was going to the office every day at 10 a.m. and I'd never worked like that before. So I told Leonard [Chess] I couldn't handle the job. I wanted to be out and free. At the time he had a lease master deal with Billy Davis and Gwen Gordy over in Detroit – Anna Records – so he said, "Why don't you go there and work in that operation, since you wanna be free. You can come in anytime you want to, you can go on the road, you can produce when you feel like it." It was an ideal situation and I'd be helping to build a new label.' So, in 1960 Harvey Fuqua and Marvin Gaye joined the Anna label which had opened a year earlier with The Voicemasters' 'Oops I'm Sorry' single. This was followed by a string of singles including The Hill Sisters' 'Hit And Run Away Love', Berry Gordy's brother Robert's 'Never More', recorded under the pseudonym Bob Kayli, Paul Gayten's 'The Hunch' and Letha Jones' 'I Need You'. Neither Fuqua nor Gaye recorded for the label.

With Berry Gordy's company Motown falling together, the West Grand Boulevard recording studios ran twenty-four hours a day, as staff writer/producer Hank Cosby (introduced to the company by a seventeen-year-old Smokey Robinson) recalled: 'In the beginning there was only one studio and it never closed down. So at one time in the early days there were about thirteen songwriters and about eight or nine producers working there at the same time. Maybe three or four were producing hit records, so we had quite a few people running around trying to get something done. It was always a challenge. We had in-house everything – engineers, arrangers and musicians. Everybody was there seven days a week, around the clock. We were just cutting records, day and night, night and day.'

One of Motown's first white executives, Barney Ales, also recalled Motown's round-the-clock operation, when Gordy would experiment with music throughout the night – 'On occasion so much noise would be heard from the studio that the neighbours complained to the police . . . [Berry] was recording in the back, and just before I came to him there was a house next to his where the people used to complain about the studio being worked so late. Because most of the guys worked either at Ford or Chrysler or one of the other factories, they worked during the day and had to record at night. So the studio had more activity from eleven o'clock to three or four in the morning than it did during the day.' Later, Berry Gordy bought the house immediately next to his and placed an eviction order on the tenants, before purchasing seven more houses in the block. It was a standing joke for several years that Motown was housed in the only seven storey block built sideways!

At this time black record sales suffered on a national scale but in their local release areas sold well. Only two national record sales charts, the Top 60 Pop chart and the Top 60 R&B (Rhythm & Blues) chart, existed. Contemporary artists like Elvis Presley and Frank Sinatra were listed on the former whilst R&B catered for black music. Berry Gordy had enjoyed R&B hits with The Miracles' 'Got A Job', the answer record to The Silhouettes' 'Get A Job', and 'Bad Girl' distributed by Chess Records, and Barrett Strong's 'Money (That's What I Want)' which was Gordy's first big seller. Smokey Robinson: 'When The Miracles recorded "Way Over There" [released in 1960 and Robinson's debut as solo producer] we put it on Motown in Detroit and it started breaking really big. So we went national. But at that time, as at any other time, when you're a new company distributors don't know if you're gonna come back with other hits, so they took their time paying you. But, we were experienced with all that by this time. Plus we were black-owned and operated which was a big thing at the time.'

Meanwhile, as their brother was slowly gaining momentum locally, Gwen and Anna Gordy reluctantly closed the Anna label in 1961 when Gwen's partner Billy Davis left to pursue other recording activities. The last singles were future Temptation David Ruffin's 'I'm In Love' and Joe Tex's 'Baby You're Right'. To replace Anna, Harvey Fuqua opened the Tri Phi and Harvey labels where the first releases were The Spinners' 'That's What Girls Are Made For' and Eddie Burns's 'Orange Driver' respectively. As a solo artist Fuqua recorded for both labels – 'Whistling About You', 'She Loves Me So', 'Come On And Answer Me', and with Ann Bogan (a future Marvelette) 'I

Hear An Echo' on Tri Phi; 'What Can You Do Now', again with Bogan, on Harvey.

Marvin Gaye's role for the new labels was not one of recording artist – Fuqua never had the time to record him – but one of session musician. Marvin: 'Apart from vocally backing several artists, I played drums on The Spinners' hit "That's What Girls Are Made For". But just as Harvey was getting [ready] to record me as a solo act, he and Gwen decided to throw in their lot with Berry Gordy and his new company.' Harvey Fuqua reputedly lacked the business acumen to keep the labels financially stable so merged them with Motown in 1963 with a combined artist roster that included Shorty Long, Johnny Bristol and Jackey Beavers, Jnr Walker and the All Stars, The Spinners and an unrecorded Marvin Gaye. Fuqua joined Gordy's in-house creative team and became Marvin's manager, leaving the running of the labels to Gordy while Gwen ran the artist development department for a time. Meanwhile, Harvey's business relationship with Gwen Gordy had turned to romance: he married her in 1960, while twenty-year-old Marvin Gaye, who was best man at the wedding, dated Gwen's thirty-seven-year-old sister Anna. Gaye visited her daily. Anna Gordy: 'Every day Marvin came to see me at four o'clock. He would come and sit in my office every day at four o'clock for two months. One day he didn't come and I looked at my watch "four o'clock, where is this guy?" And he stuck his head around the corner at four-ten and said, "You missed me didn't you?" I said, "Yes I did".'

Smokey Robinson: '[Marvin] fell madly in love with Anna . . . I could dig it 'cause I loved Anna too. She's good people. She swept Marvin off his feet. I mean, he was bonkers for the lady.'

Friends believed Gaye was looking for a substitute mother figure, but irrespective of the attraction, Anna Gordy was his first serious girlfriend, who possessed a passion that he yearned for. Yet, Gaye told David Ritz that Anna and Gwen Gordy were prima donnas – 'They had a hell of a reputation for being party girls. They were physical – that's true of all the Gordys – and spoiled. Gwen and Anna were glamorous, always dressed to the teeth and interested in beauty. They were also fiercely loyal to their brother, I admire that. Fact is, the Gordys were the tightest family I've ever seen. I rarely saw rivalry between them. No one could break into that circle, though I probably came as close as anyone.'

Being seventeen years Marvin's elder, the beautiful Anna Gordy was a worldly person and he admitted he needed a 'loving teacher' –

'From a professional point of view I have to say – and I hope this doesn't sound too cold – that I knew just what I was doing. Marrying a queen might not make me a king, but at least I'd have a shot at being a prince. Besides, Anna was into my music more than any woman I'd ever known. She'd beg me to play and sing and write, and because she had wonderful ears, she appreciated my every move. She complimented me. She called me her fine young thing. She was more forward than I was. She knew she wanted me and she got me. But I also knew what I wanted. I wanted her to help me cut into that long line in front of the recording studio.' Despite this bravado Marvin worshipped Anna, and until the day he died carried her in his heart, despite their differences over the years.

Anna Gordy was a strong-willed, ambitious woman, who with Gwen, was a major force behind their brother's success. The sisters were widely well respected as Nelson George wrote – 'Though in her mid-thirties Anna was widely considered one of the "finest ladies in the city". Visiting musicians made sure to introduce themselves, and Anna, a shrewd woman with [Berry] Gordy's characteristic business sense, introduced these suitors to her little brother. They may not have wanted to be bothered by the fast-talking little guy, but he was this sweetlooking woman's brother, so they paid attention.'

Meanwhile, Motown music was on the move, when five Detroit-born girls, The Marvelettes aka The Marvels (Gladys Horton, Wanda Young, Georgeanna Tillman (Dobbins), Katherine Anderson and Juanita Cowart) gave Berry Gordy his first national number one single with 'Please Mr Postman' in 1961. Marvin Gaye played drums on this song which was the only Motown track to reach number one twice in the US charts. The Marvelettes had been auditioned by a Motown representative and rejected because they were considered unsuitable for the inhouse writers. The girls decided to write their own material and returned with their song – the chart topper – and Gordy signed them! Also in 1961 the Motown boss was badgered into signing The Primettes, later to become the trio The Supremes (Diana Ross, Mary Wilson and Florence Ballard) and The Primes later known as The Pirates, then The Temptations (Melvin Franklin, Otis Williams, Elbridge Bryant (later replaced by David Ruffin), Paul Williams and Eddie Kendricks).

These were just three of the many heavyweight acts Marvin Gaye would compete against on record, after signing to the Tamla label, where he would stay as a solo singer throughout his Motown career.

Unlike other acts Marvin did not audition for Berry Gordy – 'I wouldn't go for an audition because I stopped auditioning when I was a very young artist. How dare I! Berry had to hear me at a nightclub because I wouldn't audition for him. I think he thought that was rather rash of me!' On the other hand, Gordy recalls that the first time he became aware of Marvin's talent was at a company party: 'In the early Sixties at Motown's Hitsville studio we were having a Christmas party and Marvin was at the piano, doodling around and playing some jazzy chords and singing some things.' Whatever the circumstances of Gaye joining the company there was one aspect he couldn't escape while waiting to record, that of working in other musical areas. Smokey Robinson: 'He was a drummer for The Miracles and me. We used to go out on the road together and our relationship started to form from our first meeting. And I went through many phases with Marvin. I'm sure he went through many with me also.'

Robinson, who nicknamed Marvin 'Dad' because he crept around like an old man, suffering as he did, from corns and bunions on both feet, recalled that one of their first appearances with Marvin as drummer was at New York's Rockland Palace. Four hours before the group was due on stage, Gaye was nowhere to be found. Minutes before showtime he returned. Robinson: 'He said, "I was out buying the gangster," using the street name for pot, "and lost track of time." He confessed in such a sweet way – sweetness was one of Dad's trademarks. I couldn't stay mad for long.'

Gaye: 'I worked at whatever they asked me to do. That was mainly drumming though. You sweated and ached and played. But you were young and your eyes were full of love and show business and music. And you were having fun and getting money for it ($5 per session). I sang background on most of the early Tamla records. Berry thought my voice was very near jazz and when they began recording me for my first disc, they were playing around with ballads and jazz. In fact, they didn't really know how to record me.'

The artist faced a dilemma because Berry Gordy felt the market place wasn't ready for another jazz singer and Motown's music was a commercial R&B sound which was, he felt, also unsuitable for Marvin. Gaye, of course, had his own ideas – he saw himself as an urbane, middle-of-the-road artist in the mould of Frank Sinatra; Gordy thought otherwise but realised he had to do something because his artist was rapidly becoming restless, unmanageable and frustrated at being a backing singer and drummer. While still undecided he took Gaye into the studios to experiment on different musical styles and finally recorded sufficient tracks for an album. From this selection, and to placate the singer, the music standards 'The Masquerade (Is Over)' and 'Witchcraft' were released under the name of Marvin Gay, as a promotional single only, in late 1960/early 1961. His debut commercial single 'Let Your Conscience Be Your Guide' followed in May 1961 and was a low-key stab at R&B. Gaye: '"Let Your Conscience Be Your Guide" was a real disaster. Berry wrote and produced it. I'm not trying to discredit him by that statement but it was one of the few lemons he'd had. He's really a fine writer, so it must have been my performance. Now I think about it, it wasn't very good.' The single marked twenty-two-year-old Marvin adding a final 'E' to his surname, a move he wanted to make for some time because 'I was tired of being teased that I was gay'. Despite his first attempt bombing, the remaining songs from the session were released as his first album 'The Soulful Moods Of Marvin Gaye' during June, which was the Tamla label's second album release following 'Hi! We're The Miracles', and second flop. His album included his beloved middle-of-the-road songs like 'My Funny Valentine', 'How High The Moon, How Deep Is The Ocean', his debut single and flipside 'Never Let You Go (Sha-Lu-Bop)'. Motown intended to market him as the next Sam Cooke or Nat King Cole and certainly at this time they would have succeeded if Gaye had been agreeable. When he refused to co-operate because he had set his sights on being the black Frank Sinatra, not because he admired his singing style, but because he wanted the women that that status would bring, the promotional idea was dropped.

Marvin Gaye's first recording sessions were noted by Mary Wilson. At the time she was talking about him to the other two Supremes: 'Somehow [he] sensed we were talking about him and we saw him blush. It was rare to see that genuine shyness in a man, and it endeared him to us all the more. We giggled behind our hands about it, but from that moment Marvin was very special to us. As I learned more about him, I attributed his lovely manners to the fact that he was a preacher's son.' Wilson also remembered that he was famous in the offices for wearing 'kookie hats' – berets, fedoras and tam-o-shanters perched on the side of his head. 'His unusual appearance was probably his way of hiding his shyness; ironically it only attracted more attention. We knew him from seeing him around the studio, but we only got to know him well when he would sing to us.' Marvin and the Supremes would regularly gather together for impromptu singing sessions; he would play the piano and the girls would cluster around in what Wilson called our most seductive poses'.

Marvin Gaye's charm was a magnet to most women as Wilson further explained – 'Other guys were cute or sharp. Marvin was beautiful. Other guys teased and joked around, Marvin was always considerate and solicitous. Being with Marvin was like having every girlhood dream come true. He was a prince, and there was just no one like him anywhere. Our attraction to Marvin was not really a sexual one. The minute we laid eyes on him we knew that we loved him in that pure, sweet way few people ever get the chance to love anymore. It was enough just to be around Mr Gaye. We were still in our early teens and Marvin was twenty-three or so; no doubt he saw us as silly teenage girls, and our attraction to him must have been comically obvious to him and anyone else. But he never treated us as if we were silly, and so we continued to hang on to his every word.' She insisted that she shared a platonic relationship with Gaye and strenuously denied any hints of being sexually attracted to him. However, twenty years later when he was exiled in London, he revealed – 'she was in love with me and because of this I avoided being in her company.'

In 1960/61, Berry Gordy had further problems with another artist, that of planning the career of eleven-year-old Stevie Wonder, real name Steveland Morris. Once again, Gordy was at a loss as to how to present the young blind boy to the public, so instructed writer/producer Clarence Paul to guide him. Paul wrote and produced Stevie's first singles, and with Hank Cosby wrote 'I Call It Pretty Music But The Old People Call It The Blues', Little Stevie's debut in August 1962. The Saginaw-born youngster waited until May 1963 before enjoying an American chart topper with a seven-minute version of 'Fingertips Part II', recorded live at Chicago's Regal Theatre. Wonder (the 'Little' was dropped in 1964) and Marvin Gaye became close friends and each respected the other's creative genius. As both grew older their careers followed a parallel exemplified in the Seventies when both fought bitter battles with Berry Gordy to gain creative control over their work. However, Wonder, a shrewd business man, avoided the pitfalls that befell Gaye, and generally conducted himself and his career with a professional attitude that Marvin lacked. Perhaps if Gaye had followed his colleague's lead, his future recording and financial catastrophes could have been avoided.

Although the two artists never competed professionally, they did clash early on in their careers when Berry Gordy introduced his 'Battle Of The Stars', where Motown acts competed against each other at a Detroit nightclub. The contest had an unexpected result as Gordy told radio DJ Stuart Grundy – 'The last show we had there was Marvin Gaye versus Stevie Wonder, and Marvin worked hard. He went out and bought a harmonica. He wanted to surprise Stevie because Stevie had his harmonica. When Marvin came out he got a great ovation, when he pulled out his harmonica he was just great. When Stevie came out, he was just sensational. But Stevie was blind and he had glasses, and he was just a tiny kid. The people went, "Oh, isn't he cute, beautiful, playing his bongos and his harmonica." Then he went off. When Marvin came back on again, they all booed Marvin. This big guy against this little kid. It was just so sad to me . . . and Marvin, I could see tears in his eyes, and I realised that that was because they were hissing at him. Marvin was so crushed by that.'

Artists also competed in their free time. Berry Gordy arranged regular company picnics where they and company staff mingled to drink, eat and play games, which included teaming up for football and baseball. Nelson George reported that occasionally the athletic competition would get fierce – 'Clarence Paul broke an arm and Marvin Gaye fractured a foot playing "touch" football.' The competitiveness was encouraged by Gordy, who expected his own teams to win. These gatherings were intended to enhance the company family atmosphere and like the Christmas parties, continued until the children lost interest.

Even though he had now recorded his own work, albeit unsuccessfully, Marvin Gaye desperately wanted to become a fully fledged member of Motown's regular working team, but his time in the studio was limited because charting acts took priority. All he could do was beaver away at his session work and concentrate on his songwriting, which he had taken up prior to joining Motown, until he felt it reached the standard Berry Gordy demanded from his writers. In 1962 Marvin finally convinced him of his composing expertise by writing 'Beechwood 4-5789' with George Gordy and Mickey Stevenson for The Marvelettes.

Another act Gaye was later to write for was Martha and the Vandellas, a trio formed by accident. Alabama-born on 18 July 1941,

Martha Reeves, one of eleven children born to Ruby and Elijah Reeves, first sang as a three-year-old in church with her two elder brothers. She was later an enthusiastic member of her school choirs and upon graduating from North Eastern High School, decided to become a performer. Reeves worked as Mickey Stevenson's secretary in the A&R department after performing with The Fascinations, Curtis Mayfield and The Del-Phis comprising Gloria Williams, Annette Sterling and Rosalind Ashford. The Del-Phis released one single 'It Takes Two' in 1961 on the Checkmate label, and performed as backing singers for J.J. Barnes among others, before unsuccessfully auditioning for Motown. While Reeves was walking through the offices she spotted an advertisement for Stevenson's secretary, applied and was hired. Reeves: 'My job was to call people and schedule them for the studio, to arrive on time and to get out.' As well as these duties she cut demo recordings for other artists, and when Motown label songstress Mary Wells failed to turn up for a recording session, Reeves and the Del-Phis replaced her. Reeves: 'Mary was returning home from a tour and was quite fatigued at the time. She had been requested for a recording session that didn't suit her schedule. So, as a stand-in for the union's sake, I sang a song which became my first recording.' The track was 'There He Is (At My Door)', with Gloria Williams on lead, originally intended as a song for another artist. However, their version was considered suitable for release and in 1962 it was issued on the Melody label. The girls recorded it as The Vels because 'The Del-Phis' was owned by their previous record company Checkmate. When the single flopped Williams left the group, and when Mary Wells missed another recording session appointment, Martha, Rosalind and Annette recorded 'I'll Have To Let Him Go', written and produced by Mickey Stevenson. Released on the Gordy label, it sold about three copies which, according to Reeves, were bought by the girls themselves!

Although in the future the media often compared Martha and the Vandellas to their sister group The Supremes, there was no contest. The squeaky, nasal vocals of Diana Ross were considered by many too twee and sugary against Martha Reeves' red-blooded, gospelly, soulful voice. Reeves: 'The biggest misconception about the Vandellas was that we were a group like, say, The Supremes. My decision to have vocal back-up was a result of my need for companionship on the road as opposed to a need for serious background singers.' Both trios ultimately recorded some of the Sixties' and Seventies' finest records but there's little doubt that as Berry Gordy was totally enamoured with Diana Ross and subsequently The Supremes, they took priority in the recording studios.

Now being active in the studios in her own right, Martha Reeves – with her slim body, classic looks and determined attitude to succeed – met other acts and remembers the first time she saw Marvin Gaye there – 'He walked around with his hat pulled over his eyes. He smoked a pipe and was kind of quiet. He was always around and if there wasn't a session on, it seemed he'd be rehearsing some instrument. If not the drums, then it'd be the piano, or melodica or something. He was just so musical and I was surprised, yet delighted, to find out he was actually a singer. As a singer he was really shy and it was our teasing, charming and speaking words of admiration that derived the results.' Also, when her regular drummer, Benny Benjamin, was unavailable for recording sessions, she recruited the shy pipe smoker as replacement. Both were easy going people, striving for the same professional goal, so a close friendship was cemented and lasted for over twenty years.

As Marvin watched Berry Gordy's other acts notch up hit records, he became panic-stricken over his own stagnant career and told his colleagues he intended to abandon it for his first love, sport. However, Anna Gordy believed in his talent and fortunately convinced him to continue experimenting with music in the studios, and involving himself with other acts' recording sessions while patiently waiting for the long queue to the studios to subside. Gaye: 'I was eager to be with music and be a part of music and I'd learn anything and do anything. Even though now I don't feel we got near the compensation for that, song royalties and everything, but it was a vehicle for us to create. I'm sometimes bitter about the money, but most of the time I'm not. I really did a lot of things in those days willingly because it was there and I wanted to see if I could do it. It was good for us all. Stevie Wonder and myself used to hang about in the studio and practise and play different things. Us and Smokey Robinson. We'd do that for hours. We might come up with a big smash during the day. We didn't make a lot of money but it was OK, because we started out with the right spirit, and I know for a fact that Berry Gordy has a big heart. Of course he's also a businessman and a good one. Having a great heart and being a businessman can be a lot of trouble but he manages very well.'

Months after Motown opened, Berry Gordy introduced a

choreography and grooming department which was, due to lack of office space, initially situated in his father's flat. Eventually one of the houses Gordy bought was split into three departments – choreography, musical arrangement and wardrobe design. Each act was trained to perform an original stage show, with dances and dialogue worked out for them. Even the adlibbing was rehearsed. Harvey and Gwen Fuqua were originally in charge of artist grooming until Mrs Maxine Powell took over by opening the company's own Artist Development School which operated for six years. Harvey concentrated on writing/producing and managing Gaye, while his wife toured with The Supremes as their chaperone and wardrobe mistress. Gwen: 'When I wasn't with the girls, I was out driving in my car, playing our records. This led me into the promotion of records.' From promotion Gwen headed the publicity and public relations department before professionals were hired to take over.

All artists were expected to attend the Artist Development School which offered its tuition free. Marvin Gaye, however, was an exception! He resisted the training and years later regretted the decision as he realised he lacked the on-stage presence that made The Temptations, for example, such visually exciting performers. Nelson George reported: 'Maxine Powell thought Marvin Gaye was a fine actor on stage – when he wanted to be. Too often, however, he was distracted and would rather have been doing something else. Technically, Marvin Gaye's only problem on stage was that he would close his eyes when he sang – another Powell no-no.' Cholly Atkins, a respected song-and-dance entertainer, became Motown's staff choreographer and believed Gaye with stage presence could easily have become another Sam Cooke, but he refused to be guided by the older man. Motown's music classes were headed by veteran band leader, Maurice King, who taught artists vocal exercises, lead and backing vocals and progressive arrangements.

'Let Your Conscience Be Your Guide', released two months after The Supremes' first 'I Want A Guy', was followed by two dismal 1962 singles – Pat Ballard's submissive 'Mister Sandman' and 'Soldier's Plea' (with The Lovetones on backing vocals) written by Mickey Stevenson, Fay Janet Hale and George Gordy. The former was based around shrill female voices over a mid-tempo-paced sound, while the latter was cluttered with a superfluous Spanish trumpet solo and a military-styled drum beat. Hardly hit material, and a disastrous start to a promising recording career. Gaye: 'None of those records were really in a commercial bag. I needed something more orientated to the teenagers. Harvey, who was my manager, kept telling me that. Berry kept telling me that, and I knew that. I was writing quite a bit but most of my things were kinda jazz-orientated.' Then Gordy and Gaye clashed over his next single. The disagreement was, Marvin admitted 'my first power encounter with him'. Gaye: 'One day I was in the control room playing around with a little song I'd written. Berry heard it and suggested I change some of the jazzier chords. I thought it should remain the way I wrote it . . . So we did it and then he said, "Now that sounds like pop. Now I think we can give you a hit."' Berry Gordy was right. That hit was 'Stubborn Kind Of Fellow', written by Marvin, Gordy and Mickey Stevenson, who also produced it. The single was issued during July 1962 and reached number forty-six in the pop charts (no 8 R&B), and was his first British release in February 1963 on the Oriole label. Rosalind Ashford, Martha Reeves and Annette Sterling née Beard provided the backing vocals on this finger-snapping tune. (The Vandellas recreated their 'Stubborn Kind Of Fellow' backing vocals on the single 'Set Me Free' recorded by a Radio WXYZ DJ Lee Alan in 1963. It was a charity release with all proceeds going to a local YMCA summer camp fund.) Marvin Gaye's long awaited success did not, however, assure him of a secure future with regular record releases because his indifferent attitude, his moodiness and short temper began annoying Motown's writers and producers, making recording sessions a nightmare. Without their assistance, an artist simply didn't record, so once again, he joined the studio queue.

Meantime, Berry Gordy's next move was to re-establish Martha, Rosalind and Annette as recording artists, following their 1962 flop 'I'll Have To Let Him Go', because he felt their voices warranted more than the confines of session work. The trio went into the studios with Holland, Dozier and Holland to record 'Come And Get These Memories' which officially launched the career of Martha and the Vandellas. Years later, Reeves acknowledged Gordy's encouragement and support at this time – 'He was a genius of a man. We being so young and rebellious, crossed his path several times, and maybe even got on his bottom nerve at times. But I think the reason for the success of the Motown artists was because of him. He was a hard-working man who knows what he's doing, has a great ear, and if one listened to him, they succeeded.' Motown's publicity department devised an elaborate story about the origin of the name 'Vandellas' and achieved plenty of media mileage by declaring that Marvin Gaye had chosen the name. It proclaimed he nicknamed them 'vandellas', the female equivalent of 'vandels', as they stole the vocal limelight from the lead singer. 'Stubborn Kind Of Fellow' is a good example of this 'vandelism' so it might have had a point! However, the real name emanated from 'Van' – Van Dyke Street where Martha Reeves' mother lived, and 'Della' in tribute to the singer Della Reese.

Six months after the release of 'Stubborn Kind Of Fellow', the album 'That Stubborn Kinda Fellow' was issued. It contained Gaye's third outing 'Soldier's Plea' and its flipside 'Taking My Time', written by Mickey Stevenson and Anna Gordy, where Gaye glided over the easy melody; the B-side to 'Mister Sandman' – 'I'm Yours, You're Mine' – and the album's title and its flipside 'It Hurt Me Too' where a gruff-voiced, deep-throated vocal wasn't immediately recognisable as Gaye's. However, as the tune progressed his familiar style returned. Both sides of his next single – 'Hitch Hike' and 'Hello There Angel' – were featured. The latter was a semi-bouncy smoocher; the sound was popular at the time with mainstream record buyers. This time male back-ups replaced the usual, and expected, female support. And another of Gaye's future singles 'Pride And Joy', and a 1969 flipside (to 'Too Busy Thinking About My Baby') 'Wherever I Lay My Hat (That's My Home)' rounded off the quality tracks. The latter song, produced by Norman Whitfield, was lyrically strong, while a profusion of trumpets and guitars turned the melody into a well-loved song which would eventually reach number one in the British charts but not as a Marvin Gaye single. The remaining track was 'Get My Hands On Some Lovin', a mediocre slice of vocal interplay where Gaye battled with high-pitched vocals presumably courtesy of Martha and the Vandellas.

The album was produced by Mickey Stevenson with the exception of 'Wherever I Lay My Hat (That's My Home)'. The front packaging showed a dapper, short-haired young singer in a dark-brown suit and tie, and white shirt with a pinned collar and cuff-linked sleeves. As was fashionable in the early Sixties, his trousers had argued with his shoes to reveal mud-coloured socks! And a small photo of Martha and the Vandellas was tucked away on the back cover. This release formed the basis of Gaye's first solo British album 'Marvin Gaye' in November 1964 issued on the Stateside label, and the standing pose of the singer on the record's front sleeve was resurrected in 1980 by Motown/EMI for the home compilation 'The Early Years: 1961–1964'.

With a hit single behind him, Marvin Gaye joined Berry Gordy's newly introduced Motown Revues, the first of which debuted at the Howard Theatre, Washington, in October 1962, and included The Contours, Singing Sammy Ward, The Miracles, Little Stevie Wonder, The Supremes, The Marvelettes, Mary Wells and the new hitmaker.

Berry Gordy introduced these Revues because television spots were rare and concert promoters were reluctant to book black acts individually or collectively, and he needed to prove to the public that the names behind the hits were capable of holding down a complete entertaining show, and weren't reliant on their past and current singles. Henry Wynne, a professional black promoter working for Supersonic Attractions, helped Gordy arrange the tour, but nonetheless it was a gamble because some of the newer acts – despite being groomed for stage work in-house (sometimes only two days before going on tour) – had not performed in concert before. However, this gave Berry Gordy an opportunity to distinguish the potential stars from the incurable amateurs, and those who failed the test were later dropped from the roster. Money was not readily available for stage clothes, so many of the female acts shared the same gowns. Thus great care was taken to ensure closing acts didn't wear the same costumes as the opening artists! But nobody cared. The youngsters were being given the golden opportunity to become entertainers and wearing second/third-hand gowns, often illfitting, was all part of making the dream come true.

Touring was the quickest way for acts to make money although the venues available for unknown performers were usually small, low-key, seedy nightspots on the chitlin circuit. The larger, more sophisticated theatres on the national circuit were reserved for established black artists, and by the early Sixties they could earn $900 per night, while unknowns contented themselves with $200 or less. However, from these fees, all expenses (booking agent, manager, backing group and so on) had to be recouped, usually leaving the artist with a handful of dollars. The tours too were long, arduous, often dangerous and exhausting by today's standards, and the Motown Revues were no different. But by using ITM, his in-house management company, Gordy was able to co-ordinate the tours, trim expenses and pocket the income,

Before leaving Detroit to start the first Motown Revue – twenty one-night stands through the Mid-west, down south and back to New York to Harlem's Apollo Theatre for a ten-day stint – Berry

Gordy insisted his artists act with dignity as they represented him and Motown's good name. He instructed male performers to sit in the back of the touring bus, with the girls in front. Once the battered vehicle – a relic from a scrapyard with 'Motor City Tour' blazoned along its sides – was out of the city, the occupants mingled. Despite chaperones in attendance, Mary Wilson remembers people were pairing off before the bus had crossed the Michigan state line. Others gambled, smoked pot, slept or rehearsed. They usually dressed for the stage en route or in a public toilet. Wilson: 'Every few days we would stop at a cheap motel to bathe and wash some clothes. We seldom got to sleep one in a bed, but compared to sleeping sitting up on a hard bus seat being able to lie on any mattress was heaven.' The Temptations' Melvin Franklin recalled the touring bus held a minimum of forty passengers at any one time – 'I used to sleep in the luggage rack. Wasn't any of us under six foot one. I can't climb like I did then, got rheumatoid arthritis. Maybe it's from being a six-foot-one sardine all them years.' 'Touring back then was murder' Thomas 'Beans' Bowles (who doubled as musician and road manager) told David Ritz – 'Berry packed far too many people on the bus. We were always overcrowded. And he booked way too many dates. The strain was bad. We had a bad accident in November 1962 when my driver was killed and we were lucky not to have others [killed]. There might have been a little weed around but no coke. Who had the money? The pay stunk. In order to protect the singers and musicians we put part of their money into an escrow account. Most of them were under eighteen, and if we hadn't done that, they'd have blown all their bread before we'd get back to Detroit. The problem was Berry didn't know when to stop treating people like kids and kept the accounts going for far too long. They wanted to be respected like adults.' Martha Reeves agreed these tours were tough but acknowledged they benefited the music – 'It was the promotion that put us all on the map, so I can't say it was a bad move. Motown knew what they were doing. It might have been tough but we made it. People died on those tours, just getting worn down, getting in the station wagon after playing on stage, then trying to drive three hundred miles.'

Marvin Gaye, on the other hand, felt exploited by the Revues – 'The people were great to be with but other than that, they were nightmares for me. It was some of the hardest work I've ever done. During the earlier years we did as many as seven shows in a day in, say, the Apollo Theatre.' He also suffered professionally on these tours as his static stage technique paled against the other acts' carefully choreographed shows. However, his cool, suave, handsome appearance did much to win him a staunch following, and as he gained more confidence, introduced a dancing troupe and backing vocalists (usually Martha and the Vandellas) on stage. Reeves: 'When we'd finished "Come And Get These Memories" we'd come off stage, change clothes, run back down and do his back-ups.' With more people performing the emphasis was lifted from him as the focal point and, in time, he even started dancing with his troupe. Gaye: 'I was the type of person who never felt the dance. I was always wondering why, what was wrong with my soul that I could never feel the dance. I don't know what I dance now, but everybody says it's really dorky. I used to go out to parties and stand around because I was really nervous. A time back I began to dance a little on stage. I mean, never before would I dance because I'd just come out on stage and pop my fingers and figure that everyone would think I chose to be cool, which is always a possibility as long as you don't try to dance. Once they've discovered you can't dance, you're really ridiculous, you've blown it.'

As black music became more popular, record sales rose and artists were in demand. Motown's charting acts were regularly included on television shows, especially The Supremes who, with Holland, Dozier and Holland songs, were consistent hit makers, and this in turn led to bookings in white supper clubs. Barney Ales, head of Motown's sales division, said the transition from stage to screen was a gradual step – 'You went from hit records to Vegas. Concerts weren't a big thing in those days. You went into nightclubs. In those days we used to call it the chitlin circuit starting in the East and working down south to New Orleans and Texas and then back up. Very seldom did they get out to the West Coast because it was too costly. When an act enjoyed a certain amount of success, they were capable of holding down a performance at the Copa. Outside of playing Las Vegas, the Copa (in New York) was the next best thing. The Supremes and The Temptations were among the first to appear but all the acts eventually played the Copa at one time or another.' For promotional tours costs were kept to a bare minimum, he said, and gave the following example – 'We couldn't afford to send The Marvelettes to San Francisco for a concert at Cow Palace. So we just sent Gladys Horton [the group's lead singer] and picked up three girls in San Francisco.'

So now, with Motown's big-selling acts touring outside Detroit, recording became difficult. For instance, should Marvin Gaye need a new single, the music and backing vocals would be completed then he would return to Detroit to record the lead. If any act stayed in Detroit, most of the time would invariably be spent recording future singles and album tracks. The finished material was then canned and issued whenever needed. Once recording sessions were completed, the artists were referred to Cholly Atkins to learn new stage routines. Interestingly, some new routines were actually memorised before a single was released so, should it be issued while the artist was on tour, it could easily be slipped into the act!

With Motown's music crossing over from the black/soul market into white/pop, record shops were unsure how to display the product. Motown's incongruous and unimaginative album sleeves rarely featured pictures of the artists. Instead a sketch or cartoon would dominate the front sleeve and sketchy notes, a track listing and perhaps a small photo would appear on the back of the packaging. However, album artwork wasn't a priority, breaking the acts was. Marvin Gaye: 'During the Sixties there was an enormous struggle for black music acceptance among whites. Before Berry Gordy it was thought of as not particularly chic to have black record collections in your home if you were white. Motown, however, did a great deal to alleviate that.' Even though Gaye was aware of Gordy's marketing dilemmas and his determination to build and expand Motown with hit acts, he insisted he receive more attention and commitment from his boss. But Gordy needed money to keep his company stable and hit records were the only way of achieving this, so any profit was immediately ploughed back into the operation to help finance the first division. So, Marvin's demands were heard and shelved until the creative staff came up with the right song for him. Unlike other acts, Gaye's wait was relatively short because he could flex his songwriting muscle.

Despite Marvin's lack of visual excitement on stage, the next single in December 1962 was named after the current dance craze and became his second significant seller, (a number twelve R&B hit and a top thirty pop hit). Gaye: 'Everybody was doing dance songs so me, Mickey Stevenson and Clarence Paul wrote one "Hitch Hike". The dance was simple, you made like you were thumbing a ride. I even invented that dance, you know. But I didn't perform it that well because I always have had a couple of left feet.' Due to the lengthy recording sessions his vocals sounded red raw on the disc, the lyrics were repetitive, the clip beat monotonous and Martha and the Vandellas' backing vocals snappy. The teenagers loved every second! And as the trio's vocal interplay formed an integral part of the song, Gaye felt they should have shared the record's label credits with him. He told Radio One DJ Paul Gambaccini this musical effect was his idea – 'And I must say with all humility that anyone can have in making one of these ego-filled statements, that this was all my doing. I would imagine I helped the producers as much as anyone. I was young and raw but we worked well together. I had lots of ideas. They used them freely, but I didn't mind.' The singer also stressed that he was the only Motown artist to use all the company acts, barring one, as backing singers at one time or another – 'And I can actually name the records! Some part of every group – The Temptations, The Supremes, The Miracles, and Gladys Knight and the Pips – have partcipated on some recording of mine. One act hasn't done background on me and I think they were The Elgins. In those days we all worked with each other with love.'

And love was also on Marvin Gaye's mind in 1963 – he married Anna Gordy! The move was expected by her family but came as a surprise to his working colleagues. Mary Wilson: 'News of the marriage came as quite a shock to all of us. I felt very close to Marvin and we were all hurt and confused when he began avoiding us. Shortly before the wedding our conversations started to centre on business and recording; there were no more leisurely afternoons spent around the piano. Of course, this match was the talk of Hitsville, for not only was Marvin marrying the boss' sister but she was seventeen years older than he. Though we no longer enjoyed our special relationship with Marvin he still liked us very much.' Yes, Marvin Gaye did change. He seemed to avoid being with any of the female artists, although these liaisons were largely innocent, and he spent less time jamming with Motown's musicians where alcohol and dope were available. By now Gaye was a regular user of marijuana and a spasmodic taker of cocaine, and used them, he said, to their best advantage. For instance, he preferred to take cocaine when recording and would snort or eat the drug; the former method was a habit for the remainder of his life.

However, Mary Wells recalled that she never saw Gaye taking drugs – 'I knew him as a sweet kind of man. He had a pretty strong wife you know, Anna never took anything. He was always mild mannered whenever I saw him. Under the influence of drugs a person can act very different. I never saw him like that.' Barbara Randolph:

'I think there was more alcohol about during those days. Everybody was into that. Mainly the drinking was among the male groups and writers. It wasn't against the law. They'd be writing and there'd be a bottle of something around. When they were in the studios they would be drinking and recording, and nobody really thought anything about it. But a couple of them ended up with really major problems. Dope wasn't fashionable then – that was something that happened later on. Cocaine was the drug you heard about. Marvin might have dabbled with a little grass or something, but I never knew him to have the kind of drug problem he ultimately wound up with.' Randolph's comments are substantiated by author Peter Benjaminson – 'When a Motown group toured by plane, the first thing they'd be asked as they strapped themselves in was, "What can I get you to drink?" One of the group was likely to answer, "Since it's morning, I'll have something nourishing. How about a Bloody Mary or a Coffee Royale?" When they arrived at the theatre, their dressing-rooms would be fully stocked with booze. Club personnel would mix everyone his or her favourite drink without being asked.'

When Marvin Gaye married Anna Gordy, it was thought Berry would have more control over him and his professional life. However, it was Anna who skilfully oversaw her husband's business affairs and became his musical adviser. Without her, Marvin probably would have stumbled through business commitments that were not beneficial to him. He needed a brick wall to lean against and support him, and Anna provided that, plus the special emotional bond known only to a loving and devoted wife. She understood him, listened to him and injected confidence when he became insecure and unsure, which was often. They complemented each other and the marriage was idyllic for as long as Marvin allowed it to be.

Marv Johnson, who released the Tamla label's first single 'Come To Me' in 1959, often came into contact with Anna – 'I didn't get along with [her] at all. I wouldn't dare speak on behalf of anyone else but for myself I can say that I had problems with her as far as our relationship was concerned. When Marvin married Anna there was a tremendous amount of – I don't know what you'd call it – it seemed to be more negative than positive sometimes. But Marvin as a person was a very artistic, sensible individual who believed in and loved music as I did.

Since he was involved with the Gordys on a personal basis maybe at some time or another he found it necessary to avoid me so that it wouldn't interfere with whatever he'd got going.'

'Pride And Joy' (also recorded under the title 'True True Lovin' which remains unreleased) was Gaye's sixth commercial single, co-written with Mickey Stevenson and Norman Whitfield. Martha and the Vandellas once again provided the backing vocals on this tribute to Anna Gaye. Anna: 'Marvin's songs were a reflection of our happiness and our joy . . . he sang what was going on with us. It was just really beautiful, really wonderful.' A black and white promotional film exists today showing Marvin dressed as a captain, standing on an upper deck of a Mississippi steamer singing the song, with Martha and the girls on a lower deck replying to his lead vocals, 'Pride And Joy', released in April 1963, became his biggest-selling American single to date and peaked at number ten in the mainstream charts (no 2 R&B). Ironically, the record also marked a change of producer. Gaye: 'I think it was felt Mickey Stevenson's productions weren't getting the best out of me as a singer. Berry decided to give me a shot with Holland, Dozier and Holland, who he felt could give me a more R&B sound.' However, the hit did little to alter his career as Gaye told Paul Gambaccini – 'It didn't change anything. That was still a struggling period during those years and I don't view them with a lot of happiness because there was a lot of pain trying to be young and not knowing the business a great deal. You know, trying to figure things out and nobody told you a lot.'

Although Holland, Dozier and Holland didn't give their best work to Marvin Gaye – The Supremes had the lion's share – they were destined to be credited with creating what the company, and later the world, called 'The Motown Sound'. Nobody has succeeded in dissecting or imitating this 'Sound' although the trio has admitted to using certain fundamental guidelines like a strong bass line to pick out the original melody. Percussion, lashings of tambourines and keyboards develop that guideline until the tight beat sets the pace for the singer. Saxophone breaks were liberally used; in fact, a listener could identify a Motown single by the way that instrument was used. The back-up vocals were sharp and squeaky, using the call and response technique and when strings were introduced the arrangements were sweeping, suggestive and low-keyed. Berry Gordy probably came the closest when he said the 'Sound' was 'a combination of rats, roaches, talent, guts and love'. And once a winning formula was discovered, the riffs would be used time and again, which is why during the Sixties so many records sounded similar.

Smokey Robinson: 'People would listen to the "Sound" and they'd say – "they use more bass or they use more drums". Bullshit. When we were first successful with it people were coming from Germany, France, Italy, Mobile, Alabama. From everywhere. Just to record in Detroit. They figured it was in the air, that if they came to Detroit and recorded on the freeway, they'd get the Motown Sound. The Motown Sound to me is not an audible sound. It's spiritual and comes from the people that make it happen. What other people don't realise is that we just had one studio there. We [had others] in Chicago, Nashville, New York, LA, almost every big city. And we still got the "Sound".'

Marvin Gaye's third album attempted to capture the excitement of his stage performances. Titled 'Recorded Live! On Stage' and issued during September 1963, it contained three singles: 'One Of These Days', 'Get My Hands On Some Lovin'', 'Days Of Wine And Roses', and two songs which to date have never been recorded elsewhere – 'You Are My Sunshine' and 'Mojo Hanna'. The album wasn't British-released, Gaye wasn't a big enough record seller to warrant a 'live' album even though the public could have heard the clarity of his voice on both ballad and uptempo material, his rapport with the audience and his nervous start turning into a confident performance. Naturally, the album with its front cover showing the singer dressed in a black dinner suit, white shirt and black bow tie, in varying performing poses, is much in demand today. Record collectors have priced the album on the old-fashioned circular Tamla logo – a globe touching a disc – sitting in the left-hand bottom corner of the sleeve.

Meanwhile, the brilliance of Holland, Dozier and Holland continued when they gave Marvin 'Can I Get A Witness', which reflected his early church influence. The simple, uptempo song was also released in September 1963, the same month as Little Stevie Wonder's 'Workout Stevie, Workout', the follow-up to his 'Fingertips Part II'. Gaye: 'Holland, Dozier and Holland came to me one day and said they had a great track for me. I said I really needed something. Diana Ross and the Supremes were in the studio and they said – "Let's use them for background voices." So Diana and the girls did the background work and I went into the studio to record it.' Eddie Holland: 'I noticed that when I was teaching him the song, he was listening to me sing it. I was getting ready to sing it down again when he said "no, no, no, I got it". And I looked at him because I didn't really believe he had because usually the songs weren't that easy for most people to sing right away. And I started the machine up and sure enough he had it. Not only did he have the song but he started improvising it, so to speak, in a way I didn't even show him. That's when I was very impressed, and became awakened and aware of his exceptional ability as an artist.' The single reached twenty-two in the pop charts (no 15 R&B) and was later 'answered' by Mick Jagger's Rolling Stones when they recorded 'Now I've Got A Witness'.

'Can I Get A Witness' was also later recorded and released by Gaye's colleague Barbara Randolph in August 1968. This was a strange move particularly as he had already been successful with it. Randolph: 'It was the choice of the producer. [We] didn't have a lot of say in our songs. There were writers there on staff and if they decided they wanted to produce an artist, they would get it approved, then they'd go into the studios and record the material with you. The only problem was you were charged for the sessions. And this money comes out of your royalties. So, now you can see why I only recorded three titles there.' Across the Atlantic, the track was given a second female interpretation when Britain's top singer Dusty Springfield recorded it, nine months after leaving The Springfields in 1963 to embark upon a solo career. The innovative songstress recorded her version on the 'Dusty' EP, released as her third single 'I Just Don't Know What To Do With Myself' entered the British top ten during 1964, and as a second 'Dusty' track 'Wishin' & Hopin'' soared to number six in the American charts. Fashionable Springfield – an international star in her own right, with her hair teased into a back-combed bouffant, panda-blacked eyes, pale face, and stiff-petticoated skirted dresses complemented by pointed toe shoes with stiletto heels – was heavily influenced by 'The Motown Sound', particularly Marvin Gaye and Martha and the Vandellas. She befriended many of the artists during visits to America or when the acts performed in Britain, to become 'one of the gang' and her admiration for this young black sound was apparent in her own recordings, prompting Cliff Richard to nickname her 'the white negress'. In time, Springfield took the unprecedented step of promoting the artists on British television.

Twenty-one years after Barbara Randolph's 'Can I Get A Witness' was released, another British singer, young Sam Brown enjoyed a

1989 hit with it thanks to the song wearing yet another musical overcoat. Thus proving good songs never die – they only sleep awhile!

As the mid-Sixties approached, the true potential of Holland, Dozier and Holland was realised and Motown artists begged for their compositions. They were in constant demand, as Lamont Dozier explained – 'If we didn't complete an average of two or three songs a day, at least we would start them. We would have parts of the songs or maybe parts of a verse done, so that at the end of the day we would have something accomplished. I guess that was primarily the reason for the success we had in such a short time. Berry Gordy trusted us to do what we wanted to do. We had a free range to pick and release what we felt was proper or would be a hit for the company.' Inspiration for songs came from a variety of sources. Dozier: 'We got ideas for songs from watching soap operas on TV, reading magazines or just dreaming up situations. Our songs were generally slanted towards girls as they made up the biggest market. We deliberately tried to be as commercial as possible and always used a very simple approach because we believed that simplicity was the key to being commercial. Another point is that our numbers were very melodic as well as having lyrics with which girls could identify. We enjoyed taking other people's songs and doing them with our own arrangements. We did this on several albums. When we were producing albums we never threw on old tracks that were not good enough for singles.'

The trio also wrote Marvin Gaye's next 'You're A Wonderful One', released in February 1964, which closely resembled 'Can I Get A Witness', although was more pop slanted. It sold better than its predecessor by cracking the American top twenty after becoming his fifth R&B hit, peaking at number fifteen and marked a format slowly being introduced into Gaye's work – his releases were slanting towards the lucrative white buying market. Marvin: 'I felt comfortable with Holland, Dozier and Holland because they were very serious producers and I understood where they were coming from. I tried very hard to interpret what they were feeling and thinking about when they wrote. It was also very taxing on my voice because I was still finding it. I was still trying to control my voice and how to sing harshly without tearing my throat out. I would get up on some of the notes, although I never quite made it in some cases. Other times I would, but my voice was in an experimental stage with their music because it needed the roughness and the softness in parts, and it was very difficult to control my voice like they wanted me to.' He also complained of being forced to record the trio's songs in an unnatural falsetto voice – 'I'd be angry at them for cutting them high, but they would always say had they not cut them like that, they wouldn't have sold like they did. You get to the point where you're about to kill yourself or have a stroke, and that's how we used to record.' Gaye wasn't alone in his complaint. Levi Stubbs, lead singer with the Four Tops, also had difficulty in reaching the high notes. Marvin: 'Sometimes his veins were popping out. His neck muscles were bulging and we had to stop the tape and spray his throat, or call in the respiratory man. And I would do the same thing and say, "Oh my God, I can't sing this song, please do something."

'It was rough, but it sold records.'

Although Martha and the Vandellas, The Supremes and the Four Tops provided the added attraction of backing Marvin Gaye on his singles, his regular in-house and touring sessioners were the female quartet The Andantes. Prior to joining Motown the quartet can be heard on 'Come On' and 'Alright' recorded by Otis Williams and the Distants, whose membership included future members of The Temptations. The singles were Detroit released on Northern Records and nationally issued by New York based Warwick. Comprising Jackie Hicks, Louvain Dempts, Pat Lewis and Marlene Barrow, The Andantes can be heard on most of Motown's Sixties recordings in this role or as 'padders' providing additional lead vocals with the principal singer. This padding is exemplified on several Marvelettes tracks and an unreleased song with The Velvelettes titled 'That's A Funny Way'.

The Andantes did record two of their own songs – 'What Goes Up Must Come Down' with Holland, Dozier and the Four Tops on the Motown label in June 1963, and a year later released '(Like A) Nightmare' under their own name on the V.I.P. label. The quartet also acted as uncredited 'Supremes' when they backed Diana Ross on the May 1968 single 'Some Things You Never Get Used To' instead of Mary Wilson and Cindy Birdsong, who replaced Florence Ballard. Doubtless there were others. Two years earlier Marlene Barrow actually replaced Florence Ballard on stage when the first signs of group conflict led to the quiet Supreme not performing.

As the public tended to support group or duet recordings during this time in the Sixties, it was difficult to successfully market a relatively unknown solo singer to his maximum selling potential.

Berry Gordy was aware of this and interrupted Marvin Gaye's 'conveyor belt' of black/pop singles to record him with his new signing Mary Wells; the first of five duet ventures. Wells: 'Berry Gordy thought the duets would make Marvin more popular pop-wise. More huge with the pop audience and it did.' The duets did much to change Gaye's public image. For a time, the cool R&B dude image was changed to the young boyfriend singing love songs to his sweetheart. The teenage record buyers immediately related to this vinyl love affair, particularly as they believed Wells and Gaye were lovers in real life. (Years later, during a 1989 interview Mary confirmed that she and Gaye were never romantically involved.) Marvin's true lover was his wife, Anna, who remained silent amidst the rumours, recognising the musical liaison as an important step in his career.

# 3. | It Takes Two

*Teaming up with Mary Wells was Berry Gordy's idea, not mine.
I couldn't really sing in those days.*

(Marvin Gaye)

*The love I had for him wasn't like the love of a lover. It was a
more genuine love.*

(Kim Weston)

*Off-stage Marvin sported the appearance of a star even though
he didn't quite have the self-confidence to carry it through in
other ways.*

(Dave Godin)

*I was making a lot of money but that didn't seem to help my
somewhat empty life.*

(Marvin Gaye)

Before Marvin Gaye and Mary Wells' debut single could be released,
Wells became Motown's biggest-selling female artist, thanks to her
American number one single 'My Guy' in May 1964, shortly before
The Supremes followed suit with 'Where Did Our Love Go' in
August. Each single stayed at the top for two weeks. Wells' love song,
her tenth for Motown, was one of Smokey Robinson's most exquisite
melodic ballads, with lyrics that melted on the tongue. More
importantly, it stood the test of time to become a soul music classic
decades later.

After working with a variety of writers and producers, it became
apparent that Mary Wells was a suitable mouthpiece for Robinson's
work, and she, in turn, gave him his first major success as a producer.
Wells was a sensitive singer whose vocals Robinson could entice to his
advantage. The combination was perfect – it was a marriage of music
and set high standards for others to follow. Her ability to adapt was
therefore a perfect vehicle for Marvin Gaye who at first had serious

reservations about the musical combination, but who was willing to grab any opportunity that might push him away from his 'conveyor belt' and finally into Motown's first league.

Gaye and Wells recorded sufficient tracks for an album, and the twee, sugary 'Once Upon A Time'/'What's The Matter With You Baby' was chosen as their first single, Marvin's ninth. Written by Dave Hamilton, Barney Ales, Mickey Stevenson and Clarence Paul (who was also producer) it was released on Wells' label, Motown, a month before 'My Guy' peaked. Gaye: 'Mickey Stevenson cut an album of us duetting but there weren't that many strong songs [on it]. The whole thing seemed to be a watered-down version of my style and her style.'

Watered down or not, 'Once Upon A Time', issued in a picture sleeve, was a hit in both America and Britain; number nineteen (R&B) and number fifty respectively, and was Gaye's British chart debut on the Stateside label. ('What's The Matter With You Baby' reached number seventeen in the R&B charts.) The album 'Together' was also issued in April 1964 and was an unimaginative collection of songs, all relatively low-key, but nonetheless all became collectors' items decades later. Both sides of the single were naturally included and due to their commerciality shone brightly against the mundane interpretations of musical standards like the Russell-Brooks composition 'You Came A Long Way From St Louis'. Both singers' voices blended easily against the often bland musical backdrop of most of the songs, particularly the album's title written by Desylva-Brown-Henderson, and 'Squeeze Me' penned by Jacobs-Pleis. The remaining tracks were 'Deed I Do', 'Until I Met You', '(I Love You) For Sentimental Reasons', 'The Late Late Show' and 'After The Lights Go Down'. (Other duets were recorded including 'I'm Yours, You're Mine', 'All I Got' and 'You Can Dance' but were canned.)

Mickey Stevenson's production differed little from others emanating from Motown at this time with its fundamental sound, often scanty orchestration, shrill grating vocals and repetitious melodies. But, like all Motown's songs, 'Together' was based on youthful enthusiasm, love, determination and pride. The novelty element of the album and the recent success of Mary Wells did much to encourage sales from the mainstream record buyers market, and would have been the perfect musical anchor for a successful and profitable career together had Wells stayed with the company.

The album's packaging was also superior to most designed for Motown at this time. At least it featured the two singers who dominated the front sleeve – Gaye's face on the left, Wells' face on the right, touching at the forehead, photographed by Bernard Yeszin. Their names were added above their heads with 'Together' inserted lower down between them. The back cover contained Lee Ivory's brief sleeve notes and track listing.

Mary Wells: 'We had a lot of success with that album. It went to number one R&B and number one jazz as well.' Despite their runaway success largely due to her solo popularity, the couple never performed together on stage.

Gaye: 'I wasn't very happy with a lot of decisions made about my career in those days. At the time I was most rebellious to a lot of decisions made. Teaming up with Mary Wells was Berry Gordy's idea, not mine. I couldn't really sing in those days. Of course, I was pure then, pure because I was younger and you could probably sense that there was something happening to my voice because every now and again a little purity would come through. So, it's true to say, I wasn't happy with my performances yet that wasn't anything personal with regards to Mary Wells. She's a great girl.' Mary Wells: 'Marvin was really a gentleman, he would do anything for me. He was an ideal man for anybody.'

Born on 13 May 1943 in Detroit, Mary Wells attended the Northwestern High School. When school work permitted, she was a solo singer in their choir before graduating. Wells' childhood was spent living on the breadline. She told author Gerri Hirshey that her mother was a domestic, cleaning floors – 'Daywork they called it. And it was damn cold on hallway linoleum. Misery is Detroit linoleum in January, with a half-frozen bucket of Spic and Span. It was just me and her. My brothers were grown and gone. I started helping my mother with the work when I was around twelve. When you get that old, and if it's just the two of you, a kid can see somethin' goin' out of her mama's face. Now church helped. She always stood better when she came out of there on Sunday. And I was singing there since I was a baby.'

It was Mary's intention to become a songwriter and at the age of fifteen she had composed 'Bye Bye Baby' for Jackie Wilson. She chose him because the song suited his style, and persuaded Robert Bateman (a member of The Satintones, originally signed to the Tamla label to release 'Going To The Hop' in 1959, the group then transferred to the Motown label) to arrange for her to meet Berry Gordy whom she knew worked with Wilson. However, when she sang the song for

Gordy he insisted she record it. Wells: 'During the time I wrote this song I really admired people like Jackie and Sam Cooke. I knew that Berry Gordy had been recording him and writing songs for him, so I wanted him to hear my song. I didn't think I could ever be an artist. I just wanted to be in the record business. I couldn't read or play music but I had to sing that song! When I got there it was Tamla Records and Tamla was huge in Detroit. It wasn't like a national thing then but the people of Detroit looked at Tamla like Columbia Records.'

After twenty-two takes, and with a more gospelly sound than intended because Wells was losing her voice, 'Bye Bye Baby' (with The Andantes providing the backing vocals) was finished and released in February 1961 to become a number forty-five pop hit (no 8 R&B). Gordy then signed the seventeen-year-old girl to his Motown label, much to her disappointment because at the time it had no credibility. Wells: 'Motown wasn't anything then, but once the record was released it stayed out a year and a half because Berry didn't have the money to take it nationally. It was just released in Detroit where it was played for six months. It was a smash. Then they took it and put it out in Cleveland and so forth. It was on the pop charts for a year and a half, on and off.'

The follow-up 'I Don't Want To Take A Chance' written and produced by Mickey Stevenson and Berry Gordy issued in the June, was the first Motown single to be packaged in a picture bag and peaked at number thirty-three in the pop charts (no 9 R&B). 'Strange Love' followed in October 1961, and four months later, Robinson wrote and produced 'The One Who Really Loves You' which reached the top ten in both the pop and R&B listings. During July 1962 Robinson's co-written 'You Beat Me To The Punch' (with The Lovetones on backing vocals) became a number nine hit (no I R&B) and her first to be released in Britain on the Oriole label. Robinson chased this with a dedication to his wife Claudette, 'Two Lovers', in October 1962, which reached number seven (no I R&B), before the double A-sided single – Holland, Dozier and Holland's beauty 'You Lost The Sweetest Boy' and Robinson's chirpy 'What's Easy For Two Is So Hard For One' – issued in August 1963 struggled into the pop top thirty and the R&B top ten.

Then Smokey Robinson wrote and produced the succulent 'My Guy' for her and the megastar was born.

With success Mary Wells became Motown's first queen of music, and she admits Motown spoilt her. For example, she was the first of Gordy's acts to wear elegant gowns on stage and, although 'My Guy' didn't top the British charts (it peaked at number five in May 1964) she was asked by The Beatles to tour with them. Like Dusty Springfield, the quartet were avid followers of Motown's artists and were also influenced by the music emanating from Detroit as exemplified on their second album 'With The Beatles', released in November 1963 with advance orders in excess of 300,000, when they re-recorded three Motown songs – The Marvelettes' 'Please Mr Postman', The Miracles' 'You've Really Got A Hold On Me' (the title is incorrectly spelt on both the album sleeve and label) and Barrett Strong's 'Money'. In April 1964 Dusty Springfield covered The Supremes' 'When The Lovelight Starts Shining Thru His Eyes' on her debut solo album 'A Girl Called Dusty'. This was later followed by versions of Gaye's 'Can I Get A Witness', Syreeta's 'I Can't Give Back The Love I Feel For You' and The Miracles' 'You've Really Got A Hold On Me' as album or EP tracks. It's thought she recorded further Motown songs including The Velvelettes' 'Needle In A Haystack' which to date remain unreleased.

Mary Wells was backed by the Earl Van Dyke Sextet on stage, and her performances enthralled the British public and The Beatles who treated her like royalty throughout the tour. And of course she was heavily promoting Berry Gordy's company by playing to standing-room-only audiences.

'My Guy' was Mary's last 'official' Motown single; her version of The Supremes' chart topper 'Where Did Our Love Go' was reputedly rejected, and two other tracks 'When I'm Gone' and 'Whisper You Love Me Boy' were scheduled for release but remained album tracks. However, with six albums and a number one single to her credit Mary Wells was at the height of her career and other companies were anxious to sign her. Wells considered several options but when 20th Century Fox courted her with a two-year contract, a reported half a million dollars and a movie deal verbally agreed with the company president, Morty Craft, she accepted. But first she had to break free from her Motown contract which she claimed was signed when she was under age. The case went to court and the outcome was in her favour. Berry Gordy was furious because he had spent over $250,000 promoting her career, and had, through his company's expertise, moulded her into an international artist. More to the point, Mary Wells' absence from the artist roster would create a deep void in valuable record sales.

Mary Wells' decision to leave Motown was probably instigated or, at the very least, encouraged by her then husband Herman Griffin, an associate of Berry Gordy's and who, apart from recording 'I Need You', Jobete's first published song, had recorded for labels like Tamla and Motown. Without his encouragement perhaps Wells would have reconsidered changing companies as she explained years later in a *Goldmine* magazine interview – 'At the time the company [Motown] was building. And we had a few problems businesswise. And if I had been more on top of knowing more about the inside of the business I probably wouldn't have left. I know that a company when it's young and struggling it needs financial backing and by this company being a family company, well, if I had been told something I probably wouldn't have left. But it was more what you'd say personal . . . When Berry wanted to negotiate I was very sensitive and more hurt than anything. It was basically business. And by being a kid and by Berry helping raise me up things weren't told to me and, you know, I think a lot of times people can become jealous.'

In an exclusive interview held in 1989 Mary Wells further explained the situation – 'When I left Motown there was this crooked female lawyer and at the time I gave her my only contract. I trusted her, she was an older lady, and she sold me out. She let them have the contract and they put more years on it. I knew Berry was gonna kill my career. He said, "If you want out, settle for this $30,000 and give up your rights." I didn't mind doing that because I was having hit singles. What happened was, when I left, one of the girl group members told me that he said, "Whatever it takes, we're gonna kill Mary Wells' career, make sure of it." They put out bad publicity, they did everything they could to stop the black disc jockeys from playing my records. The only records I got played were on the pop stations. My sales went on both sides, that's what made me so powerful. So when the records went top twenty pop, without the R&B play to take them all the way up to the top ten, for me they were dead. So, all this time I've been fighting against that set-up and it's not legal, and it's not God's law for somebody to say, "Hey, you know, you give up yourself." That music is me.'

Wells also intended to fight for her earnings prior to 'My Guy' and believed the total sum due to her would be in excess of $10 million. Wells: 'It shouldn't be less than that because Motown owe me more than that really. Up to a few years ago, when they fired this Japanese lady who was taking care of all the royalties, she told me my "Greatest Hits" album was outselling Michael Jackson and the Jackson 5.'

During her short stay at 20th Century Fox Wells recorded singles like 'Ain't That The Truth', 'Use Your Head' and 'Never, Never Leave Me', all pop and R&B hits, but she missed Smokey Robinson's midas touch. The promise of a film role never materialised. Morty Craft told author Charlie Gillett in *Making Tracks* – 'Mary Wells was coming up to her twenty-first birthday, so her contract with Motown would be up. Atlantic was after her, but I told her how if she signed with us she'd get movie contracts and be a real star. That wasn't in the contract of course, but why should I feel sorry I tricked her; if she's so crazy with overblown ambition she deserves what she gets.'

Wells left 20th Century Fox in late 1965. Further deals included Atco ('Dear Lover' – no 6 R&B/no 51 pop in 1966); Jubilee ('The Doctor', 'Never Give A Man The World', 'Dig The Way I Feel' – all top 100 pop hits and top forty R&B entrants in 1968/69); Reprise ('If You Can't Give Her Love (Give Her Up)' – top 100 R&B hit in 1974); Epic ('Gigolo' – top 70 R&B hit in 1982) and Warner Brothers. After divorcing Herman Griffin she married soul singer/musician Cecil Womack in 1966; the marriage produced two children but that too ended in divorce. Cecil later married Linda, daughter of the late Sam Cooke, and today they are the highly successful Womack & Womack duo. Mary Wells married Cecil's brother Curtis, now records for the British owned Motorcity Records, and remains in demand as a touring attraction in America and Europe.

With the duets now behind him, Marvin Gaye wanted to establish his own identity on disc. He longed to record and produce his own material but, despite his wife Anna's intervention, was instructed to work with Motown's in-house staff or else he would not be allowed to record at all. This directive hurt and annoyed him – 'I not only felt I was being shafted but I also felt like I was being puppeteered, especially with my singing. And I got into quite a few arguments.' One altercation happened with Brian Holland when Marvin was late for a recording session for the first takes of 'I'll Take Care Of You'. Gaye: 'I wasn't ready to sing. I should have been because the time was set, but I was doing something else that was of little consequence to what was really important. I remember Brian went and told Berry on me, and Berry came in and he chewed me off pretty good about it. I got mad and Berry got mad, and we had a vicious argument. It was awful.' Marvin was not actually annoyed with Brian Holland but was attempting to show his determination to become independent of Gordy's directives – 'It was a very necessary thing for me to do because it catapulted me into my own individual thing.'

When Marvin Gaye's erratic and often irrational professional attitude became intolerable, Berry Gordy would reprimand him, irrespective of the location as Nelson George reported – 'One night at the Twenty Grand [nightclub] with the whole Motown hierarchy front and centre, the band hit the introductory chords to one of his hits, he was announced and . . . no Marvin Gaye. They played it again. No Marvin Gaye. Berry Gordy went backstage and found Marvin languishing in his dressing-room with a slight case of insecurity. As a local DJ watched, Berry Gordy slapped him and "advised" him in a loud voice to proceed with his performance. Marvin proceeded. It was just one of the little dramas that the two intensely creative and completely different men played out over the years. Where Marvin was languid and worked only when inspired, Berry Gordy was a businessman and a craftsman, a nine-to-five artist of the dollar bill who had little tolerance for Marvin's flights from responsibility.'

Another example of Gaye's determination not to succumb to demands was recalled by a smiling Gordy, who attended his concert at Bimbos, San Francisco – 'We could hardly get in because the club was crowded by so many people. It was jammed to the rafters because Marvin Gaye was the number one sex symbol . . . The music played very loud and Marvin came out. The stage was black, there was a spotlight on him. He walked up to the microphone, snapping his fingers. And he started singing "Me And My Shadow". People were amazed. Here's a guy with all these great hits and he sings "Me And My Shadow"! He had a hat and cane, and he did about ten of those songs. People were in shock! Then he said, "Ladies and Gentlemen, there comes a time in everybody's life when they have to do things for money and we have to do things to make a living. So I got some songs I want to do for you that I hope you like." Then he proceeded to do "How Sweet It Is," "You're A Wonderful One", "Stubborn Kind Of Fellow", "Pride And Joy". He did them in a medley that took about three and a half minutes. Then he said, "Now that's over, let's get into some real music." "You're nobody 'til somebody loves you . . .".'

In spite of Gaye's attitude, Motown continued to support him and promoted his back catalogue with a 'Greatest Hits' album in April

1964, and released his newly recorded 'When I'm Alone I Cry' album, produced by Clarence Paul and Mickey Stevenson, in the June. The former speaks for itself, while the latter, recorded at Gaye's expense, was another collection of middle-of-the-road, film and stage material like 'If My Heart Could Sing', 'When Your Lover Has Gone', 'I Don't Know Why', 'I'll Be Around' and the album's title. This further attempt to push Marvin into a wider market again failed although the material was, by and large, pleasant to listen to. Nonetheless, the Frank Sinatra dream was rapidly becoming a memory although Marvin would have another stab at it before the end of the year with 'Hello Broadway'. Gaye: 'I'm not one to sound too sloppy and sentimental, but that could well have been a description of the way I felt when I first arrived in Detroit. Life wasn't going too good at that time, and when I [went] to Detroit you could say I was searching for something to eat.' Earl Van Dyke: ' "When I'm Alone I Cry", that was the kind of thing he loved to do. He loved jazz; he was a good jazz drummer. Basically, all the staff musicians at Motown were jazz musicians. Berry also loved jazz, but his mind was on making money.'

A month prior to the album's release Gaye began touring with his own Revue featuring a ten-piece orchestra, The Spinners (Harvey Fuqua's male group that Berry Gordy inherited from the Tri Phi label) and Hattie Littles, fêted as the new 'Queen of the Blues'. Harvey Fuqua managed The Spinners and, as they were a hitless group at the time, he devised a stage act for them that included imitations of The Beatles, Stevie Wonder, The Marvelettes and even Marvin Gaye himself. The group won public praise for this which, for the time being, alleviated the problem of its non-hit status.

The 1964 Marvin Gaye Revue broke attendance records at several American venues, including Detroit's Twenty Grand Club. The *Detroit Courier* reported – 'The show could turn out to be one of the greatest shows of the year. The versatile singer, Marvin Gaye, and his Revue that opened at the Twenty Grand Club left the audience begging for more, but Detroit has a two a.m. curfew and the folks who didn't whet their appetites for good, rousing entertainment will just have to come back for more before the show closes. Sharing the spotlight as supporting artists are Hattie Littles, who can stand toe-to-toe with any blues singer you can name, and The Spinners, a vocal quintet with harmony and class. The Spinners take-off of The Beatles, replete with long-haired wigs and instruments, will fracture you. Even in a take-off they are better than The Beatles. The star of this "reely big show", Marvin Gaye, is known for those rockin' record hits like "Pride And Joy", "Can I Get A Witness", "HitchHike" – and the current "You're A Wonderful One", but he has a way with a ballad that will push him out of the rock 'n' roll category one of these days and then it will be the posh supper clubs for Mr Gaye. Whether it's ballads or blues, Marv's timing and phrasing are flawless. The more you hear him the more you want to hear.'

Doubtless Gaye cringed at the reference to 'rock 'n' roll' because, like the mainstream market, that was the music category he wanted to avoid. He longed to capture the middle-of-the-road audience, make it his, but when the recorded projects failed he was discouraged from including the material in his stage acts. Therefore he had no option but to concentrate on the R&B and mainstream areas with the black/pop singles he said he was forced to record, obeying the instructions of others until the time for his creative independence arrived. The change would happen but not for several years yet. Meanwhile, at this developing and crucial stage in his career, Gaye, with his immaculate appearance, obvious talent and sensual behaviour on stage, knew he had star potential and was, to a large extent, indebted to his fans for their loyalty – 'I genuinely care about them but then I only owe them what I owe them. I don't owe them one hundred per cent of my time. I owe them my mind and my creativity and my purpose. My purpose is to be an artist of the people but I can't dedicate my entire being to the people. Unfortunately, I am a human being with personal wishes and desires. Not only that, I'm very misunderstood, probably because I intend to be. It's not anybody's business to understand me. What people's business is, is to like me or not to like me, to enjoy my music or not to enjoy my music.' Twenty years later a fan would be hard pressed to get an autograph from him!

When his professional commitments allowed the singer indulged in fitness programmes which kept his figure in trim and his aggression low. He also became an avid golf player – Smokey Robinson taught and partnered him – and basketball player. Not content with being actively involved in sports he, with Berry Gordy's sister, Esther Edwards, invested money in the Detroit Wheels, the city's entry in the World Football League before considering buying a WFL franchise for Memphis, Tennessee. Gaye then financed the boxer

Tommy Hanna, who was the first of several professional boxers he would own over the next seven years. He could ill afford either project but it seemed he needed to plough his energies into activities outside the music business; he needed to be wanted and feel important.

With Motown nearly five years old Berry Gordy saw his musical ambitions to provide white record buyers with popular black music reaching fruition. Modestly he told *Record World* magazine that he just concentrated on releasing songs that were human songs that made people laugh and cry – 'We put no labels on anything and we just never thought that far ahead. It was not that scientific . . . People say "hey, this is a crossover, this is pop, this is this, this is that". All we knew was that it was bringing in receipts. It helped when we had several songs of ours recorded by The Beatles. I met them and found out that they were great fans of Motown and had been studying Motown music, and they went on to become some of the greatest songwriters in history. We were absolutely delighted.' As Gordy's company expanded and prospered, his artists were pushed to maintain his high standard of recordings and live performances. As well as overseeing all the company's creative areas, Gordy continued to be actively involved in writing and producing material, and was responsible for Marvin's next single 'Try It Baby' released in May 1964. It was a mediocre pop song, yet it was lapped up by American record buyers to become a number fifteen R&B hit. Holland, Dozier and Holland stepped in to follow it with 'Baby Don't You Do It' in September 1964, which was a more basic, yet exciting track, not British released but re-recorded by the home-based group The Small Faces instead. Gaye's version reached twenty-seven in the R&B charts.

As 'Try It Baby' (his first to be packaged in a picture sleeve) climbed the charts Marvin promoted it on the Murray The K's (DJ: Murray Kaufman) 'Rock 'n' Roll Extravaganza' at the Brooklyn Fox Theatre between 12–21 September. The show featured American acts like The Supremes, Martha and the Vandellas (who were more popular than their sister group at this time because the youngsters identified with their funky, street level sound), The Ronettes, The Contours, and British artists like The Searchers and Dusty Springfield. During the show Martha and her girls provided back-up vocals when Springfield sang 'Wishin' & Hopin'' and she returned the favour by joining the trio to support Marvin Gaye. Reeves: 'You really couldn't tell the difference between her voice and mine. We struck up a friendship when I wrote to her thanking her for promoting our career in her interviews.' The Motown artists also introduced Springfield to another aspect of their lives, that of drugs and alcohol, as she told Brant Mewborn in US magazine – 'We had six shows to do and I had laryngitis. I thought I can't face this day. Then, one of The Temptations said, "Here, this'll make you feel better." It was a cup full of vodka. Typically me, I drank the whole bleeding thing! I said, "Oh, yeah, I feel better now."' She was the only white songstress on the show and spent her free time watching other black acts, particularly those performing at the Apollo. 'Everyone was partying. Wilson Pickett would come over and say, "Don't lean on her. She's with me." I was cool, like, I knew how to do this stuff, but I really didn't. I was so naive. I'd end up in hotels with no windows, really bad places in the Bronx. I was a mascot, to pimps, hookers and junkies! But I didn't know they were. It was like, "Hey, baby you want some of this? It'll make you feel good." It was glamorous to me, I was a little white girl let loose in Harlem!'

During the mid-Sixties Springfield experimented with Marvin Gaye's favourite drug, cocaine; she discovered drugs gave her confidence although she further told Mewborn – 'They also made me a complete ass. The first time I did downers, somebody gave me a handful of reds; I drank two bottles of some bad pink Portuguese wine and fell down the stairs. I was covered in bruises, but I thought, "Well, everybody does this . . ." Not everybody did that, but I was surrounded by people who did.' Springfield was luckier than most because she sought hospital treatment and was eventually able to kick her habit, although she admitted in the 1988 interview – 'There's a major repair job that has to go on.'

A month after Murray The K's 'Rock 'n' Roll Extravaganza' Marvin Gaye appeared on the television programme 'The T.A.M.I. Show' (Teenage Awards Music International) with Chuck Berry, The Supremes and The Rolling Stones.

While his product was now spasmodically released on the Stateside label in Britain during 1964, other Motown acts were enjoying success, notably The Supremes with 'Where Did Our Love Go' and their chart topper 'Baby Love', and Martha and the Vandellas with the Marvin Gaye/Mickey Stevenson-penned 'Dancing In The Street'. The song was originally written for Kim Weston but she lost it when she had an altercation with Stevenson. Martha Reeves: 'Marvin had recorded the song himself. He thought it was good but didn't actually like his version of it. So he said "Why don't you try Martha on it?" to

Mickey Stevenson. And Mickey said, "Well, why not." And I came in, I heard the melody and the track, and I liked everything about it except the key it was in . . . I came up with the song as a woman would sing it, and it turned out to be one of our biggest.' The release of 'Dancing In The Street' also coincided with the American national civil riots which prompted Governor Rockefeller to send in the National Guard in Rochester, New York State. Reeves: 'It was a bad time all over the United States and I think the writers were inspired mainly because of this. Instead of fighting in the streets we wanted to get people to dance and be happy.'

Ironically, the songstress was blamed for inciting riots with the single, and numerous radio stations banned it, although how the lyrics could be misinterpreted to support this claim was never fully explained. Reeves told author Gerri Hirshey – 'It was rough timing. Because you are black . . . a cute teen song gets viewed as some statement. People make you out to be what they think you should be . . . I never called anyone to riot. I was calling my ten brothers and sisters to the table. All I wanted was a little gravy for all of us.' The single, also rejected by Mary Wells, never topped the US charts (it reached number two to become their second million seller – 'Heatwave', a number four hit in 1963 was the first) but became the group's national anthem and one of the most popular evergreens in the history of music. The song was also later re-recorded by many acts including the Mamas and the Papas, The Kinks, and Mick Jagger and David Bowie who, in 1985, took their duet to the top of the world's charts when they recorded it secretly for Bob Geldof's Live Aid concert. Twenty-five years after Martha and the Vandellas' version was released Kim Weston actually recorded the song written for her after much persuasion by Ian Levine, owner of Motorcity Records!

In 1964 Britain was still in the grips of Beatlemania and their runaway number ones including 'Can't Buy Me Love', 'A Hard Day's Night' and 'I Feel Fine', while fellow acts like The Searchers, Billy J. Kramer and The Dakotas, Peter and Gordon, Cilla Black and The Four Pennies saturated the remainder of the listings. As the home competition was intense only The Supremes and Roy Orbison (with 'It's Over' and 'Oh Pretty Woman') penetrated the top ten to become chart toppers that year. On the album front The Supremes 'Meet The Supremes', released in December 1964, peaked at number eight, one of the first Motown albums to chart in the UK.

It was an exciting time in Britain; the country boasted of its trendsetting 'Swinging London' and musical and personal freedom, while the success of its home-grown acts overshadowed the American R&B breakthrough. Staid British record companies slowly became interested in the resurgence of American black music and began signing or licensing artists and their product. Yet it was to be a long time before R&B, or Negro music as it was called, claimed its rightful place. Meantime, British R&B followers were reliant on Radio Luxemburg to satisfy their musical needs, then rushed to record shops to order what they had heard. Stocking R&B records was alien to mainstream shops who preferred to rely on the easily obtainable and sold white/pop acts but eventually they too were forced to re-think their buying policies when pirate radio stations began broadcasting from ships moored off the British coastline. The most popular was Radio Caroline, moored in the North Sea, which was instrumental in promoting American black music including Motown, and it's possible that without their existence and DJs like Tony Blackburn and Johnnie Walker black acts would have taken longer to chart in Britain.

Marvin Gaye would join his colleagues in the UK listings with his next solo release but prior to this Berry Gordy hitched him up with a second female vocalist Oma Heard. Heard was signed to another Motown subsidiary the newly opened VIP label where, in 1964, she recorded 'Lifetime Man'. The duets were similar to those Gaye had recorded with Mary Wells but for some reason the project was abandoned. Little is known about Oma Heard and nothing has been unearthed regarding the titles, writers or producers of the duets. Marv Johnson: 'I'm not familiar with the lady but Marvin had several projects that he would work on at the same time. So it's quite possible he did record with her.' Marvin Gaye never referred to these sessions in interviews but the tapes do exist and have been heard by Motown/BMG's label manager Gordon Frewin during a trip to America. Oma Heard recorded nothing further and left the company. (See 'The Marvin Gaye Collection' at the end of the discography.) However, Gaye's third attempt as a duettist reached fruition because Mickey Stevenson, now a highly-respected and powerful A&R director, was aware of his public sex appeal with the young record buyers and felt new signing – and his future wife – Kim Weston would benefit from the gap left by Mary Wells. Nelson George summed up Stevenson's situation – 'After putting so many hours into the care and feeding of Motown's creative department Stevenson viewed Weston's stardom as his payback, the vehicle through which Motown's well-oiled machine could make dollars for his pocket . . . Another part of Weston's problem was that many at the company including Berry Gordy's sisters, resented Stevenson using his position to further her career . . . Berry Gordy's emphasis of Diana Ross as Motown's only female star ensured that Weston never became any more than a regular opening act for Motown's bigger names.'

This was a grossly unfair situation for the young singer. Weston had an innate vocal talent, an enthusiasm for her career and the position she found herself in could have been interpreted as having a damaging effect on a highly promising and profitable career, as reflected in 1989 when she toured Britain, when her audiences were in awe at being entertained by one of black music's legends.

Born Agatha Natalie Weston on 20 December 1939, and raised in Detroit's Paradise Valley, Kim sang in church from the age of three. At school she wanted to become a professional swimmer, but abandoned that for cosmeticology after graduating from high school. As a teenager she joined the gospel group The Wright Specials and later performed with The Staple Singers, The Caravans and The Mighty Clouds Of Joy and others. From gospel she moved into secular music which she felt was 'very much akin to the gospel field', and when she became a Motown artist Mickey Stevenson was assigned to work with her, while Marvin Gaye toured with the first Motown Revue. Before duetting with Gaye on record, Weston toured with him as a separate act for three years and recorded as a solo artist. Her records were superior to most released at the time; she possessed a unique, mellow, soulful voice that easily adapted from ballads – which she preferred – to uptempo songs.

Her first single, penned by Norman Whitfield and Mickey Stevenson was the stunning 'It Should Have Been Me', followed by 'Just Loving You', written by Stevenson and Alen. Both were released on the Tamla label in 1963 and both are prime examples of an exceptional talent that needed dedicated promotion. The flipside of 'It Should Have Been Me' titled 'Love Me All The Way', reached number eighty-eight in the pop charts and twenty-four in the R&B listings. ('It Should Have Been Me' was later recorded by Gladys Knight and the Pips and Yvonne Fair in 1968 and 1976 respectively. Weston then re-recorded the song in 1989 for Motorcity Records.)

Following the release of her third single 'Looking For The Right Guy' in August 1964, she teamed up with Marvin Gaye for his twelfth single. Titled 'What Good Am I Without You' and released during the October, it was co-written and produced by Stevenson to become a top seventy R&B hit. This mediocre duet was followed much later during December 1966 by another – the bouncy, singalong 'It Takes Two', penned by Stevenson and Sylvia Moy. It reached number four in the R&B charts, fourteen in the mainstream listings and peaked two places lower in Britain – Gaye's highest position so far. Also this year, Weston replaced The Supremes on stage when the trio was booked for a fortnight's stint with The Temptations at Detroit's Twenty Grand Club. The venue's management discovered that two of The Supremes were too young (under twenty-one) to appear on stage and rather than risk legal action and/or cancel the engagement, Weston stepped in to finish the dates with The Temptations.

By this time Weston and Gaye had recorded sufficient tracks for an album titled 'Side By Side'. It was allocated the prefix Tamla 260, scheduled but unreleased. Kim believed the album was originally due to be released after the August 1966 album 'Take Two', which itself was held back and was their only joint album, produced by Mickey Stevenson. Weston: 'We did a lot of material that wasn't on "Take Two" and the company still has it. I doubt if they were in the catalogues they sold [to MCA and Boston Ventures in 1988], maybe they destroyed them. I don't know.' 'Side By Side' was obviously considered for release prior to the hit single 'It Takes Two' and although the circumstances of its cancellation aren't known, it could be that some of the material to be included therein was inferior and perhaps parts needed to be re-recorded; or that 'Side By Side' was hastily included on the release schedules because at the time of 'What Good Am I Without You' in 1964 an album was expected, but never recorded. Any plans to follow 'Take Two' were shelved because Kim Weston left Motown during the release stages of the album. Weston: 'If I hadn't left Motown I guess I'd have carried on with the duets because we'd had a hit. My problem was I didn't appear to have anyone behind me other than Mickey Stevenson. And when he said he was leaving, even though he'd been offered a great deal of money to stay, I felt I could accomplish more by moving with him. For me to stay there . . . I was afraid I'd be like other artists who no one was doing anything with. So rather than stay there and let that happen I left.'

Like most artists, including Marvin Gaye at times, Weston had little contact with Berry Gordy during this period; he was too intent on planning a career for his doe-eyed beauty and future superstar

Diana Ross. Perhaps if Weston had enjoyed a better rapport with Gordy, her career with the company might have turned out differently. Weston: 'I didn't have a lot to do with Berry but I was a very quiet person at that time. I'm much older now and realise that people don't understand quiet people. And a lot of times people read the wrong things into statements because I'm the kind of person who speaks what I feel but may not elaborate on it. So consequently it may be just a blank statement and I got the reputation of being standoffish and difficult. It was actually my own inhibitions or whatever which caused me to be as quiet as I used to be.'

Thankfully the 'Take Two' album contained a more exciting selection of songs than the imagination that designed the album's incongruous sleeve. No picture of the duettists were to be seen, instead two film director chairs with the artist's name on each, and a small clapperboard reading 'take two' hidden away in the top left-hand corner graced the front. The back sleeve was worse, consisting of an advertisement for three other Motown albums, a drawing of stage lights on the right, and scanty sleeve notes written by Scott St James.

What was immediately noticeable from this album was Weston's powerful vocal range; most certainly at this time Gaye was no match for her. She also opened several of the tracks by singing the first verses, leaving him to pick up on the second, until they sang as one towards the middle of the songs. Whether this was due to Mickey Stevenson, the album's producer, giving her preferential treatment because of their relationship at the time, or how it was felt the songs would best be delivered, hasn't been determined. However, the result was a fair collection of songs that included both singles – 'What Good Am I Without You' and 'It Takes Two' – and their flipsides – 'I Want You 'Round' and 'It's Got To Be A Miracle (This Thing Called Love)'. All were co-written by Stevenson, and the latter song gives an insight into the future Gaye/Terrell duets with its easy style and the blending of relaxed voices as they weaved through the highs and lows of this tender ballad. In fact on 'Love Fell On Me' many thought Weston's vocals occasionally sounded like Gaye's future singing partner. It was an uncanny experience, particularly when this track would later sound familiar to their 'If I Could Build My Whole World Around You'. The chintzy, nightclub ballad 'I Love You, Yes I Do' was followed by an alternative version of the Four Tops' plush commercial single 'Baby I Need Your Loving'. Sparse music backed the soft, sultry vocals, while hidden away in the background shrill vocals padded out the production. 'Til There Was You', 'Heaven Sent You I Know', 'When We're Together', 'Baby Say Yes' and 'Secret Love' – where a sleepy beat dominated the strong melody of this standard encouraging the relaxed vocals to sway with the tune – completed the album.

Despite Marvin Gaye's growing reputation for being awkward in the recording studios Kim Weston had nothing but praise for her singing partner – 'I'll never forget the times we spent rehearsing and recording the "Take Two" album. In the rehearsals Marvin took the lead in developing the harmony patterns we used. He was a genius with such patience and understanding.' The two also enjoyed a brother/sister relationship – 'And the love I had for him wasn't like the love of a lover. It was a more genuine love.' Despite rumours to the contrary the duettists were never lovers. Weston was married or planning to marry Mickey Stevenson, but reputedly Gaye's wife, Anna, did not approve of their relationship any more than she liked her husband's singing liaison with Mary Wells. Weston did not know Gaye's wife that well. – 'She and I didn't have a lot to say to each other. I probably spoke with Gwen, the other sister, more than I did to Anna.'

However, Marvin told David Ritz that he was the one who had cause to be jealous – 'Anna and I had a strange sense of when we were being untrue to each other. We always knew. One night, for example, I found myself getting in the car and driving to a motel, walking up to a certain room and knocking on the door. All by instinct. How could I be so sure that Anna was in there with another man? I had no way of knowing the motel and the room number. Some force led me on. I think that's the same force that transforms my happiness to misery.'

Discovering his wife with another man both thrilled and hurt him, as he further told Ritz – 'I suppose I've always been obsessed with the notion of another man making love to my woman. In my fantasy, that man is always more powerful than me. He alone can satisfy her, while I can only watch.'

Prior to leaving Motown Kim Weston recorded two further solo singles on the Tamla label – 'A Little More Love' in November 1964 and 'I'm Still Loving You' two months later – then switched to the Gordy label (opened in 1962) to release two all-time classics 'Take Me In Your Arms (Rock Me A Little While)' (no 4 R&B/no 50 pop) and 'Helpless' (no 13 R&B/no 56 pop) released during 1965 and 1966 respectively. Weston: 'I don't remember everything I recorded because there was so much but I do know there's a lot of unreleased songs I did with Marvin that are now hidden away somewhere.' One was 'Baby (Don't You Leave Me)' recorded in 1965 which, when re-mixed, was included on the 'Motown Remembers Marvin Gaye' album released after his death. Unreleased solo Weston tracks recently discovered include 'Absent Minded Lover', 'I Know His Name', 'Look My Way', 'After The Rain', 'Build Up My Baby', 'Any Girl In Love' (using the same backing track as The Supremes' version) and a re-recording of the Mary Wells' song 'A Drop In The Bucket'. Presumably these titles were intended for her unreleased album 'Take Me In Your Arms', scheduled for release during 1968 on the Gordy label.

Weston and her husband left Motown early in 1967 when he was refused shares in the company. Kim joined MGM Records (while Stevenson worked for that company's off-shoot Venture) where she recorded, among others, the 'I Got What You Need', 'That's Groovy' and 'Nobody' singles (the latter reached number thirty-nine in the R&B charts in 1968) and the impressive 'For The First Time' album in 1967. In 1970 she recorded 'Danger – Heartbreak Ahead' for People Records and 'Lift Ev'ry Voice And Sing' on Pride Records. Both were top fifty R&B hits. She continued performing in nightclubs before 'retiring' from the business to become a tireless worker eventually for the Detroit Council Of Arts. Thirteen years on and with three hundred students She has instigated training workshops including: Instrumental under the control of one-time Supremes musical conductor Teddy Harris; Dance And Choreography with Clifford Fears who started the first Katherine Dunham School Of Dance in Stockholm; and Dress Design, using Motown's original dressmaker Margaret Brown, who still dresses Weston for her performances. Kim's dedicated work has earned her many honours, and her students have been hired by Stevie Wonder and Martha Reeves among others.

During the Eighties the songstress resumed her professional career by recording for Nightmare Records (now known as Motorcity Records) in England where she re-recorded 'It Takes Two' with Marvin Gaye's younger brother Frankie, whom she'd known for some years. Weston: 'Actually the way [the song] was done I didn't sing *with* Frankie but it was a duet. Our vocals were laid down at different times.' The two initially met via Marvin as she explained – 'The first time I went to the Virginia/Baltimore area travelling with Marvin, we went by his family's home. It was about three o'clock in the morning when we got there and the whole family got up. His mother went and fried chicken and biscuits! We sat on the porch and talked and talked until it was time for us to leave. His sister, Sweetsie, was nine months pregnant and she told me if it was a girl she was going to name her Kim. And she did. So consequently I've known the family for a long time and whenever I would go to Washington Marvin's mother and sister would come to see me. Frankie is like Marvin, he's kind of quiet too, but once I got to know him we had occasions to talk.'

Today Weston's recording career runs simultaneously with her youth training programmes.

During November 1964 and following his duets, Marvin Gaye recorded the Hal Davis and Marc Gordon-produced 'Hello Broadway' album (with a smiling singer dressed in a white frilly shirt, black bow tie and dinner jacket on the front cover) containing more show songs and middle-of-the-road tracks. Whether this album was the singer's or Motown's idea isn't known although he did explain why it was recorded – 'Back then the only way a black artist could [get established] was to do music aimed at the supper club audience. So I cut the "Hello Broadway" album. It was me with my white voice but, looking back on it now, I think it was a big mistake.' The album, with songs like 'The Party's Over', 'Hello Dolly' and 'What Kind Of Fool Am I', bombed, and once more a disappointed and reluctant singer returned to his 'conveyor belt' to churn out saleable, if somewhat meaningless songs that bored him. Marvin: 'All the audiences wanted me to do was keep on screaming on songs like "Stubborn Kind Of Fellow". I had no choice, so I did it.' Although he continued to bemoan his singles there was no doubt the black/pop flavour of his songs was successful. His next, 'How Sweet It Is (To Be Loved By You)' released in November 1964, was the best so far. It was also his biggest charter, peaking at number six in the mainstream charts (no 4 R&B), forty-nine in the British listing, and was a superb few minutes of Holland, Dozier and Holland's ingenuity, with full musical padding against an attractive and catchy hookline. Lamont Dozier: '"How Sweet It Is" is probably my own favourite of all. It was so relaxed, so nice and so Marvin Gaye. Marvin was like a natural. He did everything well. He played drums, sang, wrote, was very innovative, and was style conscious. He wanted to do things his way because he felt more comfortable doing things this way.'

To boost British sales Marvin Gaye flew to London to perform the single on the television programme *Ready, Steady, Go!*, screened live on Friday evenings. *RSG*, first broadcast in August 1963, was the most prestigious music show of the Sixties, produced by R&B fan Vicki Wickham. She had wanted to include Marvin on the programme for some time, but prior to 'How Sweet It Is (To Be Loved By You)' had no valid reason to invite him to London. Viewers saw a tall, lean singer, wearing a tight, silver-grey suit, shuffle his way through the standing audience. Occasionally a half-cocked smile appeared on his face as he endeavoured to find the right camera while miming to the song. It was an uncomfortable appearance.

Anna Gaye and Harvey and Gwen Fuqua travelled with Marvin to London where they met Dave Godin, who operated the first British Motown fan club. Godin remembers Marvin as a 'slick, ultra-cool dude who obviously knew a $300 jacket when he saw one' but an artist who felt he was regarded as second league at Motown. Godin: 'His whole wardrobe showed he wasn't short of money, but neither was he accorded quite the special treatment given to acts like Stevie Wonder and many of the various groups Motown was well known for. Offstage Marvin sported the appearance of a star even though he didn't quite have the self-confidence to carry it through in other ways. He obviously was a far more sensitive person than his outward persona suggested. Outwardly, he was a tough guy – no-nonsense and hip, but in conversation one caught glimpses of the inner man occasionally.' Godin also recognised the signs of unfulfilled and frustrated ambitions – 'Marvin had just done a duet album and I couldn't help get the idea that his contribution was regarded as very second-string. However, he had two strong allies in Harvey and Anna. Motown was only just beginning to enjoy cross-over pop, and its real strength so far as American sales were concerned still rested firmly in the R&B charts. But going pop with increasing regularity they certainly were, and Marvin was certainly sporting the public image that trends and tastes dictated in the Sixties that a male star should have. Not only did he look the complete lady-killer, but he liked to remain popular amongst the "lower ranks".' These 'ranks' were Motown's clerical and administrative staff whom Godin befriended during his visit to the company – 'I became friendly with the girls in the typing pool and Marvin certainly had the reputation for being a wolf amongst them! Of course, to acquire such a reputation doesn't really require that much hard evidence to back it up, but I certainly got the impression that he was someone who had to be kept very much at arm's length or else! Maybe he was overcompensating for his surname, because the word "gay" in the early Sixties was just beginning to emerge in the States in the sense and meaning in which it was later almost universally applied.'

To persuade Marvin Gaye to visit London at this time was a mammoth task because he loathed flying. This fear stemmed from the time when he was on a plane which hit an airpocket and subsequently fell hundreds of feet before regaining a steady course. Godin: 'The passengers were naturally panicking and Marvin resigned himself to the fact that he was close to his Maker. As a result of this experience, he told me that he'll only fly if he really has to and there's no other way of travelling.' Years later Marvin flew by Concorde whenever possible but his fear remained – 'My terror is not panic, it's inborn. I think that all of us are terrified of something or some things. As we grow up there's something that triggers this sort of response in our adulthood. I chose Concorde because I don't run away from my fears. I attack my fears, and when I attack them it makes me stronger. I have ridden an aeroplane every time I was booked to, but I don't get on them for fun. Although I'm terrified of flight, I face it.'

When 'How Sweet It Is (To Be Loved By You)' finally cracked the British charts the singer was delighted, it put him on the same level as Motown's top league acts. No longer could he be considered the company's underdog. Gaye: '"How Sweet It Is" is my favourite number from that era. When Holland, Dozier and Holland first played it to me I said it would be a smash for anyone.' He was right because many established artists including Carly Simon and Jnr Walker later rerecorded it.

Naturally an album was issued to cash in on its success in January 1965. Titled 'How Sweet It Is To Be Loved By You' (no parenthesis), it was a bestseller containing four singles – the album's title, 'You're A Wonderful One', 'Try It Baby' and 'Baby Don't You Do It'. This quartet began the album, followed by 'Need Your Lovin' (Want You Back)' where the piano introduced and dominated the song which contained familiar riffs, over which a gravelly-voiced Gaye battled against his male back-up vocalists. 'One Of These Days', where he eased his way through the lazy Mickey Stevenson composition, offered a change of pace, while another Stevenson-penned track, 'No Good Without You', reunited the singer with the Motown Sound – that wonderful musical overdrive of tambourines, strings, piano, drums and change of beat. Harvey Fuqua wrote and produced 'Stepping Closer To Your Heart' and immediately the album's mood changed once again with the introduction of a mournful organ and Gaye's young clear, almost angelic voice blending perfectly this time with his male support. Smokey Robinson's one and only contribution to this album was a mediocre 'Now That You've Won Me' where the lead and response technique returned between Gaye and his girls. The remaining tracks were 'Forever' (the B-side to 'How Sweet It Is (To Be Loved By You)'), 'Need Somebody' and 'Me And My Lonely Room'.

The album's front cover was another of Motown's unimaginative sleeve designs. It showed a sombre-faced singer on the right and a list of the album's tracks on the left over a green background, while Marvin Gaye's name was prominently placed at the top of the cover. Not an attractive sleeve by any stretch of the imagination!

Marvin Gaye might have condemned the majority of his recordings at this time but he was earning regular and 'star' money enabling him to buy a new house for his parents in a better-class area of Washington, while he and his wife continued to live in Detroit. However, money could not buy him personal happiness and although he felt his marriage was no better or worse than any other, a child would, he believed, possibly help cement the relationship. So far their marriage was childless, and as both loved children, they decided to adopt a son, Marvin III, in 1965. Gaye followed the family trait of naming the eldest or only son Marvin and not, he explained, out of respect for his own father. The relationship between the two men was by now strained; the two rarely spoke, and instead of attempting to bridge the widening gap, remained isolated from each other, thereby avoiding any possible conflicts. Anna and Marvin devoted themselves to their son, but this idyllic time was aggravated by the demands of Gaye's career.

Gaye told Smokey Robinson that after 'How Sweet It Is (To Be Loved By You)' was released he faced an unexpected dilemma – 'Women expect so much of me, Smoke, they've made me into this sex symbol until sometimes it just messes with my head.' Yes, his public image had altered and his music had dictated it to a certain extent as it appealed to the teenage market. Therefore he played up to that audience in a youthful, suggestive manner while retaining his mature sophisticated charm. Yet, what was ironic by his statement to Robinson was that being a 'sex symbol' had been his ambition. The second Frank Sinatra?

The position Gaye now found himself in would escalate to alarming proportions within a short time and his adultery would eventually lead to the breakdown of the marriage he said he was now trying so hard to save.

Being a star was enjoyable, but the pull of the fame and glamour inevitably led to family disagreements. As Gaye became more involved with the trappings of his career he spent much time away from his family, leaving mother and son to form a solid and special bond in much the same way as he himself had done with his own mother. His son's relationship with Anna annoyed him but there was little he could do – his public life demanded regular fuelling. When he wasn't touring he lived in the recording studios, ensuring a continuous string of releases. He admitted there was pressure on him to keep the hits rolling in — 'The business is tremendously competitive, especially on the chitlin circuit because blacks were not permitted to evolve to popdom. So as a chitlin circuit artist it's most essential that you continue to churn out hit after hit or you don't work. You're only as good as your last record. There is very little chance of acquiring any major security as a performer. On the chitlin circuit you must have a broad cross-over section of fans or you don't survive. I didn't have a full understanding of my business at an early age when Motown was still young; it didn't really matter. I would have paid them to let me perform. Although I look back on it with a certain degree of bitterness because I see how seriously I've been screwed, it's OK. It's all a means towards an end as I understand my purpose at this point. Certainly I've felt vindictive and I still feel vindictive, and I certainly wish those who have stepped on me will be punished.'

By the close of 1964 Motown's music had made unprecedented headlines with three-quarters of its sixty or so singles in the American charts. Mary Wells' 'My Guy' was the first number one of the year, followed by The Supremes who had broken through with three chart toppers – 'Where Did Our Love Go', 'Baby Love', 'Come See About Me'. No one at the company was prepared for the trio's runaway success, and when their true monetary value was realised, they took priority over all the other acts. Motown was geared around Diana Ross and her group, as Houston-born Barbara Randolph recalled – '[When one of] my records hit the charts with a bang, within a week it was like everything had stopped. My single went in [the charts] with a bullet, then The Supremes had a single out and everything was geared towards that. No female artist, not even Martha and the Vandellas, who were working in clubs, could get a record out. No one at that time had a record promoted. They were just released and that was the end of it. I watched this happen with Brenda Holloway and Blinky Williams as well.'

Californian-born Brenda Holloway was Berry Gordy's first West Coast signing – 'Motown's policy was to build one act at a time. When The Supremes were taking off the company would pull in records so that The Supremes could go for a million. When I asked why my records were being pulled Berry Gordy just kept telling me "wait your time". My records would go out of stock, and stores were told to re-order. It was usually at a crucial point when the singles couldn't be got, so they weren't played and didn't get into the charts. I feel Motown exploited me. For instance, they let The Supremes study my tapes and take songs from me. And as I came from a different cultural background to the others – I liked to play the violin and cello – it made me appear strange to them.'

While signed to Motown, Holloway, also a prolific songwriter, recorded a slew of soulful singles including: 'Every Little Bit Hurts' (no 13 R&B) and 'I'll Always Love You' (no 60 R&B) in 1964; 'When I'm Gone' (no 12 R&B/no 25 pop), 'Operator' (no 36 R&B/no 78 pop) and 'You Can Cry On My Shoulder' in 1965; and the classic 'You've Made Me So Very Happy' (no 40 R&B/no 39 pop) in 1967. When her contract expired she refused to re-negotiate. Holloway: 'There was no future for me because there was a long span when I was doing nothing. Then when Gladys Knight came in to do my songs that was the straw that broke the camel's back.'

Berry Gordy's chart-topping acts made him a very rich man, allowing him to indulge in his love of gambling. It was not unusual for him to blow $5,000 to $100,000 a day in bets. Money changed him in other ways too. He was known to his employees as Mr Gordy and later banned casual visitors to his office, isolated himself from the media and the daily running of the company. Nonetheless, without Gordy the artists would still be singing on Detroit's street corners, with little chance of becoming professional entertainers. He built his company from nothing, so, to all intents and purposes, he could use the profits in any way he pleased. Most certainly, Motown did not suffer financially.

Marvin Gaye: '1965 started off badly for me because I experienced certain mental traumas. I also didn't like the direction show business was pushing me into. I was making a lot of money but that didn't seem to help my somewhat empty life. Then out of the blue Smokey Robinson came to my rescue both mentally and musically.' By now, Robinson had earned a sound reputation for his work with Motown acts and with his own group The Miracles. His and Marvin's talent gelled together perfectly on 'I'll Be Doggone' released in February 1965. This was the follow-up single to 'How Sweet It Is (To Be Loved By You)', which followed Holland, Dozier and Holland's 'Baby Don't You Do It' (released in September 1964), which struggled to become a number twenty-seven R&B hit. With 'I'll Be Doggone' Gaye returned to the first division – it became his first American R&B number one. and peaked at number eight in the mainstream music charts. Smokey Robinson believed in artistic freedom and refrained from telling his artists how to interpret his songs – 'That's what was so great about working with Marvin. I'd show him a song one time and I knew he would sing it even better than the way I envisaged it. I think you should explain the basics, the melody and the lyrics, but other than that, lay down no restrictions. He'd always do something unexpected and wonderful. He sounded like he knew it before I even showed it to him. I always envisage the way the artist will sing my song as I'm writing it.' Gaye in turn credited him as his musical saviour – 'Smokey saved me during a time when I was non-productive and not even thinking about producing. I was writing some songs but I didn't have a great deal of confidence in my pen at the time because the jobs were around Holland, Dozier and Holland, Norman Whitfield, and Smokey who was a regular contributor even in those days. So it was difficult for me to have confidence in my own pen. So, Smokey saved me during a period that I needed some records. He probably doesn't know I feel this way, although we are good friends and respect each other a great deal.'

Touring America now formed an essential part of Marvin Gaye's working life and although at times he was riddled with stage fright, it did not prevent him from honouring his commitments. He had to tour to promote his records and to prove he had the charisma on stage that would continue to attract the public; an egotistical ploy to confirm his pulling power. Occasionally the plan backfired, and Marvin loathed rejection – 'Many times on stage I felt as if I was slipping, that I hadn't got it. To say I must perform, it is my job, is true but sometimes I don't really feel like singing. Then I'm supposed to say, "Yes, I do feel like singing because there are people out there."

So I get the hell out there and sing. And right away there's a big conflict. If it becomes an obligation, you're out there being dishonest.' His fears of performing remained with him throughout his career; he continued to be nervous, and was known to be physically sick before a show. He attempted to beat this – '[I let] my thoughts drift to other, non-attached things such as nature, animals and birds, and I nearly forget about the performance until I'm about to go on. Then all of a sudden a surge of energy comes through me five or ten minutes before, and I'm ready. Then all the problems that haunt a performer, that make him nervous, give him butterflies, make him forget or not and tune into his music, they're gone.'

Four months after the release of 'I'll Be Doggone' in February 1965, Marvin Gaye co-wrote his next single 'Pretty Little Baby' (originally titled 'Purple Snowflakes') with Clarence Paul and Dave Hamilton. It paled against Smokey Robinson's work, but was a good try, and struggled to become a top thirty pop and R&B hit. Clarence Paul has fond memories of working with the singer in the studios – 'I used him as my drummer during the early days of Motown, and occasionally as a keyboard player. He was playing piano on the tune "Baby (Don't You Leave Me)". In describing him, he was God's gift to a songwriter, a producer's dream.' To follow this single Marvin played safe and returned to Smokey Robinson and the Miracles to record 'Ain't That Peculiar' in September 1965. It was one of Robinson's more commercially slanted compositions, soared to the top of the R&B charts and number eight in the pop listing, and helped increase Marvin's popularity and acceptance in Britain, where Motown's releases were issued on the Tamla Motown label. Following a European visit by Berry Gordy, his sister Esther and Barney Ales, EMI Limited secured a licensing deal to open the Tamla Motown label in Britain (referred to hereafter as Motown/EMI) combining the names of two of Gordy's American labels. The first single to be released on this new subsidiary was The Supremes' 'Stop! In The Name Of Love' in March 1965 which reached number seven in the UK charts. This marked the start of Motown's European climb to fame. The music was no longer primarily black/soul aimed at a particular market, therefore Motown/EMI could promote the majority of records as pop singles. Through EMI's international network records were available in most territories of the world on the

Tamla Motown label. America was the only country to use the various other labels on a regular basis.

Motown/EMI had begun releasing attractive compilation albums in order to tempt record buyers and during 1965 'The Motortown Revue Live' was one which featured two tracks by Marvin Gaye and others from The Temptations, Little Stevie Wonder and Mary Wells. Another compilation was 'Hitsville USA' issued in time for Christmas 1965 and included 'Pretty Little Baby' and 'I'll Be Doggone'.

Also during 1965 Berry Gordy decided to send the first Motown Revue to Britain to add impetus to the opening of the Tamla Motown label. He chose The Supremes, Martha and the Vandellas, Stevie Wonder, The Miracles and Earl Van Dyke and his Soul Brothers. Marvin Gaye was conspicuous by his absence; it was felt he wasn't sufficiently well known in Britain to warrant an air ticket. British artist Georgie Fame was added to the bill to encourage ticket sales. But nothing worked – the tour was a disaster. The audiences were sparse, the promoters lost money. The failure was blamed on lack of publicity and promotion. However, while these artists were on British soil Dusty Springfield, who was in the audience of the Revue's opening night at the Astoria Theatre, Finsbury Park, on 20 March, persuaded the now defunct Rediffusion television station to build a show around them (The Temptations flew in to join them). Hosted by Springfield and titled *The Sound Of Motown*, it was screened on 28 April and was the first of its kind to be screened on British television. The black and white programme has since been released as a commercial video *The Sounds Of Motown* with Marvin Gaye footage added from his *Ready, Steady, Go!* performances.

Tragedy struck the Gordy family three months after the television spectacular when Mrs Loucye Wakefield, sister of Berry (and Motown vice-president) died suddenly. She had been a tireless worker and was responsible for the company's financial success. However, more to her credit was her unwavering availability to help out her artists, often to the detriment of her personal life. Mrs Wakefield's untimely death robbed her of one of the company's proudest achievements, that of Diana Ross and the Supremes' debut performance at the Copacabana in New York. The date of the funeral fell on the same day, 29 July, as the trio's opening night and only a few were aware of the personal grief of the girls and those attending. As a sign of respect the group paid tribute to their lost friend during their act.

At the funeral held at the Bethel AME Church several other

Motown acts likewise paid their respects in song including Martha and the Vandellas who performed 'Were You There', the Four Tops 'Nobody Knows The Trouble I've Seen', Harvey Fuqua 'What Do You Choose' and Marvin Gaye sang his childhood favourite 'His Eye Is On The Sparrow'. Both Reeves' and Gaye's performances were Motown's finest gospel voices in full bloom and it was hoped that the two would collaborate on a joint album. Sadly, that never happened. However, their tracks and other tributes were captured on record for the 'In Loving Memory' album released in August 1968 on the Motown label, the royalties from which went to the Loucye Wakefield Scholarship Fund to finance youth education. Originally the Fund was financed solely by Motown but in time it was opened to other entertainment companies. A month after the album was issued, 'His Eye Is On The Sparrow' was released as a single with Gladys Knight and the Pips' 'Just A Closer Walk With Thee' on the flipside.

Meanwhile, Marvin Gaye had returned to the studios to record the 'A Tribute To The Great Nat King Cole' album, produced by Hal Davis, Marc Gordon and Harvey Fuqua and released in November 1965. This was Motown's final attempt to push him into the highly paid, cabaret entertainer category, and once again the ploy failed. The album contained Cole's most popular songs like 'Mona Lisa' and 'Unforgettable' which Marvin reproduced word and note perfect; his pure young voice excelled against a strong orchestral backing. On 'Nature Boy' he sounded remarkably like entertainer Danny Kaye, while his voice on the mildly up-tempoed 'Straighten Up And Fly Right' was gravelly and rasping, in the style used for his singles. The album was ideal for late-night playing and upon scrutinisation it was obvious how easily Marvin Gaye would have slotted into this middle-of-the-road market. The casual way he approached the lyrics and the dreamy way his voice floated from note to note befitted the sophis- ticated image he attempted to portray on stage. Ballads always brought out the best in him; the beauty of his voice and ability to transform the most lightweight of lyrics into emotional phrases, was breathtaking. Bette Ocha who wrote the album's sleeve notes detected this – 'Although no one can replace a gentleman of the stature of Nat King Cole, there are those, also extremely talented, who will follow after . . . There are those who pay tribute and who follow in the footsteps of the past great, to become in their own way unique and famous . . . Nat King Cole now has a place in the past, a special spot reserved for the outstanding in every field of endeavour . . . It is most fitting that another young true gentleman of song – namely Marvin Gaye – should pay a respectful tribute to Nat King Cole.' The front record sleeve, designed by Bernard Yeszin, showed a piano keyboard next to which a lighted cigarette in a holder balanced in an ashtray, the sheet music to 'Mona Lisa' and a trilby hat were placed strategically on the piano stool.

The Supremes too paid homage in 1965 to another musical great by recording the 'We Remember Sam Cooke' album. Due to the trio's popularity, their tribute sold well on both sides of the Atlantic, although single-wise they were unable to repeat the previous year's UK chart-topping success because British artists like Georgie Fame, The Kinks, Cliff Richard, Tom Jones and The Beatles were dominating the music scene. However, in America the trio went from strength to strength and shattered British music's chart stranglehold by releasing four number one singles – 'Come See About Me', 'Stop! In The Name Of Love', 'Back In My Arms Again' and 'I Hear A Symphony'. Marvin Gaye: 'No one was prepared for The Supremes. It flipped Berry out, like he was playing the slot machines in Vegas and three cherries came up ten times in a row. He was gone. The rest of us felt his interest turn. Professionally he turned towards The Supremes and romantically he hooked up with Diana. Everyone saw it coming. I had predicted it and was definitely aware of being jealous of Diana. She had a power I lacked. I had Anna to talk to Berry, but Diana had Berry himself. For years I was obsessed with Diana's stardom. I resented the attention BG lavished upon her. But how could I blame him? The Supremes were making him a fortune. Besides, with Diana's drive and class, he knew this was only the beginning.' However, Gaye conceded that as the trio grew in status so the pressures laid upon them trebled – 'Berry nearly worked those girls to death. You either ride that wave or you go under. Believe me, I was dealing with the same thing.' Mary Wilson: 'The pressure was enormous by that time. So much was expected of us. We were on stage constantly, never having time to eat or sleep.' The situation was typified when during one tour Diana Ross's weight dropped to seven stone. Berry Gordy was so distressed that he checked her into hospital. Wilson and Ballard were left to their own devices.

For his first 1966 single Marvin Gaye once again relied on a Smokey Robinson composition. Titled 'One More Heartache' Robinson wrote the sugary track with his group The Miracles. When it failed to enter the top ten by peaking at number twenty-nine (no 4

R&B) another Robinson/Miracles collaboration 'Take This Heart Of Mine' quickly followed four months later in the May. The single was originally pressed in mono and later changed to stereo but it struggled to reach the top fifty (no 16 R&B) and marked the end of the Robinson/Gaye association. Nonetheless, Smokey had achieved what Berry Gordy had decreed, and elevated Gaye into an established, regular selling artist. 'Take This Heart Of Mine' was issued in Britain during June 1966, the same month as 'Ain't That Peculiar' and 'One More Heartache' appeared on yet another compilation 'Motown Magic'. Motown/EMI were determined to push the artists in every way open to them, and certainly Berry Gordy could not have criticised the company for being complacent against the stiff home-grown competition. Marvin Gaye's repertoire, for instance, was regularly re-packaged and re-promoted, and by including his material on compilations that featured hit artists, he was exposed to a wider audience. Interestingly, he was one of the few Motown acts to be adopted by the British Mod Movement which replaced the slowly declining Merseybeat era, although The Beatles' musical domination remained as strong as ever. The Mods adopted their own dress style – short, straight hair, tee-shirts, Parka jackets – rode Hondas, and frequented their own nightclubs. Marvin Gaye's records were tailor-made for the movement because they supported a fast, hard mixture of rock, soul and R&B music and went hand in hand with British groups like The Who who spearheaded the trend. Although the Mods generated record sales, it wasn't always enough to chart singles so Gaye remained a cult figure for the time being.

In America the void left by Smokey Robinson in his career was quickly and efficiently filled when he returned to Holland, Dozier and Holland to record 'Little Darling (I Need You)' for July 1966 release. Gaye: 'It was a much more melodic thing, somewhat similar to Smokey's, but it was a dance record and a big one at that.' The trio worked well with Marvin, they shared a mutual respect and a musical bond developed between them that brought out the best in the artist. Brian Holland, in particular, greatly admired Gaye's talent – 'The music industry is replete with persons possessing good voices, and in some respects, unique sounds. It is most unusual, however, for those qualities to be forged into an unerring intuition. When it does occur, that is rare artistry. Such was Marvin Gaye. The honesty in which he moved through the different music forms, R&B, pop and jazz, char-acterised his movement through life. Marvin was like an instrument, a fine-tuned, complex instrument. He pulled back the veil and revealed his artistry in all its dimensions. In doing so we the listeners were made aware of our own artistic sensitivity, never to the extent of Marvin because he was an unsheltered artist.' The single reached number forty-seven in the pop charts but fared better in the R&B listing by peaking at number ten.

Throughout the years there has been a discrepancy regarding the correct spelling of 'Little Darling (I Need You)'. It has been credited as 'Little Darling I Need You', 'Little Darlin' (I Need You)' and 'Little Darlin' I Need You'. However, as it is listed in Jobete's catalogue as 'Little Darling (I Need You)' – presumably this is correct.

Before the Holland, Dozier and Holland single was released, Marvin Gaye debuted on stage at The Cave, Vancouver. He was one of several Motown acts to test their new stage performances before a Canadian audience prior to touring the more up-market theatres in America. By using this means, any discrepancies in the act could be ironed out prior to facing the tougher American public. Following this he enjoyed a two-week engagement at Los Angeles' Whiskey A Go Go before appearing at the Copacabana. During 1966 Gaye finally became a television star by appearing on *The Ed Sullivan Show* which was screened across America and was the most influential CBS/TV variety programme at the time. Sullivan, an ex-sports reporter, gave exposure to both new and established acts irrespective of colour. The Supremes, whom Gaye considered to be his greatest rivals, beat him by two years when they performed 'Come See About Me'.

At the lower end of the promotion scales Marvin Gaye recorded an interview for Loraine Alterman's Friday 'Teen Beat' page in the *Detroit Free Press* magazine. He had been reluctant to grant the interview but conceded when he was offered the chance of further publicity by recording a jingle to promote 'Teen Beat' against the backing track for 'Pride And Joy'. Copies of the 'novelty' disc were offered free to magazine readers and local radio stations. Nonetheless, this was a most unusual move on the singer's part and naturally the disc is a collector's item today. It appeared Motown was keen to support local enterprise because also around this time The Supremes too became involved in outer-company activities when they spearheaded a campaign to encourage Detroit's young blacks to seek regular employment. Their single 'Times Are Changing' was used in the Equal Employment Opportunities campaign. This followed two

Coca Cola advertisements where the trio, with appropriate lyrics, sang over 'Baby Love' and 'When The Lovelight Starts Shining Thru' His Eyes'. Marvin Gaye accompanied them on piano for both tracks. And – ignoring the outrage from black communities – The Supremes' images were wrapped round loaves of white bread manufactured by Detroit's Ward Baking Company and, using the outstretched arms routine in 'Stop! In The Name Of Love', they convinced television viewers that Arrid Extra Dry deodorant would dry any wet spots.

Meanwhile, unknown to Marvin Gaye, his career was destined to change once more when he very reluctantly recorded a tried and tested song. Happily his objections were ignored because the single 'I Heard It Through The Grapevine' transformed him into a multi-million-selling artist. However, before that, he rose to another musical plateau when he met Tammi Terrell.

# 4. | Your Precious Love

*Tammi was very beautiful . . . she had a great style and a great way.*

(Marvin Gaye)

*I've lived and loved this business too long not to be a part of it.*
(Tammi Terrell)

*'I Heard It Through The Grapevine' was recorded at an early stage in my career when I wasn't into myself as an artist.*

(Marvin Gaye)

*It was very difficult working when I went out with Marvin because these were his troubled years.*

(Barbara Randolph)

By the mid-Sixties Motown had grown beyond all expectation. Over one hundred artists were signed to the roster, and Berry Gordy was richer than even he could have anticipated. Motown was registered under the International Revenue Code as a Sub-Chapter S company, therefore Motown's money was Gordy's money and vice versa. The company's success was exemplified in *Record World* magazine's R&B Award charts where Motown's astounding achievements in black music were registered. The Supremes were Top Female Group, followed by Martha and the Vandellas and The Marvelettes in second and third spots. The Top Group was the Four Tops, with The Miracles and The Temptations as runners-up, while 'I Can't Help Myself' (Four Tops) was top record. Marvin Gaye was named as second Top Male Vocalist, Stevie Wonder reached fifth. And Kim Weston was voted fourth Top Female Vocalist, while Jnr Walker and the All Stars became Top Instrumental Combo. Yes indeed, Berry Gordy's acts were filling his company's coffers and the 'Sound Of Young America' was making its presence felt throughout the world.

Not only did the recording side generate vast sums of money (The

Supremes alone earned $100,000 during the first six months of 1965) but also ITM and Jobete. With few exceptions, all the early compositions, including those written by Holland, Dozier and Holland, were (and still are) Jobete owned. In later years, when artists wrote their own material, they opted to open their own publishing companies, thereby securing the copyright to their songs.

The magnitude of the recording triumphs was such that Berry Gordy was unsure he could control his growing empire because there was no way he could have been prepared for the fortune he had amassed, which made him the wealthiest black man in America. Although he was relatively uneducated in certain areas, he was one of the shrewdest businessmen in the recording industry, and diligently controlled the running of Motown and his artists, even though ex-Motowners claimed his main interest was Diana Ross's career with The Supremes. Nonetheless, he always seemed to reserve time for Marvin Gaye and continued whenever possible to oversee his career and its progress. When the singer's personal life hit its current sluggish patch, and when he became disillusioned in his career because bookings for solo artists were low when compared to tours enjoyed by Motown's groups, Gordy suggested he record duets again. This time Gaye readily agreed, recognising it to be the musical diversion his career needed. His marriage had soured, the age gap between him and Anna seemed wider, and singing with a partner would be an emotional release for him: he could pour out his words of love on vinyl and not offend anyone. He wanted to remember a simple, innocent love, to recall the excitement of falling in love again . . .

Berry Gordy introduced him to new signing Tammi Terrell, a slip of a girl everyone loved and admired; a ray of sunshine to all who met her and an extraordinarily talented singer. Gaye: 'She'd been with Motown for a while, just hanging around, waiting for her turn. I rehearsed with her and really dug her voice and it seemed to fit in with my style. It was just a pleasure for me. Tammi was very beautiful. I really loved it, and she had a great style and a great way . . . I wanted to work with Tammi, I liked her. She was pretty, nice; she was soft, warm and sweet, yet misunderstood. Yes, I enjoyed working with her.' Kim Weston: 'I met Tammi Terrell prior to her coming to Motown, and I found her to be very energetic, outspoken to say the least! But she was a beautiful person. When I left Motown she was one of the few artists who stayed in contact with me. She and I went out when

I was in Detroit. When she came to California to work I'd go and see her. We had a great relationship.'

Born Thomasina Montgomery on 24 January 1946 in Philadelphia, Terrell was persuaded by her mother to consider show business as a career. However, working through school, Tammi ignored her mother's wishes to study medicine, and spent two years at Pennsylvania University. While at school she won first prize at a talent show held at Camden's VA Club, and was lured to perform in Philadelphia's Medea Club. During 1961 Luther Dixon, Scepter/Wand Records' producer, attended one of her performances. He was sufficiently impressed to sign the fourteen-year-old songstress to record for him tracks like 'Big John', 'Voice Of Experience', 'It's Mine', 'Make The Night Just A Little Longer', 'Sinner's Devotion' and Dixon's own penned 'If You See Bill'. (All these tracks are featured on the 1969 'The Early Show' album released by Marble Arch Records.) Tammi's introduction to showbusiness flopped so she returned to her university studies, before being enticed back to join the James Brown Revue for a time. Terrell became romantically involved with Brown and recorded 'I Cried' for his Try Me label in 1963. After a reputed stormy affair with him, she married in 1964. Research indicates her husband could have been boxer Ernie Terrell. It's conceivable that Tammi would have moved in boxing circles because her father was a one-time manager and her uncle, Bobby Montgomery, was the former lightweight boxing champion. Ernie Terrell was, incidentally, brother of Jean, who in 1970 officially replaced Diana Ross in The Supremes. The marriage ended in divorce although no details were publicly revealed.

Kim Weston disagreed: she did not believe Tammi married Ernie Terrell. 'She adopted the name Terrell after she came to Motown. They changed it from Montgomery to Terrell. But I don't think she had any legal ties. Actually, if I'm not mistaken they changed her name because they wanted to disassociate her from what she had done as Tammy Montgomery.'

A later recording deal with Checker Records produced the double A-sided single 'This Time Tomorrow' and 'If I Could Marry You', and by 1965 Tammi had met Berry Gordy, who signed her after seeing her on tour with Jerry Butler. In November 1965 Terrell's first single 'I Can't Believe You Love Me' was issued. The commercially-slanted song reached number seventy-two in the pop charts (no 27 R&B). It was followed by 'Come On And See Me' in April 1966 which reached number eighty (no 25 R&B). Both tracks, written by Harvey Fuqua and Johnny Bristol, were infectiously catchy and a good indication of her vocal expertise. A year later her debut duet with Marvin Gaye was issued. Titled 'Ain't No Mountain High Enough', it was a song solo Terrell had already recorded when Dusty Springfield was unable to due to contractual reasons, and was a stunning single (re-recorded by Diana Ross in 1970) featuring Four Tops' member Duke Fakir on backing vocals. Fakir: 'I remember sitting around during the time Marvin and Tammi were recording and Marvin says, "Hey man, come in here and help me sing the song because I can't make it alone."' The single was loved by everyone, it peaked at number nineteen in the pop charts (no 3 R&B) and marked the start of an enjoyable, rewarding career, where Gaye became Terrell's submissive vinyl lover. The reckless manner in which he often approached his solo work was gone, to be replaced by a timorous respect for his music. For once, Marvin Gaye was happy with his work.

Berry Gordy assigned his newly-signed writing team of Nickolas Ashford and Valerie Simpson, and established in-housers Harvey Fuqua and ex-Anna artist Johnny Bristol (who later married Berry Gordy's niece Iris) to work with the duettists. Ashford and Simpson were young, enthusiastic writer/producers, who had met in New York City during 1963, when Ashford was twenty-one and Simpson seventeen. Ashford: 'I went [there] because everyone said it was the place to make it. I was destitute and was invited to this Baptist Church. I went along to get a good meal and that's where I met Valerie . . . We got to know each other socially and talked about writing together.' Their writing collaboration won them a contract with Glover Records where, during 1964, their first record 'I'll Find You' was issued. Ashford: 'We recorded two singles but nothing happened. It was so rough, we decided we'd be better sticking to writing!' The couple moved from Glover to work for Scepter Records where they wrote for The Shirelles among others. Then, during 1966, blind soul megastar Ray Charles recorded their moody 'Let's Go Get Stoned' which became an R&B chart topper and a number thirty-one pop hit. From Scepter the couple moved to Motown. Ashford: 'It was a dream come true. We were just writers and Motown was it. When they called us we didn't hesitate. With a whole slew of artists there our songs would get the chance to be recorded. It was the best thing to happen to us.'

Record buyers were entranced by Marvin Gaye and Tammi Terrell's uncomplicated image. When she commanded, he obeyed;

when she seduced him, he responded lovingly. Their phrasing was a magical combination of devotion, their warmth and tenderness compelling. Gaye: 'I had no idea that she was as good a singer as she of course turned out to be. I hadn't got a chance to hear her before we met but some people at Motown, who were on their toes, dug her sound and realised that we may possibly make a good duet.'

With Tammi, Marvin easily fell into the man/woman role, and convinced himself their songs together represented the real love which, he felt, was missing from his marriage to Anna. He said he was trapped in that relationship and believed he had married too soon. As he was now a widely known performer he could have any woman he desired and this played heavily on his mind. In his quest to enjoy total love, he immersed himself in Ashford and Simpson's lyrics because they represented the emotion he craved for. The fact that they were (possibly) an extension of the writers' love for each other or, at the very least, an imaginative play on words, escaped him. Nonetheless, Gaye did love Terrell – no one could sing the way they did and feel no emotion – and while locked away recording, he admitted, their love would intensify within the confines of the studio, but when the session was finished they went their separate ways. Marvin: 'We worked so well together in the studio and when we sang those records we really put ourselves in the music and the story. And in fact for many moments we were lovers there doing the sessions. But it never transcended that.' Valerie Simpson: 'The chemistry between them was fantastic and while they never had a romance in real life, when they sang together "wow", they were lovers.'

Although Ashford and Simpson engineered the Gaye/Terrell success story, they remained anonymous to the public because Berry Gordy refused to allow his staff to have contact with the media. Simpson: 'I thought it was really strange because Motown wanted to keep you in the dark. Everything was Motown, that was all that was supposed to be there. At least we got our names on the records – they couldn't stop that. But you never really knew who was playing what or anything.' Today, the couple are highly paid, world successful entertainers, singing and performing their own compositions. However, when working for Gaye and Terrell neither questioned their inability to record their own material. Ashford: 'I don't think we even thought about it because we were thrilled at the fact that some songs we had written were finally out there. When you have an artist like Marvin Gaye, who was just a phenomenal singer, it's just a dream. We were real writers then and we had this voice that we could do something with. That was all the glory we needed.'

Prior to the release of 'Ain't No Mountain High Enough', Motown released Gaye's next solo album in May 1966. It was the Berry Gordy produced 'The Moods Of Marvin Gaye' which included six singles ('I'll Be Doggone', 'Little Darling (I Need You)', 'Take This Heart Of Mine', 'One More Heartache', 'Ain't That Peculiar', 'You're Unchanging Love'), plus fillers like 'I Worry About You', 'Nightlife', 'One For My Baby (And One For The Road)' and 'You're The One For Me'. The music lacked positive direction; there was little to commend the release – even Gaye looked glum on the front album sleeve! – leaving Motown's promotion department unsure of its buying market. So, the album remained a mediocre seller and a catalogue item, and was overshadowed by the magnitude of his work with Tammi Terrell. A year after the album's release Holland, Dozier and Holland's penned 'You're Unchanging Love', was lifted as a single in June 1967. It struggled into the pop top forty (no 7 R&B) prompting the opinion that the public preferred his work with Terrell at this time, although the track differed little from most of his solo commercial releases to date.

Motown's continued success with Gaye and Terrell was more or less assured but success weaved in mysterious ways with other acts, particularly The Supremes whose future depended upon a line-up change. Florence Ballard, founder of the group and original lead singer, was thrown out. As Diana Ross's role within the trio was being promoted far beyond that of lead singer, Mary Wilson and Ballard were being pushed further into the background. Ballard felt betrayed. Wilson: 'It was apparent that neither Diane nor Berry gave a damn about what we wanted.' Ballard's solo spot 'People' was subsequently dropped from their show when she objected to Gordy's and Ross's attitude, and later she was dropped mid-way through a tour. Ex-Bluebelle, Cindy Birdsong, was hired to finish it, wearing Ballard's stage gowns to ensure the audiences remained ignorant of the switch. The animosity between Ross, Gordy and Ballard grew to alarming proportions, until the fun-loving Supreme was sacked in August 1967. Ballard: 'Someone was always talking about exposing me and I never could understand why because I never did anything to expose. Yes, there were some reports that I drank and it took me a long time to realize that there wasn't anything wrong with that. I didn't drink a lot and it never affected my work. I never missed a performance because of something I did personally.'

Cindy Birdsong, meantime, officially replaced the departing Supreme on the 'Reflections' single issued in July 1967 when the label credit read Diana Ross and the Supremes. This gave Ross top billing but to soften the blow with his other groups, Berry Gordy likewise changed two more – Martha Reeves and the Vandellas, and Smokey Robinson and the Miracles.

Florence Ballard was forbidden to discuss her dismissal with the media but years later the truth became known. When she signed her group release in July 1967 she relinquished all rights and claims to all future income from the trio. Without the expertise of legal advice, Ballard signed the release which offered her $15,000 over a six-year period. Months later she realised her error and consulted lawyer Leonard Baun. He immediately secured approximately $76,000 from Ballard's joint Bank of Commonwealth account with Motown during September 1967. This amount wasn't a settlement figure but reputedly money that was rightly hers. After a series of unsatisfactory business deals not within her control, Ballard was once again penniless. She therefore instructed Baun to negotiate with Motown and The Supremes to claim unpaid monies due to her. Motown retaliated, leaving the desperate Ballard no choice but to agree to an out-of-court settlement.

Meanwhile ABC Records were anxious to sign the ex-Supreme but were unable to proceed until she had an approved separation from Motown. Ballard's release contract was eventually finalised in 1968 when it was proven that the July 1967 contract was null and void. Motown agreed to pay her the lump sum of $160,000 from two Supremes accounts and one Motown Record Corporation account.

In March 1968 Florence signed a recording agreement with ABC Records whereupon her debut single 'It Doesn't Matter How You Say It (It Is What I Say That Matters)' was issued. On Motown's instructions ABC were unable to mention in the single's promotion that she was a former Supreme. Florence's husband, Thomas Chapman, therefore hired the Joe Glaser Agency to handle her concerts and former Motown employee Al Abrams to control her publicity. The single flopped. Another ex-Motowner, Robert Bateman, who among others, introduced Mary Wells to Motown, knew Ballard and worked with her on four songs. 'Love Ain't Love', written by Van McCoy, was chosen as her second single. That also flopped.

Ballard was, by now, convinced that ABC were treating her career indifferently – 'Things looked good when I first started out as a single. I had signed with a new company and was pleased with the initial releases and even had a few engagements lined up. Then all of a sudden it seemed as if I was black-balled. My records weren't played and there were no bookings.'

Following the release of her second single and after performing at President Nixon's 1969 inaugural celebrations, ABC (under pressure from Motown?) terminated her contract and canned her album tentatively titled 'You Don't Have To'. (Due to pressure from Ballard's fans during the Eighties, ABC considered re-mixing the album with a view to finally releasing it.)

When Ballard lost the recording deal Baun informed her she was fundless, whereupon she became suspicious of his handling of her financial affairs and hired another lawyer, Gerald Dent, in 1969 to look into the matter. Dent died before the case ended; David Tate replaced him and took Motown, Berry Gordy and Diana Ross to court in 1970 in a $8.5 million suit claiming they had conspired for her to leave the group under fraudulent settlement. The suit was dismissed by the Michigan Supreme Court who ruled that Ballard's release agreement remained binding unless she returned the $160,000 to Motown. She couldn't, and she blamed Baun. Ballard was at her lowest and when Diana Ross was notified of her plight she immediately gave her financial assistance and did not ignore her as was suggested by Mary Wilson in her autobiography. Later on Ballard was mugged and robbed twice, then hospitalised for nervous strain and exhaustion. But the greatest blow of all came when the bank foreclosed on her West Buena Vista home in Detroit bought for $30,000 in 1965, despite the desperate singer selling every item of value she possessed. Once again Ross offered help.

When Ballard's husband left her, she and their three children (twins Nicole and Michelle, and Lisa) were forced to live with her mother and sister. Ballard told local newscaster Dave Diles – 'I kept saying to myself, at least couldn't I have just kept my home if nothing else? For my children's sake, couldn't that at least have been paid for?' With no income Florence and her family were supported by AFD (Aid To Families With Dependents) with fortnightly payments of $135. The ex-Supreme was seen scrummaging through vegetables to find the cheapest at the end of the day in local shops, walking home laden down with shopping because she could not afford the bus fare, and often wearing disguises so that her neighbours failed to recognise her when she shopped from second-hand stores.

A friend was so incensed by the way Ballard had been treated by Motown and was now forced to live that she informed *The Washington Post*. The paper carried Ballard's story, later syndicated throughout America, resulting in offers of work including her 1975 Detroit appearance at a benefit concert where she sang Helen Reddy's defiant 'I Am Woman' and The Supremes' 'Come See About Me' to a welcoming response. Also that year she won her law suit against Leonard Baun and received a settlement of $50,000 which enabled her to purchase a new home for her family.

Offers of work continued. Tragically it was too late. On 21 February 1976 after returning home from a shopping spree, Florence Ballard was found lying paralysed on the floor in her home. The thirty-two-year-old Supreme died the next day, following a cardiac arrest, in Detroit's Mount Carmel Hospital. The police report stated 'she ingested an unknown amount of pills and consumed alcohol'. The pills were to control her weight and high blood pressure which she took under prescription to prepare herself for her return to show business. The world mourned its favourite Supreme, a victim of tragic circumstances and one of several Motown casualties.

More changes were afoot. In July 1967 while the rest of the world was languishing in the love and peace of marijuana-influenced Flower Power, billows of smoke were seen from the Motown building. Detroit was in the grips of a riot which left over forty people dead, thousands arrested, and buildings gutted. The riot stemmed from an everyday raid in the city where low-paid blacks and whites lived in appalling conditions. Temptation Otis Williams: 'Watching the news was like seeing a nightmare. The violence, looting and burning got worse by the hour. Finally, the National Guard and the Army came into the city and started shooting near our building. You couldn't go out, but the gunfire was so close, you didn't want to stay in either. It was one of the most terrifying experiences of my life.'

The Motown complex remained unscathed by the rioters despite many threats that the building would burn, but they prompted Berry Gordy to move his $30 million business from 2648 West Grand Boulevard into a new office block, formerly known as the Donovan Building, on 2547 Woodward Avenue. He also moved up town and purchased a new three-storey mansion on Boston Boulevard, leaving Marvin and Anna Gaye to move into his old house. This was one of many moves Gaye made throughout his life, blaming his gypsy blood for his wanderlust – 'I have no home. The earth is my home at this time. I don't want to be here. I'll live here until I'm not here any-more, until I don't have to be here, however many times I must incarnate. I'm concerned with humanity and my heart is big enough, and my empathy is big enough to know it is not just my job to stay in one place. It is my job to go everywhere and to pick up and sense and report it through my music.'

Two months before Gaye and Terrell's second duet 'Your Precious Love' was issued in August 1967, Motown released Gaye's 'Greatest Hits Volume 2' compilation, while across the Atlantic, Motown/EMI prepared their own sixteen-track 'Greatest Hits' compiled from Gaye's two American 'Hits' sets for early 1968 release. 'Your Precious Love' was reminiscent of the floating Moonglows style, resurrected under Harvey Fuqua's guidance and the mellow vocalising of Gaye and Terrell. The song was the perfect romantic walkabout which enjoyed heavyweight promotion from Motown to become a number five hit (no 2 R&B). However in its enthusiasm to reap further sales from its sheet music, Jobete printed Gaye's partner's name as 'Tammy' Terrell!

Released the same month as 'Your Precious Love' was the aptly titled 'United' album where Johnny Bristol and Harvey Fuqua joined Ashford and Simpson in the composer/production credits. The album was a hit thanks to the singles it contained, like Gaye's penned sensitive ballad 'If This World Were Mine' which was seen by many as a declaration of how he would alter his personal situation if he could. As the B-side to 'If I Could Build My Whole World Around You' the song became a number sixty-eight pop hit (no 27 R&B). Other tracks included the happy-go-lucky 'Two Can Have A Party', Berry Gordy's co-penned 'You Got What It Takes' (originally recorded by Marv Johnson) and the throwaway pop song 'Something Stupid' which had been a hit for Frank and Nancy Sinatra. Clay Cole's sleeve notes seemed to sum up the album's ambience. 'When two abundantly endowed singers team together to record an album the result is a new dimension in music. Blended together, the voices of Marvin Gaye and Tammi Terrell give birth to a new and exciting sound. They display remarkable range running the gamut from fast numbers to the slower paced.'

Although Harvey Fuqua was responsible for some of the album's sweetest love songs, his marriage to Gwen Gordy had ended in divorce. She later married The Spinners' lead vocalist G. C. Cameron. Gaye and Cameron became close friends as he told journalist Scott

Taylor – 'Marvin Gaye, being my brother-in-law, allowed me the privilege of being connected spiritually as well as physically to the attributes of which he contributed. I tried to consume as much knowledge from him as I could because he was a great man, and his music will be continually great among us.'

Before the third and last duet 'If I Could Build My Whole World Around You' was released during November 1967 to become a top ten hit (No 2 R&B) and a British number forty-one, a solo Terrell single, 'What A Good Man He Is', written by Smokey Robinson and Al Cleveland, was scheduled for September/October release, but withdrawn. Also Gaye's solo work was once more exploited in Britain via his second EP 'Originals From Marvin Gaye', the nineteenth in the TME series. It mattered little to Motown/EMI that the featured tracks had already been released, their goal was to push his music beyond the ever-loyal Mod market in any way it could to secure high national chart positions. In time the company would achieve this; meanwhile it struggled.

In America, another problem arose. Tammi Terrell was giving cause for concern. Despite warnings from friends she had fallen in love with David Ruffin, a member of The Temptations.

Mississippi-born Ruffin (brother of Jimmy, a soloist for Berry Gordy's Miracle then Soul labels) joined the group as original member Elbridge Bryant's replacement to record the R&B hit 'The Way You Do The Things You Do'. David Ruffin stayed with the group for four years before being asked to leave. (Another founder member, Eddie Kendricks, left shortly afterwards.) Dennis Edwards replaced him and first appeared as a Temptation at Los Angeles' Forum in July 1968. Otis Williams remarked that although the group remained friendly with Ruffin, 'We had to let him go because of his "head thing". He would be great on stage and then he'd go off on this ego trip. He'd sit in on our gigs when he'd already left and Dennis felt obliged to ask him up on stage with us.'

The Temptations lost none of their magic despite Ruffin insisting he felt they were lost without him. Williams wrote in his autobiography – 'Motown exercised its option to keep David on the roster as a solo act. In early 1969 they released his single "My Whole World Ended (The Moment You Left Me)", a tune Johnny Bristol originally wrote with The Temptations in mind. It was a big hit, and David's solo career seemed to be getting off to a good start.' By 1978 Ruffin's hits belonged to the past and his Motown career was over.

With Eddie Kendricks, Ruffin re-joined The Temptations temporarily to record the 'Reunion' album in 1982, followed by the reunion tour of America. Late in 1982 Ruffin was sentenced to six months' imprisonment after pleading guilty at Detroit's District Court for fiddling his 1976 tax returns. He was also fined $4,500. He teamed up once again with Kendricks to record as a duet and with Hall and Oates.

Tammi Terrell and David Ruffin were inseparable, even though some believed him to be married. However, years later, Otis Williams confirmed that Ruffin was in fact single when he began dating Terrell, and added – 'Tammi was very good for David. Since she was a performer too, she had a deep appreciation for what his priorities should be – she kept him straight. She always made sure that David was on time for whatever he had to do.' Barbara Randolph also knew Terrell at this time – 'She had some wild relationships with different guys and she was a very emotional person. OK, so she lived on the wild side, but we all loved her. She was easy to love, and was a real personality. She always seemed to team up with someone who was in show business . . . She was a very sweet person, who came from a very respectable family. Her father was a preacher and she came from a religious background. When she started on the road she was sweet, innocent. But an unbelievable change happened. She just loved and trusted the wrong people.'

When her relationship with Ruffin soured, Terrell suffered horrendous headaches and took massive doses of pain killers, as confirmed by Otis Williams: 'Tammi had been complaining of excruciating headaches for as long as we'd known her but had never had it checked out . . . She'd had a rough couple of years before coming to Motown, and would have a rougher few after, but she never lost that vibrancy. When she and David moved in together, she kept a nice house and was a good cook. There was nothing she wouldn't do for David. She loved the hell out of him, and liked to be with us, so she'd come out on the road too . . . Later on they began to fight a lot. Their relationship was definitely a rocky one. But none of us knew what to do to help. Still, no matter what problems they had, one thing was certain, she loved David, and I'm sure David loved her.'

In mid-1967 as Terrell and Gaye finished singing 'Your Precious Love' on stage at the Hampton-Sydney College in Virginia, she collapsed into his arms and was carried off stage. Gaye: 'I'm not sure she knew how serious it was until she collapsed.' Her doctors diagnosed a brain tumour. Terrell's health drastically deteriorated as she lost weight and became partially paralysed. Williams: '. . . She made a valiant effort to be the old Tammi. There was some talk that she was on her way to recovering but I could see that she would never be the same again.'

It was a tragedy. Terrell was, at last, reaping the rewards of her struggling years but was now unable to enjoy them. With the powerful success of the duets, theatre owners and the media flocked to feature the duo and it was a sad, reluctant Gaye who honoured the commitments, without divulging the true nature of his partner's illness. As time passed, it became obvious that he needed a female replacement to sing with him on stage; he could no longer ignore the duets. The attractive, reserved and underrated Barbara Randolph, who to date had recorded the superb, uptempo evergreen 'I Got A Feeling', was chosen because she shared Gaye's touring manager. Randolph: 'I just approached Larry Maxwell and told him I was having trouble getting stage work, and the company didn't seem to care, even though I'd done the major movie *Guess Who's Coming To Dinner*. And he said he'd send me out with Marvin. Marvin said it was OK and everybody agreed it would be alright. This venue had booked Marvin and Tammi based on the popularity of their recordings. Tammi was in hospital so I was sent in because the club didn't want Marvin as a solo artist.'

However, Randolph and Gaye's working relationship was often strained when he, at the final moment, refused to perform. Randolph: 'It was very difficult working when I went out with Marvin because these were his troubled years. For example, I was booked to appear at the Apollo with him, and it was one of the many occasions he didn't show up. I would end up appearing there alone which was really frightening, particularly if you know anything about the Apollo Theatre! It was scary – they throw hard boiled eggs! – and the audience was waiting for Marvin. In the end I guess they felt sorry for me. Usually they don't feel sorry for anybody, but I made it through that. I reckoned I could handle any situation from then on!'

Although working with Gaye was often nerve-racking, the two never argued. In fact – and despite reports to the contrary – Randolph never heard him raise his voice to anybody – 'Personally I never heard him get into any type of loud situation with anyone. He was extremely likeable, easy going, and a very mellow person. I had the greatest admiration for him. In fact, I admired him before I ever worked with him.' Mary Wells: 'I never saw him do anything terrible. As a matter of fact, Anna used to get on at him so bad, party with him so bad. I used to be in the other room saying, "Marvin kill her, kill her".' Kim Weston: 'I never saw Anna and Marvin arguing in public, but by working with him, I could tell when the situation was tense.'

Meanwhile Tammi Terrell worked when she could. At times, she was so determined that Gaye's career wouldn't suffer because of her illness, she continued to record with him and was seen in the studios singing from a wheelchair or balanced on crutches.

Marvin Gaye's solo career continued. His next single 'You' took a hard, long look at his crumbling marriage although few people realised his anguish at the time and his cry remained unheard. The powerful song, written by Jack Goga, Ivy Hunter and Jeffrey Bowan, was released in December 1967, four months after 'Your Precious Love', to reach thirty-four in the pop charts (no 7 R&B). During the single's life, Tammi Terrell was mobile on crutches, and was seen sneaking into The Cherry Hill Theatre/Restaurant in Camden, New Jersey, to watch her partner perform. Backed by the twenty-five-piece Joe Frasetto Band which included several of his own musicians, Gaye's opening night audience was won over with songs like 'Who Can I Turn To', 'Born Free' and a medley from the Dr Dolittle film. The big band sound was punctuated by a regular bongo beat that contrasted so effectively with his voice. One critic wrote – 'Marvin Gaye demonstrated his versatility by taking over at the piano during several of his past pop recordings and later he played guitar during a group of blues favourites. His vocal repertoire ranged from R&B to jazz.'

Prior to Marvin Gaye and Tammi Terrell's second album 'You're All I Need', a taster was issued in March 1968 titled 'Ain't Nothing Like The Real Thing'. Gaye: '. . . I recall that we were trying different kinds of riffs and little things to challenge each other and that's how that song is as melodic and rifty and syncopated in the way that it is. We were really enjoying challenging each other with our riffs and little note changes, and the rises and falls. That's how it came off that way. We really had fun recording that.' It was a beautiful song and was indicative of the pending album. It shot to number eight in the pop chart (no 1 R&B) and thirty-four in the UK. 'You're All I Need', recorded in June 1968 and issued two months later, re-established their vinyl love affair. It was a superb album – they cried, rejoiced and romanced, pledged unremitting love – which included five of Ashford and Simpson's finest compositions, also their first productions, and six from Harvey Fuqua and Johnny Bristol. All the singles lifted belonged to the former duo starting with 'Ain't Nothing Like The Real Thing' and followed by 'You're All I Need To Get By' in July 1968 which raced to number seven in the pop chart (no 1 R&B) and peaked at nineteen in the British listings. The song, Berry Gordy's personal favourite with Ashford and Simpson's vocals padding out the lead voices, offered the sweetest lyrics known to lovers. 'Keep On Lovin' Me Honey' issued in the September to reach number twenty-four (no 11 R&B) carried the flipside 'You Ain't Livin' 'Til You're Lovin – which was a British top-side in January 1969, when it peaked at number twenty-one.

The album, which reached number sixty in the American charts, was a work of beauty that has stood the cruel test of time and was, quite possibly, the best of their career together. Yet, it was recorded under the dire conditions of Tammi Terrell's failing health, as noted in the record's sleeve notes – 'The Gaye–Terrell success story is documented by the number of hits they've recorded and the loyalty of their fans who have flocked to witness their superb personal performances at home and abroad. Such performances have been temporarily denied us due to Tammi's illness. It was strictly Tammi's love for her art and a quest for the spiritual rejuvenation she always received while working with Marvin that brought Tammi back to Motown to record this album. It was both a journey of love and dedication . . . a sentimental journey. Unerringly, Tammi was right. Not only did recording this album contribute to her convalescence, but added a new dimension to the Gaye–Terrell repertoire.' When the album was released, Terrell was in hospital. When she had recovered she holidayed in the Bahamas before returning home, where *Soul* magazine tracked her down to carry a rare interview under the heading 'Tammi Terrell Alive, But Can She Return?' The article read: 'Tammi Terrell, long rumoured dead or dying, is planning to go back to performing as soon as her doctor gives her the word. In a long-distance telephone interview from her home in Philadelphia, Tammi said, "I'm feeling fine. I've been staying home and recuperating . . ." Tammi underwent exploratory examination some time ago for a brain tumour following a collapse while performing with Marvin. She's been suffering from headaches and dizziness for many months. Her doctor ordered her on a limited work schedule. Mostly, Tammi said, it's a matter of when she's tired, she rests. Otherwise she works.

During her recuperation, she picked up some hobbies. "I learned to knit in hospital," she said laughing. "I feel like a grandma." And she's been cooking and eating soul food. "Am I on a diet! I went down to ninety-three pounds in the hospital and now I weigh one hundred and twenty-five." Her hair, shorn off for surgery, is "almost natural now", she said. "For a while there, my father said I looked just like him." The one thing that's pulled her through her troubles is an overwhelming desire to get back to work. At first depressed at missing shows just when she and Marvin, as a team, became popular, she's gotten over it now and is spending her time either staying at home or going to parties. Has Tammi learned anything from her blues? "I've got a lot more faith in God" – she said quietly.'

Two years later Marvin Gaye's cherished singing partner was dead . . .

A month after the release of 'You're All I Need To Get By', Marvin Gaye's solo, Frank Wilson-penned 'Chained' was issued to become a number thirty-two pop hit and top ten R&B entrant. It was a strong track and a cover version of Paul Petersen's original released on the Motown label in May 1967. Petersen, born in September 1945 in Glendale, California, and one of Gordy's few white artists at this time, had been in the entertainment business since childhood. Before signing with Motown in 1967 he had enjoyed a top ten pop hit with 'My Dad' four years earlier on the Colpix label. At Motown he only recorded two singles, 'Chained' and a pop-slanted 'A Little Bit For Sandy' in August 1968, his only British release.

Gaye's version of 'Chained' was a timely release because the lyrics related to him being trapped by marriage, and his subsequent interpretation was almost blood chilling. He admitted he and Anna were grossly unhappy, yet neither wanted to be the first to end their relationship. She was afraid of losing the momentum of being married to a star, and he was scared his career would fail without her support. According to friends, the singer wallowed in his self-imposed misery as he tried to come to terms with his wife's unfaithfulness, while expecting his own to be acceptable to her. So, the single merely accentuated his state of mind. At one point, Gaye reached the depths of deepest despair and seeing no escape threatened to shoot himself. 'Pops' Gordy rescued him although it was thought unlikely Marvin would actually commit suicide because he believed it was a mortal sin, one of the gravest against the teachings of God. This was, incidentally, the start of a run of attempts to press his self-destruct button, but whether he ever seriously contemplated suicide remains to be seen because he invariably ensured someone was nearby, or was expected. Looking logically at these attempts one could see they were cries for help, yet, it appears they went unheeded.

Unfortunately, Gaye was not afraid of dying, and was, he stressed, an act he wanted to control – 'You have to be afraid [of it] until you understand what [it] is, but once you get a pretty good realisation of what death is and why it is necessary, it need not be a fearful or a horrible thing to those that have come to that point. Like the Buddhist monks who are able to burn themselves without flinching or protesting. They are not in their bodies, they are outside viewing the body. We do know that happens, so why don't we try to emulate or get close to that knowledge. Death isn't a great problem. One who has enough power to master his body has no fear of death at all. He understands that death is another trip to somewhere else because his mind has been prepared and the body or the shell, seems nothing. All that is important is the mind.'

Following his initial liaison with Marvin Gaye in 1963, Norman Whitfield had transferred his talents to The Temptations by writing a track with Smokey Robinson for their first album 'Meet The Temptations' issued during March 1964. Two years later Barrett Strong joined Whitfield as writer/producer on The Temptations songs and together were responsible for their later major musical upheaval when their submissive, melodic sounds were replaced by raw, aggressive and funky records. The first of this ilk was the 1968 international hit 'Cloud Nine' which dealt with the hitherto taboo subject of drug-taking. However, Whitfield's productions were often excessive and superfluous as he indulged himself in instrumental orgies. His albums invariably included lengthy versions of the group's singles with ballads thrown in for balanced listening. After a run of hits, the relationship culminated with the 1973 Grammy Award winner 'Papa Was A Rolling Stone'. Even though it appeared Whitfield could do no wrong, his biggest failing was, some thought, recording the same songs with a variety of acts, and this frustrated the artists who worked with him. For example, The Temptations, Gladys Knight and the Pips and Marvin Gaye all recorded 'I Wish It Would Rain', The Temptations and Edwin Starr both recorded 'War'. Barrett Strong: 'Norman always felt he could do a song in so many different ways, but there was certainly never any shortage of material because we were writing new songs all the time.'

Nonetheless, Norman Whitfield produced a hit with Marvin

Gaye's next solo outing 'I Heard It Through The Grapevine' released in October 1968 after 'Keep On Lovin' Me Honey' with Tammi Terrell. The song had been recorded and canned some time earlier and was originally the brainchild of its co-writer Barrett Strong – 'I came up with a little idea on the piano, the bass-line figure. We thought it was great, and I had thought of this title "I Heard It Through The Grapevine" – because I'd heard people saying it so much, but nobody had ever written a song about it. We just went from there.' However there are conflicting reports regarding the record's release.

*Rolling Stone* magazine reported that Billie Jean Brown, then head of Quality Control, was searching for material for Gaye's 'In The Groove' album and found the track stored in Motown's tape library. She played it to a Chicago DJ, who was then instrumental in persuading Motown to release it as a single. The magazine further reported that Phil Jones, Motown's promotion director, received a call from WVON's Rodney Jones soon after 'In The Groove' was issued. Phil Jones: 'He said , "I played the record at the hop and they went crazy. I put it on the air last night and the phones lit up."' Norman Whitfield: 'I had the Marvin Gaye version and it was time to put out a Marvin Gaye album ['In The Groove']. So I started my campaign once again because I just wanted to get it in the album. They said they weren't going to put it in the album, so I said, "It is a number one record, it does have some name value for the album", and so forth. So they said, "Well, we guess he's right, we'll just go ahead and put it on the album". And lo and behold, the record was picked out of the album and went on to be probably the largest song in the history of Motown.'

'I Heard It Through The Grapevine' was destined to change Gaye's status within Motown for a time and the industry as a whole by transforming him into the multi-million selling megastar bracket. However, there was one drawback – another version by fellow Motown act, Gladys Knight and the Pips, released in September 1967, had sold in excess of two million copies. This version – a rousing, gutsy sound with tight vocal interplay, dominated by Gladys' deep, strong gospel voice – was also produced by Whitfield and subsequently raced to number two in the American pop charts (no 1 R&B). This winning formula set the precedent for future hits. Marvin Gaye: 'Berry decided to give Norman a shot at cutting me and we worked on the song. I wasn't keen on recording it, but

Norman had this whole new arrangement worked out and it came out pretty good . . . The single was recorded at an early stage in my career when I wasn't into myself as an artist. I was into being produceable. I simply took Norman's direction as I felt the direction he was expounding was a proper one. Had I done the song myself I would not have sung it at all like that, but there are many benefits in just singing other people's material and taking directions. The job of interpreting is quite an important one because when people are not able to express what is in their souls, and there is an artist who can, then I think that is very valuable.' Earl Van Dyke who played Wurlitzer electric piano on the single recalled that James Jamerson played bass; Eddie Willis, Robert White and Joe Messina, guitars; Jack Ashford, tambourines (which played a significant role throughout the song) and Richard 'Pistol' Allen played drums and tomtoms. The result was a divine gift which has never been repeated, although often imitated. Gaye's vocals were superbly controlled as he effortlessly moved through the moody, haunting and hypnotic slow beat that almost dragged its way across the song. Music critics glowed that the public would never need to hear another record after this. For a while they were right. 'I Heard It Through The Grapevine' sold in excess of two and a half million copies in America alone. It topped the pop charts for seven weeks, fending off Stevie Wonder's 'For Once In My Life' and Diana Ross and the Supremes and The Temptations' 'I'm Gonna Make You Love Me', both of which peaked at number two. After it became an R&B number one for seven weeks it also soared to the top in twenty-six other countries.

However, no credit was taken from the Gladys Knight and the Pips frenetic version because the two songs were totally different and both classed as classic evergreens. Despite public belief and with no admission from Gladys or Motown, Marvin Gaye recorded his version *before* them. Earl Van Dyke who also played on the Gladys Knight version: 'Maybe a month after Gladys, it was Marvin's session . . . We [the musicians] said, "What is this shit? We just cut it." And Norman said, "Now we're going to do it a different way."' (In fact, research reveals that The Miracles were actually the first to record the song which was eventually released as an album track on their 1968 album 'Special Occasion', followed by a version by The Isley Brothers.) However, when Berry Gordy heard Marvin's version, he disliked it. Gaye: 'I love Gladys very much, she's great but she always seemed to have that little number about this song. It's something that just ticks her off about the whole "Grapevine" situation. There was something unethical involved; on that score she has a beef. But the reality of the situation is that Norman cut the song on me first and Berry canned it because he didn't have a lot of faith in it; or maybe I was acting ridiculous at the time, so Berry would can it, which happened a few times. I would have done the same thing if someone was giving me trouble. And I've given him a few problems. So, as a result of the song being canned Norman knew he had a good song, so he cut it on Gladys and came out with her version first. When Motown released my version it seemed to Gladys to be a bit unethical because you don't want somebody from your own company covering your own record. But it was through no fault of mine, I didn't have any control over the situation at all.' The Pips' Merald Knight: 'We took [the song] home, worked hard to give it a new treatment and Norman hardly had to do anything. That one wasn't nothing until we took it.' Gladys Knight: 'I really believe that that was the key to our whole future. Records can determine your future and I believe that this was the magic record that started our career moving over the fence and it opened the door for Gladys Knight and the Pips.'

'I Heard It Through The Grapevine' became Marvin Gaye's first and only British chart topper in February 1969, whereupon he decided to tour the country. For some reason it never materialised, so he failed to take advantage of the success, leaving Motown/EMI grappling to keep the momentum of a number one record. Shortly after the single's success, Tammi Terrell was hospitalised for the first of several major operations. Gaye turned his back on the excitement generated by the single to become consumed by concern over his ailing singing partner. Meanwhile, the album which featured 'I Heard It Through The Grapevine', was rapidly re-named and re-promoted as 'In The Groove/Heard It Through The Grapevine'. The album's production credits stretched from Ashford and Simpson ('Tear It On Down'), Harvey Fuqua and Johnny Bristol ('At Last (I Found A Love)', 'Change What You Can' – both written by Anna and Marvin Gaye with Elgie Stover) and Ivy Hunter ('You', 'Loving You Is Sweeter Than Ever', 'It's Love I Need'). Two songs were composed by non-staffers – King/Goffin's 'Some Kind Of Wonderful' and Nelson/ Pattersoni/Treadwell's 'There Goes My Baby'. It was a musical pot-pourri indicating that some tracks were previous album cut-outs. Nonetheless it reached number sixty-three in the American charts.

While 'I Heard It Through The Grapevine' raced up the world's charts, Motown continued to make its presence felt with artists like Stevie Wonder, and Diana Ross and the Supremes and The Temptations whose 'I'm Gonna Make You Love Me' was lifted from their eponymous debut album issued during November 1968. The two groups promoted this powerfully commercial record on the prestigious *Ed Sullivan Show*. The performance inspired Timex Watches to sponsor a one-hour television special *TCB – Takin' Care Of Business* featuring the two acts. It was produced by Motown Productions Inc in association with George Schlatter/Ed Friendly Productions and represented Berry Gordy's first major television venture. A second spectacular followed titled *GIT (Getting It All Together) On Broadway*, again produced by Schlatter. Inevitably, Diana Ross coveted the star spot on both programmes even though she shared the stage with seven performers. The other artists felt they were being unfairly treated. The Temptations' David Ruffin: 'I asked some executives how [*TCB*] would be billed. They said, "Diana Ross and the Supremes with The Temptations." I said, "How in the hell can that happen because The Temptations had taught The Supremes everything they knew." To protect my interests and that of the group I suggested that the special be billed "David Ruffin and Diana Ross and The Temptations and The Supremes". A month later I was fired.'

In the light of these shows, Marvin Gaye was one of several artists who felt they should receive the same attention from Berry Gordy, but while his colleagues seethed with discontent and envy, he became withdrawn and refused to comply with the wishes of the writers and producers. Gaye treated Ross's success as a personal insult which, he remarked, gave him little incentive to record and perform. Diana, likewise, was aware of his feelings and that of the public since Florence Ballard was thrown out of the trio – 'I know some people want to attack me. It hurts but I deal with that. I never allow myself the luxury of falling apart. If things fail I'm hurt, but I'll scoop me up in my arms and minister to all my hurts and needs. I also have some very good, long-standing friends, people who listen and support when I need both and they accept that I'm a person with feelings.' Meanwhile, Gaye's intense sensitivity to the situation was a fragile instrument that needed careful handling, and when at its lowest ebb, he would hallucinate further, often negative, situations. For instance, he convinced himself that he was responsible for Tammi Terrell's illness. Berry Gordy was aware of his dilemma and did what he could, but his time was consumed by Diana Ross whom he was grooming for a solo career.

When more rational, Marvin Gaye thought of himself, his recent success and future career. He was concerned about the latter because he couldn't envisage the musical road it would now take. As much as he was delighted with 'I Heard It Through The Grapevine', it wasn't a sound he wanted to repeat, and told friends his intention was to expand his music beyond the perimeters of R&B – 'I'd like to make it as big in this business as I can, but a negro R&B singer's chances are slimmer. Only Ray Charles has made it and I don't feel he's held in the same esteem as Frank Sinatra or Sammy Davis Jnr. Although R&B, through young people, is making great strides, the older folk tend to stick to their pop singers and so their music is more successful.' Bobby Womack, who later became a leading, innovative figure in black music agreed, adding that the record industry itself perpetuated racism by the different methods used to market music – 'But music has no colour. You put people on a dance floor and play something they like and they'll all dance together. Pop has always meant white and R&B means black. It's not a good feeling to know that white groups have made millions on styles that originated in the black community. The Rolling Stones copy my songs exactly and go to number one, and that makes me ask myself what is it about my colour that makes me different? Why won't they accept this music from me?'

Motown was one of the few companies to be praised for relentlessly pushing black music into a white-dominated record market. The popularity of the 'Motown Sound' was exemplified during December 1968 when it monopolised the American top ten chart with singles from The Temptations and Diana Ross and the Supremes as solo acts or combined, Stevie Wonder and Marvin Gaye. Two acts had also broken the all-white domination of the British album charts after making heavy inroads in the singles listings. Diana Ross and the Supremes, and the Four Tops carried the Motown flag to enjoy number one 'Greatest Hits' records, unlike Marvin Gaye whose February 1968 compilation struggled to become a top forty hit.

Ironically, Motown's chart domination was jeopardised by the instigators of that success, when at the close of 1968 Holland, Dozier and Holland left the company. It was an unexpected move which prompted competitors to predict Motown's decline. When the trio's contract was due for renewal, they were stunned at Gordy's miserly offer. Lamont Dozier told *NME* in 1984 — 'In those days the music biz wasn't too big. No one was paid like they're being paid now. It was unheard of. You didn't hear of too many people having their own publishing company – the company would always have that distinctive pleasure. We wanted to participate in those dividends because we found out that they were the biggest hunks of the pie, the sharing of the publishing.' When they presented Berry Gordy with their demands, he refused to co-operate and a tedious and costly legal battle ensued, Motown filed for damages reputed to be $4 million, claiming the trio had not honoured their Jobete publishing contract for at least a year. Motown insisted it had paid them appropriate royalties, and requested the court to issue an injunction preventing them working elsewhere. Holland, Dozier and Holland retaliated by countersuing Motown, citing numerous petitions and requesting Motown's financial business be placed under receivership.

The trio's departure primarily affected The Supremes and the Four Tops; Martha Reeves and the Vandellas had of late only sung songs suitable for B-sides and album tracks. All acts were allocated new writer/producers, but the punchy hooklines, snappy lyrics and spontaneous choruses were gone. Lamont Dozier: 'We loved and respected the music. Music was the one thing that got us out of the ghettos and into better conditions. That dedication to anything, not only to music, will pay you back. At some points we'd be close to complete nervous breakdowns because of the demands on us as writers, but that's all part of the game.' As the trio was locked in legalities, they were unable to work publicly, and with little money available they opened the Invictus and Hot Wax labels and wrote under pseudonyms.

Meanwhile, at this time Tammi Terrell was desperately ill and unable to work. Thankfully, she had recorded a solo album, one of several planned, titled 'Irresistible Tammi Terrell' for January 1969 release. Harvey Fuqua and Johnny Bristol wrote or co-wrote a large proportion of this eleven tracker – 'Just Too Much To Hope For', 'I Can't Go On Without You', 'I Can't Believe You Love Me', 'Come On And See Me', among others. Holland, Dozier and Holland contributed their much-recorded 'This Old Heart Of Mine (Is Weak For You)' while Smokey Robinson wrote 'He's The One I Love' and co-wrote with Al Cleveland 'What A Good Man He Is'. No production credit was given on either the record label or album packaging but presumably Fuqua and Bristol handled the bulk. The release was a godsend to Terrell fans but held nothing spectacular in the way of compositions. All were attractive, simply constructed and pleasant to hear. What was startling, however, was Terrell's voice. She tackled each song with a confident ease, her expertise was a delight, even though the tenderness of her duets with Marvin was lacking. Nonetheless, she showed the potential and dedication of a future megastar. The front album sleeve portrayed her wearing a straight-haired black wig falling over her shoulders, transparent red cubes dangling from short silver earrings and heavily mascaraed eyes. She sat crossed-legged and was dressed simply in a squarenecked, long sleeved shapeless dress, patterned in orange, yellow, grey and purple which matched her loud orange tights and shoes. Ed Ochs wrote in the sleeve notes — 'The soul purr 'n' soul power, Tammi's way with words, in and out of music – is always music. And her performance on record is as popular and persuasive as Tammi, the person. Which is to say, it's hard to resist the irresistible Tammi Terrell.' Perhaps this was part of the singer's problem – she was too nice! Today of course, the album is a classic and much in demand by collectors.

However, Motown needed more duets and when Terrell had a respite from her illness she had been able to start recording a third album with Marvin Gaye. Sadly, the sessions were shortlived as her health deteriorated so drastically that only half an album was completed and she was once again hospitalised. To keep their public love affair alive, one finished track was released as a single in January 1969. 'Good Lovin' Ain't Easy To Come By', was a jewel in the crown; the perfect love tale which reached number thirty in the pop charts (no 11 R&B) and twenty-six in the British listings. This was quickly followed by Gaye's solo 'Too Busy Thinking About My Baby', issued after much deliberation by its writers Whitfield, Strong and Janie Bradford. The follow-up to an international number one single is a dubious and risky task for any artist, but Marvin needed to prove 'I Heard It Through The Grapevine' wasn't a fluke. This new track fell short of its predecessor; it was insipid in structure, with a simple chorus yet buyers flocked to support it, pushing it into the American and British top five after topping the R&B charts for six weeks! The flipside of this unexpected smash was the poignant 'Wherever I Lay My Hat (That's My Home)' which remained lost to the general public and was appreciated only by Gaye connoisseurs until British singer Paul Young took his version to the top of the UK charts in 1983.

'Too Busy Thinking About My Baby' introduced the next solo

album 'MPG' (Marvin Pentz Gaye) in May 1969; nicknamed the 'miles per gallon' record by his British fans. The sombre, darkened sleeve showed the singer staring blankly into space, with his personally drawn 'MPG' logo in the corner. The album followed no particular musical pattern – 'There Goes My Baby', 'Some Kind Of Wonderful', 'This Magic Moment', all previously recorded by The Drifters, his next single 'That's The Way Love Is', and on scrutinisation thematic tracks like 'It's A Bitter Pill To Swallow', 'Memories', 'More Than A Heart Can Stand' and 'Try My Life' which emphasised the torment that festered in his soul, as his marriage finally crumbled. If the listener cared to strip down the sweeping melodies and superfluous orchestration, the true impact of the lyrics, and Gaye's tortured interpretations, were obvious. However, as the public at this time was ignorant of his personal dilemma, the general reaction was, 'Oh, Marvin's singing those sad songs again!' Nonetheless, it was his first album to crack the American top fifty. 'MPG' marked the end of Gaye's working relationship with Whitfield and Strong, which, while it lasted, was profitable, although Marvin's reluctance to promote his work by touring possibly prevented their full sales potential being realised.

The dull 'That's The Way Love Is' was issued during August 1969 and this time critics stressed Whitfield was wrong to expect further mileage from this track. He proved otherwise when it soared to number seven in the pop charts and number two in the R&B listing where it stayed for five weeks! Surprisingly, Marvin Gaye wasn't perturbed at recording another tried and tested song; instead he boasted his interpretations were always superior – 'I know what I have, what I am and what I can do if I want to do it. And I can be what I want to because I have that gift. God gave it to me and nobody can take it away from me. I'm not insecure in this business either, and never have been.' Not every cover version he recorded was a hit or even an enjoyable album track, a fact he tended to ignore, claiming he rarely studied the charts, preferring to tot up the sales credited on his royalty statements! Realistically, he was thoroughly bored with his music, and this discontent was heightened by his colleagues' disinterest in his opinions. He needed to break free from the predictable 'conveyor belt' hit syndrome and wanted to create his own music. Each time he discussed the possibility with Berry Gordy or his creative staff he was told his compositions were unsuitable for him to record. So, with a probable touch of defiance, he ploughed his energies into fellow-act The Originals who recorded for Gordy's Soul label and excelled in tight harmonies in The Moonglows' ilk. Comprising Walter Gaines, Freddie Gorman, Henry Dixon, C. P. Spencer (who was replaced by Ty Hunter in the early Seventies) and prior to working with Gaye, they were session singers for him, Stevie Wonder, Jimmy Ruffin, and numerous female acts. They had also recorded several superior but non-selling singles since joining Motown but, like Marvin, had reached a stagnant, indecisive period in their career.

Gaye: 'I was getting tired of all the pressures, tired of all the fights I was getting to have with Motown's administration. and tired of being in the hands of other producers. I started telling them I wanted to produce myself. I'd never actually tried to learn production but I'd seen so many producers at work in the studios twiddling knobs that I just picked it up. When I produced The Originals and got a number one hit that really showed Motown that it was absurd putting me with a producer.' Marvin and his wife Anna wrote the touching love song, 'Baby I'm For Real', released in August 1969, for The Originals. It seemed ironic that this strong emotional track with tender lyrics could be borne from a couple who were constantly at loggerheads. Gaye explained the situation to Ritz – 'You have to understand me. One day I'd be throwing bottles at Anna, and the next day I'd be loving her, like we'd just met. Fighting stimulated us. Besides, Anna was always good for my music. She'd give me ideas and push me any way she could. I'm the sort of artist who can always use a push. My moods can get a little heavy.' Freddie Gorman: '"Baby I'm For Real" was classed as a doo-wop song by various programme directors and disc jockeys on the radio stations. Before we did that it had been a few years before the group had done doo-wop. Marvin, being an old group man himself, having sung with The Moonglows, wrote this song with that in mind. We were just fortunate to be available at the time to record it.'

The single shot to number fourteen in the pop charts and became the top R&B single for five weeks. The follow-up single 'The Bells', another smooth song released in January 1970, was also penned by Marvin and Anna, with assistance from Berry Gordy's niece, Iris, and Elgie Stover. It reached the top twenty (no 4 R&B) and was followed six months later by 'We Can Make It Baby' which Marvin co-wrote with James Nyx this time. It was the least successful of the trio (no 74 R&B/no 20 pop) but, nonetheless,

Marvin Gaye had proved his point and his ego was fulfilled!

Once again, Stevie Wonder's career inadvertantly ran a parallel with Marvin Gaye's because he too helped a fellow-group's career by co-writing 'It's A Shame' for G. C. Cameron who had some time earlier been auditioned by Marvin Gaye to sing lead with The Spinners. The song was released as a group single on the VIP label in June 1970 to reach number fourteen in the pop charts (no 4 R&B) and, under the name the 'Detroit Spinners', number twenty in the UK charts. During 1989 Cameron would re-record the single for Motorcity Records and would duet with Martha Reeves on a re-make of the Gaye/Terrell single 'You're All I Need To Get By'. Cameron told Scott Taylor he was delighted to have the opportunity of working with Reeves – 'Martha is a superstar, always has been. I respect her very highly and she is and always has been, a number one artist in my opinion. Being with her just automatically elevates the character of my artistic qualities.'

Meanwhile in 1970 Stevie Wonder also co-wrote The Spinners' follow-up 'We'll Have It Made' which struggled to number eighty-nine in the pop chart (no 20 R&B), and three years later attempted to salvage The Supremes' flagging career by giving them 'Bad Weather'. Unfortunately, not even Wonder's commercial talent could lift the girls from the doldrums.

While 'Baby I'm For Real' climbed the American listings, Diana Ross and the Supremes and The Temptations competed with 'The Weight', their last joint single, The Marvelettes issued 'That's How Heartaches Are Made', Smokey Robinson and the Miracles released 'Abraham, Martin And John', a song Marvin Gaye would record, and Martha Reeves and the Vandellas 'were taking love (and leaving me)'. Not all the acts enjoyed automatic hits, nor did they work regularly, but money still ploughed into Motown at a staggering rate. However, major changes were afoot which would seriously affect the roster of artists.

After years of grooming Diana Ross as lead singer of The Supremes, Berry Gordy decided the time was right for her to embark upon a much-speculated solo career. The trio's last single with Ross at the helm was 'Someday We'll Be Together' in October 1969 (originally recorded by Johnny Bristol – who produced this version – and Jackey Beavers in 1961 on the Tri Phi label). Bristol's voice was featured on The Supremes' single which was recorded by a solo Ross backed by The Andantes. The demure Jean Terrell, signed and recorded by Gordy as a soloist, replaced Ross. And the Jackson 5 joined Motown. The young family group would monopolise the Seventies in the same way as The Beatles had dominated the Sixties. Never before in the history of Motown had an act made such a huge impact on the world. Gordy used Diana Ross to introduce the brothers to the media, claiming she had discovered them. In truth, Gladys Knight and Bobby Taylor first saw them perform and recommended Berry Gordy sign them. Nevertheless, Gordy's ploy was successful, garnering mileage for both his acts. So now, artists were faced not only with Diana Ross and outside competition but also that emanating from the young group. It was a tough future.

The next and last change affected Motown itself. The company outgrew Detroit and moved to Los Angeles. Gordy was anxious to expand into television and films with Diana Ross as the main attraction, and tragically many acts who built the company's reputation were left behind. Also, most of the musicians responsible for creating the company's distinctive music during the Sixties couldn't afford to move, so new sessioners were hired and the magic of Motown was lost for ever. Motown moved into offices on 6255 Sunset Boulevard, where the television wing, Motown Productions Inc was opened, alongside a new recording studio, Hitsville.

Naturally, the move was a spiritual blow for Detroit's black community since Motown symbolised success. Gordy too moved house again to Beverly Hills, and later to the Bel Air estate 'Vistas'. Motown was moving uptown at, some said, the expense of the artists who had made the company. Hank Cosby believed Motown lost its whole creative structure when it moved to Los Angeles – 'Motown had to change the whole thing, and their costs zoomed way up. When they were in Detroit they were able to do business at a very moderate rate. In LA everything sky-rocketed and it never came down. In Detroit we had our own village. We had a whole block of buildings, and then there was a real, tall city building. But what we really had then was a warm feeling and when it became a big corporation that feeling had to go.' Smokey Robinson: 'We lost Detroit, and for a long time after we left it was hard for us to get our records played in Detroit. I think it felt let down by us. The newscaster on the television the day we actually closed the building made it sound like an obituary. He was standing in front of the building on Woodward and really looked sad. It was a big let down for the people there, and it was our roots so we were sad too. We'd put Detroit on the map for something other than automobiles. It was a hard blow for everyone, but moving to Los Angeles we were able to get off into many other avenues of entertainment. We became more than just a record company, we became an entertainment complex, getting into movies and television, things we could never have done in Detroit.'

Meanwhile, the music continued while the move took months to complete. One priority was Marvin Gaye and Tammi Terrell. As she was obviously the public's favourite, Motown was determined to exploit that in every possible way. When the recording sessions for the third album were halted, a compilation album 'Marvin Gaye And His Girls' had been issued in May 1969 featuring tracks with Mary Wells, Kim Weston and Terrell. It bridged the chasm and struggled to 183 in the American listing. What was needed was another new album but Terrell had only recorded sufficient tracks for one side. So, the duo's writer/producer Valerie Simpson, who recorded Terrell's demo songs, replaced her in the studios. A devastated Gaye strongly objected to Simpson's intervention because he believed it deceived their public. He was persuaded to change his mind when Berry Gordy told him Terrell's family would benefit from royalties. Because Valerie Simpson mimicked Terrell so perfectly (or vice versa?) – the accent and phrasing were identical – it's extremely difficult to distinguish her from Tammi. However, Simpson confirmed she sang with Marvin on 'What You Gave Me' and 'The Onion Song', but with diligent listening more tracks appear dubious. The result was the 'Easy' album in September 1969 which featured Carl Owens' shoddy, dark brown painting of Gaye and Terrell on the front record sleeve. The material within, however, was magnificent, especially the singles ('Good Lovin' Ain't Easy To Come By', 'How You Gonna Keep It (After You Get It)' and 'The Onion Song'), while 'I Can't Believe You Love Me', previously featured on Terrell's solo album contained Gaye's over-dubbed vocals. Several cover versions were included like the Four Tops' 'Baby I Need Your Loving', James and Bobby Purify's 'I'm Your Puppet', the 5th Dimension's 'California Soul' and Brenda Holloway's unreleased original 'Love Woke Me Up This Morning'. Regardless of how 'Easy' was conceived, the public was conned into believing it was a genuine Gaye/Terrell album, and this was a recording ploy which remained a closely guarded secret for some years because the magic of the duo had to be kept alive! The album peaked at number 184 in the American charts.

During October 1969, Motown/EMI took the initiative by recognising the potential in 'The Onion Song' and secured permission from the American parent to lift it for single release. Even without the duo's promotional support, it became a top ten hit, and in March 1970 was issued in America as the follow-up to 'What You Gave Me' released during November 1969 (no 6 R&B/no 49 pop). 'The Onion Song' only reached the top fifty (no 18 R&B), despite being pressed in red vinyl as an added selling attraction.

As Motown celebrated its Tenth Anniversary in 1970, and grossed $39 million in record sales, Diana Ross performed for the last time with The Supremes. Marvin Gaye attended the farewell concert with other members of the Gordy family and company acts at the plush Frontier Hotel, Las Vegas, on 14 January. The highly charged performance marked the end of a fairytale era, while opening the door for two new careers – the solo Ross and the 'new' Supremes. During the performance Jean Terrell was introduced to the audience, although she had been rehearsing (with Ross's guidance) with Mary Wilson and Cindy Birdsong for some time. One of the concert's highlights was centred around 'Let The Sunshine In' where Diana walked into the audience, encouraging individuals to sing verses of the song. She gave the microphone to a reluctant Marvin, after acknowledging the Gordy sisters, who sang a verse before hurriedly returning it to Ross. Despite cries of encouragement, he refused to sing further. Diana Ross: 'It was a sad night but I can't say that I was sorry to see it happen. We [The Supremes] had stopped communicating and if I hadn't left, something else would have had to change because we couldn't even be sure of the group sound any more as far as having guaranteed hits. I had to turn down a lot of opportunities as well because I didn't want Cindy Birdsong and Mary Wilson with nothing to do. There was a lot of pressure and it was an emotional thing for me . . . It was a difficult decision in some ways, easy in other ways.'

Marvin Gaye's next solo album 'That's The Way Love Is', released in January 1970 as a belated cash-in on the single, failed to reach the American top hundred. Two of Norman Whitfield's re-worked tracks previously recorded by The Temptations and Gladys Knight and the Pips were included – 'I Wish It Would Rain' and 'Cloud Nine' – while two further songs became singles. The first, 'How Can I Forget?', pressed in red vinyl, had been American-released only in December 1969 to reach the top fifty (no 18 R&B); the second, 'Abraham, Martin And John', written by Dick Holler, was a diamond.

Once again Motown/EMI believed in its potential and lifted it as a single in April 1970, to become a number nine hit, the same position as 'The Onion Song' six months earlier. The song, not issued as a single in America, was originally recorded by Dion (DiMucci) in 1968 when it reached the US top five, and Smokey Robinson and the Miracles a year later when it didn't!

Marvin Gaye's mellow interpretation of the disturbing song which immortalised the deaths of Abraham Lincoln, Martin Luther King and John Kennedy was spine-chilling. Gaye: 'The song was recorded late at night. There was nobody in the studio but Norman Whitfield, myself and the engineers. And I remember the lights were strangely lit that night and I felt sincere when I recorded that song. It may well have started me thinking about social problems and the world situation, and the situations that confront all of us socially.' When the singer was eventually aware of his British success he was delighted, but retorted – 'Nobody told me the song was a hit. I don't go round seeking out news like that and I don't get any charts or anything. To me it's too commercialistic and that's not where my head is. You have to get to England to learn these things. But I'm just the singer, the artist. I take the music, I sing it and can't really get into the business end of it. I can only be upset with the business part of it. But on the other hand, not being in control of the business, Motown do pretty much what they want. They, who are in control, either choose to promote a product or not. If they choose not to promote then that's too bad, and in America, for example, that's what happened to "Abraham, Martin And John".'

Sales of black/soul music had slumped in Britain unlike the previous two years when it had maintained a flourishing position against heavy white competition. However, Motown held its own. Underground clubs that diligently supported American soul music had been replaced by hard rock music establishments and the gentle marijuana was replaced by the hallucinatory LSD. Therefore when 'Abraham, Martin and John' became such a big seller black acts and record companies took heart. The future wasn't as bleak as envisaged, but the automatic soul hit was a thing of the past.

Amid the excitement of Motown's Tenth Anniversary came tragedy when Marvin Gaye's beloved singing partner finally died weeks after the company's publicity department jubilantly circulated a press release stating she was on the road to recovery. Twenty-four-year-old Tammi Terrell lost her two-year battle against a brain tumour, despite seven attempts by surgeons to eradicate it. Terrell died at 8.55 p.m. on 16 March 1970 in The Graduate Hospital, Philadelphia. Gaye told *Rolling Stone* magazine – 'Tammi's death hurt so much, not because she and I were lovers. I wish we had been, but the relationship was platonic. I was hurt because such a talented and beautiful human being died so young.'

Three thousand rain-soaked mourners joined fellow performers four nights later in an emotional, tearful farewell at the Jane Memorial Methodist Church. Prior to the service The Temptations, Four Tops and The Miracles paid their respects by filing past her body, shrouded in pale pink, in a gold and bronze coffin. The Reverend Henry Nichols delivered the final eulogy; he praised the courageous young woman whose early death brought a tragic end to a promising career – 'Tammi was a girl who was always kind and loving, and she in turn was loved by nearly everyone who knew her. She is gone, but she has left behind her music and her songs so that we can remember her.' The choir sang her favourite hymn 'How Great Thou Art' which she once sang with them. Her distraught and inconsolable singing partner tearfully delivered his own personal eulogy, and told of her immense courage during her prolonged ordeal and of her continual optimism and refusal to abandon her hope of one day recording again. Tammi was buried the following morning in Mt Lawn Cemetery. She had once said of her career – 'I just wouldn't be happy doing anything else. I've lived and loved this business too long not to be a part of it.' Terrell was survived by her parents, her sister, her uncle Bob Montgomery and cousin Lynda Lawrence, a future member of The Supremes, among others.

A certain amount of speculation surrounded Terrell's death and nineteen years later, Barbara Randolph probably summed up the public's thoughts – 'I felt very saddened, as everybody did. It was a very shocking thing to happen to her at the pinnacle of her career. And she was a very lively, zestful person and it made everybody wonder what is this all about. Tammi had paid her dues so to speak. She'd been out on the circuit and finally she'd gotten to Motown and she'd had success. I saw her all the way down to crutches, when her motor capabilities had just vanished. It was very disturbing to everyone. There are so many rumours about her death. The only thing anyone knows for sure is that she suffered from an inoperable brain tumour which, I imagine, in this day and age they'd probably be able to do something about. But in those days . . . well . . . it was said she was hit by a telephone and that injured her. Oh, many things were said, and I don't know if I believe any of it or not, but I'll tell you this, it's possible, very possible. Maybe certain people felt she was leading a reckless life, but nobody deserves that.'

Kim Weston: 'There's something I would like to say. I know a lot of people have blamed David Ruffin for being responsible for her death. I will not name the person's name but Tammi told me it was a very famous artist who kicked her in the head and down a flight of steps. A plate had to be put in her head because of that. Tammi told me this – this is not hearsay. And this happened before she came to Motown; she didn't even know David Ruffin then. I don't think anyone has ever written on that yet so please put the record straight.'

Marvin Gaye was heartbroken for longer than he cared to admit – 'It's not easy to lose in this life someone you love and someone who you like and get along well with. And we were both relatively young . . . it really affected me tremendously. So much so that I didn't perform for a couple of years. I had such an emotional experience with Tammi and her death that I don't imagine I'll ever work with another girl again. She was a singer who was still developing and her talent was denied her and so many others. I loved her very much.'

His career was now in jeopardy as he was swallowed up in the aftermath of her death. The intensity of his mourning startled his friends as they attempted to pluck him from his gloomy depths and back into reality. All ploys failed because he had slipped into a self-imposed exile; he refused to record and abandoned touring altogether. In tribute to Tammi Terrell's talent a 'Greatest Hits' package of previously released duets was issued during May 1970. It struggled into the top 180 in the American charts and fared much better in Britain by reaching number sixty. This album was quickly followed by another, 'Super Hits' in the September, featuring Gaye's most recent solo singles. The album sleeve was another Carl Owens' original. This time the artist portrayed the singer as the cartoon character Superman, flying through the air with a scantily dressed woman hanging on to him. Even if Marvin had agreed to be the courageous demi-god, the sleeve was too childish or melodramatic for most record buyers. Staunch Gaye fans dismissed the cartoon as appalling, annoyed that he should be so shabbily treated. The album sold badly, and struggled to get into the top 120 of the US chart, a poor placing for a 'Greatest Hits' package. The album formed the basis of the British compilation 'The Hits of Marvin Gaye' two years later, which contained fourteen tracks including additional newer material.

Diana Ross's solo career was underway, Berry Gordy ploughed $100,000 into her debut concert in Massachusetts but her immediate recording success was dampened when her first single 'Reach Out And Touch (Somebody's Hand)' (originally intended as her final single with The Supremes) crawled to number twenty in the mainstream charts. However, that situation changed when her second single, a glossy, dramatic re-make of 'Ain't No Mountain High Enough' raced to the top of the pop charts. Meanwhile, Stevie Wonder married Syreeta after a four month engagement, and The Supremes debuted at The Frontier Hotel, Las Vegas, the venue of their final performance with Ross fronting. A slew of Tenth Anniversary albums flooded the market including The Temptations' 'Puzzle People', the Four Tops' 'Soul Spin', Edwin Starr and Blinky's 'Just We Two' (Motown had hoped this duo would repeat Gaye/Terrell's success: unfortunately they didn't), Diana Ross and the Supremes' last studio album 'Cream Of The Crop' and a five-album box set 'The Motown Story', which featured artist narration between the company's best known songs. The Jackson 5 were going from strength to strength with their debut 'I Want You Back' single, followed by 'ABC', 'The Love You Save' and 'I'll Be There', while Smokey Robinson and the Miracles enjoyed their first British chart topper with the bouncy 'Tears Of A Clown'.

Before 1970 ended, Marvin Gaye's version of another Gladys Knight and the Pips' song was issued. Titled 'The End Of Our Road', it was American-released only to become a top forty hit (no 7 R&B), and seemed to sum up his unproductive career at the time. Motown's publicity department unashamedly went to great lengths to smother his inactivity by announcing he was locked in the recording studios working on a new project. The truth was nobody at Motown knew what he was doing; communication between record company and artist had broken down. Marvin Gay Snr: 'I think Tammi's death triggered something in him. I would phone Marvin and ask why he wasn't working. He'd say he was tired of his music but his excuses didn't satisfy me. It just didn't sound like him. I had to attribute the fact that he wasn't working to Tammi's death.'

Although Marvin Gaye didn't realise it at this time, his period of mourning and self-imposed exile would give him the strength and inspiration to produce his finest, and most controversial, work ever . . .

# 5. | What's Going On

*I was terribly disillusioned with a lot of things in my life.*
(Marvin Gaye)

*Marvin educated so many people with his 'What's Going On'
album.*
(Michael Jackson)

*When the money ran out, I couldn't pay the Vandellas and I lost
them. It was as simple as that.*
(Martha Reeves)

*I hate the hassles and restrictions of touring and I hate getting
up on stage in front of a lot of people.*
(Marvin Gaye)

While Marvin Gaye lived in exile in Detroit, his brother-in-law Berry
Gordy languished and worked in Los Angeles with Diana Ross. Gaye
used the time to lament over his career and the prospect of a future
that offered nothing but despondency and uncertainty, He would in
time likewise move to the West Coast but for the meantime he whiled
away his life smoking marijuana and living a hermit lifestyle. He
refused to leave his home – some days he stayed in one room – and
reputedly showed little interest in his family. His mind was troubled
about Tammi Terrell's death, he felt a part of him had died when she
did, but no words of comfort helped him. He didn't bother about his
appearance and discarded his chic suits and urbane image for casual
attire, like track-suits and training shoes. He also grew a beard which,
when fully grown, gave him a distinguished, mature look, and helped
to avert eyes from the beginnings of a bald patch on the crown of his
head. Gaye liked his new carefree image and intended to keep it
because it represented the start of a new life. However, the music
business beckoned because Motown insisted he start working on a
new album, but the more they urged, the more he refused to co-

operate. The singer wandered further away from reality and became totally introvert; being a big name recording artist now meant little to him. Success had so far only brought with it temporary happiness and money, for which he had little respect. It's conceivable that at this point Gaye would have abandoned his career entirely to spend the rest of his life in an animated limbo. He reflected on this time in a later interview – 'I was terribly disillusioned with a lot of things in life, and in life in general. I decided to take time out to try to do something about it. In a sense the rumours that suggested I had quit were true. I had retired, but only from the personal appearance end. I did that because I had always felt conspicuous on stage, and I'm not the sort of person who is like an exhibitionist. I spent the three years writing and producing and reflecting. Reflecting upon life and upon America especially – its injustices, its evil and its good. Not that I'm a radical. I think of myself as a very middle-of-the-road person with a good sense of judgment.'

After a lengthy period of being alone and depressed, Marvin found solace in his beloved sports – his third obsession next to women and music. His love of baseball, basketball and golf during the mid-Sixties had been overtaken by an all consuming passion for football, a sport previously forbidden by his father. The singer's obsession for the game convinced him that he could fulfil an ambition of joining the Detroit Lions, and to this end he befriended two team members, Lem Barney and Mel Farr. Naturally, the ambition was a pipe dream but he was granted permission to train with the team as Nelson George reported – 'Marvin was working with weights, bulking up from 160 to 207 pounds [this forced him to purchase ten thousand dollars' worth of new clothes for his new body] and asking when to report to rookie camp. "It's like me saying I'm going to sing at the Copacabana," said his buddy Farr. "He's never trained for it, but being a football player is a real obsession with him."' Needless to say, Marvin's ludicrous request to join the team was denied for obvious reasons and the fact that the Lions' insurance didn't cover a million-dollar artist risking life and limb battling against the odds on a pitch. Undeterred, he joined Detroit's King Solomon Gym to continue his training. Gaye: 'I just happen to enjoy physical activity and sports, but in all honesty it does give me a feeling of . . . the ego part of it makes me feel more masculine. Supreme, that's the word, but more chauvinistic maybe. I like feeling that way.' This love of sport had not only angered his father but also Berry Gordy because on more than one occasion the singer was known to have abandoned a recording session, at considerable expense to Gordy, to watch The Lions on television. Yet another of his idiosyncrasies that the Motown boss was forced to tolerate!

Meanwhile, Stevie Wonder was consumed with creative frustration. Tired of the pop songs he was forced to record and co-write without due regard for his growing talent. Again, his career crossed with Marvin Gaye's; they had both reached musical crossroads and were indecisive about future moves. So strong were their feelings that Gaye said they had discussed the possibility of opening a record company together simply, they said, to ensure they controlled their recorded work. However, after much deliberation, Marvin decided the move would be a disastrous one for him – '. . . You're caught in the same old trap because we'll get eaten up too if we don't play the game the way the rest of the biggies [large record companies] are playing. We couldn't possibly survive. I realised, after giving it a little thought, it would be a pretty hypocritical thing to do because I can't have my views on record companies and think that I'm going to have a record company that's going to be successful where I can do something other than what these big fellas are doing. So I would rather never have a record company. I don't want to deal with it. I may have a label, a record label that Motown would distribute for me. But I could never be into the record manufacturing business. Never in my life. That would be like asking Michelangelo to sell everybody else's paintings.'

Pondering over opening a record label at this time wasn't a priority, recording a new album was. Motown's goading did little to persuade the reluctant artist, but eventually he eased himself back by two diverse means, neither directly connected with the company – his brother Frankie and writer/producer Al Cleveland. The latter told Nelson George that although he was aware Marvin had no intention of working, he had left him a tape of a song he'd written with Four Tops' member Obie Benson titled 'What's Going On', before leaving Detroit to go to Los Angeles. Cleveland: 'We begged him for about a month to do the tune. He hadn't had a record out in a year and a half, and he wasn't doing too good financially. As a result he was not in a good frame of mind.' Benson: ''What's Going On' came easy. Al and I were sitting down one evening writing and we just happened to come up with this tune. It sounded like something Marvin could sing so we presented him with the idea.' Frankie Gay returned from active service in Vietnam and spent hours telling his elder brother of the horrors, cruelty and destruction the war had brought. Marvin was stunned to the core. Someone, he felt, had to stand up and condemn the man-made horrors – 'It's so weird man, what is happening God, what is happening Lord, what is going on with life and people? I don't know' – and an urgency developed as he became consumed by a necessity to tell the story. Gaye: 'I think it was around 1969 and 1970 when I stopped thinking so much about my erotic fantasies and started to think about the war in Vietnam and my brother who was there. He told me some pretty horrible stories about the war. It caused me to think hard about society, and something happened with me during that period, and I felt the strong urge to write music, and write lyrics that would touch the souls of men and that way I thought perhaps I could help.' Frankie: 'I was drafted in 1964 when I was twenty-two and discharged in 1967. I came home destroyed by what I had seen. The whole experience had been a horrendous nightmare. I wanted to get back to reality again and I'd become very withdrawn and I just wandered around aimlessly. While I'd been away Marvin had become a very big star and I didn't want to progress as a singer by riding on his coat tails. I became a doorman at the Fairfax Hotel and would just do the occasional show as well as helping other guys to rehearse their acts and put their music together.'

Al Cleveland, Obie Benson and Frankie Gay, therefore, were instrumental in pushing Marvin back into the music business, and should be credited for lifting him from his meandering, depressive, soulless exile, and giving him the will and encouragement to record again, although at the time Gaye probably would not have acknowledged this.

After living with the rough, taped version of 'What's Going On' for some time, Marvin Gaye thought it would be an ideal song for The Originals to record because, once again, they were desperate for good material. After further thought he changed his mind. The song was tailor-made for him, the lyrics brought alive his thoughts about Vietnam and the low-keyed melody haunted him. It was a musical style he could adopt and was totally different from his past recordings. Standing his ground against outside influence, and in Cleveland's absence, Gaye went into the studios, recorded the track and was delighted with the result. However, there was one draw back, Gaye had no album to accompany it and this was vital for marketing. Nelson George further reported that Marvin, with arranger David

Van De Pitte's assistance, began recording an album prior to Cleveland and Benson's return to Detroit, which annoyed them. Cleveland: 'We'd talked about the concept for the album when we wrote the song, but Marvin had started without us.' One of the project's session musicians, Johnny Griffiths: 'One day Marvin came in an hour and a half late with a bucket full of chicken. He said, "We're gonna do something different this time. . .", but it wasn't a surprise to us. Seven or eight years before he used to say, "If I ever get the chance I'm gonna get into something different."' Gaye: 'I wanted to write an album that could be translated into any language, and it would hold its meaning, and not be particularly an ethnic statement that other people and nations couldn't get into. It took a little time to think about that philosophically because I was much more incensed and wanted to write stinging things to music that would make people say "he's after us" and incense them also.' An inner, possibly a sacred, force prevented him from telling all the story – 'It was a divine project and God guided me. I don't remember a great deal about it because I was in a sphere or dimension or enwrapped in something, so I don't have a great deal of recollection about the project.'

'What's Going On' was Gaye's first self-produced album although, in the end, none of the tracks were written by him unaided. But he did conceive the majority and made the final decisions. For the first time in his career the many participating musicians and the song lyrics were listed on the album packaging. This was a reluctant move on the singer's part because he believed the public would think he was no longer capable of working alone which, to a certain extent, was true. Approximately forty musicians were involved in the project, including soloists alto saxophonist Eli Fountain and tenor saxophonist William 'Wild Bill' Moore. Marvin played piano and presumably many tracks were actually recorded with him sitting at the keyboards. In the personal credits he acknowledged his immediate family, friends and close colleagues, including his wife. his parents, his sisters Zeola 'Sweetsie' and Mable Jeanne, Frankie, Aunt Zeola and his son Marvin Pentz Gaye III. Berry Gordy's name was conspicuously absent.

The album sleeve marked another debut. Marvin Gaye personally wrote the sleeve notes which began with some ridiculing – 'After some several days of reflection and pondering and general thought (which is very unusual), I still can't think of any non-complimentary things to write about myself . . . If you like an artist well enough to buy his or her album, you don't have to be told how groovy it is, or which tunes you should dig; or how great his or her majesty is. I mean the fact that people just won't let us think for ourselves really bugs me! Now just because I like "Mercy, Mercy Me" and the one that says "Save The Children" shouldn't influence anyone . . . And you shouldn't have to pay any special attention to the lyric on "Flyin' High In The Friendly Sky" just because you think you ought to . . .' Then he dictated in print – 'Find God: we've got to find the Lord. Allow Him to influence us. I mean what other weapons have we to fight the forces of hatred and evil. And check out the Ten Commandments too. You can't go too far wrong if you live them, dig it. just a sincere and personal contact with God will keep you more together. Love the Lord, be thankful, feel peace. Thanks for life and loved ones. Thank you, Jesus.'

The front album cover was startling when compared to his tacky previous work. It showed Marvin standing in the pouring rain, in a mature, conservative pose, wearing a wide-collared raincoat over a dark suit, yellow shirt and kipper tie, staring into space. (Incidentally, on the British album's back cover the Tamla logo, manufacturing and publishing credits were badly disguised.) The American inner record sleeve showed a montage using photos from the Gaye and Gordy family archives, while the British sleeve was plain.

Apart from the excellent. thoughtful artwork 'What's Going On' also marked a drastic change in Gaye's vocals. Gone was the past rasping, guttural, almost sweaty voice, synonymous with his hit singles, in particular the torturous straining with the Holland, Dozier and Holland tracks. In its place he adopted a velvety, relaxed voice, inspired by listening to the moody music of horn player Lester Young, as he ploughed one vocal on top of another, ensuring every pure dimension of his range was used to full effect. Marvin: 'When I first started singing, I wondered how I could be a famous singer at all. My friends could sing so well, and I always felt they could beat me at singing. Those guys could blow bad baritone voices. I could sense they had something – power. If you notice I sing a lot of different ways. I sing rough, falsetto. I don't have a classic voice that comes from the diaphragm. I am not a total singer. I don't think I do anything according to Hoyle. Voice I did not possess, so I developed a style. I figured out how to make my performances as pleasing as possible, and tried to please the listener.'

The album's opening minutes set the musical pace, laying down the foundation of the thematic tunes, where Gaye begged for peace, cried to his parents and his brother for help. Assisting him on back-up vocals for the album's title track were Bobby Rogers (of The Miracles), Lem Barney and Mel Farrer (from the Detroit Lions), while The Andantes were brought in to work on the remainder of the album. When Motown's A&R staff heard the song 'What's Going On', they demanded Marvin use professional session singers. He refused, insisting he preferred the informality of the relaxed atmosphere. Gaye: 'It worked just perfectly. "Hey man, what's happening, hey baby!" Slap thighs, slapped hands. Man, it was great, just what I wanted. And football players are very good about talking-it-up and getting the conversation going because they're full of energy. You just had to hold out on the profanity. So because they were to be on record, they didn't say any curse words.' This wasn't the only track Motown objected to; the whole album was rejected and considered unsuitable for release. Nobody saw any commercial value to it at all because the music was alien to anything the company had handled before. Marvin Gaye quickly retaliated to this decision and told Berry Gordy – 'If you don't issue it I'll never do another album for you!'

This was identical to the situation Stevie Wonder faced when he recorded, with the help of his wife Syreeta, the 'Where I'm Coming From' album in April 1971. This release was Wonder's first without Motown's creative input and the last under his 1960 recording contract which expired when he reached twenty-one years old in May 1971. The album was a poor seller but Wonder was determined to win creative freedom. His loyalty to Motown was therefore questionable.

'What's Going On' was music from the soul for the soul, a work dictated by human conscience. Apart from the title track, the content was alarmingly accurate and haunting. On 'What's Happening Brother' Gaye spoke with Frankie's voice returning home from Vietnam – the questioning of that war's purpose and result. Gaye's reliance on drugs was well documented in 'Flyin' High (In The Friendly Sky)'. He admitted the stupidity of his habit while enjoying its effects. 'Save The Children', possibly the hardest hitting track, echoed the thoughts of millions that if the world was to continue, children should be a protected species. Gaye: 'I have a great affection for children. I love children, children are tremendous. I think I wrote [the song] because I was trying to think of something, some why, that I could get . . . even a man who is hard in his heart, who refuses to receive any thoughts of goodness, who hardens himself to words, compassion, and that sort of thing . . . I figured it was the only object I could see which was a real object to me. So I saved the children, and I think that having been a child oneself that same hardened man will perhaps say "well, I should save what I've been".' Two songs, 'God Is Love' and 'Wholy Holy' were semi-hymns where Gaye begged for family harmony while pledging his trust to God in the former, and praised the Lord's work and rulings in the latter. He touched on the destruction of Mother Nature in 'Mercy, Mercy Me (The Ecology)', and attempted to minimise the social gap between the wealthy and the poor in 'Right On'. And 'Inner City Blues (Make Me Wanna Holler)' exemplified his anger at the brutality of modern day life, and his hatred of the tax system – a possible first inkling of his future financial problems.

Unbeknown to the singer, Motown decided to quietly release the single 'What's Going On' in January 1971 and when it flopped, their point would be proven. However, quite the reverse happened. 'What's Going On' blew wide open! Within twenty-four hours record stores had re-ordered substantial quantities of the disc and within a week in excess of 70,000 copies were sold, making it Motown's fastest-selling single. It raced to number one in the R&B charts where it stayed for five weeks and number two on the mainstream listing for three weeks. The Temptations' 'Just My Imagination (Running Away With Me)' and Three Dog Night's 'Joy To The World' prevented it from reaching the top. Barney Ales, one of Motown's presidents at the time, told author Nelson George – 'I remember Berry called me in and said, "How could you release that? It's the worst record I ever heard." He had me on the coals. From that point on, Berry didn't get involved in anything [Marvin] did.'

Thirty-one-year-old Marvin Gaye was nonplussed over the single's astonishing success. It had only proved what he'd been trying to say for years that, given the chance, he was capable of writing and producing without any guidance from Motown.

When the single was released in Britain during May 1971 it struggled to reach the top hundred listing although it was afforded plenty of airplay. Motown/EMI were mystified at its failure. True, the music was totally alien to Gaye's previous 'conveyor belt' releases which the British public had lapped up, but the company had hoped his name alone would spur sales. It was a pipe dream because the British en masse weren't interested in intense, soul-searching issues dictated by an American when they could enjoy throwaway bubblegum music from the Bay City Rollers, Sweet and Rod Stewart; loud 'bovver' sounds from Slade and The Who; light political epics from ex-Beatles George Harrison and John Lennon and the attractive yet simple sounds of T-Rex, headed by the elfin Marc Bolan.

The 'What's Going On' album was released during May 1971, four months after the single in a rather belated attempt to cash-in on its success. If Motown had not initially been so reluctant to issue the album, presumably it would have been available the minute the single charted. Gaye: 'There was not the total confidence in it that most record companies have when they release a project on an artist because it was different and innovative, and they felt like they were taking a chance. But Berry, having an idea that I had something – everybody always told me all my life you have something special, that they feel some day, somehow, someway, I am supposed to do something that was supposed to have affected somebodys' lives – and viewing me in that manner, he probably felt that whatever I did, he would take a chance with it. I used to have spiritual battles with him and I said, "God will take care of it, trust me and that sort of thing." So he looked at me awhile and said, "Put it out." 'Within two months of its release, 'What's Going On' peaked at number six in the pop charts! This success wasn't helped by Motown's publicity department who distributed a ludicrous press release to accompany promotional copies of the album. An extract read – 'God must have known that He was moulding Marvin Gaye from the good black soil of His Earth and that this God-fearing man would one day view the radical madness, the injustices, the chaos threatening the existence of man and join the thunder from the heavens to demand "What's Going On".' Thankfully, record critics ignored the written word and concentrated on the music! In Britain, the album floundered and bombed. With a non-charting single Motown/EMI had little hopes of enjoying success with the album but as it was contractually required to release all product by major signings, the company did the project proud. Advertising was rife and radio play excellent, resulting in an abysmal top hundred position, although critics and diehard Gaye fans glowed in their praise. Over the years, public opinion changed and the album became one of Motown/EMI's regular top ten selling projects.

Gaye was alarmed when the full implications of 'What's Going On' were told to him by reviews, journalists and fans. His project had touched millions, something he had failed to grasp at the outset. Some people saw him as a preacher, saviour, while others believed he was conservationist or, more startling, a demi-god. Gaye was modest in his response – 'I'm only human and when you get lots of pats on the back for something, it makes you go on these ego trips. I was only the instrument in the album. All the inspiration came from God Himself. It's true the album is social commentary but there's nothing extreme on it. I did it not to help humanity but to help me as well, and I think it has. It's given me a certain amount of peace of mind. The album [only] shows the sort of emotion and personal feelings I have about the situations in America and the world. I think I've got a real love thing going. I love people. I love life and I love nature, and I can't see why other people can't be like that.'

On the other hand, he believed he was a pioneer of music and that the work was his first attempt to publicly explain his thoughts on certain issues, as previously confirmed by musician Johnny Griffiths. Gaye: 'I've always said from the very beginning that I'm going to do something to change music. I've always thought that music the way it is isn't all there is, there has to be more. There has to be something besides the scale. If I can even unlock the secrets of music, unlock the whole new musical world for people, set a whole new scale, a new dimension outside of what we know now, I think that would be fantastic. I would say that I'm a pioneer in the sense that "What's Going On" was my first attempt.' He further told *Crawdaddy* magazine – 'I hope to refine [music], study it, try to find some area that I can unlock. I don't quite know how to explain it but it's there. These can't be the only notes in the world, there's got to be other notes some place, in some dimension, between the cracks on the piano keys. Why isn't there another horn, or another saxophone? Why can't you have five or six saxophones, and another trumpet, or another kind of texture, and different colour? But I can't study what another man has done. Those are their trips and they're beautiful, but I can't even listen to records because it'll cloud my mind. I wouldn't be starting fundamentally.'

Marvin was always generous with his praise of other artists who, he felt, had an exceptional talent. Not all were black and contemporary. For instance, he felt that American composer George Gershwin – who died in 1937, and wrote stage shows like *Porgy And Bess* and *Lady Be Good*, and jazz tunes like 'Rhapsody In Blue' and 'I Got Rhythm' – came close to expanding musical boundaries in the same way as 'What's Going On' had done. Marvin: 'You can hear other things in his music, other than what you're used to hearing. His feeling went outside of music, while still within the bounds. But it always seems new. There's something about it and it's that kind of thing I'm talking about. What made it different? He did it within the bounds of what is accepted and made it a very personal thing. I'd like to take it outside the bounds of what is accepted and make it a very personal thing, either to dig it or not dig it: leave it for generations to come and judge, was it good or was it not? Is it something that a writer can take and move it, develop something out of my basic creation? Maybe I won't live long enough to do this, but if I leave enough for somebody to come along and say, "Marvin did this, let me take this and do this to it", that's all I need to make me happy.'

The maestro of bedroom soul Barry White believed 'What's Going On' was the first universal album – '[Marvin] spoke for every depressed man and woman, every person who feels battered, abused, misused by the system. People who dealt with war, people who were actually in the war. "What's Going On" was a question the world was asking itself. Marvin Gaye came out musically and made that statement and I salute him.' And during 1979, prior to the release of his first solo CBS album 'Off The Wall', Michael Jackson likewise spoke of the album to the media – 'I don't like talking about religion and politics because people are too quick to listen and it's a tremendous responsibility to have so much power. Whatever we say in our music, the kids will listen, more than to the news or newspapers. We can educate them through our music. For example, Marvin Gaye educated so many people with his "What's Going On" album. He opened so many minds by first asking that question. It was great.'

Gaye was also praised by his fellow Motown artists. Lionel Richie: 'I think it was the first true concept album. And its message was street. It was not about pie in the sky, or some love relationship gone astray. It was straight, basic, street-related messages.' Otis Williams: 'I remember driving along a Detroit street one day in 1971 when "What's Going On" came over my radio. It so amazed me that I had to pull over and park my car until it was over.' Smokey Robinson: '"What's Going On" , Marvin Gaye's masterpiece, the greatest album, in my opinion, ever made by anyone . . . Marvin surprised us. Marvin seduced us with a new sound, funky as hell, that soared with spirituality . . . "What's Going On – was a sacred work . . . Most important though Dad took [Motown] out of the age of the artist. He made musical history.'

It was the general consensus that Marvin Gaye would win several Grammy Awards – at the very least one for top album – for 'What's Going On'. He believed he deserved to receive the music industry's recognition for his work. but sadly he had to wait ten years before the Academy decided to acknowledge his talent. Motown and Gaye were surprised and disgusted when Carole King's 'Tapestry' album swept the board, while Lou Rawls walked away with the R&B Male Vocal Performance Award, one Marvin was convinced was his. Stevie Wonder: 'We were all very sorry he didn't receive a Grammy for that album . . . I think that that was not only the best album at the time for him as an artist but for all popular music.' Nonetheless, 'What's Going On' received numerous other awards and honours, including the prestigious NAACP's Image Award.

Meanwhile, following his twenty-first birthday, Stevie Wonder with a few half-written songs and $1 million which had been held in trust for him by Motown, locked himself away in a New York studio to work on a new project, once again without Motown's interference. Before the work was completed, Wonder's lawyer had negotiated a new recording contract where the synthesised 'Music Of My Mind' album was the first release. Stevie concluded a deal in a 120-page contract that allowed him total creative freedom (Motown had to accept whatever he delivered, within reason), ownership of his future compositions via his own Black Bull Publishing Company, a higher royalty rate, and the opening of a production outlet, Taurus Productions.

Motown's A&R staff were unhappy with 'Music Of My Mind' because it lacked potential singles, an unheard of situation under his last contract. Nonetheless, the album was extensively marketed, in the light of the new deal, and 'Superwoman (Where Were You When I Needed You)' was reluctantly lifted as the first single to become a top forty hit. The release might have failed by Wonder's standards but Stevie hadn't. He had followed Marvin Gaye's precedent and had likewise stuck to his beliefs and his talent. Gaye insisted that Wonder had known of his plight with 'What's Going On' and had benefited greatly from his own struggles.

'What's Going On' and 'Music Of My Mind' pushed Motown into the Seventies in a way that Berry Gordy could never have envisaged. The music was alarmingly diverse from the rapidly stagnating late Sixties when, some believed, the company became rather complacent and rested on its laurels. With these two albums to its credit, Motown had changed its musical policy, marketing ideas and promotional activities to keep abreast of the mixture in musical tastes. It had to face the prospect of moving with the times or staying static; Gordy chose the former although success wasn't as spontaneous as it had been in the Sixties. Gaye: 'The Seventies were rough for Berry Gordy because the artists' time had arrived. The old days when the producer ran the show was over. People like me, Stevie and Diana knew that. There was no more "Motown Sound" in the Seventies, just a string of separate singers doing their own thing. It wasn't easy for Berry Gordy. He always lived through his artists, and now all of a sudden his artists were running their own careers. He felt left out, and was nervous. We were nervous too. He wasn't there to take care of us like he used to.'

'Mercy Mercy Me (The Ecology)' was the second single from 'What's Going On' in June 1971; 'Inner City Blues (Make Me Wanna Holler)' followed three months later. Both earned gold discs, topped the R&B charts, reached numbers four and nine respectively in the pop listings and together sold four million copies. Neither charted in Britain, although 'Save The Children' which followed 'What's Going On' in November 1971 struggled to the number forty-one position.

Away from his music, Marvin Gaye once again turned his attention to acting. Ever since Diana Ross and the Supremes appeared as nuns in a television episode of *Tarzan* in October 1967, he had been agitated because he hadn't been afforded the same attention by Berry Gordy. *Tarzan* was Gordy's first major deal with NBC-TV, and it was apparent to many that he used the programme to boost Diana's career more than that of The Supremes. Prior to the trio's small screen debut Berry Gordy had in fact offered Gaye the chance to star in a full-length movie, playing the late Sam Cooke in a film of his life. Marvin had immediately rejected the idea, claiming it to be in extremely bad taste and shuddered at the thought of playing a soul singer who was shot to death.

Quite frankly, Marvin Gaye was a natural successor to Cooke. Even their personal lives suffered the same conflict of joy and pain. The build-up of tensions and paranoia prior to both men's deaths were similar and the outcome, of a killer bullet, unavoidable. Mary Wilson: 'If they ever made a movie of Sam Cooke's life, I could think of no one better to play him than Marvin Gaye.' Once again, Gaye stuck to his guns and the movie idea was dropped. This time, his decision was wrong. Nonetheless, he was convinced he had actor potential, once he had shaken off his own complex personality. Marvin: 'You have to put yourself in somebody else's place – live the part; it's a real special kind of person to be. But I think I could psyche myself into it. I like physical stuff though – running, jumping, riding. Or maybe I could do a situation comedy because I've got a little funny bone that needs exercising, so that would be a nice outlet also.'

The nearest the singer got to being a film actor was appearing in two television movies. Marvin hired Stephen Hill as his manager and joined the William Morris Agency. The outcome was unspectacular. Gaye accepted a small acting role, playing a soldier in a television film *The Ballad Of Andy Crocker*, starring 'The Fall Guy' Lee Majors, and in *Chrome And Hot Leather*, an American International Pictures film devoted to motorbikes, his favourite pastime. Neither role attracted critical acclaim or further offers, so he left the agency after a year claiming it was bogged down with named actors and had failed to support him in the manner he deserved. Gaye: 'I've never had the chance to try to see if I have any real ability. I like dramatic things. I would prefer a drama to a comedy, although I also like westerns very much. I like dramatic heavy roles, the ones like [Sidney] Poitier sometimes plays. I believe in those kinds of roles. In fact, that would be a direction to aim for.'

The direction he craved for was Hollywood and once established there he intended to pursue two careers – music and films. Interestingly, prior to Gaye's television debut he was seriously thinking about two movie projects. The first using the 'What's Going On' album as the basis. Marvin: '. . . I'd like to do [it] about a returning soldier from Vietnam and how life has changed or not changed since he's been gone. How things are, maybe, even worse than they were. He would come back and he would discover all the evils of life and say "what have I been fighting for?" Like a philosophical thing.' For some reason, probably lack of finances, the project was dropped and the singer never mentioned it again. The second concerned slavery. *Rolling Stone* magazine described it as being loosely based around a slave ship *circa* 1810. Many of the slaves became ill on the voyage to America except for a few strong, tall men. On arrival this handful was sold to work on a plantation, but there was something uncanny about them. For example, when their bodies were cut the wounds instantly healed. In time, it became apparent that these slaves originated from another planet, and being disgusted at the way in which they were treated on earth, decided to return to their home. Before they left, they handed the white plantation over to the slaves left behind. Again, this film was aborted with no reason given.

So, Marvin Gaye returned to his music. This time he co-wrote Stevie Wonder's 'What Christmas Means To Me' for November 1971 release, and recorded demos for the newly signed entertainer Sammy Davis Jnr. A year earlier Berry Gordy had bought the worldwide rights to Davis' Ecology label to which Davis was the only artist signed. Marvin presented Davis with several songs on tape (not having learned to read or write music) which included 'I Thank God For My Wonderful Life' and the Norman Whitfield/Eddie Holland track 'Happy Go Lucky'. Gaye: 'I often wondered if Sammy knew I wrote him an album. It was a beautiful album, all original songs. I had a great deal of respect for Sammy at the time and when he was supposed to sign with Motown I went to Berry and asked if I might write an album. It's still in my trunk!'

Despite the Gaye/Davis musical relationship being blocked, Davis did later record for the Motown label but when he disagreed with Berry Gordy about Ecology's future musical direction their collaboration also ended. However, the material Gaye intended for Davis was not lost, some tracks were found and released after his death. Meanwhile another collaboration had also finished – that of Motown and Gaye's close friend and mentor, Harvey Fuqua, who left the company to join RCA Records. Fuqua became involved with four acts – Mint Juleps, Alan Frye, New Sound and The Nite Lighters. These artists also formed the New Birth group, but none became as successful as his original solo protégé.

Before the end of 1971 two more of Marvin Gaye's colleagues gave him cause for concern – Martha Reeves on a personal basis, Diana Ross, professionally. Martha had suffered several nervous breakdowns, she was having problems in keeping the Vandellas working in the absence of hit material and when Motown had moved to Los Angeles leaving her in Detroit she reluctantly concluded her career with the company was over. Reeves: 'There were money problems within the Vandellas. We didn't have any records released so our bookings dropped off. We couldn't have continued in that position so it was decided to call it a day and find something else. When the money ran out, I couldn't pay the Vandellas and I lost them. It was as simple as that. When Motown moved away it left most of their business behind in a right state, there was no one for me to speak to. I wasn't asked to go along with them so I felt I owed them nothing. They didn't seem that bothered with the way I felt. I loved being with Motown and they'll always be part of me, but I felt disheartened in the way they treated me towards the end.'

A five-month legal battle ensued between Motown and Reeves to release her from her contract which reputedly still had three years to run. The terms of her release were never publicised but it's thought her freedom cost her $200,000 when she signed away all future royalties earned from her and the Vandellas' recordings. Over the years it was discovered that several tracks remained unreleased including 'I'm Willing To Pay The Price', a version of The Marvelettes' 'Someday Someway', 'Spellbound', 'Keep Steppin' (Never Look Back)', 'All That Glitters (Ain't Gold)' and 'It's Hard To Walk Away From Love'. Naturally her loyal public hope these will be released in the future, meanwhile they content themselves with bootleg versions.

While Reeves embarked upon a solo career away from Motown, Diana Ross began rehearsing for her first feature film in December 1971. She was to play the late jazz/blues singer Billie Holiday in *Lady Sings The Blues*. When Berry Gordy was approached by producer Jay Weston and director Sydney Furie to finance the film, they suggested Ross should play Holiday. Gordy subsequently altered the script before submitting it to Paramount Pictures after Fox showed little interest in it. Paramount were nervous about sinking millions of dollars into an unknown actress so Gordy finally financed the whole project. When the shooting was finished Diana Ross faced an onslaught of (unwarranted) criticism, but the film broke box office records – it grossed in excess of $6 million in its first week – and garnered numerous awards. But not the most prestigious – the Oscar. Diana Ross lost out to Liza Minelli for her performance in *Cabaret*. Ross: 'I really worked hard on that goddamned film and I really felt that I deserved that Oscar. But just because I didn't get it doesn't mean to say I won't try again.' To date Ross has appeared in two further movies, *Mahogany* and *The Wiz*, neither of which won her the coveted trophy.

Meanwhile, in 1971, Marvin Gaye felt his status within Motown slipping despite the unprecedented triumph of 'What's Going On'. Realistically, he was now one of the company's top-selling artists – a position he had yearned for – but something was missing. He wanted the support Berry Gordy gave Diana Ross. But that would never happen. And when *Lady Sings The Blues* became such a runaway money spinner Gaye knew his relationship with the Motown boss was almost over. However, while Ross concentrated on the big screen her recording career began to suffer, and when two years later Berry Gordy asked Gaye to consider recording with her, he surprisingly agreed, even though it meant breaking his word to Tammi Terrell.

# 6. | Let's Get It On

*I might have got a film score award if more people had seen the movie.*

(Marvin Gaye)

*Don't go any further – you're supposed to be a minister's son.*
(Marvin Gay Snr)

*It's well known that certain drugs will open up one's creative facilities and perception banks.*

(Marvin Gaye)

*I've wanted to do something with Marvin for so long.*
(Diana Ross)

In the spring of 1972 Marvin Gaye was persuaded to perform again, although right up until the last minute nobody was convinced he would actually honour the commitment. His reputation for cancelling or postponing dates was now widely known. For example, he had recently cancelled hosting the first Martin Luther King Birthday Gala in Atlanta (King was assassinated in Memphis, Tennessee, in 1968) although, when criticised for his action, he claimed the engagement was never confirmed. This 1972 concert, arranged by Gaye's junior high school colleague in conjunction with Guy Draper's Congressional Entertainment Complex and the District of Columbia Bicentennial Commission, was to be held on I May at the John F. Kennedy Center for the Performing Rights. It was the first concert to be held in the Center's short history and was a charity event for a newly launched self-help organisation, Pride Inc.

To honour the artist's return to Washington the city's mayor was encouraged to dedicate 1 May as 'Marvin Gaye Day' and several activities were arranged by way of celebration. However, the organisers were so worried that Gaye would also let them down that they asked his mother, Alberta, to intercede on their behalf. Indeed, they had cause for concern because the singer was undecided; he was terrified of performing before an audience but more importantly felt the celebrations were hypocritical, as he told David Ritz – 'Why should they all of a sudden love me, now that I've sold a few records? Where were they when I needed them . . . I resented the whole thing and I desperately didn't want to do it.' Nonetheless he did – for his mother.

During the morning of 1 May Marvin, conservatively dressed in a light-coloured jacket, dark sweater and trousers and for some reason, tinted glasses, addressed an assembly of students at his old school, Cardoza High, warning them of the dangers of drug-taking! Then, with his parents, he travelled in a motorcade to be presented with the key to the city by the mayor, Walter Washington. The ceremony was conducted from behind a rostrum, advertising 'Mr What's Going On, Marvin Gaye – his first and only public appearance in three years'. After receiving the city's key, he seemed to settle into his surroundings to enjoy the accolade and quipped – 'I've often wondered what to do with a key to the city. I wonder if it will do any good if I get stopped by a police officer and show it to him!'

Before his concert later that evening Gaye attended a reception at Capitol Hill hosted by city dignitaries, where he enthralled them with his warm manner, his charm and enthusiastic conversation. His long-awaited performance was a triumph. Attended by two thousand and seven hundred people he was preceded by Renee Morris, a local artist. Backed by ten Motown studio musicians, augmented by a twenty-piece brass and string ensemble directed by Gene Page, and The Andantes as backing vocalists, Marvin Gaye walked on stage to be introduced by Pride's Marion Barry and to listen to a telegram of congratulations sent by Mrs Coretta Scott King, widow of Martin Luther. The audience, which included leading Congressmen, rose as one to welcome its home boy as he sat at the piano to open his performance with a medley of familiar songs like 'I Heard It Through The Grapevine', 'Can I Get A Witness', and a selection from 'What's Going On'. It was an emotional evening and taped for a possible future album. In his closing statement Marvin, flushed from a triumphant return, told the audience that his music was designed to bring people together in love, peace and harmony and he hoped nothing would change that. Tom Zito reviewed the concert for *The Washington Post* – 'It was Marvin Gaye's evening from the moment he walked on stage . . . an almost exclusively black audience rose in a tumultuous and spontaneous display of appreciation for a man responsible for radically changing the style of soul music, adding to it equal amounts of instrumental sophistication and social conscious- ness.' Zito concluded his review by noting that the singer, a perfectionist with nothing but respect and love for his audience, repeated 'Inner City Blues (Make Me Wanna Holler)' and 'What's Going On' to satisfy the audience's craving for more – 'For those at the Kennedy Center last night, he probably could have sung them ten times over!'

Throughout his stay Marvin was treated as grandly as a returning war hero, and his parents who had originally arrived penniless in Washington D.C. had now been elevated into public figures.

Following this concert, it was inevitable Gaye would be in demand as a touring artist. The public wanted to see the enigmatic man behind the hits, to enjoy once more the intimate moments that his shows offered. Subsequently, dates were booked – and cancelled! One was a prestigious concert at the Oakland-Alameda County Coliseum. (This date would eventually be honoured two years later when Marvin confidently appeared before an audience of fourteen thousand!) Naturally, during this time, tour promoters were rapidly growing wary of Gaye's attitude – some refused to consider working with him at all. He was a liability but he was unperturbed, insisting – 'I hate the hassles and restrictions of touring and I hate getting up on stage in front of a lot of people. I know part of it is a crazy ego thing. I want to be liked and I would hate it, I mean, really hate it, if the audience didn't like me. It's a real hang-up for me.'

Meantime, his record company, Motown, also had a hang-up, that of persuading their artist to record again. Since 'What's Going On' he had toyed around with several ideas but none had reached fruition. In desperation and to quell Motown's impatience, Marvin hastily recorded and delivered a sample of his next thematic project. Titled 'You're The Man Parts I and II', the single was issued in America only during 1972. Motown/EMI knew they would have problems in selling the multitracked, personal opined political statement, so issued 'Inner City Blues (Make Me Wanna Holler)' instead. As the American single struggled to become a number seven R&B hit, the British release bombed. When 'You're The Man' failed to make the US pop forty, Gaye was puzzled and upset; he expected automatic success following 'What's Going On'. He also realised that if the sample had been rejected by the public there was no point in progressing with the project which was scheduled for June 1972 release. Gaye: 'I had a whole album planned around that track because I very much wanted to work in the movie field and I wanted to use this music as a soundtrack.'

A re-think was needed to gain public acceptance once more and Motown was cautious about taking too many chances with his work. Marvin knew it was impossible to follow 'What's Going On' – 'It has been categorised as a classic album and I now think I should leave it at that. But "What's Going On" was also an attempt to unstifle myself and my creativity, and flex my artist's muscle and do something that had some meaning.' As he changed his attitude towards his music so did Motown, although he believed the company was more influenced by the country's economy than his progressive talent. 'When we started out the dollar was worth a lot more, and the record company could do a lot more. Attitude-wise I think they've always remained primarily the same over the years. If anything, they have become much more liberalminded with regard to me. My hardest times with them were in the early years. Motown is alright really. They can be an incredible company, but record companies are record companies, and to be successful there is just about one way they can do that and make money. I understand that my big fight has been one of creative freedom.'

Having achieved a certain degree of creative freedom did not mean, as Gaye believed, the company would automatically release his future work untouched. In reality if Motown considered a project unsatisfactory, it would be returned to him for correction, irrespective of how long it took and how many times the work was given back. There were certain standards to maintain and Gaye knew this. He generalised on the subject – 'Berry loves music, but he's also a businessman in a way that I admire. I think they were very serious about their music making, though I don't know if they knew what they had early on. Once they discovered what they had going for them, they started to really get off on it. At one point they were leaders, but then they became followers, doing material that was good, but very much a part of what the going thing was. Stax [Records] was a threat in the mid-Sixties but I don't believe it ever overtook Motown. It was a whole other sound and market, more roots, more guts, more blackness.'

So, this was the Marvin Gaye of the early Seventies. Every aspect of his life conflicted but he believed he had succeeded where others had failed, to shrug off Motown's musical dictatorship to prove himself a capable independent and a saleable commodity by providing the company with its fastest-selling album to date. Whether he could have achieved this without the tragedy of Tammi Terrell's death or the horrors of the Vietnam War will never be known, but it seems the two events gave him the incentive to record serious, meaningful music and abandon once and for all what he often referred to as his lightweight, throwaway pop with a lifespan of a few months. His work prior to 'What's Going On' might have seemed inferior to him but time was to prove him wrong because it lived on through the decades, attracting new generations.

As Marvin Gaye's personal life changed for the worst, his career expanded further. Ironically, these two aspects of his life were due to cross because of an unexpected court decision, but meantime Marvin attempted to live one day at a time. No one really knew how he was spending his time during this period; his contact with Berry Gordy and Motown was non-existent because — 'There were disputes over financial matters, over promotion, over a whole heap of things. Also my marriage was beginning to run into difficulties. Anna and I had in fact separated.'

Marvin did return to work and his next project was an unexpected move and once again stretched Motown's promotion department to the limit. In the wake of black music stalwart Isaac Hayes-penned movie soundtrack for *Shaft* and the growing popularity in low budget, semi-violent black flicks, Gaye jumped on the merry-go-round to write his only film score *Trouble Man* – quite an apt title for him at this time! It's feasible that he resurrected the music planned for the aborted 'You're The Man' project as he worked on the soundtrack in both Detroit and Los Angeles, where he had now bought an apartment. (A year later he, his wife and their eight-year-old son Marvin III moved to Beverly Hills, after lodging with Anna's sister Gwen. Gaye also moved his parents from Washington D.C. to a new house he had purchased in Gramercy Place, Los Angeles.)

Gaye totally immersed himself in *Trouble Man*, adopting the role of the film's main character 'Mr T' to write the whole album. The result was moody and jazz-tinged – almost a sinister reflection of his darkest moments. Gaye: 'I've had "Trouble Man" within me for a long time but it took a serious piece of negativity to bring it out. It was an indication of my ability to do music that would not be categorised as blues or soul, which I had never had a serious opportunity to delve into commercially, because Motown – and all record companies actually – are only interested in strong commercial stuff.' Many of Gaye's own frustrations and anger were channelled through 'Mr T', who, like him, was anti-establishment and ignored society's rules and regulations. A perfect vehicle for Gaye – he could condemn and ridicule without damaging his own reputation. 'Mr T' was a central figure in the worst of Los Angeles' urban black ghettos, rife with racketeers, gamblers, pimps and so on. The film's plot was based around the hero being hired by two gamblers – one white, one black – to crush the conflict between their gang and several rival racketeers. The ensuing story revolved around his escapades involving the obligatory cops, hoods, women, shoot-outs and double crosses. Filming began on location in Los Angeles on 17 April 1972 with television actor Robert Hooks playing 'Mr T',

Despite offering film-goers similar ingredients as the other 'black flicks', *Trouble Man* flopped, much to Gaye's annoyance – 'I might have got a film score award if more people had seen the movie. I wanted it to be different and I wanted it to have sensitivity and all the things that make me, and then I wanted to also say that I could divert from "What's Going On" – and actually go into another area completely.' More importantly, the singer needed, once again, to prove his musical longevity to Motown and his public by creating diverse music and not be pigeon-holed in one market. Gaye: 'I can write soul and I can write operettas. I have a symphony in two movements which I wrote four or five years ago and got disenchanted with. Now I've finished it and I think it's very good. I've also written two screenplays but I'm not happy with them yet, they need a little work.'

Without the film's visuals to back up the music much of the excitement of *Trouble Man* was lost, although connoisseurs appreciated the overall sound which was excellent. The atmospheric start, 'Main Theme From Trouble Man', with lashings of brass, climaxed in the choruses while the remainder of the track was held together by a moody sound. That sound was noticeable throughout the album as was the 'Trouble Man' theme, a distinctive few seconds of music. 'Poor Abbey Walsh' was one of the vocal tracks; thoughtful, reflective, and remembered for its dramatic hooklines. Gaye's voice calmed the mood before snatches of double tracking led into a further instrumental. Interestingly, his voice could be heard somewhere on most tracks if only for a few seconds, perhaps adding his hallmark. A long introduction led into 'Cleo's Apartment' where Gaye's humming eased its way into 'Trouble Man' itself, the vocal single. 'Main Theme From Trouble Man' followed where his wailing led into 'Life Is A Gamble', another track with a vocal introduction. The last three titles 'Deep In It', 'Don't Mess With Mr "T"' and 'There Goes Mr "T"' wind down the soundtrack within a short six minutes, but not before an eerie indication of Gaye's destiny. After stressing more than once that the hero was trouble on the last track, a simulated gun shot was heard; the music stopped; the album finished! Perhaps this inclusion suggested Marvin actually had an inkling of the circumstances surrounding his demise? In fact, the album's front sleeve showed his name and 'Trouble Man' riddled with bullet holes beside a serious looking singer sitting on an upright chair.

The soundtrack album sold exceptionally well although, naturally, not up to the standard of 'What's Going On'. The title track, released as the only single in November 1972, a month prior to the album's release, peaked at number seven in the mainstream chart (no 4 R&B). The album reached fourteen in January 1973.

'Trouble Man' was not the official follow-up to 'What's Going On', it was, Marvin claimed, a project he was determined to do as a diversion, to perhaps ease the pressure built up to write another commercial blockbuster. Gaye: 'I think to write a score for a film one must either be very sensitive or extremely mechanical. If you are mechanical you write the standard sound for a certain scene or emotion. In my case I depend on my feelings towards the characters in the scenes.' Gaye realised he would be open to criticism with his first film score but felt it wouldn't attract as much attention as his predecessors because – 'I don't think you would classify my soundtrack with any of the highly entertaining ones such as "Superfly" or "Shaft". I wrote specifically for this motion picture out of the classical soundtrack mould because, quite frankly, that's how I've always viewed writing for films.'

He loathed the way artists had to be categorised in order to sell their music, and he stressed, this was another vital reason why he willingly composed 'Trouble Man'. He refused to be labelled, a trait that remained with him throughout his career; he was true to his art and followed his instincts, ignoring Motown's occasional adverse attitude. Gaye: 'This is a very set industry and people seem to go along with the flow. But I'm just artistic-minded.' However, he accepted his work needed to be commercial to a certain degree to sell

– 'although what I feel I'm making commercial may not be the commercial thing of the day. I don't think I'm easily categorisable as a soul singer. People might want a musical categorisation but that's not the deal.'

In January 1973 when Motown was named by *Black Enterprise* magazine as the top black-owned business with record sales estimated at $40 million, Berry Gordy resigned as president of Motown Records to become chairman of his new entertainment arm, Motown Industries Inc. in Los Angeles, which included his film, television and publishing interests. Ewart Abner II, Motown vice-president of six years' standing, replaced Gordy as president. Meanwhile, the music machine continued as usual. Marvin Gaye's ex-producer Norman Whitfield had transferred his talent to his new protégés The Undisputed Truth, who filled the gap left by The Temptations when they severed their working relationship with the producer. Actor/singer Bobby Darin joined Motown, Diana Ross issued her 'Touch Me In The Morning' album which featured her self-produced version of Gaye's 'Save The Children'. Ross was pregnant during the recording session which may, she said, have inspired the album's baby theme, although several tracks were recorded and canned including 'Baby I Love Your Way' which was eventually issued in her 1983 'Anthology' package. 'Touch Me In The Morning', written by Michael Masser and Ron Miller, was an American chart topper and nominated for a Grammy in the Best Pop Vocal Performance – Female Section. And The Supremes, minus a pregnant Cindy Birdsong and lead singer Jean Terrell with replacements Scherrie Payne and Susaye Green, recorded the Stevie Wonder-penned song 'Bad Weather', while Wonder's own 'Superstition' from his 'Talking Book' album had recently topped the US charts.

For his next musical project Marvin Gaye wrote and sang about two of his passions – women and sex, although when he planned the concept his ideas were sketchy, his working schedules erratic. Gaye: 'I don't know what I'm going to do. I know what I ain't going to do and what I ain't is come back with something pretty much like what I've done already. To me, that's a job finished and I'm off to new adventures.' The adventure would, he smiled, present Motown with more headaches, particularly as it wanted pure musical commercialism. He felt the company was now paranoid – 'about something that might be a little different. There are two mentalities in this business. There's the performer who's primarily mechanical, and somewhat mercenary, and good and brilliant many times, but surely not an artist. He is in the business to make money, and that's how he approaches it. An artist, however, isn't generally concerned with the money-making prospects of the industry. He's concerned with doing something, telling something, predicting something. Giving something that has depth, meaning, that someone can go to later on when they need it, and put it on, and pull themselves back together . . . because life is tough. That's an artist. If he's good and if he's true to himself he can be just as wealthy as the other type of individual. But even if he never gets wealthy, he's wealthy anyway. And he'll always be rich.'

The new work was indeed commercial but the content risky. Titled 'Let's Get It On', it shot to number two in the US album charts, while the title song issued as a single in June 1973 soared to number one in both the pop and R&B charts (it stayed at the top for six weeks in the latter). When released in Britain it peaked at thirty-one, his first hit since 'Save The Children' in December 1971. The British single's flipside was Gaye's version of Gladys Knight and the Pips' 'I Wish It Would Rain' (taken from the 1970 album 'That's The Way Love Is'). This harmless track was chosen in case radio stations rejected the topside as unsuitable for peak daytime airplay. After all, very little had been left to the imagination with the single; the sexual implications were clear and direct, representing the erotic mood of the entire album which followed in August 1973. Happily, most of the songs were eagerly played uncensored on both sides of the Atlantic. When Gaye's father heard the single he told Marvin – 'Don't go any further, you're supposed to be a minister's son.' In defence of his work Marvin explained – 'I think sex is great! And I'm a fantasy person. I think there's a point where you can live out your fantasies and not go over into perversity. I also think society makes people creep and crawl about and it only accentuates perversity. I suppose that makes it more fun for the pervert though.'

Some believed 'Let's Get It On' was 'What's Going On' with a lyric change, conceived in similar circumstances – it was someone else's idea. For 'What's Going On' Al Cleveland and Obie Benson wrote a song which inspired Marvin to work on an album. On this new project Ed Townsend gave him the idea for the title song and ultimately co-wrote half the album. Marvin lacked the initiative to start a project, he needed the injection of another's imaginative talent to start his own creative juices flowing. If Gaye had been left to his own devices it's feasible that the calibre of music to date would have been drastically inferior. Like Cleveland and Benson, Gaye had known Townsend for some time – '[We] have been good friends for years and Ed came and told me he had a good idea for a song called "Let's Get It On". I knew immediately or instinctively that the phrase alone, the terminology "let's get it on" was a smash. Then he sat and played the melody for me, and I knew the melody was beautiful. Then I just did the lyric and it worked. I hope it won't advocate promiscuity. I tried to think that my records are honest and that what I sing about should be dealt with in honesty, not total promiscuity and a muckness, but I don't have any restrictions, any boundaries. I can't be dictated to, I can't be told what kind of music to release. I have to release the kind of music my soul tells me to release.'

While locked in the recording studios with his music, Marvin Gaye was introduced to his future wife, sixteen-year-old Janis Hunter. She was a friend of Ed Townsend, his working partner, who had invited the young, shy girl and her mother to the studios to meet the singer. Instantly, Marvin was struck by a thunderbolt; Hunter was the answer to his wildest dreams as he fell under her young spell. 'Let's Get It On' began to take on a whole different meaning. Hunter inspired him; no longer was he forced to sing to and plead with a fantasy figure. He now had his own perfect image of womanhood, his delicate angel. Thankfully, Marvin Gaye guarded his thoughts, checked his feelings and paced his actions, as serious reservations about this pending relationship sprang to mind. He was thirty-three years old with a wife seventeen years his elder, a son, and he was widely considered as a drug-taker and womaniser. Janis Hunter was a minor and, he said, he was naturally worried about possible future legal implications plus the reaction of his family and friends should a relationship develop. So, from the outset he conducted himself as a suitable suitor with honourable intentions; he did not intend to lose his precious jewel, his God-given gift.

To a great extent Janis Hunter's presence was felt in 'Let's Get it On'. The sensitivity and delicate multi-tracked vocals against the haunting, compulsive melodies that encompassed the whole project, could not possibly have been the result of his imagination. Even the harsher tracks, the title song and 'Keep Gettin' It On', both of which carried a similar message and style, indicated a mighty outside influence because Gaye was at his persuasive peak, cajoling his partner to consent to his loving demands. In 'Please Don't Stay (Once You Go Away)' he pleaded for his lover to remain with him, afraid of being alone, while 'If I Should Die Tonight', with its dramatic introduction, settled into a mellow, highly orchestrated song with a sweet sax solo. 'Come Get To This' and 'Distant Lover' (later to become a favourite in-concert highlight especially for British fans) opened side two, signifying the end of the Gaye/Townsend written tracks, arranged by Rene Hall. 'Come Get To This' Marvin wrote alone, while 'Distant Lover' he penned with Sandra Greene and his wife's sister Gwen Gordy Fuqua. Both were drenched in a powerful delivery of all human emotions as he tore out his soul. 'You Sure Love To Ball' had connotations that speak for themselves and if portrayed as a movie in the cinema would have instantly warranted an X-rated certificate. It was considered crude and vulgar by many, especially when sexual simulation from Madeline and Fred Ross backed the lead vocal. It was also considered a sexist statement by the singer with undertones of voyeurism, and not the submissive lover he intended to portray. Finally, 'Just To Keep You Satisfied', written by Gaye, his wife and Elgie Stover, brought to the listener's attention his pending divorce, the finality of the relationship and the tragedy of a broken love affair. However, a diligent listener could read other implications and suggestions into the lyrics but there was little doubt about Marvin's intentions here.

'Let's Get It On' was a woman's album from an artist who believed he was the ultimate lover, the conquering hero, a woman's fantasy. To millions he was and they loved it. Others, including feminists, loathed it because it typified everything they stood against; the dominant egotistical male, the selfish, demanding lover, the male who clearly saw women as sex objects to oblige as he commanded. Marvin Gaye was undeterred and stood his ground – 'I was talking directly to the girls out there, but I hope it will be an aid for men as well. Maybe it'll have some aphrodisiac power. I had a lot of fun doing it too. It just killed me. Try the album sometime when you've got a difficult girl on your hands. Put it on and see if it helps. One time don't use the album, and the next time you have her, just put it on and you'll really see if it works or not. I'll bet you anything she'll be nice; she'll come round a lot nicer than the first time.'

Once again Marvin wrote the album's sleeve notes which in themselves were offensive to some and included – 'I can't see anything wrong with sex between consenting anybodies. I think we make far too much of it. After all, one's genitals are just one important part of the magnificent human body. I have no argument with the essential part they play in the reproduction of the species; however, the reproductive process has been assured by the pleasure both parties receive when they engage in it . . . I contend that sex is sex and love is love. When combined, they work well together, if two people are of about the same mind. But, they are really two discrete needs and should be treated as such. Have your sex, it can be very exciting, if you're lucky . . . I hope the music that I present here makes you lucky.'

With this album Gaye's intention was to look at physical and emotional love in a freer, more explanatory manner than he'd previously been able to do at the hands of dominant producers and writers. With him as overall producer here, he said, he had the last say, yet in the sleeve notes he credits Cal Harris who 'practically produced this thing and didn't ask for anything'. Also Marvin Gaye faced the same dilemma here as he did with 'What's Going On' because he had to list his composing associates on the album sleeve. The move was again reluctant, he wanted his public to believe that he alone had conceived the project. What he failed to grasp was that only the most dedicated fans would have noticed or cared, the majority preferred to enjoy the music. The record's gatefold sleeve showed the singer wearing his red knitted hat, denim shirt over a light brown vest and heavily belted jeans. Some poses, all photographed by Jim Britt, showed him in a working situation while others pictured him smoking and relaxing. Unlike 'What's Going On' the songs' lyrics were conspicuous by their absence. Possibly this was an obvious move as some of the poetic rhymes would have been classed as obscene at the time.

Marvin Gaye was overjoyed with the public's response to the album – one UK journalist referred to it as 'the most incredible collection of screwing music available' – but surprisingly admitted he had, to a certain extent, deceived his fans because he'd given them nothing new. He conceded the music had been written using the same techniques as 'What's Going On' and some of the melodies were inspired or left over from that work. It was an intentional move, he cautiously explained, because he believed he owed it to listeners to keep the musical momentum alive by using 'The kinds of changes, interjections, the sensitive things, the rocking things with the message on top of it.' Yet in another interview he confessed – 'Quite frankly, my heart isn't in this one as much because all I can do is expound on what I said before. There have really been no changes to write about. I hope that eventually I make it to the plateau where I'm able to sing romantic songs and torch songs and songs of love and life, and this will be the accepted mode. That's where I'd like to be, and be very secure.'

'Come Get To This' was the second single lifted from the album in October 1973 to become a twenty-one pop hit (no 3 R&B) followed three months later by 'You Sure Love To Ball' which reached number fifty in February 1974 (no 13 R&B). Motown/EMI passed on this single knowing it was a pointless move. Without radio exposure the vinyl would merely collect dust on record store shelves.

By this time Marvin Gaye admitted he had a regular drug habit and had in fact been arrested for carrying dope. Motown had bailed him out before the media could sensationalise the arrest. He had said on numerous occasions that he took drugs to stimulate his creativity – 'It's well known that certain drugs will open up one's creative facilities and perception banks. Colour and sound centres can become more apparent by the use of drugs. So, in some cases they can play a part in creativity but certainly one can reach those levels without the aid of such drugs. Also, the abuse of stimulants can be very detrimental and harmful. It's all a question of balance and maintaining control.' He may well have been able to sustain a balance at this time, but by the late Seventies the scales had tipped drastically against him.

He treated cocaine with respect and reverence although occasionally lost control. He told David Ritz why he chose that particular drug – 'I like the feeling. No one will ever tell me it's not a good feeling. A clean, fresh high, especially early in the morning, will set you free – at least for a minute. There are times when blow got to me, and sometimes I know it built up bad vibes inside my brain. I saw coke, though, as an elitist item, a gourmet drug, and maybe that was one of its attractions. Was I corrupting myself? Slowly, very slowly.'

Since 'What's Going On' Marvin Gaye became more aware of world politics, international debates and social issues, subjects he'd ignored or had no time for previously, being a slave to his music. He began speaking fluently on past and present international events, and became intensely aware of the cruelty and obscenity of war, the killings and the tragedies of isolated and full-scale warfare. By studying influential works on nuclear war and holocausts, he became passionately preoccupied with thoughts of saving the world from total destruction. He believed that despite efforts by mankind to annihilate the world, it would survive and based his theory on man destroying himself instead. Gaye: 'There will be an earth and there will be people left, and life will go on, and it will start all over again, and let's see if we can do a little bit better the next time. People who love peace and who are evolved and who can see, think and feel, know that. It's those people who will be the survivors and the only ones. And they should prepare now.' Part of that preparation, he insisted, included strict and general abstinence – 'Soon there will be nothing, and one has to get used to living on little. The countries that have always enjoyed good food and conveniences will be the hardest pressed because the countries where people know hunger and have learnt to live on very little will do much better. I think these times are potentially the times of the greatest crisis that the earth will ever face, in this lifetime, or any other, and I think the crisis will become very evident within the next twenty years. I think these are the times when, if one is wise, one will get into the study of survival.'

He would spasmodically refer to this subject in the future together with his newly acquired knowledge of psychic healers and alternative medicine, where he voiced particular concern regarding the ease with which doctors prescribed pills for patients without respect for other remedies. Gaye: 'Instead of suggesting that their patients eat a few vegetables instead of that stupid pork, say, and that they take a jog around the block once in a while, most American doctors would rather give them a pill and take their money week after week, so they may be rich doctors like their mommies always dreamed they'd be. It's really a cold conspiracy and a trap.' On the other hand, he stressed, there were great surgeons and doctors whose aim was only to benefit mankind, without any thought for financial incentives and personal gain. It was simply a few who gave the wrong impression. Marvin: 'I'm not knocking medicine at all but I am knocking the way medicine is structured momentarily, and I am knocking the knowledge that doctors don't have, or the knowledge they do have but refuse to dispense to their patients. But I praise the new wave doctors who say you have this, this and this. Now I can send you to a surgeon and he can cut it out, but I feel you can get rid of it with some discipline. If you drink these teas, eat these herbs, do not smoke any cigarettes, cut out liquor, go to these baths, do these particular exercises, then you will get well. On the other hand, if you don't have the discipline to do this, then take your butt over to the surgeon and let him get cutting on your organs and get you well and suffer the rest of your life with internal pains and things. And that's bullshit, and the doctors who are aware know it's bullshit.'

In this same interview with the *NME*, Gaye said he had also studied the different forms of cancer and concluded that it wasn't the disease that killed, but the victim's terror of it. He explained his reasoning – 'It is the mind that kills most cancer patients. The fact they feel if they have the disease their chances of dying are very strong. Your body cannot heal because for all the good and positiveness it wants to do you, you're always telling yourself subconsciously, "Oh God, I'm going to die because I have cancer." The smart doctors know that this is probably why fifty per cent of people succumb to the disease, but do you think that the cancer institutes and all the money they raise for cancer is going to be stopped over somebody telling them that. They'll just say "you quack, get outa here". There may have been many cases where terminal cancer patients who have had a chance to deeply concentrate from the mind perspective have had phenomenal results in curing their own disease. If people think it's quackery, I can tell them it's certainly not. It goes back to the original principles, and if you can use your mind to cure cancer, then you can use your mind to never getting it. People should get into their own mind power and control their bodies and their diseases with their minds, but it's difficult in our society because the senses are clouded with meat and pus and drugs and stress.'

As Marvin Gaye was ploughing his energies into non-musical activities, his fellow artists continued to earn Motown money. Shortly after 'Let's Get It On' was issued, Stevie Wonder returned to the charts with his own personal statement on social issues with 'Innervisions', his first self-conceived album which went on to win five Grammy Awards. Three days before 'Innervisions' was released Wonder was nearly killed in a car accident in North Carolina. He made a complete recovery but still bears facial scars. And one of Berry Gordy's better signings, the Commodores with Lionel Richie transferred from his defunct West Coast label Mowest to Motown, Jermaine Jackson began promoting his solo album 'Come Into My Life' following a sell-out tour of Japan with his brothers, and Diana Ross, now a mother of two (Rhonda Suzanne and Tracee Joy), debuted as a soloist on the British concert circuit as part of her European tour.

In October 1973 four weeks after her opening night in Birmingham, England, the unthinkable happened – Marvin Gaye broke the vow he made when Tammi Terrell died and released an album with Diana Ross.

Following the ex-Supreme's 'Lady Sings The Blues' and 'Touch Me

In The Morning' projects in 1972 and 1973 respectively, Berry Gordy was determined to restore and maintain her vinyl selling power. Once again he thought of the past successes with duets, and decided this ploy would work again, particularly if Ross sang with an established partner. He asked Marvin Gaye to record with her even though he was at the time finishing 'Let's Get It On'. Before he would agree to participate he insisted Gordy paid him extra royalties and top billing in the same way as he had with Wells, Weston and Terrell. Gordy refused. But Gaye agreed to the duets anyway! Some felt he made this move because he might, in the future, be afforded the same treatment Ross received from Gordy, while she said she had nurtured a desire to record with Gaye for some time.

Eighteen tracks in total were recorded (some completed, others not including 'Alone', '5, 10, 15, 20 Years, Of Love', and 'Live It Up', later recorded by Jermaine Jackson), but only ten were released. Berry Gordy personally selected the repertoire and asked Hal Davis to produce the bulk of them. The album 'Diana & Marvin' was preceded by the beautifully constructed 'You're A Special Part Of Me' written by members of The Devastating Affair, Ross's one-time vocal backing group and artists in their own right. The single became an American number twelve (no 4 R&B) and a British struggler at the close of 1973.

The project was an ambitious gamble. Two giant artists, both used to demanding and receiving individual attention to feed their egos, warranted careful handling, discretion and patience. Hal Davis told J. Randy Taraborrelli that he handled both artists with kid gloves and worked with the utmost diplomacy – 'I would get my artistic points of view across without hurting either one. Of course, we had some touchy moments in there, but you're bound to have that when you've got two major stars working together like that. They had their individual opinions and I had to be the mediator.' Nonetheless, taken as a whole, the album was luxuriously presented, certainly the novelty alone guaranteed sales.

However, some tracks were surprisingly lacklustre – 'Pledging My Love', 'Love Twins', 'I'm Falling In Love With You'. Others were familiar, like the two tried and tested, Stylistics' sophisticated ballads 'You Are Everything' and 'Stop, Look, Listen (To Your Heart)' both penned by Linda Creed and Thorn Bell, and released in 1971 and 1972 respectively, and Wilson Pickett's recorded and co-written 'Don't Knock My Love', a low-keyed smooth funk track which became his own second million seller in 1971. Even the brilliant commerciality of

Ashford & Simpson – who had originally been asked to produce the whole album – that worked so well with Gaye and Terrell had lost its sparkle on the soulless 'Just Say, Just Say'. Nevertheless the album was rifled for singles and its highlight, the chirpy, mid-paced Pam Sawyer and Gloria Jones' track 'My Mistake (Was To Love You)' was the second in January 1974 to become a number nineteen pop hit (no 15 R&B). Motown/EMI opted for familiarity and issued the melodic ballad 'You Are Everything' in the March and the gamble paid off when it raced to number five in the British charts. The third American single was the infectious mover 'Don't Knock My Love' in June 1974 (no 25 R&B/no 46 pop), while Motown/EMI flushed with success lifted the second Stylistics' coverversion 'Stop, Look, Listen (To Your Heart)' which reached the top thirty. This was followed by the second American single 'My Mistake (Was To Love You)' in October and lastly, in July 1975, 'Don't Knock My Love'. The mediocre 'Pledging My Love' remained untouched!

When the album showing Ross and Gaye sitting back to back on the front sleeve, which cynics believed indicated an unamicable association, was first issued, Motown's publicity machinery cranked into action with idyllic stories of the two megastars recording together. The picture painted was entirely harmonious and the public lapped it up. Gaye was pleased with the public's support as he told Paul Bernstein in a *Crawdaddy* interview – 'Diana and I have known each other since the outset of Motown. This is a good duet album. We liked to think we could do it better than most people . . . I'm hoping the album will be a classic one day. I'd like it to stand for several years. I like change anyway and this project afforded me with that change.' He even hinted at a possible movie venture with his new singing partner – 'It would also be nice to do a love story with Diana because I think I have the sensitivity to pull that off . . . Maybe a film with some sort of tragic implications; lost love or some really emotional kind of thing. I'd like to do anything with her quite frankly.' Despite his enthusiasm at the time Marvin insisted the recording project was a one-off album – 'I never had any thoughts that my singing with anybody could possibly injure my progress . . . it's always enjoyable to work with someone. It's something new, a new excitement in my life. But I don't follow my footsteps and my shadow. Singers are afraid to branch out and try something new and exciting, but I wasn't.' This time he kept his word.

The publicity machine rolled on and on to sell the album and singles by the million, and the romantic ambience of its conception remained untarnished until 1976 when Marvin Gaye told British researcher Jim Hegarty that he was not always in the studios with Diana Ross, therefore many of the songs were recorded separately. This was later confirmed by another source who revealed that although Gaye had said he had the highest regard for Diana's immense talent and her recent achievements in the film world, he felt intimidated by her. She appeared to him to be insecure, lacking the confidence she usually exuded, and was pregnant with her second child. Her professional relationship with Berry Gordy was reportedly strained, and Marvin aggravated the recording situation by smoking dope and drinking alcohol during the initial joint sessions.

At this time Gaye invariably recorded under the influence of marijuana and would be seen smoking his way through numerous songs while in the studios. Should anyone walk into one of his sessions, the air was so thick that only the outline of his sitting figure could be seen. This situation understandably upset Ross who feared for the health of her unborn baby and prompted the individual recordings. Gaye admitted to Ritz that he didn't handle the situation properly – 'Musically I may have overplayed my hand. I was too cavalier. I should have done everything in the world to make Diana comfortable . . . I could have been a little more understanding. But I'm afraid I went the other way. It's hard for me to deal with prima donnas. We were like two spoiled kids screaming for the same cookie. It was definitely not a duet made in heaven.'

American taste in mainstream music diversified during the early Seventies. British acts were making their presence felt once more with solo Beatles, Paul McCartney and Ringo Starr, and the flamboyant Elton John who competed against Carly Simon, Cher and Helen Reddy, among others. Nevertheless, Motown held its own because its music had changed drastically. No longer could a single be recognised by its opening bars or chorus. It was flexible to the public's differing tastes and the company's move to Los Angeles was blamed, and credited, for this. It was in this unpredictable and fast moving environment that Marvin Gaye had presented and succeeded with his finest music which had not pampered to public dictation.

It's true to say, Stevie Wonder had inspired him not only to trust his own judgment by recording music he believed in, but also to follow his example when re-negotiating his recording contract in 1973. All contracts were exclusive and could run for seven years with options to renew or terminate at Motown's discretion. Royalty rates continued to be low, usually between 1.8 per cent and 2.7 per cent although research suggests some were higher. There is no reason to suppose that Marvin Gaye's original contract differed from other Motown artists to include provisions for management, publishing and recording costs, which invariably were high because musicians could earn $60,000 a year. If a record bombed and/or the artist was dropped from the roster, Motown swallowed the expense. A selling, working act with a regular income, however, was obligated to repay all costs from royalties. While it was reported that Martha Reeves owed Motown $200,000 when she left, Barbara Randolph's debt was higher even though she only recorded three tracks ('I Got A Feeling', 'You Got Me Hurtin' All Over', 'Can I Get A Witness') for the company. Upon receiving her first royalty statement she was horrified to discover she owed Motown approximately $300,000 in studio costs – 'I can't tell you how! They had a little bit that I had supposedly earned from sales, something like a couple of thousand dollars. And then they had the "you owe us" bit and they subtract that from what you owe them. And its still $300,000 or something. So it takes you a long time to catch up. I only imagine that other acts who recorded albums were in debt to Motown for life.'

Barbara Randolph also reiterated Gaye's past grievance when she said one major problem was the artists' inability to choose, or have any control over what material they recorded – 'There were writers there on staff and if they decided they wanted to produce an artist, they would get it approved, then they'd go into the studios and record the material with you. The only problem with that was you were charged for the sessions! And this money comes out of your royalties. So now you can see why I only recorded those three titles there. Today, the album comes first, but in those days it didn't. You did a forty-five and if that was a success you did an album. And I guess I thank God in a way because if I'd done an album I'd probably have ended up owing them $5 million!'

When Marvin Gaye signed his new multi-million dollar recording contract which, among other things, allowed him total control over his recordings from their inception, he also insisted that his first advance be Berry Gordy's personally signed cheque for $1 million. The Motown head agreed although he probably smiled, realising he was bowing down to a Gaye whim. A whim that would contribute to his future financial downfall. But to the singer the cheque and the new contract which incorporated all his demands, proved he was now a powerful artist with immeasurable potential. However, instead of returning to the recording studios to flex his newly acquired muscle, Marvin Gaye turned his back on his career once again, and with his pocket full of cash, devoted himself to his new young love Janis Hunter.

# 7. | I Want You

*I'm not a whore. I'm promiscuous, yes, but very selective.*
(Marvin Gaye)

*Marvin Gaye's return was not a concert; it was an event.*
(San Francisco Chronicle)

*[Marvin gave] me the impression of a haunted victim, of a condemned man.*
(Cliff White)

*I don't know why I shaved my head, I'm as crazy as any of us artists, I suppose.*
(Marvin Gaye)

To all intents and purposes 1973 and 1974 were possibly the most interchangeable musical periods of the decade and artists had to ride with the changes or be left behind, and those who opted out for whatever reason found their return precarious. Marvin Gaye was one of these artists, his interest in music was infinitesimal following 'Let's Get It On', and his eventual return would be a struggle even for the powerful and influential Motown. Not only did Gaye neglect the music business but also his everyday life when he took Janis Hunter into hiding in the Topanga Canyon, a few miles outside Los Angeles. He rented a large wooden cabin in the picturesque mountain range and set up home with a record player, a phone, a piano, a couple of jeeps and guard dogs. The cabin was set in an isolated location and was a deliberate attempt by the singer to escape from the outside world. Once more he claimed he was weary of the demands now made on him to act in a responsible fashion that befitted his superstar status. He ignored those demands and spent his days lazily – walking endlessly and aimlessly, going nowhere through the Topanga Canyon, driving one of his jeeps through endless miles of Mother Nature's unspoilt countryside, or religiously reading the theories of Don Juan,

Nostradamus and Carlos Castaneda. At times he thought of the past and attempted to plan his future without coming to any conclusions. He composed at the piano, played records, smoked marijuana, and ate the simplest of meals. Yes indeed, it was an idyllic haven for a man unashamedly in love with a woman seventeen years his junior.

This peaceful ambience that enthralled Gaye so much prompted him to consider other areas of music. For instance, the quietness and seclusion accentuated nature's own sounds, something he had never noticed before, and this inspired him to listen out for particular noises – certain birds singing, insects clicking, rabbits noisily running through the undergrowth and the cacophony of animals at war. His school-days' interest in nature returned as he absorbed every glorious moment and he began thinking about using these sounds in his music. He later tried to explain his feelings to Paul Bernstein – 'We're not the only ones who really enjoy music. There is music in the flower. You just have to have your senses acute enough to pick up on it. What is music to a flower? What is music to a bee? What is music to an ant? To the trees? The wind certainly must play a certain music that trees must love. And the rain plays a certain music to the flower, and the sun must play a certain music. It's that area I'd like to get into, to invent something that would portray this, an instrument, a device for sound that I could incorporate into notes as I know the notation system now, as I have it in my head. And to make a new musical scale, something that's completely universal. The very fact that a guy playing flute drew rats out of the place is indicative, man. It's there – you just have to unlock it.' In retrospect, this way of thinking may well have inspired Stevie Wonder to write the soundtrack for 'Stevie Wonder's Journey Through The Secret Life Of Plants' for 1979 release, a project that took three years to complete. It was an imaginative and sensitive piece of intricate music and was used in the film based on American author Peter Tompkins and biologist Christopher Bird's book of the same name and, like Marvin Gaye's 'Trouble Man' before it, failed to reach its expected potential because the movie was not widely screened.

In the real world outside Topanga Canyon, Marvin Gaye's wife Anna was silently suffering. She knew their marriage was to all intents and purposes finished but nonetheless she waited for his return knowing he'd need her when he once more faced reality. The pain of his shameless philandering must have been intolerable for her, yet she maintained a calm and dignified front befitting a sophisticated and sensitive woman. Marvin admitted he was being selfish by flaunting Janis Hunter to his family and colleagues, but he was hopelessly enraptured by her dazzling beauty and innocence. Anna's brother Berry Gordy was also worried, but for different reasons – Marvin Gaye had recorded two million-selling albums for Motown and had turned his back on that success to live on a mountaintop, leaving nothing suitable in the can to release. There were of course the songs Gaye had intended to give to Sammy Davis Jnr but these all needed dedicated re-mixing and Gaye's approval before the tracks could be touched – something Motown knew it would never receive.

This situation had to be rectified but by now Motown knew there was little it could do except to drop heavy hints in Gaye's direction. The singer stood his ground as he explained in a later interview – 'If you are an artist and you adhere strictly to the guidelines of what is supposed to be an artist, then you don't move out of this mould. I am true to my art and I am true to my artist. The fact is you can even die from it, or starve to death. If you have this power placed in your hands, it's rather impossible in the way the world is geared economically. Today in our system of government, you would be a complete idiot if you got all involved in the politics of running a big corporate organisation when you need to be relaxed and not worry about anything else. Be an artist, strictly an artist, and whatever wealth and fame you receive, is earned and is blessed . . . and it's yours.' Nonetheless, he insisted he'd never leave Motown as he felt a certain loyalty to the company, to Berry Gordy because he understood their workings – 'Over this period of years we've worked out a pretty good working relationship. I go nuts one time and they go nuts the next, and we just still go nuts together. Meanwhile, the years keep passing and I hope that my career keeps going the way it's going. I'm a very patient man, I know that whatever is supposed to happen in my life, I'll have it, so long as I keep my attitudes proper.'

Meantime, Motown realised he worked when he wanted to, released product when the mood took him, seemingly ignoring the terms of his recording contract. He refused to release a constant flow of records – even though he knew this was what Motown wanted – because he saw it as 'selling out and too commercialistic'. Gaye: 'I want to put out something, something that you can feel. There's only so much in this world that you can write and sing about. It's the same thing over and over again anyway, and to me it gets a little boring sometimes. You have to be intelligent to be a true artist because you will definitely be exploited beyond any reasonable expectations. But you still have to remain an artist and the fight and struggle is a very difficult one.'

While Gaye was languishing in Mother Nature's bosom, a solitary single was issued to keep his name before the public, a 'live' version of 'Distant Lover' in September 1974 (no 12 R&B/no 28 pop), while Motown/EMI concentrated on his duets with Diana Ross, and re-issued his solo 'I Heard It Through The Grapevine'. The company had also plundered his back catalogue to lease certain songs to an organisation specialising in releasing and promoting low-priced compilations, an area Motown/EMI had not yet ventured into successfully. The leasing provided sufficient material for two albums 'How Sweet It Is (To Be Loved By You)' in August 1973 and 'The Onion Song' in March 1974.

These releases confirmed to the public that Gaye was no longer active. However, what wasn't realised at the time was that it would be at least another two years before any new material would be available from him. Motown knew there was only so much it could do to keep Gaye's image alive and 'Greatest Hits' packages were already available. It needed a new marketing angle to sell catalogue items so the 'Anthology' collections were introduced, showcasing the hits of Motown's top acts like Diana Ross and the Supremes, The Temptations, Smokey Robinson and the Miracles, Martha Reeves and the Vandellas and Marvin's three-album set which included a booklet containing assorted pictures of an overweight singer in his Topanga Canyon hideaway. When released in Britain the 'Anthology' was reduced to a two-record package losing the much-in-demand 1972 non-UK released single 'You're The Man' which, if successful, Gaye had hoped would have elevated him into the position of a respected black leader. Today the disc which mocked the priorities of American presidential contenders is a British collector's treasure, exchanging hands for extortionate prices.

In Marvin's absence Berry Gordy's other acts were busy. For example, Stevie Wonder released his 'Fulfillingness First Finale' album which later scooped five Grammies, Mary Wilson married Pedro Ferrer in the Candle Light Chapel, Las Vegas. Her sister Catherine was bridesmaid and her adopted son, Willie, best man. Ex-Temptation Eddie Kendricks issued 'Boogie Down', Smokey Robinson, the 'Pure Smokey' album, and the Commodores with Lionel Richie began their recording career in earnest.

At this time Marvin Gaye's public was unaware of Janis Hunter's existence in his life; it believed he had temporarily retired, like he had when Tammi Terrell died. This was a deliberate ploy on his part because once Hunter became exposed to his professional, public life she would no longer be his exclusively. However, his concern was unwarranted as was later confirmed when she rarely strayed from his side. More to the point, there was possibly another more important reason for keeping his young love secret from the world. Marvin was afraid of the media's reaction when it discovered Hunter was a teenager because any adverse publicity could have caused irreparable damage to his career, in much the same way, years earlier, when rock 'n' roll giant Jerry Lee Lewis married his thirteen-year-old cousin. His determination to keep her within arm's length heightened when she miscarried their first baby. The loss brought them even closer together and made Marvin understand the fragility of life and the preciousness of Janis.

So why was Marvin Gaye besotted by this young girl? His close friend Dave Godin: 'There are remarkable qualities about her which become apparent in a very gentle way after a short time. It became obvious to me that she has had a powerful and very sustaining effect upon Marvin, and he is so much more secure and obviously happy.' Gaye: 'She's helped me regain my sense of youth and my spirit and my love for my music. I'm very much in love with her and being in love with someone will bring out a lot of things. She adds a lot of inspiration to me.' On the other hand, this brought problems – 'I'm really having the same battle with Jan that my wife had with me, and that is a struggle for identity and power. I refuse to be less than a man. Control and power and that sort of thing. And being a man who is a ram I shall survive at all costs. And, of course, I'm seventeen years older than Jan.'

Unlike the other women Gaye loved during his lifetime, Janis Hunter had a staggering effect on him. She was responsible for his changing moods, and was capable of predicting his every move and thought. It was an almost telepathic vibe between them which few couples shared or, at the very least, imagined could exist between two people. And Janis, like Anna before her, would love and protect her man in a way he really didn't deserve.

Meantime, the outside world persistently beckoned via his only contact, the phone. News of 'Let's Get It On' was relayed alongside proposals of high-financed tours to cash in on its success, plus offers for more film roles. Marvin ignored them all despite his burning ambition to become an actor, preferring to stay in the seclusion of his mountain hideaway. These weeks in Topanga Canyon were probably the happiest of his life and despite his determination that nothing would interfere with his paradise on earth, he knew the time would come when he'd be forced to return to the world he had left behind. That time came in 1974 when his financial situation was rock bottom and he had no choice but to return to the stage. Gaye agreed to appear at the Oakland Coliseum in a concert promoted by his colleague Wally Cox and Mel Reid, his partner. It had been two years since Marvin had performed a full-length show (apart from the Pride Inc. performance, he had appeared on stage briefly during 1972 for the Push Expo Benefit in Chicago to promote 'Save The Children') and the thought of this Oakland concert terrified him. So much so that the concert's original November 1973 date was postponed until he gave the go-ahead for January leaving the promoters with very little time to promote the night. With such short notice the concert was understandably disorganised from start to finish. During the afternoon prior to the show Marvin completed his sound check in the empty Coliseum while Motown personnel (who shrugged off the singer's non-co-operative attitude towards them) rallied round to rectify the chaos to organise the thirty-three musicians and their conductors, lighting and sound technicians, stage hands, assistants . . . and *their* assistants!

It has been established that when showtime was minutes away and following Ashford & Simpson's superb opening act, Marvin Gaye's paranoia of appearing in public was so overpowering that he sent his young lookalike brother Frankie on stage to test the audience's reaction. The welcome was deafening, leaving Gaye, who was waiting in the wings, with no doubt as to his public's attitude. After a hesitant start, the artist relaxed into the show and with a handful of songs behind him his confidence returned. Dressed like a member of the teenybop group the Bay City Rollers, in faded denim jeans, high platformed silver army boots, woollen cap to hide his balding crown and one earring Marvin inspired a critic from the *San Francisco Chronicle* to write – 'Bedlam promptly ensued and recurred steadily for [an] hour, dependent only on Gaye's whim. At such time as he sat at the piano and quietly sang a new ballad like "Jan", all was pacific. But, on his feet and singing through "Let's Get It On" or a medley of past hits – fists clenched in emotion, arms shooting upward, clomping from one side of the stage to the other, teeth flashing, an occasional waggle of the hip or thrust of pelvis; yet never seeming to seek the easy contrived Isaac Hayes-Tom Jones tin-horn tight pants titillation trip – well, friend, screams and yowls filled the air and nubile young bodies crammed toward the well-guarded stage like so many billiard balls on the break. The actual performance at a concert like this, the niceties of voice, phrasing, pitch and all that, is fairly immaterial; all were fine but that's not the name of the song. Marvin Gaye's return was not a concert, it was an event; a gathering of black pride and star-gazers. Some look to the comet Kohouter; some don't.'

It became apparent that the Oakland Coliseum was a test run for a fully fledged tour although it was impossible to persuade Marvin to commit himself at this time. He wanted to put any plans on hold because Janis Hunter was pregnant with their second child and his immediate intention was for them both to return to Topanga Canyon, possibly until the baby was born. Unfortunately this wasn't to be, due to a series of odd incidents which unhinged Gaye, one of which he relayed to Ritz – 'Someone slit the throats of my Great Danes. That scared the shit out of me. I had nightmares for weeks. I knew there were bad people out there after me, and living where I did – so high up and isolated – I was extremely vulnerable. In comparison, being on stage didn't seem so terrible. It was time. I had to come down from my mountain.' Whether this and other incidents were coincidental hasn't been established but this could well have been an early indication of the singer's bizarre paranoia regarding his safety which escalated to inexplicable proportions later on.

Weeks after the Oakland Coliseum concert and despite his concern for Hunter's condition, Rolling Stone magazine carried an interview with Marvin Gaye who had reportedly flown alone to San Diego to watch one of his boxers Lee Mandingo fight Duane Bobick. Prior to this fight, the singer had regularly jogged and exercised with the boxer whose six-foot six, twenty-stone frame towered above Gaye. Mandingo lost the contest but Marvin was, at the time, confident of the giant's potential as he told journalist Tim Cahill – 'He's a good fighter. He has all the tools, everything. For a big man he's phenomenal. He's fast, he's agile, but exhaustion killed him. Because he got so excited, and started thinking like "I can win. I actually hit him. God! I actually hit him!" It was terrible. I looked at him and thought "you're not tired Mandingo. Jesus Christ, don't wobble like that." Oh, it was terrible man. He fell on the ropes and they thought the whole fight was gonna come up.' Did Gaye consider his profession similar to boxing, Cahill asked. Marvin: 'I don't know. If there is something to be learned, I'll get it subconsciously and maybe it'll help me at a later time. I don't know what it could be, unless it's something about controlling my mind.'

While Marvin Gaye was concentrating on pleasing himself Motown was anxious to issue an album of the Oakland Coliseum performance but, of course, the final decision to make the tapes available to them rested with Gaye. He spent weeks listening, editing and mixing them at Motown's studios in Hollywood before eventually releasing them. He said he was satisfied with the result, except for one sequence, Wally Cox's spoken, overindulgent enthusiasm. Gaye: 'When [he] finished the show with "the marvellous Marvin Gaye, ladies and gentlemen, a legend in time. Marvellous Marvin, ladies and gentlemen". . . . Oh, that's terrible. I wish he didn't do that.' The show was reported to have equalled that by The Beatles years earlier, another point that distressed and surprised Gaye – 'God, it was unbelievable. I'm thirty-four and at Oakland, I mean, some of them were little girls, really little girls. I don't understand it. I'm flattered but I don't understand it.'

The album was released in June 1974 to become a US top ten entrant, with the track listing broken down into sections – 'The Beginning' including 'Trouble Man', 'Distant Lover' and 'Jan'; 'Fossil Medley', his 'pop' singles and 'Now' with 'What's Going On' and 'Let's Get it On'. Ewart Abner was executive producer while Gene Page directed it all except the 'Fossil Medley' directed by Lesley Drayton. Motown/EMI originally scheduled the album in the STML listing (the numbering system used for single jacketed albums) before releasing it in July 1974 under an STMA number, the company's de luxe listing which carried a higher selling price.

With the 'live' album behind him and now settled in Hollywood, Marvin Gaye once again needed money to survive and reluctantly left Janis Hunter to return to the stage. Once a starting date could be agreed upon, the tour got under way in August 1974 and was to include twenty dates across America, his first tour since Tammi Terrell collapsed in his arms on stage during 1967. Gaye: 'I just don't have the desire to perform. To me, there's something false. Possibly the next time I perform I will try to perform with total honesty. Whatever happens happens. I'll try to be happy, try to enjoy my work because that's the only way to look at it. If you're honestly trying to give, I think the audience can feel the vibrations. I'm into a big thing about vibrations and mental communication, being able to read thoughts or at least get a feeling of how the vibes are. I think if you get on a good plane as a performer, then the audience will be on a good plane. It still bugs me a bit that somebody might call out "sing 'Yellow Rose Of Texas'." But I guess I can get by with that.'

For this tour, to alleviate his timorous attitude towards an audience, Marvin Gaye engaged a dance troupe to take the visual emphasis away from him, a twenty-piece orchestra and Ladies Choice, a female vocal backing quartet to cover mistakes he might make like fluffing a line or verse or not reaching a note. And to help placate troublesome and melodramatic moments Gaye's mother Alberta was asked to travel with him, a move she would make regularly in the future. Marvin's insistence at appearing on stage dressed in a denim shirt, with blue jeans rolled up around ankles to show off unsightly platformed boots was ludicrous, and hardly the seductive attire of the cool epitome of love, the sophisticated young man of the Sixties who was capable of breaking a woman's heart with a single glance! He chose these clothes because he wanted to do something different; he wanted them to represent his new future career and not that of the past which he wanted to ignore.

The tour was a dazzling triumph – standing room only audiences, a succession of accolade and worship which would have delighted any celebrated demi-god. Was Marvin Gaye pleased? No. The tiring and disciplined travelling, illness and pressure from his promoters to keep to deadlines and so on, so exacerbated the non-subservient artist that he couldn't wait for the tour to finish. To be fair, Gaye was worried to the point of distraction about the imminent birth of his second child, and worried to a lesser degree about maintaining his increased drug intake which he now relied upon to sustain him on the road. It was thanks to his loyal and determined entourage who indulged his every whim that, against all odds, the tour was honoured in full. There was little doubt that the strain of performing and touring had taken its toll on the singer; he was physically and mentally exhausted, and his body began to show the tell-tale and sad signs of cocaine misuse. Nevertheless, he was a wealthy physical wreck, and recovered in his newly acquired luxurious apartment in Brentwood, Los Angeles.

During this time there remained a problem, that of calming the vicious snipes from the media who, after seeing Gaye in concert and hearing no new material, claimed his creative juices were exhausted, having peaked with 'What's Going On' and 'Let's Get It On'. Annoyed that his talent should be questioned, let alone attacked, Marvin retaliated by claiming he had in fact finished another album – 'I think [it] is very strong and the only reason I've held it back is because I haven't been able to use the music I want. I haven't been able to find the particular kind of sound that I want to accompany what I've already recorded. When I'm close to that, and if politically I am able to go about my work in a positive manner with Motown, then I'll finish the album.' It seems unlikely he was referring to the future 'I Want You' project at this time because that, like his two previous million-plus selling albums, would involve third party inspiration, and he would again have to be bullied into recording it. More likely, he was referring to the partly-finished Sammy Davis Jnr tapes, or at the very least, some ideas he had which weren't started. However, as was typical of his turbulent life, Marvin Gaye had other things to occupy his mind at this time although for a change it was nothing he had done personally.

His name was the centre of public controversy when in 1974 Elaine Jesmer, a one-time Motown press agent responsible for Gaye's publicity, wrote a book titled *Number One With A Bullet* based around the lead character Daniel Stone who bore a remarkable resemblance to Marvin. The publication delved into the corruption within a family-owned American record company (the Gordys and Motown?) and its artists, particularly Stone and his struggles to record his own work and to control his career. It was possibly one of the first publications to tarnish Motown's squeaky clean image however loosely disguised, and was naturally a much sought after book. Following its American publication and prior to it being published elsewhere, Motown sued its publishers for libel and when unsuccessful bought the book rights presumably to prevent the film rights being sold elsewhere. But while Motown went to great lengths to protect its image, Marvin Gaye was quite unperturbed by Jesmer's work and told *Ebony* magazine – 'Elaine Jesmer pretended she was in love with me – or maybe she wasn't pretending – to extract information out of me so that she could write the book. Daniel Stone was supposed to be me. There was a lot of truth in it, but a lot of fiction also.' For example, Stone was a sexual oralist, unlike Gaye who claimed – 'I'm a dominant sexual partner usually, but she made mention in the book of some sexual activity that isn't in my character. I'm not a whore either. I'm promiscuous yes, but a very selective one.'

How typical of the singer to comment on the sexual references rather than the misleading statements about his recording career! Nevertheless, he did concede there was indeed a distinct similarity between him and Jesmer's hero – 'But I certainly wouldn't say that's an accurate description of my character because it's not. I don't think anybody could accurately describe my character because I don't think I'm even able to do that.'

On a more serious and happy note the real Marvin Gaye became a father again in September 1974 when Janis Hunter gave birth to a girl, Nona Aisha. Once more Gaye's career took a back seat as he devoted himself to his family. He again fell into the role of father and when time allowed continued with his studies, searching for answers to centuries-old questions, avidly devouring prophetical and scientific works, particularly his old favourite Carlos Castaneda, whose writings continued to fascinate and enlighten him even though certain aspects of his teachings, like his appraisal of selfmastery, made Gaye feel uneasy. Marvin: 'It takes a special kind of individual to get involved in spiritualism and meditation, and even someone who is very evolved, to accomplish these tasks.' He condemned the use of drugs as a means of mastering these objectives as he told *NME* – 'You're going to have to have something deeper than that before you can achieve any of the feats that marvellous Indian reputedly achieved.' While, on the other hand, his interest in Rastafarianism led him to condone their high drug intake although he did not approve of drug taking per se. (At this point in Gaye's career the general public was not aware of his own habit. He wouldn't talk openly about it for at least another two years.) Marvin further told *NME* – '[Rastafarians] smoke a lot of bush but they have the capacity to smoke so much because it's inbred. It started a long time ago and they're able to. Besides that, the spiritual revelations and the degree of attunement that they receive is worth it, and really shouldn't be scrutinised, because the religious overtones of their smoking far outweigh the bullshit of physical addiction. It's ridiculous to say that smoking marijuana is bad, when the only thing that can be bad about it is that you smoke yourself to death. But you can drink yourself to death, even drinking enough glasses of water can kill you. So it depends on the individual entirely. That's the message of personal freedom that the individual should have control of.'

Although the singer never claimed to possess psychic powers as such, he was, he said, able to predict the future – particularly his own and that of the world as a whole. Gaye: 'I study and amass facts, coming to the obvious conclusion that there's something very deep here that needs to be looked at from a serious point of view. I've simply made my studies and listened to people I believe to be worthy and I've thought, "Jesus Lord, it looks like they're right to me." He cited the example – 'If Atlantis went under at one time, then maybe New York did come up.'

The works of the French astrologer and physician Nostradamus, known for his prophecies and who died in 1566, particularly fascinated Gaye as he mentioned in the same *NME* interview – 'When one checks the religious people who can interpret "Revelations" properly, with the psychic people who can see beyond what we normally see and interpret the future, and even with the scientists, who are mostly atheists and don't believe in God, who will give you strict scientific data? When all this information you gather starts to pin-point a certain date and time, you know instinctively that you are on to something that isn't very nice. And all this information does correlate.' Even though the strength and authenticity of Gaye's ability to predict the future could have been due to his imagination, he was able to speak convincingly and prophetically about the infinitesimal effect of nuclear war when compared to his own inner, future vision of the earth's destruction – 'Mother Nature will wipe out most of civilisation, when she's decided she's had enough . . . When Mother Nature starts to feel a little sick, and all her oil is gone and you're poisoning her old body with nuclear waste, then she's going to decide she's feeling restless and shift a little bit, and it's going to be all over. She'll only shift for a moment, but she'll do her little number. It will be the end for most people, especially those who are ill-prepared.' However, he stressed, there would be relatively safe places on this earth should she move, and cited Canada as an example – 'Other safe places would be those parts of the world which remain relatively peaceful, where people are good. There seems to be some energy in these places that is concentrated and that will hold. There are places in America and Europe that will hold. People should be concerned with various things like living behind massive mountains on the other side of the oceans. One should be concerned with water, and where water is. Things like that are important. I wouldn't give much for England's survival. Countries that are far inland are going to be much better. It's going to be pretty rough – it's the floods, the tidal waves and so on. A giant wave coming off the Atlantic could wipe out much of the UK.'

Genius or charlatan? Well-read or full of imagination? No British journalist questioned him to find out. However, when Marvin Gaye indulged himself in these orgies of non-musical subjects during interviews, reporters have been known to wonder and comment upon his sanity – he was a musician not a scholar. It wasn't a malicious thought but one based on the effects from his drug taking, which many journalists were aware of at the time but refused to print. Like most artists Gaye was asked by his record company to grant interviews to coincide with a record's release or a pending tour, as an extra means of promotion. This free publicity, naturally enough, required the artist to talk about the subject to be advertised and not, as in the case of Gaye, his meandering beliefs about science, world annihiliation, theocentric opinions or some other diverse topic. Needless to say, he was often criticised for his attitude and the topics of conversation discussed in his interviews; several members of the media called him a 'crank' or 'eccentric'. But he merely shrugged them off, refusing to be intimidated, with – 'I don't care. I'm only speaking about my personal convictions. Nobody has to believe them, if they don't want to. However, if they choose not to then when and if anything happens, it's going to have been rather like smoking and catching cancer, and knowing you're going to die from it, and feeling twice as bad because you know you gave it to yourself. Mind you, I refuse to do anything but talk about it, so I'm ridiculous because I'll feel bad too!'

It was generally agreed that interviewing Marvin Gaye was an art in itself. For example, when he lived in London and met the media Motown/EMI warned interviewers of every possible aspect that could go wrong prior to the meeting. It wasn't that Gaye didn't want to talk, he just 'didn't get round to it'. Once the first hurdle of ensuring he did indeed intend to honour the arrangement on the right day – the timing was immaterial – the interviewer knew he was in with a chance. All interviews were booked for the afternoon, Marvin never rose before noon, needing to sleep off the night before.

The second hurdle once the reporter and Marvin Gaye had met or were connected to the phone, was the length of the interview; some would be cut short, others could last for hours. Often he would disappear into another room to make a phone call, meet visiting friends, take cocaine, or whatever he felt, leaving the journalist to wonder whether the interview was concluded or not. In one-to-one situations like this, interviewers noted he would be 'spaced out', and peer through half-closed eyes or hide behind sunglasses and be anxious to get the interview finished, but would inadvertently elongate it with his soft, slow drawl. While staying in London, Gaye, under extreme pressure from Motown/UK to honour a mutually agreed valuable interview, conducted his conversations from his bed, while the scribe sat by his feet. No, talking to Marvin was not a journalist's dream, but wherever he went they persistently pursued him with tape recorders and notebooks!

Early in 1975 Marvin Gaye's estranged wife Anna began divorce proceedings, instigating a two-year legal fight which would practically bankrupt her husband. In typical fashion Gaye turned his back on his future financial predicaments, and continued to spend money freely and lavishly. He designed and had built his own recording studio on Sunset Boulevard, near the Motown building, called 'The Marvin Gaye Recording Studio'. He intended to recoup the money spent by renting out the facilities to musicians but inexplicably this did not include anyone connected with Motown. Smokey Robinson wrote in his autobiography – 'One of the reasons Marvin got his own recording studios was because he loved the art of making records. To watch him come into a control room and lay layer upon layer of his own background voice to a recording was a truly exciting experience. I guess that kind of creative spark was kindled at the age of two when he used to sing gospel songs at his father's Church of God in Washington D.C.'

Marvin – whose earnings were probably the highest of his entire career – also opened the Righton Production company to oversee the studio's business and his other financial interests. And when Janis Hunter fell pregnant again he moved his family into a ranch fashioned on the Spanish style on several acres of land in Hidden Hills in the San Fernando Valley.

Money was also ploughed into numerous non-music businesses, like boxing, where Marvin was one of several backers of an April 1975 heavyweight exhibition featuring George Forman. He was spending money in a big way, refusing to listen to his advisers, continuing to show an irreverent respect for the dollar bill at a time when he should have been saving. He not only showed little respect for the dollar but also his family, particularly Hunter. He admitted his intentions of being the perfect father and lover had soured, marred by his need to belittle Janis whenever he could. Marvin seemed determined, intentionally or not, to destroy the happiness he had craved for with the woman he adored, and there is no doubt he idolised Janis, his madonna, the goddess of his dreams. Hunter, a light-coloured beauty, was everything he desired, needed or wanted in a woman, yet he set out to attack her innocence. He reverted to what he called his 'wild and wicked ways', forcing Hunter to retaliate. He encouraged and instigated arguments between them, he loved her as much as he hurt her. It was a no-win situation. Regrettably, all Janis wanted was his love, loyalty and devotion, and to ease his troubled life. Marvin often admitted he expected his partner in love to serve him, be totally committed to him, and in Hunter's case that included fuelling his often perverted fantasies exemplified by his instructing her to have affairs with other men. When she refused, his anger reached bursting point. In short, Marvin Gaye wanted to somehow destroy the purity and beauty Hunter brought into his life, to turn his princess into a whore. He told David Ritz – '. . . I couldn't stop picking on the relationship, bending it, twisting it, perverting it. The more I lived with Jan, the more I loved her, the more I made her miserable. It was a vicious circle, and I know, as hard as I tried, that it could never stop. I was afraid of the thought, but here was another woman, aside from Anna, destined to destroy me.'

Irrespective of what Gaye told people, Janis Hunter was committed to her partner, even during his blackest of moods. Her strong character was similar to the other influential women in his life – his wife and his mother. Thankfully, tranquillity and contentment did reappear in the Gaye household when Frankie, nicknamed 'Bubby', was born in November 1975, and with a second child to care for Gaye began thinking seriously about marriage. However, it was a move he wanted to avoid, still being sore from the breakdown of his first one. In any event, time was on his side, he could do nothing until his divorce was final.

It's probably true to say that if any future marriage was to work his wife needed to be older than him, or at the very least, his own age, and someone who refused to share his perversions. She needed to be the dominant figure ensuring his professional life ran as smoothly as the home she would provide for him. Gaye's friends told him Hunter was too young to be that influence, but in time they were proven wrong because in her own determined way she kept Marvin under control, even though she failed to wean him off drugs.

Marvin Gaye's next recorded work 'I Want You' was once again instigated by a third party, signifying that he was still incapable of starting a project alone. That is not to say since 'Let's Get It On' he hadn't attempted to recapture some of his magical inspiration, because he had. However, none grew into anything more than ideas and rough songs. Gaye fobbed off his lack of new material to journalists by claiming he now felt stifled by the record industry itself – 'The business I'm engaged in, outside the artistry of it, has not afforded me the opportunity to do any more albums than I've done.' He compared his music to that of an artist's painting which, when completed, they were compelled to witness being merchandised and handled by strangers. Gaye: 'I make lots of money on it, sure, but that isn't the first priority. If it's good and you're a good artist, and you're true to your work, the money and fame will come. Just hang on in there strong, and these forces will bless you. It's got to happen; it's law, and it always works, especially if you're talented and blessed with it.'

He accepted he had now escaped from the 'follow-on album syndrome' since 'What's Going On', because it was a project that stood entirely on its own. To a certain extent 'Let's Get It On' was the same although, of course, the theme could be used time and again. Gaye had deliberated for some time about the viability of trying to re-create the magic of both albums – 'Perhaps "What's Going On" was that good that I could have followed it with a similar album, and people would have still enjoyed it. And maybe "Let's Get It On" – was good enough that had I followed in its footsteps a little more closely, or stayed within the guidelines of it a little more musically, people would also have enjoyed that.'

Gaye wasn't worried about this indecisive situation, he was confident he had an inbuilt mechanism to create, a gift he could never fully describe or appreciate, to share with the public – 'to keep their heads and hearts strong, give them a release, a way to release the evil one. Music to play, to reminisce by, whatever the mood, we are very important people to people. I don't think we're really thought of in the right light because there are other people in the industry who are so commercially minded that the artists are closed out.'

After several arguments with Berry Gordy about his inactivity, Marvin Gaye agreed to work with Leon Ware and Arthur 'T-Boy' Ross. Gaye recalled Gordy telling him – 'Listen man, dammit, you've got to do something because you've been fooling around here for months. Now here's some material that Leon Ware went into the studios to cut, see if you like it.' Gaye had little choice but to do as Gordy wished, although the future liaison was not as unpleasant as he first thought. Marvin: 'I had known Ware for some time. I met him when he was teaming up with Diana Ross's brother 'T-Boy' who was quite prolific with his writing too. I think I met the two of them socially at a party or something like that.' Ultimately, Marvin Gaye ended up recording several songs written by Ware and Ross which were intended for their own personal albums, and with Ware wrote 'After The Dance', 'Feel All My Love Inside' and 'Since I Had You', and with 'T-Boy' Ross, 'Soon I'll Be Loving You Again'. All were already recorded and only needed Gaye to transform them into his own.

Ware, a well-respected and experienced in-house singer/composer, formed his first group The Romeos in 1954 with Ty Hunter and Lamont Dozier, before working for ABC Records for four years. In 1964 Ware joined Motown to work with The Isley Brothers and then moved to Groovesville Music as an independent producer for two years, followed by a spell at Bell Records. During 1969 he worked with Johnny Nash, Kim Weston and the Righteous Brothers before writing the 'Nuff Said' album for Ike and Tina Turner. Four years later he collaborated with Quincy Jones on the 'Body Heat' album released on A&M Records. He then returned to Motown to work with Marvin Gaye. Ware's own album 'Musical Massage' was issued in September 1976 on the Gordy label and featured Playboy magazine centrefold model Azeree being massaged by the artist on the front sleeve. Ware: 'I had actually recorded "I Want You" and "All The Way Around" and they just happened to be among the first ones Marvin and I worked on. That's why there's such a similarity between the sound of my album and "I Want You". It's similar because it was my concept that was turned over to Marvin and I couldn't have been more thrilled about it. I think I respect Marvin as a man and a talent more than anybody else in this business.'

Arthur 'T-Boy' Ross, an ex-law student, had been signed to Motown for some time but had not yet recorded his own work. 'I Want You' was his first major project and was an introduction to his pending 'Changes' album due for release in February 1979 on the Motown label. 'I Want You' was originally intended to be his album. Ross: 'But Berry Gordy explained to me it would be better if I gave the project to Marvin because it would build up my reputation better that way. And I understood how hard it would be to break a brand new artist at the time so I went along with it. Marvin was such a fine, versatile performer that I was proud to hear him doing my songs, although he didn't sing them exactly the way I wanted which is why I included "I Want You" on my album.'

Although Gaye liked Ware's songs, he didn't at the time of recording them plan to release another album devoted to emotional and physical love. He felt 'Let's Get It On' had adequately portrayed his feelings on the subject to the extent it was 'the most profound and paramount part of life', and believed the public would criticise him for using the tried and tested formula. Gaye: 'Perhaps it is boring to know that the message is the same, some might feel that I'm not creative enough to go somewhere else. But that wasn't it. It's just that I wasn't doing anything, and I didn't intend doing anything,' Nonetheless Ware, Ross and Gaye worked well together although Marvin didn't take instruction well. His working itinerary was erratic; he either walked out of the studio for no apparent reason, or was late for a session. His domestic situation was blamed because, he moaned, it was not the ideal set-up for a creative man to be involved with. While recording the album and, against Marvin's wishes, Janis Hunter sat in on some of the sessions held at his own and Motown's studios. It seems likely she attended to ensure he actually worked. Even so it took over a year just to complete the vocals!

'I Want You' was finally released as an album during March 1976, followed a month later by the album's title track which raced to number fifteen in the pop charts (no 1 R&B), while the album soared to number four (two places higher than 'What's Going On' and two rungs lower than 'Let's Get It On'). It sold in excess of one million copies in America alone yet, like his previous block-busting albums, failed to attract any Grammy Awards. The album concentrated on foreplay rather than the sex act itself, where Gaye teased and seduced his listeners into submission. It was Janis Hunter's album, he said, all the tracks were dedicated to her and expressed his feelings for her. More importantly, during the track 'Feel All My Love Inside' he proposed marriage to her. Hunter: 'Some of the tunes on the album Marvin would tell me he was singing to me and that made me feel good.'

The album's title track opened the work – intricate vocal interplay where Gaye pleaded for an affair, frustrated with a one-sided relationship, obviously depicting his careful attitude with Janis. His intentions were made perfectly obvious, a complex clash of minds.

While 'Come Live With Me Angel' – a repetitious, barely audible track – was more direct in approach. The gentle goading of co-habitation was replaced halfway through the song with 'freakish pleasures' and 'experienced company', accentuated by spasmodic heavy breathing. A profusion of guitars and keyboards dominated 'After The Dance', one of three instrumentals, although the other two both titled 'I Want You (Intro Jam)' were short. The inclusion of these instrumentals was questionable; presumably they were either album fillers or mood dictators to prepare for the following tracks. Simulated intercourse which Gaye indicated he loved to hear, thus implying his voyeuristic tendencies, somewhat dominated his proposal of marriage in 'Feel All My Love Inside', while the few seconds of the next track, the mid-paced 'I Wanna Be Where You Are', where Gaye says goodnight to his children, had the makings of a commercial track. He never explained why this song remained unfinished.

The second side of the album started with a taster of 'I Want You' which led into 'All The Way Around', a more catchy track with less seductive vocals, where Gaye attempted to tackle the complexities of a love affair, while arriving at no decision. His love of the spoken word conflicted with his multi-tracked vocals on 'Since I Had You' where once again the writhing moaning of sexual passion interrupted the song's flow. His obsession with the vocalities of intercourse had by now become aggravating and to some, unnecessary, because the listener's attention was dragged away from the lyrics. A liberal use of the bongos introduced 'Soon I'll Be Loving You Again', arranged by the established Paul Riser, which drummed home again the message of the preceding tracks. The only deviation this time had been muted, where Gaye howled like an animal in agony. The final track 'After The Dance' could have been interpreted as a continuation of 'I Want You', where once again he attempted to persuade his lady to take him to her home at the end of an evening. Certainly the hooklines here were the strongest on an album that overdosed on sexual play, in some instances superfluous to the construction of the low keyed songs.

Although Leon Ware produced the entire album, Berry Gordy and Marvin Gaye were afforded the courtesy credit of executive producers, while 'T-Boy' Ross and Hal Davis were acknowledged as associate producers. Gaye: '"I Want You" was a quick album, an album I made without much enthusiasm.' He felt this way because Berry Gordy had bullied him into it, and because it had done little to alleviate the problems that existed between them – 'Motown keep me mad all the time by not treating me properly. I'm like a fine race horse, but they don't treat me like one. At least a race horse gets a rub down after a race. I don't even get that! I had no plans to produce anything on myself because ninety per cent of the time, when I get mad I get unproductive.' Despite his feelings, he said he was pleased with the album as a whole, particularly three tracks – 'After The Dance', 'Come Live With Me Angel' and the title song. He believed these were the superior songs and had sold the album. However, what had excited him the most was the record sleeve upon which he had spent a great deal of time. Gaye: 'As part of the package one has to consider the cover, one that will be interesting because I like to bring something into people's lives. I didn't simply want to use a photo, so I went to great lengths of buying a painting. I even held up the cover because I wanted the picture to be right. It had pretty good connotations and it was ethnic and was something that people who are not coloured or black, can look at and say "here's a study of us".'

Regrettably, not everyone shared his enthusiasm. The original 1976 painting by Ernie Barnes was loaned, not bought as Gaye indicated, from the Los Angeles Company of Art. It depicted a Saturday night 'hop' with dancers and musicians cavorting their elongated bodies across a dance floor. None had their eyes opened as they sang, drank and danced through a rather dull, dark background of gaudy colours showing banners hanging from the ceiling announcing a dance contest, a welcome to The Sugar Shack advertising 'Big Daddy' Rucker, Gaye's new hit 'I Want You' and radio WMPG. Once again no lyric sheet was included in the record's packaging and sleeve notes were also omitted, confirming the speed with which the project was completed.

With this album's release Marvin Gaye was for the first time prepared to listen to his critics. In the past one aspect of criticism which had depressed him greatly was the media's inability to grasp the full meaning of, and the intentions behind, the subjects he was trying to expose. And 'I Want You' similarly confused the reviewers; the delicate melody and lyric was, he felt, lost to them, as they continued to mourn his past music with its basic, spontaneous, easy to understand slam-bang effect. Gaye: 'People in the arts should be listened to, particularly if they're legitimate. They visit and see a lot of people and pick up a lot of energies and vibes, and somehow the truth seems to filter through because of their association with so many people and situations.' He was also wary of possible retribution when it was realised he had once again used another's input. It's quite possible this train of thought urged him to comment – 'Leon Ware contributed almost as much as I did!'

When, after a lengthy wait, British journalist Cliff White succeeded in interviewing the singer in his Knightsbridge hotel suite for *NME* in 1976, the 'I Want You' reviews were discussed. Gaye said he had not received good reviews from England and cited one in particular – White's own review. 'Gaye: "You did it?" White: "Yes, I must confess it was [me]. Am I now going to be thrown out?" I ask half-jokingly, although you can never be too sure these days. Anyway, no panic, Marvin is a gentleman. Gaye: "No, I'm not the type. I'm not vindictive. But I must tell you it was a very fair review . . . because, you see, many times when you hear . . . when you're writing a review you have to figure that although an artist may be disappointing, think of the work behind it."'

During the time spent with Marvin in the hotel suite White noted – 'He spends a lot of time gazing absently across the rooftops as he speaks, perhaps focusing on the distant chimneys of Battersea Power Station, radiating the aura of a guru who's about to wax mysterious and levitate himself sideways out of the window. At other times, he turns inwards, on the room and on himself, sitting with head bowed, playing idly with the stem of his wine glass – or slowly smoothing the creases in the table cloth, giving me the impression of a haunted victim or a condemned man. There's undeniably an unreal, slow-motion atmosphere pervading the whole conversation. His speech is not slurred; on the contrary, he had a clear precise voice, higher than I'd anticipated – but the conversation is erratic.'

Before 1975 ended Marvin Gaye was persuaded to appear in concert again. This time he stunned his audience, not with his performance but his shaven head, his protest against the incarceration of Rubin 'Hurricane' Carter, who was serving a prison term for a murder he claimed he didn't commit. Gaye: 'I don't know why I shaved my head – I'm as crazy as any of us artists, I suppose. Most of us are a bit touched!' The concert, held in November, was staged in San Francisco and the proceeds went to the Glide Memorial Church, headed by the Reverend Cecil Williams. Gaye appeared on stage wearing a white suit and was backed by The Gentlemen's Quartet. The shaven look lasted for as long as it took his hair to re-grow!

By the New Year 1976 it was apparent Marvin Gaye was once again in financial difficulties. Touring was the quick answer but promoters were reluctant to work with him because of his habit of cancelling performances at the eleventh hour. However, one promoter took the chance and booked a date in Denver, Colorado. Motown insisted he perform. International journalist David Nathan attended and reported that no one knew quite what to expect – 'His stage appearances are rare events because [we understand] he prefers to work in the studio and at home. However, he offered an excellent selection of material from his three major albums – his latest "I Want You" set, "Let's Get It On", and his historic "What's Going On". Aided on occasion by two dancers and with a fine orchestra with tunes like "Come Get To This", "Trouble Man" and, seated at the piano, "Inner City Blues", "God Is Love" and "What's Going On". His rendition of "Save The Children" was superb and it's only when you see the man in person that you can fully appreciate his vocal capability. Earlier he had everyone swooning with "Let's Get It On" and his sex appeal is unquestionable – it's more sensual appeal than anything else but he certainly gives Al Green a run for his money when it comes down to getting to the ladies. Closers were "Distant Lover", "I Want You", "After The Dance" and "I Wanna Be Where You Are", and the only point to raise regarding the presentation was Marvin's disappearance from the stage for over five minutes whilst he completed a change of clothes – from black to white. The necessity for doing such is questionable. But overall, the man is a star and the quality he possesses – a certain magic that is strictly his own – came over with no problem. The only adverse comments we heard pertain to the fact that the man doesn't leap all over the stage, but then songs like "Distant Lover" hardly call for acrobatics!'

The next time Marvin Gaye performed on stage was in London, England, but it wasn't a visit he had planned . . .

# 8. You're All I Need to Get By

*I've never been called 'boy' so many damned times in my life.*
(Marvin Gaye)

*He sat on the couch, Janis at his side, smoking a joint.*
(Jim Hegarty)

*I got something more than I dared dream of . . . from English fans.*
(Marvin Gaye)

*I knew . . . he really wasn't as stubborn as people made out.*
(Dave Godin)

Anna Gordy Gaye's divorce proceedings were now well under way but despite this Marvin Gaye continued to see her at regular intervals. It's thought he didn't encourage an amiable relationship between them and when they met communication was strained. It's possible he didn't truly believe she would see the divorce through to its bitter end or that she would demand financial support from him. However, his daydreaming came to a sudden halt when, at Anna's lawyer's hand, he faced imprisonment during 1976 for non-payment of $6,000 in child-support and alimony.

When the warrant was issued for Gaye's arrest he had no money to pay the debts. Reputedly Motown bailed him out (Gordy to pay Gordy?) and it was suggested that he leave America for a time. A European tour was arranged to start in September 1976 with promoter Jeffrey Kruger of Ember Concerts to include Marvin's first major visit to Britain in ten years. To ensure the tour ran smoothly Gaye's entourage included Wally Cox, his sister Zeola and Janis Hunter. Motown/EMI had prepared for the tour well in advance, although not believing its good fortune to actually have him on home soil and likewise hoping he would respect their wishes by undertaking some promotional activities to help boost his record sales. To coincide with the visit the company re-promoted 'I Want You' and released 'The Best Of Marvin Gaye' containing fourteen tracks (including 'That's The Way Love Is', 'Too Busy Thinking About My Baby', 'What's Going On, 'Let's Get It On' etc) to become a number fifty-six hit. London was fly-posted with his tour dates and radio stations up and down the country were swamped with his material. No stone was left unturned for Motown's recording giant. 'After The Dance' was the current UK single – after creeping into the American top eighty and the R&B top twenty – and 'I Heard It Through The Grapevine' was issued as the flipside to 'I'm Gonna Make You Love Me' by Diana Ross and the Supremes and The Temptations.

To guarantee Marvin Gaye received the warmest of welcomes at London's Heathrow, Motown/EMI announced the flight details through the media and enticed fans to welcome him personally by giving all attendees at the airport free 'I Want You UK Tour '76' tee-shirts to wear. Gaye was scheduled to arrive at 8 a.m. from Los Angeles on Sunday, 26 September. Researcher Jim Hegarty: 'Marvin arrived late, but his band came in on time. His charming sister Zeola accompanied them. At midday Marvin and Janis arrived. He wore flared jeans, cream tee-shirt and cardigan, and talked for a few minutes before leaving in a black limousine for his hotel, The Carlton Towers.'

Marvin Gaye's opening night was at London's Royal Albert Hall, opposite Kensington Gardens, on 27 September where he performed at 6.30 p.m. and 9.15 p.m. Further dates included The Apollo, Glasgow (28th); The Empire, Liverpool (30th); ABC, Manchester (1 October); Bingley Hall, Birmingham (2nd); and The Winter Gardens, Bournemouth (5th). Another two shows were added on 3 October at the London Palladium due to an overwhelming demand for tickets.

His support act throughout the tour was Motown's newly signed, distinguished songstress Rose Banks, sister of Sly Stone, a former DJ and record producer who led his group The Family Stone through a number of soul-laced psychedelic singles like 'Dance To The Music' (1967), and three American chart toppers, 'Everyday People' (1969), 'Thank You' (1970) and 'Family Affair' (1971). Banks joined her brother's band as a keyboardist for a time before embarking on a solo career. Her husband, Hamp 'Bubba' Banks recorded a selection of songs with her and arranged for a Motown executive to hear them. Banks: 'When I first arrived I felt part of the family but it seemed they weren't pushing my album as much as I'd have liked. Basically, I wanted Rose Banks to have had the support of Diana Ross. I mean, who knew her when she first arrived. It seems I'll always be known as Sly Stone's sister but I wanted to establish memories of my own.' The album, 'Rose', had been British-released in July, followed by the 'Darling Baby' single a month later. Banks rarely came into contact with Gaye as, she said, he tended to keep himself private, spending most of his time confined to his hotel room. He avoided arriving at theatres early, preferring to arrive within minutes of performing. Regrettably, once Banks had completed touring with Gaye she left Motown and reputedly retired from the entertainment business.

Prior to Marvin Gaye's British debut in London, Motown/EMI hosted an exclusive reception in his honour at the plush, expensively decorated Carlton Towers Hotel's Ballroom, where tables threatened to collapse under a mountainous array of food including specialties iced in aspic, laced in rich sauces and mouthwatering creams. Statues carved in ice melted slowly while every type of drink was readily available. Unobtrusively smart waiters attended tables or offered trays of cocktails to guests dressed in evening dress, jeans, sweatshirts and track suits. And it was here that the American superstar, dressed in a three-piece, peach-coloured suit that emphasised his athletic build and fuller stomach, met the British media, publishers, clinging photographers, promoters and others who had wheedled their way in after discovering a loophole in the invitation-only reception, later hailed as the year's finest. The attendees were astonished to be warmly greeted by an unassuming thirty-five-year-old Marvin Gaye who looked younger than his years due to his smooth, almost transparent pale brown face, sharp darting eyes and inaudible voice. A quiet, shy Janis Hunter wearing little make-up and a simply cut summer dress stayed in the background, preferring to let Gaye enjoy the company of his guests. During the evening the singer sat next to Hunter at his table to drink white wine and nibble white meat, while music softly emanated from a discreetly placed disco console. The lack of Motown material was noticeable because Motown/EMI had been forewarned of Gaye's dispute with the American company. At one point during the evening he and Janis returned to their suite, while company personnel covered for him. When they later returned, Gaye placed a pair of bongos between his knees to give an impromptu exhibition even though the majority of the guests had already departed. Dave Godin and Marvin Gaye were reunited at the reception and went on to spend much time together. Godin's general impression had changed little from their first meeting in 1964 – 'His wry sense of humour, his tremendous and quite genuine interest in the British soul scene, and his own thoughtfulness, remain as they were.' The singer's soulmate recalled a particular incident during their first meeting when he had attempted to promote Gaye's career in England – 'Try as hard as we could, it was impossible to get any bookings for him to appear anywhere. Nobody wanted to know, and although we didn't tell him this in so many words, he must have put two and two together in his mind. When he left he complained: "I've never been called 'boy' so many damned times in my life as I have here on this visit" and I think any explanation was too late to heal the hurt. Even the word "woman" in those days was a taboo word in black circles and always one had to be sure to use the polite term "lady" if one didn't want to give offence. "Negress" was even worse, and Marvin couldn't believe his eyes when he saw the word freely employed in the British press to describe the female performers at Motown. So, in my opinion, another Motown artist had come to Britain and had returned without having conquered.' Happily, Godin laughed, that situation had drastically changed now. Marvin Gaye had returned to London to be greeted by a legion of eager, loyal and enthusiastic fans which, he said, would 'slay 'em back home', where it was widely thought he would fail abysmally in Europe.

One point, however, did bother Godin and that was his friend's ability to handle the label of 'international star' and all that went with it. Godin: 'I hope he's still the same guy who took such care to help Hattie Littles (a blues singer signed to the Gordy label in 1963 and who toured with Gaye), who had infinite time and patience with his fans at receptions, and who, when I told him I was just too tired to go on to that party with him, understood and ordered drinks instead. I knew then that he really wasn't as stubborn as people made out but someone who keeps his real self private and secure.' Godin had little cause to worry at this time – a few years on his worries would be justified – because Marvin did show an interest and tolerance with his fans. This is exemplified by Jim Hegarty who visited him at The Carlton Towers Hotel – 'I knocked on Marvin's hotel door and moments later Janis opened it and asked me in. She said Marvin was in the shower and would be out soon. She offered me a drink and as she was talking about this trip being her first to London, Marvin appeared wearing an African robe, his hair still wet. He shook my hand, and was kind and human, signed autographs for me and sang a few lines of "Your Unchanging Love" after I said it was my favourite song. He sat on the couch, Janis at his side, smoking a joint but didn't offer any to me. I want to stress that. Before leaving I asked Marvin if I could have something of his. He thought for a minute and said, "How about my beard comb?" I thanked them for their time and Marvin thanked me for my love and support.' Gaye: 'The truth is I didn't believe the reception or the true, honest vibes and feelings, and I got something more than I ever expected or dared dream of getting from English fans.'

So, this then was the man who confidently strode out onto the darkened stage at London's Royal Albert Hall on 27 September 1976 to meet the British public. It was an historic and highly charged event, the atmosphere was subdued yet electrifying, the audience curious to see the man behind the music. Many were quick to criticise, while the majority devoured every note he played and sang, every word he spoke. Gaye's nervousness and awkwardness were overcome as the opening bars of 'Let's Get It On' were heard. The appreciation shown at the close of the song encouraged him to relax and warm to the standing-room only audience. Numerous artists have 'died' playing at this arena-like monument because the acoustics were unsuitable for modern day performing equipment. However after a handful of feedback 'squeaks' Gaye's sound was modified to a near-perfect pitch. When he had digested the uproar from his opening number, the music moved on while he familiarised himself with the stage to coo and groove to the women in the audience. Then he shed his green jacket, yellow tie and waistcoat to boogie with two dancers before leaving them to fill the void as he re-dressed to play 'Trouble Man' at the piano. As soon as he was seated members of the audience clambered up onto the high stage to touch and kiss him, much to his amusement. The mood changed, Marvin put on his yellow knitted hat, and introduced a somewhat jumbled medley of his solo hits like 'Ain't That Peculiar', 'You're A Wonderful One', 'Little Darling (I Need You)' and 'I Heard It Through The Grapevine'. Although very well received, the audience would have preferred these songs to have been performed in full. The dancers now likewise wearing yellow hats re-appeared, whereupon Gaye momentarily joined them for some casual foot tapping before all threw their hats into the audience at the end of the routine. The mood changed again as he relaxed into his 'What's Going On' project, during which the audience sat motionless, hypnotised by his music. A further medley was introduced, that featuring his duets and Florence Lyles took the place of Gaye's partners to sing a handful of favourites like 'Ain't Nothing Like The Real Thing', 'Ain't No Mountain High Enough' and 'You're All I Need To Get By'. The Marvin Gaye legend was real, the public welcomed him with open arms, and this scene was repeated up and down the country and throughout Europe.

At this time Motown/EMI was unaware of the extent of Gaye's arguments with Motown. The company didn't, at this point, realise Gaye felt strongly against Berry Gordy and *his* attitude, *not* Motown itself. When he later raged to the British press about the situation, Gaye said 'What's Going On' was the brunt of one disagreement – '[Berry Gordy] made me tame down some of the political content. I'm allowed to write virtually what I want, but it's toned down somewhat . . . Berry is so control-conscious and power-orientated, and I feel I am an artist and not meant to be treated as a marionette.'

Through Gaye's interviews it became apparent that these disagreements arose when he was unable to have his own way, and he vented his temper on Gordy, who, to his credit, more than once turned a blind eye to the artist's antics. Should Gordy be forced to stand his ground on an issue – often to benefit Gaye in the long run – it angered Marvin sufficiently to tell his version to the media, even though such a move was not always a wise one. And it was during this visit that the British press gained its first inkling of a rift between artist and record boss, although whenever possible Motown/EMI encouraged Marvin to speak about his visit and his recent professional past. Subsequently, his quotes would be ambiguous and be something like – 'I've been touring quite a bit in the States for the last two and a half years. Well, not as much as most American artists do, but I have been able to make a living.' However, he was genuinely sincere when he said he was touched by his public's reaction, particularly after the long absence from the British stage – 'I'm so happy to see the response is or has been what it is because in my early years I was never a visual performer. I was a struggling performer in the States and I didn't feel that audience reaction. Now it seems to be at the level that I can appreciate it as an artist.' He said he was particularly astounded at the reception because he had been advised his European record sales were low. Gaye: 'I didn't get paid a lot of money in American royalties for English record sales. The fact that I'm sold out on most of my British performances has obviously nothing to do with the fact that I don't sell records! Actually when I arrived in England to find out I'd not only sold out the tour but that an extra show had been added, it made me wonder what the hell was going on. [Not selling records here] signified to me that not many people were buying records, so there was no point in touring Europe as much as I'd always wanted to.' He also claimed that when he asked Motown personnel about his overseas business he would be told – 'Yeh, you're probably right, you have sold records.' Gaye: 'Then they'll go on not paying me my English royalties and I'll be happy like dumb artists are supposed to be.' It was never proven whether this statement was true or not but it's highly unlikely that overseas record sales did not at some point show up on his royalty statements unless, of course, his contract differed drastically from other Motown acts.

When American artists toured abroad they usually relied on the tour promoter and/or local record company to advise on their shows' content because European audiences flocked to hear familiar repertoire, and not album tracks and songs confined to the American market. Marvin Gaye used this system although he refused to sing some of his most popular Sixties tracks in their entirety. Marvin: 'I got a list of songs from my promoter. He told me all the tracks that were popular in England and I just put them into medley form for a few minutes because I hadn't done them in years. In fact, when I sing them in the States people go for popcorn and hot dogs. The only way you can perform an old record in the States is if you are very animated about it because Americans don't want memories. They're not nostalgic people. So, I can't understand why British audiences want to hear the old stuff because to me some songs are very painful, especially those with Tammi Terrell. For the most part though they [Americans] don't want to hear a bunch of old material, they want to think very progressively. We're a very progressive-minded society, if not an aggressive-minded society. We don't have a lot of time to think about the past because we're trained that way basically, and regimented like that.'

While in England Marvin Gaye agreed to conduct interviews from his hotel room, when he talked openly on a wide range of subjects. However, one topic that arose time and again was that of his back catalogue of music including what he called 'his best work' and that Motown would never see it – 'I don't think Motown would handle this work correctly and I don't think they deserve it. Without sounding too petulant I don't think I'm treated properly.' He elaborated to *NME* – 'I have so many albums in me and so many ideas that I can do stuff on just about anything and make a product of it, a complete statement. I have that gift. But I won't give these innovations away for nothing. Because that's how our society is constructed, and although I don't believe in it, I'm not a fool either. So I'd rather do nothing.'

In the same interview he stressed he had a respect for music that few musicians had, and it had been difficult to find fellow artists who shared his respect – 'If I ever find those musicians we will play music that the world will never forget as long as there's a world. And I won't do my music until I find them and if I never find them my son will do it for me. I have only scraped the beginning. I have a lot of music in me. I have written a lot of music that's unpublished that I think is great. But I cannot afford to do it.' At this time, the singer had little unreleased finished material in hand, so it's unclear to pinpoint what work he was referring to. On the other hand, as is more likely, perhaps he was allowing his imagination to work overtime. However, Gaye's son, Marvin III, did in fact follow in his musical footsteps, but it would take him five years after his father's death to prepare a portfolio to present to British record companies. The resemblance to his father was eerie, although the repertoire was typical mid-Eighties and could conceivably be the route Gaye himself would have taken should he have lived.

Several high profile promotional activities were arranged by Motown/EMI to ensure Gaye was regularly featured in the press during his 1976 stay. However, one appearance was largely unpublicised upon the company's instructions because it was felt he could have been accused of giving preferential treatment to his race, while another source felt he would garner adverse media attention by supporting ethnic minorities in the semi-volatile environment of an integrated London area. All Gaye did was to visit Ladbroke Grove, one of the city's highly cosmopolitan bed-sit areas where he spent time at a children's centre in Powis Square. Not all the kids knew him as he later recalled with a smile – 'A youngster stared at me and asked, "Are you Mohammed Ali?!"' – He then visited the Mangrove Restaurant to talk to the leaders of local black communities, followed by a short stay at the Black People's Information Centre and the Metro Club where he was scheduled to lecture the youngsters. The talk was aborted when Gaye opted to play table tennis and sign autographs instead. As the afternoon drew to a close, the singer dressed handsomely and expensively in a fur-collared leather coat, returned to the Mangrove Restaurant for a meal of rice, peas and curry.

Marvin Gaye's appearance at the London Palladium in October 1976 was spectacular, emotionally special and recorded for future album release. The splendid, revered theatre in the heart of London's West End is one of the world's most prestigious, and is used for various types of entertainment: mostly musicals and television spectaculars.

The theatre has strict rules regarding the calibre of act who will grace its stage; for example, rock and punk bands are prohibited. So, for an artist to appear there is quite a professional triumph, possibly second only to performing at the Royal Albert Hall. With this in mind Marvin Gaye gave one of his finest performances of the whole tour there. He stunned his audience, the adrenalin swept from stage to arena until finally both were exhausted. However, following the performance one journalist suggested the strain of this debut had seen Marvin and his entire band 'doped up' on stage. Instantly he denied it then added – 'I've not smoked a lot in the past year and a half, but I've been drinking a bit though.' The journalist was probably right in his observation but Gaye was not prepared to agree, adhering to Motown/EMI's wishes that his public image should be untarnished. However, he did concede his body had taken a beating from junk food, and exhaustion because he found sleeping difficult. Gaye: 'When the moment finally comes to sleep, I fight it. Every day of my life I've fought up to that last drop-off into sleep because I don't want to be there.' Gaye's sleeping habits were highly erratic anyway. Like Stevie Wonder, time had no meaning to him, he had little regard for the clock and those who worked by one. He would work and play until he dropped, sleep and eat whenever he wanted, and constantly refused to acknowledge day or night. Probably the most aggravating aspect of Wonder's lifestyle was his friends were at his beck and call twenty-four hours a day.

Gaye then told *NME* – 'I've also done many seven-day fasts which I do just to create control within myself. But there's more for me to do, and much more strength for me to get, and much more discipline to be had, and much more study to do in survival.' Using nature as an example, he rambled on – 'Being able to recognise what plants and roots can be eaten, because those are the sort of things that one will have to know in order to live. There'll be no grocery stores and one will have to know how to test water for radioactivity because lots of water, food and plants will be poisoned.'

'Live! At The London Palladium' was released in March 1977, his second 'live' album in three years. Nonetheless it reached the American top five. Three sides of the record accurately captured the magic and atmosphere of those stunning performances including his three medleys – pre-'What's Going On', his Seventies work and his duets with Florence Lyles. The fourth side contained one eleven-minute studio dance track 'Got To Give It Up' written by Gaye and recorded in Los Angeles. This poorly orchestrated disco tune, with his brother Frankie and Janis Hunter (it was the only time she was allowed to sing with him) on back-up vocals, was one of Gaye's most exciting performances in a long time as the music was entirely different to his most recent work. He had been under pressure from Motown for some time to cash-in on the disco boom where the company had enjoyed two American chart toppers – Diana Ross's 'Love Hangover' and Thelma Houston's 'Don't Leave Me This Way' – plus a slew of club hits, and dancefloor favourites from William Goldstein. Berry Gordy's artists competed hungrily against the disco boom led by Gloria Gaynor, Donna Summer, the Bee Gees, Van McCoy, KC and the Sunshine Band and a host of acts who contributed to this relatively new and often monotonous musical explosion. Marvin's contribution was a reluctant move although he had nothing against dancing itself – 'People don't dance enough. What people should do is study their roots, they should incorporate their roots as they take themselves back. It's good for the soul. You have your different feelings which you communicate through the dance, from your soul. And whatever your soul does, this is how your dance comes out. That's why everyone does different dances, the Indians and the Irish, and the Scottish, and the Africans, everyone does their own. In Africa they have their little different dances, tribal things, and it's very good for you physically for relieving tension, for letting your emotions out, for expressing sexual desires or feelings, for getting rid of inhibitions, the dance is very necessary in society.'

Unfortunately 'Got To Give It Up' was not a single that would be remembered as a highlight of the disco movement because it lacked the musical depth and fullness of its competitors. However, it was a song to which Marvin gave a lot of thought. Gaye: 'It's a funk tune meaning it's got a chant to it. It's got a round-type of overplay, like, at the end it's got two chants going simultaneously and the bass line is hypnotic. Straight disco music is more monotonous.' He played piano on the track and credited Bugsy Wilcox as drummer, Jack Ashford, tambourinist and Johnny McGhee as guitarist. 'Got To Give It Up (Parts I and II)' was released in March 1977 to become another million seller and a number one US hit in both the pop and R&B charts and when issued in Britain it reached number seven, his third-biggest selling UK single behind 'I Heard It Through The Grapevine' (no 1 in 1969) and 'Too Busy Thinking About My Baby' (no 5 in 1969).

Once again Marvin Gaye had total control over his finished work, this time the concept of 'Live! At The London Palladium' and the double-sleeved package design featuring Richard Young and Hiro Ito's photographs. The front sleeve showed the singer in a full-length, legs apart pose taken on stage as he wailed into the hand-held microphone in front of the large word 'Live' situated below his name which was centred at the top of the sleeve.

While Gaye was basking in his number one success, his third duettist Kim Weston had just left the cast of the musical *Selma* when Detroit's newly-elected Mayor Coleman persuaded her to head a series of training programmes for the city's young people. Therefore she was unable to maintain regular contact with her ex-singing partner because of her workload and because she didn't know Janis Hunter that well – 'And knowing that Marvin had marital problems before, I didn't like to push myself towards him. He came to Detroit and emceed a programme, and later he was not far from Detroit and I went to see him, but I wasn't really able to keep up with him.'

During the same month as 'Live! At The London Palladium' was released Anna Gordy Gaye divorced her husband and the settlement was unusual to say the least. She had asked for $1 million, and knowing that Gaye had no assets at all, the judge agreed with his lawyer Curtis Shaw's suggestion that he could pay a total of $600,000 to his wife with his next album (his advance: $305,000, album's earnings: $295,000). Anna agreed and the divorce was granted on those terms, leaving Gaye free to marry Janis Hunter.

Months later, Marvin was again at the centre of a financial dispute. *Variety* magazine reported that four of his musicians had alleged he had not paid them for a year. They took him to court and were awarded approximately $196,800 in unpaid wages. The outcome was not published, so it's unclear whether the musicians were paid or not. However, Marvin Gaye seemed unperturbed. He was due to work

The Fifties doo-wop group The Moonglows featuring
Harvey Fuqua (right) and minus Marvin Gaye. He joined
the revamped group which recorded for Chess Records
© Wiltshire Music

One of Marvin
Gaye's first pub-
licity shots show-
ing a 'killer-diller'
moody image
© 1963 Motown/
EMI

Marvin Gaye and his fourth duettist Tammi Terrell. This publicity shot promoted their biggest UK hit, 'The Onion Song', in 1969
© Motown/EMI

Marvin Gaye performing during a Seventies concert, wearing his
beloved woollen hat which would later hide his balding crown
© *Blues & Soul*

Marvin Gaye broke his vow when Tammi Terrell died and recorded
one album with Diana Ross. Titled 'Diana & Marvin', issued in
1973, the album spawned several hit singles, particularly in Britain
© Motown/EMI

Berry Gordy, owner of Motown, and his daughter
Hazel Joy, following her marriage to Jermaine Jackson.
Picture taken at the Beverly Hills Hotel
© Motown/EMI

Marvin Gaye appeared on stage in 1975 with a shaven head as a protest against the incarceration of Rubin 'Hurricane' Carter. The new look lasted for as long as it took his hair to grow back!
© *Blues & Soul*

Showing his drumming expertise, Marvin Gaye gave an impromptu performance at his 1976 reception held at The Carlton Towers Hotel, London

Florence Lyles joined Marvin on the Royal Albert Hall stage to sing
a medley of hits made famous by his various singing partners
© *Blues & Soul*

After cancelling one British tour, Marvin and his son
'Bubby' finally arrived at London's Heathrow to honour
the rescheduled dates in 1980
Photographer: Peter Vernon

Diana Ross and Marvin Gaye joined Stevie Wonder on stage at
Wembley Arena, London, in September 1980
Photographer: Justin Thomas

The front sleeve for 'In Our Lifetime', Marvin's last Motown
album issued in 1981. The singer sketched the artwork before
commissioning a UK artist to complete the design
Sharon Davis Collection

News of Marvin's sudden death on 1 April 1984 hit the
British press within hours. The world mourned the
tragedy while Gay Snr sat in a prison cell
Jeff Tarry Collection

with Dionne Warwick and was asked to produce ex-Supreme Mary Wilson's debut solo album. Wilson's husband/manager Pedro Ferrer, who was blamed for the demise of The Supremes, had negotiated a new recording contract with Motown for Mary ensuring her $1 million a year for the next five years. As was to be expected, Gaye failed to honour both commitments. Wilson generously explained – 'It didn't happen because he had some work of his own to do, so we decided to look around for another producer. We chose Hal Davis.' However, the Wilson/Gaye liaison was feasible because Pedro Ferrer told British reporters he had taken over Marvin's management. Ferrer: 'I plan to bring him back to the UK because he was so knocked out when he came the last time, and he wants to come back as soon as possible. At the moment he's finishing up another album in the States, in fact, he's going through a productive period at the moment. Then I'd like to put a show together with him and Mary – A Gentleman And A Lady – like Dionne Warwick and Isaac Hayes did.'

Presumably Gaye's 'productive period' referred to him working on the 'divorce settlement' album although that wasn't made clear at the time. However, what was clear was his reluctance to re-marry, but he knew if he refused to make a commitment, Janis Hunter would despair of his intentions and leave him taking their children with her. He was now caught between having the freedom he craved while wanting to be a responsible family man with the children he loved. Gaye did the right thing, and following an autumn tour with Luther Vandross he married Janis Hunter in October 1977 in a secret ceremony in New Orleans. Gaye's friends and family felt the union would stabilise him, encouraging him to become reliable and thoughtful with his family and in his career. Was he happy with his choice? Not really. Marvin said that marriage had made his relationship with Janis different, he felt it was deteriorating, yet prior to this they had enjoyed each other and the romantic thoughts of marrying. Hunter rose above the complications to cope with her husband's idiosyncrasies and shoddy behaviour, while he told the media – 'There are a lot of things I desire. I desire peace and happiness and love and understanding. That sounds ridiculous to a lot of people. "Who is this guy wanting all that?" Another trouble maker.'

# 9. You Can Leave, but it's Going to Cost You

*I wouldn't ask any other person to adapt to my lifestyle.*

(Marvin Gaye)

*['Here, My Dear'] is not as original or inventive as some of his earlier works.*

(The Daily Mirror)

*Marvin remains uninhibited in his subject matter and the portrayal of his feelings.*

(Curtis Shaw)

*[Marvin] recently swore that [Motown] would have to kill him to get him back into the studio.*

(The Temptations)

Marvin Gaye was destined to face another period of frustration and indecision; some said he was a broken man, a man without a purpose. He couldn't settle at home nor adapt to a committed family life, and spent much time travelling around, staying with friends or being alone. Although his divorce from Anna Gordy was settled he still had to honour the financial commitment as decreed by the judge – that of paying her the advance and royalties from his next album. Added to this, bankruptcy charges were instigated against him from which he had no escape. Curtis Shaw told *Rolling Stone* magazine that he attributed the singer's disastrous plight to hiring unqualified friends and members of his family – '[He delegated] duties to people who were incompetent. I couldn't even get Marvin to hire an accountant. In fact, the Federal Bankruptcy Judge told Marvin in court, "Mr Gaye, we are all working hard to get you out of all this terrible trouble but I already know the pattern." '

Yes, indeed Marvin Gaye was troubled, and friends worried for his welfare, believing him to be on the verge of a nervous breakdown.

Also, he was in no hurry to finish his 'divorce settlement' album – parts of which were already on master tape – and it took friends months of persuading to get him back into the studios to complete it, thereby honouring his debt to Anna. He later said he had deliberately taken his time because of a new spate of disagreements with Motown – 'I was involved in some political fighting with Motown and then the Federal Court felt the album was part of my estate for bankruptcy. At first I thought I'd put out a lot of garbage for the album because all I had to give was one album. There was no stipulation that it had to be a good one, so Anna was taking her chances here.' However, part way through the recording sessions at his studio he changed his mind – 'I thought of my fans when I started recording. The more I cut, the more I got involved. After a certain point I forgot I was mad and angry, and did some decent work. The result was, I think, pretty fair. I listened to it for over a year and I felt poor when I realised I wasn't going to make any money from it.'

Many said it was a hefty pay-off for a marriage particularly as Gaye speculated, but never confirmed, that Berry Gordy had financially helped his sister in the court case. Uncharacteristically, Marvin was not bitter about the action, although he fervently disagreed with the legal structure surrounding divorce proceedings as a whole – 'I like the institution of marriage, although this album makes it look as if I don't. There's a terrible imbalance with the whole divorce thing and I don't like it. It doesn't matter who's right or wrong, the man must pay the wife everything. Pay for the divorce and give over to her the custody of the children, and yet the man can still take care of his child because a father can be a mother too. American law cannot see that and it's horrible.'

The 'divorce' album was titled 'Here, My Dear' and contained cynical, personal statements from Gaye, intimate details concerning his two wives although occasionally it's difficult for the listener to distinguish the difference between the two. The thematic work was devoted to discovering and sharing love, the loss of that love and the bitterness and pain caused by that loss. In other words, it was a breakdown of his fourteen-year-old marriage and of the joy in discovering a new love. Due to its intense personal nature, the album was, for a change, Gaye's own work (although this was later disputed) with the exception of three tracks – 'Sparrow' and 'Everybody Needs Love' which he wrote with Ed Townsend, and 'Anger' with Townsend and Delta Ashby. Quite possibly more people were involved than the three mentioned, but all he would say on the subject was – 'The album was recorded under a certain amount of strain and I don't like to work under those conditions. It was a painful necessity, best done and best forgotten.' London DJ Graham Canter: 'Marvin said, and I think the quote was, "At least I've got the darned album away. Let her have her money." He was talking about Anna, and he never spoke to me about her again.'

When the recordings were completed Gaye insisted that Anna visit the studios to hear them and irrespective of her feelings afterwards she maintained her dignified silence. It was obviously distressing for her to hear their private life reiterated in detail for public consumption, yet Gaye was adamant he had done nothing wrong – 'Anna is a very beautiful person, she's great . . . and it was a very painful and bitter situation that left me somewhat frustrated and beaten a bit . . . I just felt I'd write about what was true . . . I would not like to suggest this would hurt Anna because I'd love to see some happiness in her life.' He also insisted he had included both sides of their marriage, the bitter tracks that stung and the respectful songs that portrayed their wonderful love. Gaye: 'The trouble with marriage is that one has to put up with little differences and it's these things you have to look out for because they eventually become monumental things. There are great people and there are people who aspire to greatness. If one's mate isn't really of the same mind and feeling, then I can't see it working. And my way of thinking is such that I wouldn't ask any other person to adapt to my lifestyle.'

'Here, My Dear' was simultaneously released in America and England during December 1978 because when Motown/EMI was notified of the pending US release date it shipped in five thousand copies to sell with over-stickered UK record prefixes to stem import sales which would not be registered as British sales, thus losing valuable chart points. British pressings were then made available under the deluxe TMSP series when the imports were exhausted. On both sides of the Atlantic many Gaye fans were appalled with the concept; they were tired of his self-inflicted depression, the impassive songs of doom forced upon them, and once again pined for another 'What's Going On' or, better still, those glorious, carefree sounds of the Sixties. Cliff White's review was generously compiled – 'On the first few hearings it doesn't seem to be a wholly commendable album; over-sentimental in some places, carelessly padded in others. But when it's good, it's very good, especially if we're to assume it's all straight from the bleeding-heart-Marvin-Gaye-tells-it-like-it-is sensation.' While the *Daily Mirror* stated – 'It's not as original or inventive as some of his earlier works.' Yes, the media was confused, somewhat cynical in its opinions, and this was later reflected by his fans.

To ensure nobody was in any doubt why the double album was recorded Gaye introduced the listener with a message to Anna which included the following – 'I guess I have to say this album is dedicated to you . . . Although perhaps I may not be happy, this is what you want, so I have conceded . . . I hope it makes you happy . . . There's a lot of truth in it baby . . . I don't think I'll have any regrets baby.' He then embarked on a stinging attack about being prevented from seeing his son before adding – 'So here it is, enjoy, reminisce, be happy, think about the kisses and joy . . . the other times cloudy and grey . . . you taught me that was life . . . think of me, the way I was. This is what you wanted, here, my dear, here it is.' Thus began an often vindictive resumé of the breakdown of their marriage starting with a mellow, moody 'I Met A Little Girl' where he chronologically revealed his time with Anna – when they first met, their marriage and divorce, his fantasy woman who turned into reality and the promises they sealed with a love that was strong enough to stand the test of time. Marriage vows were sacred and eternal, he said, and this introduced the lengthy 'When Did You Stop Loving Me, When Did I Stop Loving You', a slightly more aggressive song both musically and vocally. Here Gaye attempted to unravel the spider's web that led to the breakdown of their marriage and why he should be the one left with the $1 million debt. 'Lies and Ties' was the theme of this self-indulgent cross-examination, until 'Anger' took over, a lightweight, slightly offbeat funky song overflowing with the most powerful of emotions. Gaye's dissection was unsatisfactory against spasmodic shrill backing vocals.

Side two opened with the mellow 'Is That Enough' which dealt with possessiveness and jealousy, and Gaye's inability to accept the decision made by the divorce judge. His drug habit was referred to fleetingly, prior to a sultry brass solo leading into a lengthy instrumental section. 'Everybody Needs Love', a testament to those he felt would benefit from love irrespective of their standing in life. Predictably 'Time To Get It Together' dealt with his favourite subject, albeit a subdued reference this time. 'Sparrow' opened the next album, a poignant tale of Gaye's wise and weathered feathered friend, against a strong melody where the lazy, cumbersome horns almost ruined the song. Not so 'Anna's Song' – 'baths of milk, satin sheets, all night love' – a tender love song. Side four began with 'A Funky Space Reincarnation' followed by the biting yet lacklustre 'You Can Leave, But It's Going To Cost You', Gaye reflected on meetings at Anna's sister Gwen's house, where they thrashed out their problems; the familiar story of attempted reconciliation and the high price of freedom. Finally, after the separation and break-up the 'Falling In Love Again', the joys of rediscovering love, presumably with Janis Hunter, with references including 'she's pretty, she's wonderful'.

The gatefold double album packaging was, many thought, Gaye's most inventive to date. Like 'I Want You' before it, the colouring was dull, dark, punctuated by splashes of insipid red. The sleeve when flattened showed a statue of an embracing couple depicting Rodin's *The Kiss* with a pair of pink roses at its base. A black statue of Gaye wearing a toga stood in the foreground. Behind these, two plaques were etched into facing walls, one reading 'Pain And Divorce', the other 'Love And Marriage', and a further statue of a couple hugging, partially engulfed in flames. High in the middle of the sleeve a decaying tower-like structure overlooked what could have been a section of a Roman monument, possibly a courtyard or roofless hall. which had suffered from the ravages of battle. Fire burned in places and blood stains streaked the walls. The dramatic scene sketched by Michael Bryan was a confusing dash of good and evil, and a pictorial indication of Gaye's imaginative, disturbed mind.

Bryan was also responsible for drawing the inner sleeve to Gaye's design, depicting a board game entitled Judgement and similar in design to the Monopoly board. On the right of the picture a red-fingernailed woman's hand hovers over a pile of $500 bills and a couple of coins, a mansion, a limousine, two dice, insects and a dress ring. On the picture's left a man's hand clutches a record, under which is a Revex tape machine, a piece of recording equipment, a grand piano and a single dollar bill. A short-stemmed red rose, a burning chair and a skull dominate the foreground, while at the top left back a mass of human faces press against a church window, while in the opposite corner what appears to be either burning lava or a city skyline dotted with red flashes can be seen. Obviously a slew of personal messages were hidden within this design, some obvious, some not, but as a whole the graphics depicted a pretty dismal picture of Gaye's life at this time.

Curtis Shaw wrote the sleeve notes to include – 'Marvin Gaye has done it again. He being a creative genius and having the guts to express to that special someone things we all sometimes find difficult, may have inspired this masterpiece . . . Marvin remains uninhibited in his subject matter and the portrayal of his feelings. He testifies through "Here, My Dear" – and takes us on a musical trip through a personal experience we can all relate to . . . I wondered through it all if Marvin would be able to capture and then convey all of the feelings that one experiences while undergoing such an ordeal; not only has he done all of this, but as only Marvin Gaye can do . . .' This album wasn't Gaye's only ordeal because shortly after its release Janis Gaye, now presumably at the end of her tether, filed divorce proceedings. Fortunately Marvin was able, by some means, to persuade her to drop the action. Nonetheless this move typified their volatile relationship.

No musicians were credited on the sleeve of 'Here, My Dear' except for an ambiguous 'Special thanks to all the musicians who are too numerous to mention but who are all superstars'. Gaye explained this away – 'It's mostly the musicians who played with me in London and on the road, musicians like Bugsy Wilcox and Fernando Harkness. The musicians are really pissed with me that they're not on the credits. In fact one of them's suing me. He says I stole his ideas for "Anger" and "A Funky Space Reincarnation". But he volunteered his chords. I didn't steal them.' Whether this was true or not remains to be seen, but this wasn't to be the first time the singer was accused of plagiarism! It was later discovered that Marvin was unable to list the musicians' names because he used them without permission from the Musicians Union. Prior to 'Here, My Dear', his relationship with the Union had soured.

Gaye: 'I'm not very well liked at the Union because I don't believe [in them] – for myself that is.' This stemmed from his persistence in cancelling performances which, in turn, meant that the musicians hired to play with him would be cancelled also. When this happened it was often too late for a musician to find employment elsewhere. Therefore the Union stipulated that any performances proposed by Gaye should be backed by a $40,000 performance bond which should, at the very least, ensure he would honour the commitment, or, if not, the musicians would receive some payment. Naturally, Gaye was furious with this stipulation and exacerbated the situation by cancelling an appearance at the Hollywood Palladium!

'Here, My Dear' reached number twenty-six in the album charts and was a very sluggish seller in Britain. The most commercial track 'A Funky Space Reincarnation Parts 1 and 2' was reluctantly released as a single in January 1979 to struggle to number 106 in the pop charts and number twenty-three in the R&B listing. 'Anger' was scheduled to follow this mid-year but was withdrawn. The project was a failure and Marvin Gaye's career had taken a knock. Only he was capable of retrieving his status, his past glory, but sadly he didn't seem to be fully cognisant with the severity of the situation. He knew the public hadn't supported him in the way he'd expected, but believed this was simply a temporary setback due to Motown's inefficiency in promoting his work. This time, he was wrong. So, where to now? Speculation ran rife in music circles that his career was over; Gaye, on the other hand, boasted it had only just begun – 'I write all the time but the problem is putting my writing across. I can now do what I want, more or less. I can get involved if I want to. All I have to do is assess what I am going to do. After this album I now think I'm ready.' He hinted that his next album might be devoted to death and dying simply because they were subjects ignored by his contemporaries, but knew such a project would cause problems – 'Death is as big a force as life itself and you cannot play with death. You must be careful when dealing with it or even talking about it, as you have to be careful about how you feel about love and life. I feel that all these things are powers and that earth is put together with these powers. The power that makes up life is primarily dormant and the other side is where we live. One side is where we go to sleep, and the second side is where we wake up.' His idea never reached fruition, but it wasn't a figment of his imagination either because he touched on the 'life and death' concept in his last Motown album 'In Our Lifetime' in 1981.

It's hard to imagine what Berry Gordy felt when he first heard 'Here, My Dear'. On the one hand he had another non-commercial Marvin Gaye project which needed diligent marketing and promotion as the follow-up to 'I Want You'. On the other hand, by releasing the album he'd be responsible for exposing to the world the personal life of his beloved sister. Doubtless it would have been futile to have argued with Gaye about changing the concept or at the very least some of the tracks, to perhaps ensure a modicum of decency. It's possible that at the end of the day Berry Gordy had no choice but to release the album and suffer the consequences. There's little doubt that 'Here, My Dear' widened the already growing gap between the two talented men, but Gaye took the situation one step further by telling a British reporter that he was an exploited artist, that his work suffered because of this and that he had little or no control over the way in which his music was marketed once the tapes were delivered to Motown – 'I'm easily exploited because when I'm giving up material, I'm giving up honesty, heart and soul and pure love. Pure love of my music and my respect. I'm pouring it out when I'm doing something, or I won't do it at all. And when Motown get something from an artist, myself or any other artist in this business, then it's something special. An artist has to make a living like anybody else. It's very simple – record companies have decided that this is the vehicle by which music shall reach the people and I have no control over that. If this is the only vehicle, then I have one choice. I can either be an artist and accept the fact that this is the only vehicle from which my music can reach the people, or I can say I don't like this vehicle and I don't like this business, and I don't like the way things are done to artists and people, so I won't do anything. I also know, on the other hand, to use this vehicle to get a message across to people is a great thing, even though they're making a lot of money doing it and heaven knows what they're doing with it. I mean, I don't get a lot of it. They have an awful lot of overheads and stuff like that and record companies probably don't make as much money as people think. I still don't think that in proportion to what the artist is giving that he makes near enough money from the total sales. After all, artists generally are the source; you're tapping the mine, and when the mine runs out, you simply go and get yourself another mine. They can tap you for years, and for that you deserve fantastic awards. It's like you either play the game or you get eaten up. It's a vicious, vicious circle.'

While Marvin Gaye was completing 'Here, My Dear' the music industry was being strangled by the second John Travolta dance film *Grease* which spawned two multi-million-selling singles 'You're The One That I Want' and 'Summer Nights' recorded by Travolta and his co-star Olivia Newton-John. Motown too was enjoying another prosperous period thanks to the Commodores finally breaking through with their runaway international love ballad 'Three Times A Lady' written and sung by Lionel Richie. The company also garnered sales from High Inergy, a young female trio being groomed as the new Supremes with their debut 'You Can't Turn Me Off (In The Middle Of Turning Me On)' and 'Love Is All You Need', and the newly-signed funk 'n' love master Rick James whose career was just beginning on the Gordy label with 'You And I' and 'Mary Jane' (his pet name for marijuana). James would in time give Marvin Gaye cause for concern because he felt the newcomer was stealing his younger audience. That was nonsense because at this time James lacked the sophistication of Gaye: James' approach was hard-hitting and often crude whereas Marvin's was subtle and sensual. David Ritz wrote of further problems – 'Gaye was convinced that Jan was in love with Rick James [and] Slick Rick hung around Gaye's studio a great deal and called his idol Uncle Marvin.' Apparently, Gaye loathed this term of endearment, saying it made him feel old, instead of treating it with the respect it deserved.

However, Uncle Marvin had more important issues to contend with when his financial situation reached boiling point, leaving him no option but to file two voluntary bankruptcy petitions before the Los Angeles Federal District Bankruptcy Judge, Richard Mednick. *Billboard* magazine reported – 'Gaye is petitioning in a personal bankruptcy situation, correlated with a petition for bankruptcy for his Righton Productions. Both were filed early this year [1978]. What appears to be the latest filing in his personal action is an undated plan submitted to the court estimating that Gaye would pay off debtors in less than three years "if reductions can be accomplished". No totals of assets and liabilities were available for this petition.'

The Righton petition consisted of an estimated $1.8 million in liabilities and assets of $1.27 million, and Gaye agreed to an arrangement to pay $7,560 monthly less an administrative fee of $832 for disbursement. His personal petition appeared to be taken up with outstanding legal fees estimated at $1.5 million to Carlton Robinson, Patrick Cavanagh and Gregory C. Burgin, and revealed he owed $522,314 in returns for the years 1974/75. His 1976/77 returns were being finalised, likewise his debt to the State of California, while his unsecured liabilities were estimated at $7 million. *Billboard* further stated – 'It is evident that Gaye, who produced his own masters which in turn were turned over to Motown by Righton Productions, was slapped with a bill for sales and use tax by the California State Board of Equalization. The state's tax unit tried to assess a 5% tax on all such industry dealings in the early Seventies. The attempt to tax masters fell through when an industry group was able to gain a legislative bill which kayoed the board's move. But not before a number of labels and producers were hit with hefty tax levies. The court record shows Gaye was advanced $176,000 by Motown Records in January 1978 to make an unidentified payment to the Equalization Board. The advance is shown as a liability.' Various other monies paid to and by Gaye were taken into account particularly those relating to ASCAP.

The court trustee in Marvin's personal action estimated that he'd earned in excess of $1 million in recent years, with Motown paying him $350,000 per album. Personal monthly earnings were estimated at $40,000 against personal expenditure of approximately $35,000 per month. It was a dismal picture but the singer really had no one to blame but himself. He had avoided paying his taxes, had surrounded himself with what he later called unscrupulous people, extortionists, and had suffered from the cost of his divorce about which he said – 'American courts are very imbalanced. I think it's becoming the same all over the world. Anna is getting the proceeds from the album. I don't wish her any ill but something's wrong. If the scales are imbalanced to that extent, something's wrong. I think "Here, My Dear" – is a last-ditch effort to maintain whatever supremacy I have.'

Marvin Gaye would, in a couple of years time, refer to this period of his life as his 'crazy era' – his personal life was one upheaval after another. 'Here, My Dear' was his poor selling controversial soul bearer and he was hounded by the IRS and numerous debtors. His predicament was burning him up and when the media latched on to the situation the reports were wildly exaggerated and hurtful. In an attempt to put the record straight, he told journalists – 'I heard I owed six million dollars, although the press say it's around three million. It's more like two million which I owe my manager. I got into that state because I prefer to handle my own life and affairs, and I guess I'm not the smartest in business. Anyway, there's a lot of people saying I owe them a lot of money. I don't know why I'm involved in any law suits either. I always thought I was such a decent person. I'm involved in them, I suppose, because of my unswerving faith in human nature. I never learn. I wish I could stop believing in people. I'm an easy mark, and now I'm not sure I've even got the best legal counsel in the world. I'm not, though, what the authorities call a poor bankruptcy.'

While Marvin Gaye suffered so did The Temptations, unhappily signed to Atlantic Records. The group was on a promotional trip to England when Marvin's name cropped up in an interview given to *Black Echoes* magazine which reported the group members 'were not shy about slagging off their former record company'. The group cited Gaye as a prime casualty of Motown's politics that had soured their own relationship – 'Marvin is just coasting because he can't get away. He recently swore that they'd have to kill him to get him back into the studio.' 'But hasn't he just recorded a new album?' asked one of the party. 'Yeah, but have you heard it?' retorted a Temptation. 'It's just a reproduction of his early, early work, "The Moods Of Marvin Gaye" and you know how far back that goes.' The Temptations were mistaken. Gaye's 1966 album had been reissued as part of an American archive series, and, of course, had no bearing on Gaye's inability to produce a new album!

Back in America, as an annual survey revealed Motown Industries was the top black-owned business for the seventh year running with revenues of $50 million, ninety-year-old 'Pops' Gordy died. He had devoted half his life to Motown and its artists and became a vital figurehead in the organisation. As a special, and loving tribute to this sadly-missed man Diana Ross, Stevie Wonder and Smokey Robinson joined Marvin Gaye to record the 'Pops We Love You' single, written by Pam Sawyer and Marilyn McLeod, and released in December 1978 to become a pop 60 hit (no 26 R&B). The record, pressed in green vinyl and a limited edition in heart-shaped red, was originally written as a birthday surprise for Gordy Snr but tragically it became his epitaph. An album of the same name was also released during April 1979 featuring a host of artists including Tata Vega, Jermaine Jackson, the Commodores and Marvin Gaye's duet with Diana Ross, 'I'll Keep My Light In The Window' written by Leonard Caston and Carolyn Majors and left over from the 1973 'Diana & Marvin' album, and Gaye's remixed version of 'God Is Love'.

As usual Marvin Gaye was in no hurry to record again, whereas other artists might conceivably have been eager to follow a poor-selling album to prove credibility. However, Marvin didn't doubt his ability to be creative because 'Here, My Dear' was a masterpiece in its own way, and a loving tribute to his talent. He was given a special gift, an almost theocentric skill which he didn't use to its full advantage and which few artists possessed. The reason he was hesitating now, he said, was because he was scared to lay that gift before the public again. There was little about his life that was now sacred, his innermost soul had been exposed, and he felt he had nowhere else to go, or when he did discover a usable avenue, he was worried about the music itself. Irrespective of these worries, he knew the eventual result would be phenomenal because – 'If I stay with my music and keep my head in a proper level, I'm going to do some fantastic music.' He fully realised that any future work would need to be more commercially slanted and that it would take time for him to adopt a style that had been alien to him since his 'conveyor-belt' hits of the Sixties. He said many a time that he wrote and sang to satisfy himself, not what popular music trends dictated and, although he rarely listened to the radio to keep abreast of changing styles, he was aware of the way different instruments were being utilised in contemporary music. He also followed the various breeds of musicians, became interested in those not afraid to experiment and used the following to exemplify his meaning in *Crawdaddy* magazine – 'They take strings and acapella voices, contralto and soprano voices generally, and they put these voices deep in echo and they use strings and you get a very eerie sound. That does something to your senses, makes you feel a certain amount of emotion. If you're watching a horror movie you tend to get uptight because the music is suggesting that you should be uptight. Only because of what we have been conditioned to. The only reason you can't envision this music that I'm speaking of is that you have nothing to go back on. You say, "Well, I can't imagine it because there's been nothing in my life to make me know what you're taking about." It would be foreign if I ever did it for a second or a few minutes, and people have to get used to it, and say it's a bunch of crap – and maybe it is, but to try is the thrill.'

Marvin's favourite instrument at this time was the synthesiser, an instrument he was to become extremely fond of because he believed he was sufficiently sensitive in his art to garner the best from it. Stevie Wonder shared his opinion – 'It has allowed me to get certain kinds of sounds and play them for myself and create arrangements using those sounds . . . There are machines that will write out the parts of a song, say for a string section or a reed section or a brass section or a woodwind section. But I like instruments, real instruments. The synthesiser is just an extension of what you can do.'

Marvin Gaye also intended to record without lyrics, chords or beat, a difficult task he admitted but one he felt he could do – '. . . I have a thing where I just put my hands on the keys, I don't care where they fall. And it's got to where I can't sound a bad note. There just aren't any. I don't care where my hands fall, they always sound fantastic. I don't care if they're wrong, but they don't sound wrong. Don't say I gotta put this note here because it sounds good, that's the way it should be – bunk! Music is what you feel. All notes are good, there are no bad notes.'

Towards the end of 1978 and early into the next year Gaye did deviate from the music for which he was publicly known. He recorded several tracks with Bobby Scott, songs that appealed to him, showing another side to his talent. Gaye: 'The arrangements were such genius . . . I was really flabbergasted. Every time I tried to sing against these arrangements I became terribly frustrated because I felt inadequate musically.' The songs were mostly ballads and included 'She Needs Me', 'I Wish I Didn't Love You So', plus jazz-tinged versions of 'Funny' and 'This Will Make You Laugh', and 'Why Did I Choose You', 'The Shadow Of Your Smile' and 'I Won't Cry Anymore'. At the time Marvin complained that Berry Gordy wouldn't consider these tracks for release because they were alien to his selling image. Even after Gaye's death Gordy's attitude didn't change. The majority of the tracks remain unreleased but thankfully three escaped – 'Why Did I Choose You?', 'The Shadow Of Your Smile' and 'I Won't Cry Anymore' – to be featured not on a Motown record but on the posthumously issued album 'Romantically Yours' – released by CBS!

# 10. | Life's a Game of Give and Take

*I started to witness [Marvin's] demise because he started to go off into the cocaine thing very heavily.*

(Smokey Robinson)

*[Marvin] was emaciated because he had just been eating bread, and looked like death.*

(Jeffrey Kruger)

*[Marvin] would be either spaced out or laid out.*

(Roger St Pierre)

*I suppose [Marvin] is the Judy Garland of the soul world.*

(Graham Canter)

With the loss of The Supremes, the Jackson 5 and The Temptations, Motown concentrated on pushing the new signings like the Missouri six-piece band Bloodstone, the white, blonde Californian, and Rick James' protégé Teena Marie who was heavily influenced by Marvin Gaye, the young, enthusiastic Patrick Gammon and Dr Strut, a jazz outfit. Many failed to develop into major acts because they claimed too much emphasis was placed on promoting Stevie Wonder, Smokey Robinson, Diana Ross and Marvin Gaye. However, these and other established artists like Syreeta, Rick James and the Commodores were not a continuous threat to the newcomers as they preferred quality releases rather than quantity. However, it's true to say that when a 'star' product was released it was afforded more expensive marketing campaigns to ensure top sales to keep Motown financially stable. With its expanding artist roster of new young acts and diverse types of music, there was now no indication of the public loyalty of the last decade; Motown had become just another record company fighting for hit records in an industry that had by now reached near saturation point. Through Motown's mid-price label Natural Resources, mainstream release schedules were padded out with re-issues and

'Greatest Hits' compilations, but with a new decade looming consistent support had to be given to new faces if the company was to remain successful. Dance music continued with a vengeance with runaway hits from Chic, Amii Stewart, The Village People, Anita Ward, Gloria Gaynor and Sister Sledge among others, while young British acts offered competition with their own brand of rock/punk music (The Skids, Generation X, The Sex Pistols) and new mainstream groups like Squeeze, Police and Dire Straits.

Marvin Gaye made two significant appearances during this time. The first with his friend and fellow master of sensual love Teddy Pendergrass (ex-lead singer of the soul outfit The Bluenotes) headlining San Diego's Kool jazz Festival; the second with Stevie Wonder at a surprise birthday party thrown for his wife Janis. Both events were significant because they showed that Gaye was making an effort to succeed both professionally and personally. Meanwhile, one of his original backing singers and Vandellas' leader Martha Reeves had finally settled into a new career, having recently released the 'We Meet Again' album, produced by ex-Motown producer Hank Cosby, for Fantasy Records. Harvey Fuqua would also join this company when he produced the late 'You Make Me Feel Mighty Real' superstar Sylvester. Reeves' deal with Fantasy followed a recording association with Arista where she recorded the much-acclaimed 'The Rest Of My Life' album after leaving MCA Records. While with MCA she enjoyed an American hit single with 'The Power Of Love' taken from her eponymous album produced by Richard Perry, and contributed three songs ('Willie D', 'King Midas', 'Keep On Movin' On') on the movie soundtrack 'Willie Dynamite'. When not recording Reeves was in constant demand on the American and European touring circuits. Throughout she maintained contact with her Motown colleagues, both those in her home-town of Detroit and in Los Angeles, and kept a close eye on Motown's releases, particularly the re-packages that included many Martha Reeves and the Vandellas albums.

However, re-packaged material was not what Motown wanted from Marvin Gaye – the company needed a new album, and a commercial one at that to compensate for 'Here, My Dear'. Unlike previous instances where an album was desperately needed and there was nothing in the can, this time Gaye had been writing spasmodically for some months. Unfortunately he had little to show for it except one song which he delivered to the company to appease the pressure. Titled 'Ego Tripping Out (Parts One & Two)' and released in September 1979, it wasn't an exceptional piece of work but rather a bloated indulgence in self-expression which did little to placate the public who were becoming disillusioned with his work. Respected music critic John Abbey, a long-time admirer of Marvin's work, was generous with his review – 'For his new single Gaye reverts to producing, arranging and writing his own material. If the unusual but hypnotic track is anything to go by, we're in for a dynamic album. Strange rhythm riffs dominate the musical support and Marvin's highly distinctive double-track vocal style is perfectly suited to the crisp rhythm track.' Notwithstanding heavy marketing the single sold badly. It failed to register in the pop charts and struggled to become a number seventeen R&B hit and was later deleted from the company's catalogue.

Marvin Gaye's career was at its lowest ebb. No longer were the hits automatic, no longer was his name a saleable product. Yet it was only a few years ago when he was being hailed as a musical genius, a leader of his people, America's conscience. It looked as if he was losing the battle – and he needed money. With no album pending, therefore no advance, there was no alternative but to tour in late 1979. It was a brave move, one that few artists would have made in the wake of recent failure. To avoid flying from date to date, Gaye bought a comfortable fourteen-seater bus, complete with sleeping facilities, small kitchen and bathroom for travelling the hundreds of miles around America. Without a hit to his credit since 'Got To Give It Up' in March 1977 his concerts were poorly attended. This demoralised him but sadly this is part and parcel of the fickleness of showbusiness – no hits, no standing room only audiences – which applied to all acts, not just Gaye. Regrettably, he was learning the hard way and his past erratic behaviour where performances were cancelled after the tickets had been sold, also had to contribute to the public's unresponsive attitude.

Part way through this tour, Marvin collapsed from exhaustion and spent several days in a Tennessee hospital. Drug abuse was suspected although not publicly announced. It was a lengthy American trek fraught with problems, apparently aggravated by Marvin's moodiness and unpredictable behaviour. Some concerts were cancelled simply because he preferred to play hooky in nightclubs or to enjoy the women who flung themselves at his feet. Gaye: 'I've never had any problems with women. Having been one of the world's greatest womanisers they've probably had more problems with me.' Yes, the singer appeared undisciplined, isolated from Motown's badly needed guidance and still in debt, owing inescapable amounts to the IRS. He had hoped to win sufficient money to pay off these and other debts when his boxer Andy Price beat Sugar Ray Leonard in a Las Vegas match in the autumn. But it wasn't to be. Andy Price lost.

As if to ensure Marvin also suffered the after-affects from one of Sugar Ray's punches he was told that Janis had taken their children, Nona and Bubby, to move in with her mother. David Ritz reported the singer visited her, whereupon he ended up in a Los Angeles hospital! Janis had phoned the police because she was afraid her husband would kidnap the children and when he refused to leave the house, a fight ensued. A policeman hit Marvin, bruising his cheek, blackening his eye and after a short stay in hospital he was released. As usual, his mother Alberta rescued him and took him home with her.

In November 1979 Motown – after being assured by Marvin that he would deliver – confidentially notified its licensees that a new album had been scheduled for release. Titled 'Love Man' the tracks included 'Life's A Game Of Give And Take', 'Life Is Now In Session', 'I Offer You Nothing But Love', 'Just Because You're So Pretty', 'Dance 'N' Be Happy', 'Funk Me, Funk Me, Funk Me', 'Lover's Plea', 'Songs Are To Learn From' and the last single 'Ego Tripping Out'. A decade earlier 'Love Man' had been a title used by Otis Redding – who died in a plane crash in Lake Monoma on 10 December 1967 – for an album and single which became American top fifty and top eighty hits respectively. The single also became Redding's last British hit. This did not deter Marvin Gaye, the title stayed because it was tied to the conceptual nature of the album's content and was designed to warn off imitators. Gaye: 'At the time we were trying to combat the disconcerting tide of the young black male, supposed sex symbols and pretenders to my throne, and I had this idea to come up with this concept to quietly dispel those pretenders.'

The album's artwork, showing Gaye in a sexually provocative pose – arms outstretched, legs open, the conqueror of women – had been completed and circulated to Motown's various overseas licensees in readiness for its release. All they required were the finished tapes for duplication. Days turned to weeks, weeks into months; international planning and marketing schedules were postponed, record presses put on hold, until all plans were eventually abandoned. The artwork and track listing, already circulated to excited record company salesmen (a new Gaye album always promised healthy orders and they were told this one was his best since 'What's Going On'), were filed away and projected release dates scrubbed. Motown had rejected the album as unsuitable for release and returned it to Gaye for re-working. He retaliated with some hostility claiming Berry Gordy had once again undermined his creative ability – 'I took the tapes of "What's Going On" to Motown and they didn't like it and said it was no good. I took them the tapes of "Live! At The London Palladium" and they said it was no good, and they didn't like it, and it wouldn't sell because it didn't have any new material on it. I'm the type of artist who, if I do something that's revolutionary or innovative, or just hasn't been done before, then everybody starts to panic. They can panic if they want to, but if they put "Love Man" out it'll sell too because I've got it, and they're afraid to admit it!' He cared little for the outside competition, knowing the record company would take the responsibility for the marketing and promotion – 'I don't care about them worrying whether it'll be a hit because Michael Jackson's flooding the market with a different sound, or Quincy Jones' sound is in, bull, I'm me. I'm not taking anything away from them, or any other artists because they're brilliant too and I love them. I need a record company who knows what they have, who knows that I'm different and I may have a miss or two, but what the fuck.'

When the returned 'Love Man' tracks had been re-worked to its satisfaction, Motown guaranteed the album would be released. However, the record's title could not be altered. Gaye: 'The company has already printed up four hundred and fifty thousand sleeves so they said if I wanted to change the title then I'll have to pay for the re-run myself. So I'll just stick with it. The album itself is quite controversial. I can describe it best in just two words – sensually social. Some of the songs may be changed around a bit but the material itself has been settled and most of it is completed. The tracks are all up-tempo or midtempo.' He spoke about some of the songs to a *Blues & Soul* reporter, starting with what he called his most controversial 'Funk Me, Funk Me, Funk Me', then 'Songs You Can Learn From' – 'It deals with legitimising the word "funk". It's used in many derogatory ways that it's hard to legitimate its use. If one can honestly say "fuck me because I love you" then what's wrong with the word? It may be offensive to puritans and prudes when it's said in public, but I'm sure that even they use it in intimate moments behind closed doors. And "Songs You Can Learn From," well, the point I'm making here is that songs can have a heavy influence on people and that influence can be either good or bad. I'm telling kids to be aware of what they are getting into and that they should beware of getting influenced by bad songs.'

Of 'Love Man', the album's title track, he insisted it was another concerning being 'funky' – 'The word "funk" itself has been much misused and misunderstood. It was Motown's bass player, James Jamerson, who first came up with the word in its modern context. He used to tell us "let's get the funk pressure high" or "get down to the funk". It's a word that can be more easily understood than explained. Being funky really means being yourself. You can be funky, have a good time and still have a higher consciousness.' When he explained 'A Very Heavy Love Affair', Gaye surprisingly revealed for the first time to a British journalist that his second marriage had failed – 'This song refers to my relationship with my present wife and the break-up of our marriage, but seen from a positive rather than a negative point of view. I've just gone through another very heavy love-hate relationship and I'm trying to show young people that what they should really look for is a relationship with a true soulmate, someone with whom they are really compatible.' When asked to elaborate he declined saying he only wanted to talk about his music. Gaye: 'The next track "Love Party – is my foreboding song, a warning about the end of the world as I see it. I feel the prophesy of Revelation is coming true with frightening speed. I'm saying to my woman, "Be more God-conscious and truly loving." It's very much a message song thing.' His thoughts on depression dominated 'Let Your Love Come Shining Through' – 'Despite them being spiritual, they get themselves locked up into their own dark sides. I'm trying to say to them "open up and let the love that's in you shine through" – even if it's only for one hour a week. It's got a very positive message too.' And finally, with 'I Wish I Had Someone To Love Me' he generalised on his present personal situation without giving too much away – 'The song has a self-explanatory title. I've gone through quite a tragic few years with the ladies I've loved and I haven't exactly had much luck in that direction. I truly do wish I could find a real soulmate to love and be loved by.'

It's ironic that it was only six years ago when Marvin believed he had actually found his soulmate, his partner for life. And he had nearly ruined his career by pursuing her. Now he said he was looking for someone else, indicating that he had abandoned any thoughts of him and Janis, who had bloomed into a desirable young woman, working together to save their marriage. He seemed to have forgotten how badly he had wanted her, and how he had referred to her in 1973 as his precious jewel, his God-given gift. He admitted he still loved Janis, still wanted to be with her and their children, but couldn't live with her. It was a contradictory situation. So because of this attitude he was ruining four lives, theirs and their children, insisting their helter-skelter relationship continued. However, Marvin was forced to face up to the unhappiness he was causing when Janis reputedly absconded with Teddy Pendergrass taking their children Bubby and Nona with her. This was a move forty-year-old Gaye had not bargained on: his wife and his close friend, the principal characters of many a love ballad crooned by a broken hearted singer with tear-filled eyes. Marvin Gaye was furious, and in time that fury turned into illness, which would in turn jeopardise his future, and be the start of one of the most hellishly emotional and destructive periods of his life from which he would never fully recover.

To ease his situation Marvin agreed to tour again, and before 1979 closed, he had performed in Hawaii followed by a short tour of japan, with a European trek pencilled in for the New Year. The American promoter wasn't contractually able to handle the European itinerary because the Continent belonged to Jeffrey Kruger who had promoted Gaye's 1976 tour. Following the Japanese visit Gaye opted to return to Hawaii instead of Los Angeles because all his assets had gradually been grabbed by the IRS in their attempt to retrieve the millions owed in back taxes. Gaye: 'I've lost my home and my studio. I've never really given a shit about where my money went and I don't think I'm going to change now, so I'll probably be in trouble again.' His main problem, like so many other Motown artists, was not saving a percentage of his earnings to cover taxes. Gaye: 'I don't know how to hold on to cash for Uncle Sam. If someone needs help, needs money, I'll give it to them and always forget I have a tax bill coming in at the end of the year. As for my creditors, well, most of them are just pure extortionists. Still, at times like this you learn who your real friends are. There are a lot of people around who I lent money to years ago and never asked for it back, but when I got into trouble they didn't rush to help me. On the other hand, Harvey Fuqua, who I hadn't heard from in years, sent me some dollars to help me out as soon as he heard the trouble I was in. He was one of the few people to seek me out and offer to help.'

When Marvin was settled in Hawaii Janis attempted to patch up their marriage. *Rolling Stone* magazine reported – 'He invited Janis to visit, but they wound up fighting. "I nearly killed her," Marvin said. "I had a knife about an inch from her heart." He persuaded a friend to abduct his four-year-old son, Frankie [Bubby], and bring him to the island – an act that resulted in the filing of criminal charges against Gaye back in Los Angeles.' The singer couldn't stoop any lower. The genius that was Marvin Gaye was now numbed by his addiction to cocaine. He also had no money. Smokey Robinson also visited him and told radio personality Tony Blackburn – 'I started to witness his demise, you would say, because he started to go off into the cocaine thing very heavily . . . he was just surrounded by people who were like to me leeches, who were there because he was Marvin Gaye and he had money to buy cocaine and what have you. He wanted to get this money from me and we sort of had a falling out because I wouldn't give it to him. I felt if I gave him the money that he was only going to buy cocaine with it. Right after that he went to Europe.' The leeches followed or re-appeared under another guise in London and Robinson wouldn't speak to Gaye for another three years.

Jeffrey Kruger worked hard to secure dates for Marvin Gaye to ensure that he was away from America for some months during 1980. In December he announced the tour – even though the singer was booked to appear in Los Angeles – where the British leg was due to open at 'The Biggest Disco In The World' at The National Exhibition Centre (NEC), Birmingham on 19 January 1980. This was to be followed by performances at The Usher Hall, Edinburgh (21), The Philharmonic Hall, Liverpool (23), The Royal Albert Hall, London (25), The Rainbow Theatre, London (26), The Centre, Brighton (2 February), The Apollo Theatre, Manchester (6) and The Venue, London's new exclusive nightspot, on the 7th for a farewell concert at 10 p.m. Gaye's support act was the likeable Edwin Starr, originally a Ric Tic artist before being transferred to Motown when Berry Gordy bought the label during the Sixties. Starr, adored by British soul fans, had now left Motown after a string of hits, and had recently enjoyed two top ten singles with 'Contact' on 20th Century Records and 'H.A.P.P.Y. Radio' on RCA Records. All the dates were sold out. Marvin and Janis were due to leave Los Angeles on flight TWA 760 on Wednesday, 16 January 1980, to arrive at 11.40 a.m. at Heathrow the next day, while the musicians were due in London on the 18th. Following Gaye's performance at The Rainbow Theatre he was scheduled to fly to Rotterdam, Holland, then France and Switzerland before returning to England for the remainder of the dates. The entourage was booked to return to America on 8 February.

Meantime, it was reported that early in 1980 Janis had visited her husband for a second time, presumably to collect her son who was staying with his father. Gaye said he honestly had attempted to repair the damage between them but had reluctantly concluded his endeavours were futile – '[I] may have had successes in the entertainment business but in the marriage stakes I'm a two time loser. That's not to say that I've not had my fair share of good times, I have. It's just that I don't seem to be too well equipped mentally and emotionally to handle a long-term relationship. I must have been difficult to live with but I don't regret any of it. Marriage is a very personal thing between two people and it's their business, nobody else's.'

At the beginning of January 1980 'The Biggest Disco In The World' date was cancelled through a breakdown in negotiations between the promoters and the venue, and by the end of the month Gaye's entire tour was postponed! Jeffrey Kruger, who had invested a lot of money in the tour, issued a press statement explaining the situation was due to Gaye's personal problems, coupled with extreme physical and mental exhaustion which had left him unable to travel. It then mentioned that Janis had in fact left Gaye, taking their baby daughter to live with Teddy Pendergrass, before including a brief message from the distraught singer – 'I'm very sorry to disappoint you. I have fond memories of previous visits and the warm receptions I received.' As much as the public sympathised with Marvin's dilemma it was a bitter pill to swallow. Jeffrey Kruger immediately flew to Maui to ascertain the extent of Gaye's illness, and to secure a firm date from him for a future tour. Once they had met Kruger was convinced beyond doubt that the singer was incapable of travelling and performing, as he told a British journalist – 'He was packed and ready to leave when I arrived, but his doctor said he was in no way well enough to travel. He was in a pathetic state. He was emaciated because he had just been eating bread, and looked like death. He just couldn't hold himself together. He said he couldn't do the January/February tour and would need time to get himself together. He would come in May or June he told me.' Coupled with Gaye's physical illness Kruger noted his drug intake had become so excessive that for the most part he was incoherent, irrational, and he had attempted to commit suicide by eating cocaine!

Eventually Marvin Gaye was persuaded by his mother to reduce his drug intake and take stock of his life. He had promised Kruger that he would honour a 1980 British tour and the only way this could be achieved was for him to cleanse his system, enabling him to perform. Subsequently, Gaye spent much of his time enjoying the warm sunshine and sea air, walking along the beaches, eating a basic diet of junk food and ice cream. And taking lesser quantities of cocaine. It wasn't, of course, an ideal lifestyle for the young Bubby (Janis had flown home without him) but he must have been aware of his father's addiction, and overlooked it. At his very lowest Gaye convinced himself that the whole world was against him. The enemy wasn't the world, of course, just the IRS and he couldn't blame anyone but himself for that. The money he would earn in Europe would be exempt from American taxes, therefore at the very least he could pay off some of his debts; although there's no evidence to prove that he did. During this drug hazed recuperation period Gaye at one point lived in a milk truck which he had converted into some type of home — 'It wasn't that I couldn't afford a conventional home, I just wanted to be free to float around and that's exactly what I did. It was a wonderful therapy because I like being close to nature, and Maui is a beautiful place although very expensive.' He conceded he was in a weakened state of depression – 'And in an artist that can be dangerous. For all our sensitivity and love of life creative people can fall into deep pits of despair where the heart is concerned and become very self-destructive. I'm not worried about the money matters at all. Matters of the heart are more important.' However, behind this brave façade Gaye was crying out once again for someone to care for – 'I just wish I had someone to love me for myself, someone who didn't care about my moods and my entertainer's nature. 'I'm a ram and a fire sign, I might singe, but I'm full of love and sensitivity. My kid, Bubby, keeps me balanced now but it's been a problem trying to see he's properly looked after. Fortunately, I've had very strong support from my family.'

While Gaye stayed in Maui Jeffrey Kruger had to keep the British public interested in the singer and through regular snippets to the media stressed that the 1980 tour would be rescheduled, and that ticket holders should hold on to their receipts unless a refund was required. To ensure Gaye actually honoured the revised commitment this time Kruger contacted his friend Mrs Jewel Price. Not only did she persuade him to *leave* Hawaii to tour but accompanied him to Europe with Alberta, his mother, an aunt and Gordon Banks, his musical director. Bubby wasn't due to tour with his father but as confusion arose over his collection prior to Gaye leaving Maui he had no choice but to join him. However, it was thought that Gaye had deliberately avoided returning Bubby to Janis because he'd later refer to this action as kidnapping his son.

Once Jeffrey Kruger was satisfied beyond doubt that nothing would go wrong, the new tour was confirmed. The original dates were changed several times because venues were not now available, so the new itinerary read something like this – Royal Albert Hall, London, 13 June; The Odeon, Birmingham (14); The Rainbow, London (15); The Fulcrum Centre, Slough (18); The Centre, Brighton (19); The Apollo, Manchester (20); The Usher Hall, Edinburgh (21); The Theatre, Southport (22); and The Venue, London, on 4 July where Gaye would host a special American Independence Day Celebration with tickets at £10 per head. As well as these concerts he was booked to perform at a Royal Gala to be staged at The Lakeside Country Club, Camberley, on 8 July before HRH Princess Margaret. A close friend of the Princess had approached Jeffrey Kruger prior to Gaye's arrival and had asked him to recommend an artist to star in the charity event. Kruger: 'When I suggested Marvin, Lady Patricia Neatrour was thrilled to bits and asked if I thought he would agree to stay on for it. It seems the Princess is a great fan of Marvin's records. Marvin will be the star of the show and afterwards he and his mother have been invited to dine with the Princess which is a tremendous honour for them.' The date was therefore confirmed.

The timing on Gaye's travelling from Hawaii was tight; he and Bubby arrived at London's Heathrow on the morning of his first concert! The singer looked tired, emaciated and older than his forty-one years, wearing an ill-fitting jacket and trousers, with a tie knotted inside his crumpled shirt collar, his woollen hat on his head and his son on his arm. He had little luggage with him, what clothes he did possess were creased and unwashed; stage attire was practically non-existent. Interestingly, an April tour of Britain by Teddy Pendergrass, also arranged by Jeffrey Kruger, was cancelled via a terse telegram from the singer's management. Rumour, naturally, suggested this had happened because of the situation between Gaye and Pendergrass although no statement was issued to that effect. Perhaps in this instance coincidence was stronger than fact!

'We finally made it. We've had a few problems and what can I tell you? We like to keep you guessing!' laughed Marvin Gaye on his opening night at the Royal Albert Hall, by way of explaining his five month postponement. *Blues & Soul* music editor, Jeff Tarry, attended – 'There was certainly a good measure of joy to be gleaned from merely being present on such an auspicious occasion. Good vibes filled the hall and Gaye's staunch followers had a field day identifying each song from the merest hint of an introduction. But sadly, Marvin's rather intimate projection failed to reach many parts of the audience and seemed better suited to a far smaller venue. His material for the evening stretched back to "I'll Be Doggone" and "Ain't That Peculiar" and included a medley tribute to the late Tammi Terrell with songs like "Ain't Nothing Like The Real Thing" and "Ain't No Mountain High Enough". Having melted a few hearts with "After The Dance" he announced that he felt like dancing and invited a lucky lady up on stage to move around with him for a few bars. Marvin's own touring band was good and solid throughout, and the vocal trio perched unobtrusively to one side of the stage were especially effective. Here and there Mr Gaye took to the electric piano to conjure a few bars, but his instrumental prowess appeared to be somewhat limited. "How Sweet It Is" – and "Come Get To This" were among the highlights which served as vehicles for Marvin's slinking and weaving stage craft, but it was classics like "What's Going On", "Let's Get it On" and "Mercy, Mercy Me" – which drew the greatest roars of approval. After a strangely subdued "Inner City Blues (Make Me Wanna Holler)", the climax of the evening, there was as usual no encore, despite the stomping pleas. Instead Marvin chose to introduce his young son on stage. All in all, a belated qualified success with the degree of audience satisfaction depending on where you happened to be sitting. Edwin Starr opened the show with a performance which on most other bills would have served as a worthy headliner.'

It should be noted that the 'lucky lady' chosen to dance on stage with Gaye was found before his show began by a member of his entourage. She then stood at the side of the stage or in a prominent position to hop alongside him when she heard her cue. Invariably, the young girl is then invited backstage for a drink after the performance. Jeffrey Kruger first met Marvin Gaye during 1974 in a New York nightclub. The singer was one of his idols as he told a Sussex newspaper journalist – 'He was like the Elvis Presley of black entertainment. I walked into the Winchester Club with my wife and we were the only two white people in an audience of three thousand blacks. I was very hesitant when I was taken in to meet him and I thought he had given a terrible show. He said, "How did you enjoy my show?" and I said, "Do you want to hear the truth?" I told him it stank. He looked at me and said, "Here's the first white monkey who ever told me the truth!" 'The two men came to an agreement that they would work together in Europe. Kruger: 'We could have doubled the dates, and I had a lot of time to talk to him as we travelled through Europe. Marvin is an intellectual, very serious, and dedicated to his music, but totally unbusinesslike, He just didn't care about the details of life.' The singer's money problems, he said later, were due to his lackadaisical approach – 'Marvin left tax bills unpaid and got in with the wrong people. Instead of facing up to his problems he made himself a martyr and just hibernated in his woodland home in the hills.'

One of Europe's foremost promoters of black artists, Kruger had succeeded where others had failed, by working with Dionne Warwick, The Supremes, Gladys Knight and the Pips, and The Jacksons among others. Gaye said Kruger's success was due to his ability to become personally involved with the artists – 'from the moment a tour is first mooted until we get on the plane to return home at the end of a tour and even then his work doesn't stop.' The promoter only worked with artists he admired and with twenty-five years of experience then behind him, he was in a position to select those acts he wanted to represent. Kruger: 'I believe it's easier to give an artist the day-to-day comforts they require, rather than leave it to chance. We prepare a questionnaire requesting full details of their favourite drink, food, travel likes and even go as far as finding out whether they prefer female or male company. We try to leave the artist free to concentrate on his performance and nothing else.' The British soul public were among the most loyal in the world he confirmed – 'Their support for an artist does not relate simply to a current record success or tour, but matures and grows through an artist's career. Marvin, for instance, was truly amazed at the welcome he received from his British fans, even though he hadn't been over for a while, had no recent chart success, and the tour had been on-off, on-off and on again since January.' The two men formed a close personal relationship as Gaye was quick to mention – 'Jeff Kruger is helping me get myself straightened out. He's looking after my business worldwide and we will be working closely together to further my career, not only here but back in the States too.'

However, in a very short space of time Jeffrey Kruger had no choice but to publicly denounce Marvin Gaye . . .

Journalist and press agent Roger St Pierre was hired to handle Gaye's tour promotion and publicity, and had a high regard for the singer – 'But he shot my work schedule to pieces. He'd never be in the right place at the right time; he'd either be spaced out or laid out. We could never be certain he'd show for a gig or for an interview until he was on the premises, and even then we had to keep a constant eye on him.' For his part, Marvin was experiencing bouts of painful insecurity and admitted he now felt extremely susceptible to the strains of touring and being an entertainer. This state of mind worried him sufficiently to mention it to St Pierre. Gaye: 'An artist must be like a sponge and absorb everything about life, use his senses to pick up and store experience. Just look at the lives of people like Van Gogh and Beethoven. It makes you very vulnerable if you're not strong. It's like taking on the world's problems and storing them up inside. But you don't know pleasure if you don't know pain. To cope, you have to learn from your experiences, develop a wider wisdom of what life is all about. I get tired sometimes and I feel I'd like to become spiritual again, but then the zest of life comes through and I know I'm in the right place at the right time.'

The tour more or less ran smoothly although on stage Gaye often forgot the running order of his songs, occasionally stumbled over the lyrics, repeated verses or improvised. Those who knew him attributed this to his cocaine intake, while his audiences believed his stage inadequacies were a result of his broken marriage. Behind his public face Gaye was a thoroughly depressed and sad man who hated to be in his own company, hence the friends and hangers-on who followed him around. Gaye: 'There are still times I feel unhappy and I must smile, and there are times I want to cry and I must laugh. Unfortunately, that's the business I'm in and I have to put up a good face for people no matter how I feel. So, I tuck up my face and put it away. People rarely see the real Marvin Gaye.'

Performing before British royalty is always a highlight of any entertainer's career; many are considered but few actually are chosen. The publicity surrounding such an invitation can ensure an act's popularity long after his last hit record. However, Marvin Gaye's performance before HRH Princess Margaret at The Lakeside

Country Club on the evening of 8 July 1980 was a fiasco! It was an embarrassing disaster and, for a time, did untold harm to his reputation. Tickets for the event cost £10, £15 and £20 each and the evening's proceeds were to go to the Dockland Settlement of which the Princess was president. Motown/EMI's promotion manager Les Spaine decided to ensure Gaye honoured the date and visited him in his hotel, The Britannia, on his way to Camberley. Spaine found the singer languishing despondently, talking incoherently, angry because of a reputed misunderstanding with Jeffrey Kruger. When it became apparent to Spaine that Gaye had no intention of performing that night, he notified Peter Prince, Motown's vice-president based in London. Gaye also refused to co-operate with the quietly spoken Prince, a placid, experienced music business veteran who began his career by promoting Motown acts for EMI Records during the Sixties. The evening passed slowly by, getting more tense by the moment, when shortly before midnight the Lakeside management received a message saying Gaye had cancelled his performance as he was too mentally exhausted to do justice to his act. After this message was received, another followed which indicated Gaye had left his hotel and was actually *en route*! The change of heart was the result of a phone call by Peter Prince to Berry Gordy which was made in sheer desperation. He was the only person on earth who had the power to persuade Gaye to honour the commitment. Gordy, a strong admirer of Royalty, considered it a privilege for his artists to be invited to perform – also such appearances and ensuing publicity boosted their status in America, proven by the previous command performances by Diana Ross and the Supremes, and the Jackson 5. So there was no way in which Gordy would permit Gaye to shrug off the performance. Unfortunately, the damage had already been done because by the time Gaye arrived at the club – despite Surrey's chief constable, who was among the guests, arranging for a police escort along the usually congested M3 – to go on stage forty minutes later to give a thirty-minute performance, Princess Margaret had left. Jeffrey Kruger had the unsavoury task of explaining the incident to the awaiting press.

It became apparent from what he was saying that Marvin had known of the Gala for three months and had even brought members of his family to meet the Princess. Kruger: 'Then he waited until they were all dressed up in their finery and broke their hearts. He disgraced the American people, his own black people, his profession, and will lose the admiration of hundreds of fans when they read about this.'

The promoter then left the club stating he would never speak to the singer again – 'Princess Margaret is a fan of his, and of course she was disappointed but she was very charming. I am absolutely disgusted by his behaviour and words cannot express what I feel about this. It is a snub for the Royal Family and he has absolutely no excuse for his behaviour.' Lakeside Country Club's manager shared Kruger's anger, telling the local press that as far as he was concerned Marvin Gaye disgraced himself, no one else – 'I also feel he insulted us and the Royal Family but he is the loser because it reflects on him. In future we will be looking very carefully before we book any similar acts to Marvin Gaye from America. I would not have let him go on stage but people had paid to come and see him.'

Days later the Kruger Organisation issued a press statement which did little to further explain Marvin Gaye's behaviour – 'We are very disappointed with what happened. We fully realise that Marvin is going through enormous personal and business difficulties but we have bent over backwards in an attempt to resolve these problems for him and to make the tour as pleasant and free from strain as possible. That is why we fell in with Marvin's wishes and didn't set up a heavy press and radio interview schedule. Marvin did some great shows but sadly he still has not got his head together and consequently there were considerable problems involved in trying to fit in with his somewhat erratic approach to everything.' The Lakeside performance was a great honour for the singer, the statement continued – 'And we were totally astonished when he blew it. It caused enormous embarrassment to everyone associated with the tour. He let down his record company, the tour promoter, the charity, his fans, the Princess, but most of all – himself. There is no real satisfactory reason we can offer as an excuse. It is quite inexcusable.'

Weeks later Gaye told Lady Edith Foxwell, a member of the British aristocracy, a prominent, well-respected figure in London's society and a tireless charity worker, that he acted in the manner he did because he was angry with his wife. Foxwell: 'There was a lot of trouble. He was in a bad way and he told them to stuff [the evening] up their rear end. He wasn't going. Then Les Spaine apparently talked him into going, but he got there too late. Princess Margaret had to leave and that made him very upset. He said he didn't mean to be rude, he was very depressed.'

Months later he told *Melody Maker*'s Paolo Hewitt that he was controlled by his emotions and feelings – 'And if they say I shouldn't do something because of a very strong principled position that I must take, then in spite of the consequences, in spite of all that is facing me from a detrimental point of view, then I have to remain true to my artistic nature. That was a decision I had to make involving my pride and my dignity and it had nothing to do with the Royal Family.' Then he stressed – 'I'm dreadfully sorry I had to make such a decision. The fact is that nobody was snubbed despite it being written I snubbed Royalty. Because of the pressures put upon me, I couldn't go out there and sing. I refused to do it until certain people who were social-climbing and everything were removed. So, when I got there, Princess Margaret had gone, but if she'd stayed a further fifteen minutes, she would have seen my show.' It's unclear whom Gaye considered to be social climbers, certainly not his entourage and family, and his explanation failed to satisfy the media's curiosity. He then dropped his defensive attitude in Hewitt's interview to boast – 'If I do good music, I'll overcome everything anyway. If the music is good, people don't really care because they go out and buy your music anyway.'

Gaye's music, or lack of it, was now of prime concern to Motown on both sides of the Atlantic. His last British album was 'Here, My Dear' in 1978 which did little to boost his career and the last single was 'Ego Tripping Out' a year later. Despite Motown being told he had been recording in Hawaii, there was still insufficient tracks for an album and any possible single needed extensive re-working. Due to Gaye's ongoing strained relationship with Motown/USA he was reluctant to work with its British offshoot even though he knew he would, in the long run, benefit by co-operating. Eventually, after careful handling by Motown/EMI, he agreed to become involved in certain projects although sometimes the results were unsatisfactory and, at their very worst, damaging to his career. For example, Gaye agreed to be interviewed on London's commercial radio station, Capital Radio. The programme was actually on air as he travelled to the studios in Marylebone Road, with the DJ not knowing whether or not he would contribute to the programme. The singer eventually went on air to mumble his way through a few minutes' chat which listeners could barely decipher. It was a disgraceful exhibition and a waste of airtime.

By now, it didn't take a crystal ball to realise that Gaye's regard for the media was negligible, yet without its support his career would be finished, and this was instilled into his mind time and again by

Motown/EMI's promotion and publicity staff who also for the first time came face to face with his cocaine habit of which he made no secret. Naturally the company strenuously denied his involvement for fear of him being prosecuted and arrested, while Marvin merely shrugged off the possibility of legal action! Occasionally he requested money from them offering numerous excuses why he needed the cash because he knew that record companies, like other business corporations, hold 'grey area' budgets for various uses. However, no company or company staff can be seen to supply cash for, or condone the use of, drug-taking although of course it does happen. Motown/EMI refused to finance Gaye's habit but the legitimate money it might have given him for his living expenses or other certain items probably ended up in a dealer's pocket. It was a no-win situation!

It was also unfortunate that as fast as the British company issued denials of Gaye's cocaine habit, he hinted or confirmed it to journalists including *NME*'s Chris Salewicz who interviewed him one afternoon and evening. Salewicz told David Ritz – 'Marvin snorted quantities during the interview . . . it had an adverse effect on him . . . he began to feel ill and explained this was due to the dodgy substance the cocaine was cut with . . . he attempted to clean out all the impurities from the cocaine . . . snorted the purified powder to blast the rubbish from his system.' Finally Motown/EMI had little choice but to abandon all hopes of maintaining his cool, clean image and reluctantly shrugged off responsibility for him in this respect. London DJ Graham Canter possibly summed up the company's position during this time – 'What could they do anymore? I think Motown in America were frankly very worried about it but the UK really didn't have the clout to do anything about Marvin Gaye. They were largely the puppet sitting on the knee of Motown/America, and in the end they couldn't have given a damn.' Lady Edith Foxwell: 'Marvin was very open with me about his drug taking. I've never taken any drugs, I don't even smoke cigarettes. I just thought it was a shame because I saw so much of it when I was connected with The Embassy [nightclub]. It ruins people. I didn't speak to Marvin about it because it wouldn't have done a lot of good. If people are determined to do something they'll do it.'

Another interview Marvin Gaye conducted also gave cause for concern, not because of its content but because he mistook the female reporter for a hooker. Graham Canter: 'Marvin was in a West End hotel and he had a series of press interviews that day in his room. The night before he'd had a knock on his door and it was a lady of the night offering her services. Marvin already had company and said, "No, no, not tonight, thank you. Come back another day." The next day there was a knock on the door and a very attractive young lady was standing there. She didn't say anything particularly interesting to Marvin. Well, Marvin being the sexual being that he was had this lady's top – I think halter tops were in fashion at the time – removed and was playing with her breasts. She wasn't objecting. I walked in and shouted at him to stop and told him who she was, a national newspaper journalist. He didn't stop, he just carried on until she ran out in tears. If I hadn't come along at that stage I think it would have gone a lot further. He might have been fathering her children. Afterwards he just went to the loo, I don't think those things bothered him.' Canter identified the journalist but as she still works in that field, he requested her anonymity.

Bob Killbourn, editor of *Blues & Soul* magazine, was another to fall foul of a Marvin Gaye interview. This time it was the singer's lateness which would have discouraged the most devoted and diligent of reporters. However, their eventual meeting did lead to a remarkable, honest relationship, one Gaye rarely cemented with a journalist, and which lasted up to his death. Killbourn waited in the singer's London apartment from mid-afternoon until late evening while he languished in his bedroom next door, doing nothing in particular except being obstinate and sending out messages via a member of his entourage for him to remain. The interview was eventually conducted from Gaye's bed. Two years on, Gaye again wanted to speak to Killbourn whereupon a telephone link was arranged between Los Angeles and London. For five nights Killbourn sat by the phone waiting for the singer to call! On the sixth night he did and one of the first questions asked was – 'Marvin, don't you like interviews?!' Gaye said he didn't – 'I don't enjoy them and I don't like being misquoted!'

Ignoring Gaye's sarcasm Killbourn continued – 'Do you like the atmosphere of interviews?' Gaye: 'Frankly? No. I prefer to be just quiet and to be the quiet dark horse who emerges occasionally to do his little number and then sinks back into his solitude. That way, people wonder what the hell I'm up to, and I like that.'

Using another tactic the next question concerned the singer's obligations to share his life with his fans, a point regularly raised by the press who felt he ignored his public. Gaye thought otherwise: 'I don't feel obligated to share my life, but I do. I'm extremely honest and I do share my life with my fans because of a desire to let them know what's going on or because I want something back in return. I am simply being honest and I don't have anything to hide. My life is an open book. Why should I hide anything? Nobody's going to get in the casket with me. Besides, twenty years from now, there won't be anybody who'll give a shit anyway.'

After several minutes had passed Gaye indicated the conversation was over. Killbourn fired a last question, was there anything specific in his career he wanted to achieve? There was, he said – 'When I was a very young chap I always had this dream that I was singing to a multitude of people – a larger sea of people than I've ever seen the Pope enjoy. Anyhow, when I finished my performance, I was acclaimed the world's greatest singer. I used to dream that dream quite often and I imagine that those early childhood dreams are what drive me on. Perhaps one day that'll become a reality.'

As Marvin Gaye's British tour ended, promoters Marshall Arts announced dates for 'Stevie Wonder's Hotter Than July Music Picnic' concerts for September 1980 as part of his European tour, his first in six years. Six nights at Wembley Arena were secured and instantly sold out. Gaye had intended to return to America before his colleague's tour began but when the time came to depart he shuddered at the thought of facing the unholy mess he had left behind and deliberately missed his flight. Forced to move from his hotel, he settled into the first of several apartments with his mother, and his musicians. Situated in Rutland Gate, a stylish area of south-west London, Gaye and his entourage stayed in an expensively decorated, luxurious apartment until it was 'wrecked'. The furious landlord demanded that Motown/EMI rehouse Gaye and his musicians before he contacted the police. The musicians being penniless following a misunderstanding about unpaid wages, had actually slept on the apartment floor waiting for the problem to be resolved. Eventually, Motown – possibly the London-based Motown International – paid for them to return to America, while a colleague found Gaye another apartment where he stayed until the lease expired.

Frankly, Marvin was oblivious to the trouble he had caused and the upsets in his personal life seemed forgotten because he was now free – no commitment, no tour schedules, no one telling him what to do. London was everything he had dreamt of and more. Easy access was available to all the pleasures he indulged in, particularly freely available cocaine and an endless string of obliging women. Even so, in time this wasn't enough; he pined for Janis, his family and the love they had shared. He pined for his career. He became a lonely man, a sad figure, people felt sorry for him.

His newly-found freedom took him into London's nightlife: he was seen regularly with a handful of playmates at the most exclusive of clubs and the more prestigious of concerts, and also at the seediest hang-outs night-time London can offer. He was photographed with many of the city's glitterati including Princess Margaret's son, Viscount Linley, and his name was linked with Lady Edith Foxwell, then co-owner of the exclusive Embassy Club opened during September 1980 in London's Piccadilly area. Foxwell was the former wife of the film magnate Ivan Foxwell, and she first met Marvin Gaye at the opening of another nighterie, Cheeks, in the East End, when she, like Gaye, had been invited as a celebrity guest. Foxwell was incapacitated by a broken foot which necessitated using a walking stick but she was determined this wouldn't prevent her from attending the function. Lady Edith Foxwell: 'On arrival I was asked have you met your other celebrity and I asked who it was. Marvin Gaye! Well, I'd heard of him of course but had never met him. So we were introduced in the pitch black, I couldn't see one single thing. We had to give prizes for something that I've now forgotten and I asked him if he'd like to come back to The Embassy with me. He said it sounded good and we sailed off. What I hadn't realised was that a whole lot of people had come with him, including his bodyguard called Cool Black. So we *all* went back to The Embassy!'

After this evening a close friendship developed between the singer and the aristocrat, so much so that she was able to break down Marvin's emotional barrier to discover the real man hiding within. Foxwell soon realised that the inner man was looking for someone he could trust sufficiently to confide in – 'I don't know if he trusted me, maybe he did. We got on terribly well and I honestly don't know why. We had a very good relationship and maybe that's what he liked. I liked him a lot, he was a very sweet person. He was also a very sad person, had a very sad quality. He wasn't stupid, he was a very deep thinker. And he used to tell me all about his problems, his troubles, his marriages that had gone wrong and his family life.' Gaye's sadness during this time was likewise detected by Graham Canter who also remembered him to be painfully shy – 'If I had had a monster talent like him I'd have been much more extrovert, but he seemed shy of his talent and shy at meeting people. When you got to know the man, he was fun with an extremely dry humour and was caring for people although a little eccentric in his behaviour. He was not the sort of man who tolerated fools gladly and I think if you gave him a lot of bullshit would be inclined to dismiss you from his company. You'd be in his company physically but he'd tend to ignore you in the conversation.'

While Marvin Gaye partied the night away, his young son, Bubby, was cared for by his nanny, said to be either Patricia or Eugenie Vie, his girlfriend and/or his secretary who wanted to marry him. Canter remembered two women being in Gaye's life at this time – 'And that's one thing that surprised me about Marvin. He would immediately be attracted to a woman and he would have a period of longevity with a woman, rather than some American artists I can mention saying "I've got to have everything in sight and now." Marvin wouldn't. During a period of say six months he would only have two, maybe three girlfriends and for an American artist he was really going well. And this was pre-AIDS days although I don't think Marvin would have cared less about that. I think he knew he was destined to die one way or another.'

Often Gaye was criticised for his treatment of women particularly when he used them as playthings or treated them in a shoddy manner. One such shabby incident, remembered by a close source, concerned a young lady who adored him but whom he disliked, and instead of telling her this, he led her on – 'She came to me one day and said, "Marvin has asked me to lunch." I said, "You'll be lucky to see him at that time." He'd invited her to his flat in Rutland Gate, so I asked him why he had done that. "Ah well," he replied – you know how he used to go – "she doesn't understand. I think she needs a little understanding." Anyway, the great day dawned and passed. Then she phoned me. "What's he done now?" I asked. She told me, "I went to the apartment, knocked on his door. Someone came and said Mr Gaye was otherwise disposed or something and couldn't take me out." So I said, "What did I tell you!" When I spoke to Marvin afterwards he said, "I thought she needed teaching a lesson!" I believed that was very unfair of him and told him so.'

From time to time Marvin Gaye felt that London was hemming him in and escaped to Lady Edith Foxwell's family residence in Sherston, Warwickshire, purchased by her father in 1940. In typical fashion, Gaye wouldn't travel alone so Foxwell was forced to entertain his rapidly growing entourage. She remembered their first visit –

'They were coming at one o'clock for lunch. Eventually, after numerous phone calls they turned up at nine at night. There were about six of them including his son, the nanny, Cool Black, Felice, but no girls, not even his fiancée. It was a very funny time. They all stayed, and then sort of eased their way back to London. Marvin came down numerous times because he loved it there. He liked the ambience.' During these visits Gaye would play the out-of-tune piano in the nursery, and when it was later tuned spent hours behind closed doors working on new ideas. Foxwell: 'He also liked to go to the village pub for a beer. The locals knew who he was and he loved it. Or he would wander about enjoying the countryside and my garden, where he was very much by himself.' This was an idyllic situation Gaye would again find himself in but next time Belgium was his host.

When Marvin enjoyed London's nightspots and other people's hospitality he never paid for anything, having little or no money of his own as noted by Foxwell – 'He never made any bones about it either! I used to take him to a lot of things. It was no big deal. But as regards a slap-up meal at Claridges, no, we didn't have anything like that. I used to entertain him a lot at Sherston though.' Graham Canter: 'I never actually saw Marvin spend any money. In fact, I never saw him with money. His minions and helpers layed it out for him. Anyway, the only time I ever saw him needing money was for drugs and half the time he didn't pay for them because he was Marvin Gaye, and at the time there were many people who wanted to latch on to him and be with him.' The money Gaye earned from his last tour had been spent almost before the dates had finished, and in desperation he had sought help from fellow Motowners Stevie Wonder and Smokey Robinson, who both declined to offer assistance, knowing why he needed the money. Both abhorred drug-taking, although Robinson was at one time a regular rock cocaine user, and did not intend to fuel Gaye's habit. Even fellow artist Rick James had abandoned his wild drug-taking binges following several spells in hospital prior to the release of his fourth album 'Garden Of Love'. James: 'I wound up being over-tired and my liver was in bad shape. It has meant that I have had to cut out a lot of things. No drugs, no alcohol, although I still smoke my Mary Jane. It was a case of live or die and I realised that I had been taking too much alcohol and coke.'

For a time Marvin Gaye's presence in London and the problems that went with that stay were pushed aside as Motown/EMI staff scurried around to ensure 'Stevie Wonder's Hotter Than July Music Picnic' concerts (1–7 [excluding 4] September) and his stay in England passed as pleasantly as possible. Arrangements included organising a playback reception for his forthcoming album 'Hotter Than July' at EMI's famous Abbey Road Studios, purchasing his favourite chocolate chip cookies from Harrods and ensuring his limousine driver was black, a stipulation laid down by his management. At the same time, Motown/EMI hoped he would make himself available to film a promotional video for his 'Masterblaster Jammin'' single which had just been issued. (Wonder agreed, but only if it could be shot in two takes at Wembley Arena on his day off! It was.) Also, Motown/EMI asked whether he would consider meeting the media (very few interviews were granted) because 1980 was a special year – Motown celebrated its Twentieth Anniversary. Even though the celebration was a year late, as the Tamla label was opened in 1959, Motown records and merchandising carried a specially designed logo to celebrate the achievement. More acts visited England this year than ever before and due to the exceptionally high standard of music, Motown enjoyed its best year in terms of record sales since the Sixties heyday. Motown/EMI alone sold in excess of one and a half million albums and three million singles, a staggering success in a climate dominated by spiralling costs within the record industry. Since the British subsidiary Tamla Motown opened in 1965 approximately thirty million singles and twenty-five million albums had been sold, and their office walls sagged under the weight of silver, gold and platinum records, awards, certificates and a host of other honours.

The Twentieth Anniversary also coincided with the return to Motown of Berry Gordy's beloved Temptations, a move encouraged by Smokey Robinson, where their first releases were the 'Power' single and album in April 1980. The quintet contributed to Motown's British success alongside artists like Stevie Wonder, of course, Rick James, Teena Marie, Jermaine Jackson, Billy Preston and Syreeta, the Commodores and Diana Ross with her Nile Rodgers and Bernard Edwards-conceived 'Diana' album which spawned three 1980 hits – 'Upside Down' (no 2), 'My Old Piano' (5) and 'I'm Coming Out' (13).

Maybe the success that emanated from this Anniversary inspired Marvin Gaye to think favourably about Motown once more because he visited the temporary UK offices in Mortimer Street, situated immediately above a family planning clinic (which invariably brought a smile to visitors' faces!) and opposite the Middlesex Hospital where one of the world's best loved actors Peter Sellers died. Gaye called at the offices to discuss a recording schedule to complete the 'Love Man' album among other things, with the company executives. He initially appeared awkward and his soft drawl was difficult to understand immediately, yet the atmosphere on this warm afternoon was relaxed. Several young autograph-hunting secretaries burst into the Motown office, taking Gaye by surprise, something he loathed. However, instead of retreating he welcomed them with a shy warmth, his halfcocked smile twitching. The youngsters sang his praises for days afterwards!

Unfortunately, the Marvin Gaye magic was not always successful because a short time later he failed to patch up his marriage when his wife Janis flew to London with their daughter Nona. Lady Edith Foxwell: 'He used to talk about a divorce . . . they were separated and not really amicably so. I don't know whether they actually divorced or not. I saw them together but it was for a very brief period.' Friends longed for a reconciliation, their hopes fuelled when Marvin indicated he intended to follow his wife back to America. He never did, and all hopes were finally dashed when Janis threatened to snatch back their son Bubby claiming Marvin had kidnapped him. Gaye: 'You might say I have kidnapped my own son, but I love him and he loves me, and he's happy. I don't have custody of him. My wife lives in Los Angeles and I don't suppose she's too thrilled about it.' His son wanted for nothing; he had his father's love and attention albeit spasmodically, but he was bored with no one of his own age to play with. It appeared he lived on fast foods, and asked visitors for money for ice-cream and toys. However, nobody could blame Janis for her concern, particularly if she chanced to see the newspapers which occasionally carried items about her revelling husband, the man about town. It was a situation more befitting the pages of a Hollywood novel than an everyday occurrence in London town!

Before the lease on his second apartment had expired Marvin had befriended the employees of Lagos International, a company based in Bryanston Street, London. In time the company would handle Gaye's next tour, but meanwhile they helped him move into a permanent home situated off the busy Edgware Road, where he remained prior to moving to Belgium. This cramped apartment on Park West Place, near Kendal Street, London W2, became a home for him, Bubby, his girlfriend and members of his entourage. The set-up was disorganised, little housework was done, and the tiny kitchen rarely used. Gaye's wardrobe was crammed, bursting to the seams, usually with unwashed clothes even though there was a washing machine in the apartment. When he visited Lady Edith Foxwell, she would arrange for his washing to be done in her laundry and if he had a record company or 'official' function to attend, Lagos International's Gloria Dale or Motown/EMI's Noreen Allen arranged for laundry services or personally took his clothes to the dry cleaners.

From this apartment, and in between entertaining – it was known for him to greet visitors from his bedroom, while sitting on the toilet, or refuse them entrance at all – Gaye began negotiating another British tour. It was to be quite some time before this actually happened; Motown/EMI were notified of the negotiations but remained silent, waiting for the outcome. Another Marvin Gaye tour was not what they needed, new product was, but as he desperately needed money, the company knew it couldn't force him to finish the 'Love Man' project. Also the company was involved with Stevie Wonder's tour, promoting 'Masterblaster Jammin' and planning marketing campaigns for his pending 'Hotter Than July' album, as well as keeping a high profile for the Anniversary year. Then the unbelievable happened, Motown's queen of song Diana Ross flew to London on a private holiday with her boyfriend Gene Simmons. the swirling-tongued member of the wild rock group Kiss, who were appearing at Wembley Arena after Stevie Wonder. Before dating Ross, Simmons had been her best friend Cher's boyfriend, and this was, many said, a mismatched relationship. Prior to her arrival, Ross insisted she had no intention of working, but when she discovered how tirelessly Motown/EMI staff had promoted her career she agreed to host a press reception at the Inn on the Park Hotel, off Park Lane. During the lavish reception she warded off questions concerning her affair with Simmons, stressing it was a private matter, and happily accepted the numerous awards from Motown/EMI for British record sales and delighted the media with her good humour and quick wit. Needless to say, she graced most newspaper front pages the next day!

With Diana Ross's arrival Motown's top three solo acts were on British soil – Marvin, Stevie and Diana! And how Motown/EMI must have prayed that this godsend could be utilised publicly. It was a chance of a lifetime, the *crème de la crème* in promotion and a perfect climax to this Twentieth Anniversary. Unfortunately, following discreet enquiries, the company reluctantly abandoned the pipe-dream. But what it hadn't reckoned on was the pulling power of Stevie Wonder . . .

# 11. | A Heavy Love Affair

*[Marvin] spoke of a deep hatred of Motown, from Berry Gordy down to the packers in the distribution department.*

(Graham Canter)

*I'll certainly not give Motown another album.*

(Marvin Gaye)

*Marvin was such a happy-go-lucky, laid-back sort of person who didn't want any hassle.*

(Lady Edith Foxwell)

*I said, 'Marvin, why don't you let me just marry you and take you away from all this.'*

(Mary Wilson)

Motown history was made during Stevie Wonder's British tour because the three megastars not only met up but performed together on the Wembley Arena stage on 7 September. Diana Ross and Gene Simmons were already seated in the exclusive artists' enclosure situated at the side of the awesome stage when Wonder began his show. Marvin Gaye arrived later, driven to the venue in a pale-coloured mini which was later parked in the vast aircraft hangar-type area that was immediately behind the newly designed stage. Gaye did not go into the auditorium, he preferred to wander around backstage. A member of Wonder's entourage went on stage to tell the singer Gaye and Ross had arrived, whereupon at his earliest convenient break he invited them both up front. When Diana was told of Wonder's intention she immediately resisted claiming she wasn't suitably dressed for an appearance, yet she looked stunning in a simply cut outfit, a make-up-free face, her long hair pulled back, while Marvin, dressed in a striped, light-coloured shirt and suit, was unsure what move to make.

Both artists were escorted to the stage to find themselves facing a disbelieving audience of eight thousand! The earth-shattering reception the three stars basked in was of the highest accolade. Hysterical fans rushed uncontrollably to the stage, causing pandemonium. Within seconds stage security was trebled while hand-chosen photographers hidden in the stage pit climbed over themselves to point their lenses at one of music's historical events. When the thunderous reception had finally died down Gaye sat at Wonder's piano to play 'What's Going On'. He improvised the lyrics on the first verse before leaving it to his co-stars to pick up the song. After ten or so minutes the spectacular was over and two happy stars left the stage leaving Wonder to somehow retrieve the remainder of his musical programme.

The three artists were also reunited for a while backstage (much to the annoyance of Gene Simmons who felt Diana Ross should remain with him) where people milled around requesting autographs, where security men stood shoulder to shoulder to prevent members of the public from sneaking through the several backstage exits and where the assortment of authorised personnel completed their assigned tasks before the venue closed for the night. Jim Hegarty, who had first met Marvin Gaye during 1976, was backstage, amidst the mayhem – 'Marvin, Stevie and Diana stood together so that I could take some photos. Unfortunately Gene Simmons was next to Diana and was included in the shots. When he realised this I had to take the film from my camera and give it to him. The creep. Just because he had no makeup on. I felt so sick about that, because few people believed I actually was in the presence of the three Motown legends. Sadly, this was the last time I spoke to Marvin.'

Another ex-Supreme also in London, Mary Wilson, was part way through a tour of Europe and was using the city as her base. Wilson would occasionally meet Gaye in the fashionable Tramp nightclub where they would spend evenings together, she trying to lift him from bouts of intense depression where he would openly cry regardless of his surroundings. She also visited him in his apartment where he played her songs he intended to record. During one of these visits Gaye said she spoke of marriage (even though she was already married to Pedro Ferrer) and how she felt deeply about him. Wilson: 'I said, "Marvin why don't you let me just marry you and take you away from all this."' It was probably a playful remark on her part but Gaye said he was wary of her motives. On the other hand, he too suggested marriage, not to Mary Wilson but to Lady Edith Foxwell as she laughed – 'It was a joke really. He said, "We should get married and then you'd be Lady Gaye." It was very funny . . . that would have taken a lot of explaining too, wouldn't it?'

During this time in exile in London Marvin Gaye's battles with Motown and Berry Gordy grew to frightening proportions. The two would speak occasionally over the telephone but their wounds never healed. Gordy was anxious that Gaye should straighten out his life and offered to help where he could. Derogatory publicity about Motown instigated by the singer didn't help the situation but no one could stop him criticising and condemning the company which had stood by him throughout his career. No sign of loyalty was shown towards Berry Gordy either; the man who had patiently groomed and later invested vast sums of money into the young inexperienced singer with sky high ambitions. Graham Canter: 'Marvin was constantly complaining about Motown. It was one of the bees in his bonnet and when I spoke to him about it, he spoke of a deep hatred of the company, from Berry Gordy down to the packers in the distribution department.' Canter felt the Motown boss had tried to distance himself from the singer's personal problems at this time and this hurt Gaye – 'Marvin was in a situation where he needed a father figure but not his own father. He needed someone to say "Look Marvin, you're in trouble. Get yourself sorted out!" Someone to take on all his financial worries and to encourage him to work. If he didn't want the advice after that – then OK. There's nobody in this world who's indispensable, even to Motown!' .

A month after appearing on the Wembley stage Gaye delivered his next album to Motown in November 1980 for early 1981 release. The reluctantly finished project largely comprised those tracks intended for the 'Love Man' album, re-recorded and/or rehearsed in the Seawest Recording studios in Honolulu, Hawaii, and his own Los Angeles studio before it was snatched by the IRS. Several of the songs were completed in the Odyssey Studio, London, following his British tour. Gaye: 'I finished off the album in London because the energy is something incredible. When I recorded my "live" album at the London Palladium I recognised a different energy than I had in the States, and it's like a lift for me at this point. I've been in this business for twenty-four years now, which is a long time, but I think it's an achievement rather than an age thing . . . I think a lot of people are envious because I still have my energy, and I still can do an hour and a half of a high-energy show.'

It appears that Motown/USA had issued Marvin with an

ultimatum to complete the new project within a certain period of time or else it would not be released at all, and in this event, Gaye would probably be asked to return the financial advance! So he had no choice and the record's masters were duly dispatched to America, or as Gaye claimed – 'Motown simply confiscated the masters before I had finished and they released [the album] in that unfinished form. They released it to make money. So at the end of the day I can't really claim this piece of work as my production because the liberties taken by Motown were appalling. In fact I disavow publicly this being my work.' The reason for the 'confiscation' was simple. Berry Gordy had given him ample time and finance to re-mix the work, and had to prevent him from spending more money on the project which was already wildly over-budget. Nonetheless Gaye was furious at Motown's action — 'The album was taken from my hands and taken back to Los Angeles and done with what Motown saw fit to do with it. They have the control, they have the album, and they'll do what they jolly well please!'

In the light of recent events, it was obvious his crusade against Motown had finally come to an end. Neither seemed able to reach a compromise, and the only way he felt his career had any future was to leave the company and begin again, as he pointed out to a *Melody Maker* journalist – 'There's a horrible conflict between us. If one's artistic nature is true, then he or she is more likely to run into tremendous difficulties with those who are concerned with deadlines and commerciality and control and all those nasty little words which make us very ill. I can't imagine I'll ever record another album with Motown unless a miracle happens . . . I'm not bitter or anything like that. It's experience and it's a step upwards for me actually. I feel that if I can find another record company that's interested in my qualities as an artist, rather than a single; if I can find a company that is more interested in me as a complete entity of artist, producer, arranger, musician and who recognises those qualities in me and who feels that these qualities are essentially good and that I should be respected and that one should be treated special if one is special, then that is the company I'll sign for.'

Irrespective of Gaye's attitude, Motown put its wheels into motion by pressing and marketing his new album now titled 'In Our Lifetime'. Marvin had personally sketched the album's sleeve design which was then given to British artist Neil Breedon to complete during a meeting at Motown/EMI's offices now re-located at EMI's headquarters at 20 Manchester Square, London. The finished copy was then sent to Motown/USA (Berry Gordy?) for approval. Reputedly the copy was rejected but the go-ahead was given anyway, thus avoiding any further friction with the singer.

The record's front sleeve, edged in red, depicted good and evil. On the top half of the sleeve Gaye the God and Gaye the Devil faced each other across a checkered clothed table upon which sat an exploding world against a background of black clouds in a darkened sky. A dove sat behind God on a high-backed antique chair entwined with flowers, while a motionless bat was suspended in space behind the Devil, with a long snake replacing the entwined flowers on his chair. Below the clouds swirling at their feet, was America, with it's peaceful welcoming symbol, the Statue of Liberty, fragmented in a nuclear explosion, while Mother Nature's induced tragedies were pictured alongside including earthquake and flood. These earthly devastations over which human beings have no control were balanced by man-made inventions like war, space ships, pollution, air travel, electricity and so on. It was a complex insight into the singer's confused and perhaps egotistical mind (who else would have dared to impersonate God in such a way?) and had little to do with the album's content, even though Gaye's original intention was to show the contrast between God and the Devil – 'These two forces are good and evil, positive and negative, light and dark, however you want to put it. I wanted to show with music – and the illustration on the cover – that this is an area we would be concerned with. But I didn't get the chance to clearly illustrate that with this work because I was stopped about three-quarters of the way through, conceptually speaking.' The album's back sleeve listed the tracks and the obligatory recording credits, to the left of which the killer-diller Gaye provocatively posed in a silver grey, open-necked shirt, with its matching handkerchief flopping from his black velvet jacket's top pocket. The photograph, presumed to be some months old, was taken by Ron Slenzak.

It was only when the album was pressed and packaged that Marvin realised to his horror the title was incorrect. It should, he moaned, have read 'In Our Lifetime?' but the question mark was omitted from the final artwork, despite being included on the draft. Motown promised to correct it on the reprint but it was thought sales didn't warrant further copies being pressed at this time.

Although the majority of the songs included were old Gaye was emphatic that they should not be treated as dated – 'Most of the songs that were going to be on "Love Man" are now on this album, but they're all changed. If I were an artist who painted pictures I have just erased half of the image I put on canvas, and I'm going to replace it with something else.' The first side of 'In Our Lifetime' comprised tracks originally destined for the 'Love Man' album – 'Praise' previously titled 'Let Your Love Come Shining Through', followed by 'Life Is For Learning' previously 'Songs Are To Learn From', 'Love Party' and 'Funk Me' originally 'Funk Me, Funk Me, Funk Me'. Side two opened with 'Far Cry', arranged by Frank Blair, where Robert Ahwry's guitar expertise battled with Fleecy Joe James' percussion before the song changed from its jumpy sound into a moody melody. Snatches of Isaac Hayes' 'Shaft' were apparent, Marvin's tribute to the musician's talent. The remaining tracks were, by and large, almost nondescript. 'Love Me Now Or Love Me Later', partly narrated, told of Gaye's conversations with the Gods of Good and Evil, while 'Heavy Love Affair' offered lashings of soft vocals behind his lead, reminiscent of his Seventies work. The almost monotonous beat was thankfully broken by Raf Ravenscroft's sax solo, better known for his work on Gerry Rafferty's 'Baker Street'. The final track was the album's mid-paced title where the lyrics were barely distinguishable. 'In Our Lifetime' was a disappointment; the songs were weak, the music jaded, the commercial appeal practically nil, and certainly was not a fitting finale to his Motown career.

Promotion and marketing are vital roles in selling product to the public, and the record business is no different; records need specialised and expert attention because the competition is aggressive due to the short life span of a single. An album can live forever. On occasion, record companies will combine with another entertainment entity like a particular radio/television programme, a magazine or nightclub to promote records and/or artists. Motown/EMI was asked if Marvin Gaye would make a guest appearance at a north London nightclub. Gaye agreed to attend during December 1980, whereupon a car collected him from London's West End to travel the forty-minute journey across the city, battling against the Friday night traffic. On arrival at the nightclub, where a standing-room only audience waited, Marvin was ushered by the theatre's security and Graham Canter (who accompanied him for the evening) through the entrance and quickly upstairs into a management office. Within minutes of Gaye's arrival lines of cocaine were spread across the office desk for him and for others who participated. Canter: 'I think Marvin not only anticipated it but he expected that. I don't think he was getting a fee for the appearance he was making but I think he wanted his narcotic requirements satisfied. It wasn't in lieu of payment, no, it was like a band, after they've finished or before they've started a gig to expect Southern Comfort or Tequila in their dressing-room.' Meantime, a late guest arrived and being incensed at the open display of the drug, swiftly swept what was left on the table down to the floor. Marvin laughed uncontrollably, he thought her actions were both courageous and amusing; not so those waiting to indulge!

As Gaye waited to perform on stage he often quoted lines of prose, and tonight was no exception. Canter: 'I asked if they were his words. He said, "No, it's Shakespeare", and laughed.' It really was his which he hadn't written into a song yet. When I asked him if he often quoted his lyrics he replied "only in moments of great joy or in moments of great sadness".' When Gaye walked onstage, the nightclub's resident DJ played the twelve-inch version of 'Got To Give It Up' over which Marvin would sing. Canter: 'The song's introduction went on forever, and Marvin walked about the stage very cool, very calm, as thousands of kids went absolutely crazy. He walked along to the front row, shaking hands, microphone tucked into his jacket pocket. Four bars before he was due to sing, he whipped the mike out, spun it in the air, turned round, caught it and sang. The performance was the most emotional thing I've ever seen.' After a short stay to sign autographs Gaye was quietly smuggled outside and driven home. The following week, Motown artist Jermaine Jackson made a similar personal appearance when the strongest substance available in the upstairs office was orange juice.

'In Our Lifetime' was released simultaneously in America and Britain during January 1981, and 'Praise', considered to be the most commercial track for radio play, was the first single to be lifted a month later in America, (where it failed to make the pop chart but fared better in the R&B listing by reaching the top twenty) and during March in Britain. The track was re-mixed and edited to bring it into line with competitors' product and was coupled with the more compelling 'Funk Me' which was heavily played in nightclubs. When the single bombed on both sides of the Atlantic, Gaye was not bothered, nor was he concerned about the adverse publicity surrounding its release – 'I am not unduly worried about any negative publicity that people choose to put out about me. I believe in being true to myself and to my art [which] will ultimately transcend all that other garbage.' However, being true to himself was not the answer at this time. He desperately needed to re-establish himself as a selling commodity to enable Motown to recoup the money advanced to him, and as much as his fans continued to support him, their disappointment in 'Praise' was reflected in its abysmal sales. Likewise 'In Our Lifetime' was a steady seller from its release but not sufficiently to chart it in the top fifty. The failure of this work, Gaye pointed out, simply underlined what he had been saying for some time, that Motown was suppressing his natural creativity, was meddling with his art and was not supporting his career. What he failed, or perhaps refused, to acknowledge was that 'In Our Lifetime' was a mediocre record, devoid of singles, yet Motown backed it to the hilt with extensive, costly marketing and promotion more befitting potential chart toppers.

As Marvin Gaye's career started its decline once more, Stevie Wonder fulfilled one of his ambitions by leading a rally in Gaye's hometown, Washington D.C. to celebrate the birthday of the late Dr Martin Luther King. Approximately two hundred thousand people shrugged off the thirty degree weather to participate in the march that left the Capitol steps at 10 a.m. on 15 January 1981 to march to the Washington Monument grounds where his two-hour programme of music began at noon. Also this was one of Wonder's most successful periods, thanks to his highly commercial album 'Hotter Than July' which had to date spawned the American top five hit (and British number two hit) 'Masterblaster (Jammin')', and 'I Ain't Gonna Stand For It' which reached the top twenty in both countries. However, the next single 'Lately' was the *crème de la crème* – a beautiful, poignant ballad which went on to become a music classic. During the same month, January, Motown/EMI released two movie title songs – Diana Ross's 'It's My Turn' from the film of the same name and 'Take Me Away' by The Temptations, from the *Loving Couples* film. Both singles had been American-released late in 1980. And Smokey Robinson celebrated his silver anniversary in the music business by releasing his sixth American chart topper and first British solo number one 'Being With You' lifted from his thirty-third album named after the single. Meanwhile Mary Wilson was unsuccessfully trying to re-form The Supremes due to the success of the Broadway musical *Dreamgirls* loosely based on the rise and fall of the Motown trio.

As Berry Gordy, now chairman of Motown Industries, announced that he intended Motown Productions to produce films as well as television specials under the presidency of Suzanne de Passe, Diana

Ross was planning to leave Motown. For some time she had felt disappointed with the company's accounting of her royalties and took the unprecedented move of over-seeing her business affairs without Berry Gordy's involvement, and when 'A Diana Ross Production' ran in the closing credits of the television spectacular *Diana*, rumours that had circulated the music business of her pending departure were confirmed. She had reluctantly severed the umbilical cord. Gordy had no choice but to let his protégée leave because she was asking for a re-signing advance Motown could not afford. In terms of record sales Ross was not, as the industry believed, a big seller in America, the majority of her sales emanating from Europe although nowhere near the scale Motown reported publicly. Therefore her departure didn't leave a void in Motown's market percentage and wouldn't, as was predicted by industry magnates, damage the company's overall sales figures. Ross's defection affected some of Motown's artists more, as they had looked to her as the company's backbone, the company's financial security, while others were delighted to see her defect, hoping they would, in her absence, be afforded the same exclusive treatment she had enjoyed for years.

Before *Diana* was screened in England, Ross had signed a seven-year contract with RCA Records in March 1981, reputedly worth $20 million for Canada and North America. Capitol Records, a subsidiary of EMI Records, signed her for the remainder of the world. Interestingly throughout Ross's career (with and without The Supremes) her European releases have always been via Motown's licensing and distribution arrangement with EMI! Berry Gordy was understandably extremely shocked and annoyed by Diana's disloyalty as he told *The Sunday Times* magazine – 'I felt personally insulted and very hurt. And to leave as she did strictly for money. I would think that if any person leaves for that reason then they should not be with Motown. If they don't understand what we did for them, understand about the care and love and all the other stuff they had, and rate everything in dollars, that to me is not very bright. But with Diana I felt even worse, because I had spent a tremendous amount of time with her. I felt like a failure. I will always love her, but I will always be disappointed in her too.' Smokey Robinson: 'Diana was always regarded as family within Motown and it's always hard to lose a member of one's family . . . Nobody could ever replace her, she was and is a very special and unique talent. However, we do have one or two other acts still at Motown!'

Diana Ross's new recording contracts required her to deliver one album per year but without Motown's teamwork her future career was a struggle – not only did she have total business and creative control but also produced her own recordings. The security and help offered by a loving Motown was gone, she was now on her own to fall and rise on her own initiative. The move was a brave one even though her colleagues and fans felt it was one she'd never make – Diana Ross without Motown was unthinkable – yet those same people supported her new career. She told J. Randy Taraborrelli why she left Motown – 'All of a sudden I felt like here I was thirty-seven years old with three children and through a divorce, but yet not able to take full responsibility for my own decisions. I don't want to pick up the phone and call Berry Gordy, Motown or anyone if I want to buy a car. I want to know where my bank accounts are.'

For her first RCA/Capitol single Ross chose to record a version of 'The Teenagers' featuring Frankie Lymon's 1956 million seller 'Why Do Fools Fall In Love' which reached number seven in America's national listing, number four in Britain during November 1981. The single was the first to be lifted from the album of the same name, which went on to become a platinum record. Two months prior to the single's release Motown issued Ross's 'All The Great Hits' compilation and the company continued to re-issue her product, and that of The Supremes, up to the present day. (Incidentally both Ross and Mary Wilson receive royalties on re-issues.)

As Ross departed, Marvin Gaye – annoyed that she had once again pipped him to the post by not only leaving Motown but by ensuring she had another record company to go to – was determined his public voice about his pending move became louder. It literally boomed from the pages of *Blues & Soul* when – much to the annoyance of Motown/EMI and Berry Gordy – Gaye told the magazine – 'I want out! I want to be free! I'll certainly not give Motown another album, and you will never hear my voice on another Motown album that hasn't been previously pre-recorded.' He had defiantly slammed the Motown door behind him, even though he knew his recording contract had some years to run, without having a key to open a new record company door. But he cared little – 'I've given the best part of my life giving to Motown. They have reputedly sold Jobete Music [the publishing house] for thirty plus million dollars and they wouldn't have been able to command such a high figure if it hadn't been for people like myself, Diana Ross, Stevie Wonder and Smokey Robinson. I doubt very much if we'll get fifty thousand dollars apiece [from the sale] and I think that's appalling. But that's the nature of the business.'

To date, Berry Gordy still owns Jobete although its future is uncertain because during 1988 he did the unimaginable and sold Motown Records to MCA Records and Boston Ventures Ltd, an investment company, for $61 million at a time when Motown was said to be generating in the region of $20 million a year, a fraction of the millions it garnered two decades earlier. Motown Productions, the television and movie company, Stone Diamond and Jobete were excluded from the transaction. Nonetheless Motown fans were horrified at the sale, the company they had lovingly supported for over twenty-five years under Berry Gordy's guidance had been handed over to a stranger, MCA's executive Jheryl Busby to run.

Frankly, Motown had been struggling for some time; money had been heavily invested in new acts that bombed, television specials that were unwatched, and the company seemed to lose direction as records remained unsold. When a lavish Thirtieth Anniversary gala was planned to be held in Detroit during June 1988 then aborted, the industry knew something was wrong, particularly when Michael Jackson and Diana Ross were pencilled in as headliners.

Berry Gordy sold Motown because he was tired, music was no longer fun to him and the artists he associated with were, he said, 'a bunch of spoilt brats'. However, it was heavily rumoured that he would not leave the industry entirely and would reopen the Gordy label and personally supervise the recordings, no mean feat for a sixty-year-old man. To date, however, he has kept a low profile, reputedly heading up the Gordy Enterprises Corporation, while Motown, now without the support of its stalwart fans, ploughs money and energy into new signings leaving Lionel Richie, Stevie Wonder, Smokey Robinson and The Temptations among others, and a wealth of memories in its back catalogue as its only connection to the company's glorious past.

Meanwhile, in 1981, Rick James who was basking in the accolade surrounding his million-selling album 'Street Songs' was quite adamant that he wouldn't fall into the same trap with Motown as artists like Marvin Gaye had done. He told *NME* what he meant – 'Artists at Motown are in control of their own destinies just like everyone else. They just aren't coming up with the songs. As much as Motown means to me, I can sit back and say that a lot of those cats want to come down out of those fucking hills and get their asses back on the street.' If Motown inaccurately accounted to him regarding his record sales, James said he would leave the company to find one he could trust. Unlike the company's established acts James did not grow up under Berry Gordy's guidance, therefore he felt he owed him nothing; he grew or fell on his own talent.

Rick James had simply related to certain aspects of Marvin Gaye's Motown career. But for Gaye it was too late. True, he now appeared to be standing his ground even though he had not secured an alternative record deal and the likelihood of him retracting his condemnation of Motown was negligible, although it's thought Berry Gordy would have welcomed him back once their differences had been rectified. It's also true to say that record companies have always been interested in securing successful Motown acts because of their status in the market place. When a recording contract was due, and if Berry Gordy was interested in retaining an act, negotiations would begin long before the contract's termination date. So, if an act wasn't approached prior to their contract expiring, Motown intended to drop them from the roster.

It's unsure exactly what was going through Marvin Gaye's mind at this time. He knew he needed the security of a record company; if only he could have sorted out his dilemma with Berry Gordy comments like the following would have been unnecessary and the hurt caused to Gordy avoided. Gaye: 'Motown are commercialists. They are exploitative-minded and motivated. I'm not mercenary or prostitutive of my work and music. If you're not the kind of person who has those principles and that morality it makes it difficult to have to deal with people who are commercial and cold, and strictly business.' His music was his life, he pointed out, his very being; his pain and pleasure, his master – 'I love it, and I'd love to think that someone was as interested in it as I was. Alas, they're only interested in making money.'

Gaye had always considered his music was God's gift to him, and his more innovative work was God Himself, which was why he was so concerned when that gift was treated like dollar bills. He attempted to explain his reasonings to an *NME* reporter – '. . . [Music is] one of the closest link-ups with God that we can probably experience. I think it's a common vibrating tone of the musical notes that holds all life together. I'm not sure that it can ever be found or played, or perhaps even heard. It hurts one to see it abused and misused when music is thought of as money for example, and that money and music go together . . . The ideal solution would be to work out some sort of peaceful coexistence between God and commerciality!'

This infatuation between music and God left Gaye open to ridicule. Weren't some of his albums dripping with erotic lyrics, simulated love and seductive suggestions? A misuse of that divine gift surely? Not so, according to the gospel of Marvin Gaye – 'I won't say sex is God's greatest gift. I'd prefer to say the act of creation was the greatest gift that God gave us. Sex is a continuation of that, a continuation that wasn't meant to be.' And in defence of his lyrics – 'I think if you listen closer you'll find a spiritual connotation in all my songs, even the ones that appear to be highly sexual. There's nothing wrong with sex, but nowadays one has to be very careful.' Sexually transmitted diseases were, he insisted, caught for a reason – '[God] and Mother Nature have got it together and they know how to cut down on all this madness down here – simply send in the herpes bug! Sex is okay as long as certain morals, honour and principles are adhered to. It's how one gauges it, not the act itself, that is the problem.'

In the same interview he revealed that at some later stage in his life he would be called upon to actually serve God, although he was unsure what that would involve. Until that calling came he felt he was in his own small way following a divine instruction by devoting his life to his music – 'I feel that my records are successful because I need credibility and to have media coverage so that I can become very popular worldwide. So that if and when I do this particular thing that I'm going to do for my God to save people I'll be ready. I think we are very near the end of our time as we know it because I feel the world is going to experience a cataclysm which happens about every seven years.' The number 'seven' was prominently figured throughout his career – he even called this time in his life 'his seven-year shit period' – as it did in most creative people's careers. The earth too also experienced seven-year rebirths and was, he was convinced, coming close to the end of one period – 'You need only to look at society and see what's going on every day and one would certainly ascertain that we are coming to an end of something. It certainly can't go on this way, and you needn't be terribly intelligent to assess that. I can see myself being alive when the new world comes . . . When this thing happens there won't be any recording studios left. The first thing to go will be show business, which won't be a sad thing for me.'

It was generally thought that instead of conducting interviews of this nature Marvin Gaye would have done better to have talked about his music, especially 'In Our Lifetime' and prove to the media that he planned to continue with his career. Motown/EMI struggled on to promote the album and 'Praise' in the hope of securing high chart positions, but they needed Gaye's help. One source revealed that he was eventually told in no uncertain terms that if he expected more money from the record company 'he should get off his butt and earn it'. If record sales were reasonable, he would benefit accordingly. With this directive it became apparent that Berry Gordy had no intention of releasing Gaye from his contract, that the success of his future career depended on the work he now did in conjunction with Motown/EMI who had been instructed to push his career as much as it could. Gaye considered the ultimatum and decided to obey as long as his working schedule began after noon each day. One of the first projects arranged by Motown/EMI was a photo session and after three cancelled appointments, and on a crisp winter's day in the newly renovated, highly commercial Covent Garden area of London, Marvin Gaye and Lagos International's representative Gloria Dale arrived, thirty minutes late, to honour the appointment at the Floral Hall Photographic Studios. The photographer, Peter Vernon, was well versed in working with both the newest and biggest names in music, and the fact that Gaye and his unreliable reputation was his subject did not deter him.

An irritable singer, dressed in an ill-fitting black suit, the trousers were held up by braces under a bulky black overcoat, reluctantly sat before one of the several large dressing-room mirrors while a make-up artist set about her task. Slowly his mood melted, he nibbled chicken sandwiches and sipped white wine, while quipping jokes like – 'you'll have to hide my bald spot!' or 'don't you think my best side is my backside'. Very little face make-up was actually applied although he requested that his eyes be emphasised in a subtle yet vivid manner because, he explained, they were glazed, red and swollen through lack of sleep. He then pointed out he was not in a photogenic mood but, turning to the attending Motown staff, smiled he had been instructed to comply with the company's wishes.

Gaye had brought no change of clothes with him, a necessity for a record company shoot. All he had was the dreary suit he had worn to the studio. A local clothes store was persuaded to loan him some of their most expensive cashmere sweaters among other things, on the understanding all were returned at the end of the session. All were, except one cashmere jumper which was marked by make-up stains, a ploy instigated by Gaye who had decided to keep it. The next time he was seen wearing the jumper the stains were still noticeable!

As the session progressed, Gaye relaxed and succumbed to Vernon's lenses; occasional bursts of laughter wafted over the top of the high screens in the studio, erected because Gaye insisted on privacy. Outside shots were then required and without objection the singer retrieved his overcoat, pulling the collar up around his neck against the chill winter wind for a further thirty-minute session in the attractive Covent Garden complex. When the shoot was over he took the Motown staff aside and told them his animosity with Motown had no bearing on his relationship with Motown/EMI and as they had treated him with respect and dignity befitting an artist of his standing, he would, he grinned, consider working with them again!

He kept his word and during February 1981, after a series of rearrangements, he conducted a string of press interviews in his apartment. Journalists were invariably ushered into his small bedroom where they noted the bed had recently been slept in and had remained unmade. The room itself was littered with empty food cartons, overflowing ashtrays, bundles of clothes, an assortment of books and mountains of notes written on small pieces of scrap paper. For some interviews Gaye wore a white, terry towelling dressing-gown hiding his thin body while he quietly and slowly answered questions fired at him.

Gaye was serious about keeping his side of the bargain with his record company but occasionally he lapsed by falling into deep depressions. At times like these he turned to cocaine, to indulge in free-basing the drug, and spent days unable to rise from his bed. Visitors were barred as he isolated himself in his self-imposed prison. Remarkably he survived. Naturally the singer was again fundless, but yet again he was rescued when an American colleague flew to London to give him several thousand dollars for living expenses. Months later Gaye repaid the kindness.

Also in February 1981 Marvin Gaye was rescued again when he met Freddy Cousaert, a boxing promoter who was an admirer of his music. When Cousaert learnt of Gaye's struggling existence in London he volunteered to help him. He knew the singer was anxious to leave the city (visa problems?) and arranged to transport him, his son Bubby and girlfriend/nanny Eugenie Vie to Ostend, Belgium, where he initially housed them in his small hotel run by his wife, before moving them into a desirable residence on the seafront.

Freddy Cousaert, who also loaned Gaye money, took excellent care of him, and even persuaded him to return to work by experimenting in the recording studios. Cousaert also arranged press interviews and the occasional concert for him, while ensuring he met influential society members including Prince Charles of Belgium. (A picture of the two was published in 'A Heavy Love Affair Tour 1981' programme.) Gaye: 'The Prince and I got to be good friends. I stayed at his place for a few days on and off. He's a great artist. He would paint a lot while I was there. He's quite an outcast in his family though because he likes black music for example, and his brothers and sisters don't appreciate that sort of thing. But he's a marvellous man and I love him dearly.' Cousaert then arranged for Marvin to be the subject of a local television programme *Marvin Gaye – Transit Ostend* which was later screened twice by Channel 4 in Britain. The programme included sequences of him rehearsing with his group, and also at a piano situated on stage in an empty theatre where a solitary spotlight reflected upon his single earring. Seafront scenes were idyllic as he sauntered along the pavements or jogged across the sandy beaches, but the highspot of the entire programme was his heart-wrenching a cappella rendition of 'The Lord's Prayer' emotionally delivered in a deserted church.

Gaye soon settled into the Belgian way of life, and his routine followed that of his neighbours which was a far cry from his lifestyle in London and Los Angeles. He spent much of his time cleaning out his system – running, dieting on fish and light meals to regain his athletic build and mingling with the local inhabitants in the street bars where he drank beer and played darts – badly! Naturally, Marvin became a local celebrity but few people bothered him for autographs. Gaye: 'I like the Belgian people. They are very simple, they eat simple food and they are very strong willed, and I found that to be a quality I admired. The people here are the same as people everywhere in the world from my black eyes.' However when he first arrived in Ostend, he was aware of staring faces, and felt a certain animosity towards him. This disturbed him until he was told the Belgians see few black Americans. Gaye: 'If you speak to them they'll be very nice and if you act stand-offish they won't say anything either because actually they are quite respectful – as most Europeans are towards visitors. I grew to love the Belgian people.' He also grew to love himself again; within a relatively short period of time the damage caused by his reckless stay in London was more or less rectified. His outlook was calmer and more logical, his mind clearer and physically he carried the figure of a twenty-year-old.

Meanwhile in Britain, negotiations opened for Marvin Gaye to undertake another tour. NEMS Enterprises reached agreement with him and advertised a string of British dates following the completion of a European tour which included performances in France, Holland and Germany. The tour was cancelled before the print on the tickets had dried! And in May 1981 promoters Outlaw/Kiltorch/IMCP announced further British dates which, they assured the public, Gaye would honour. By a memorandum dated April, a Motown International executive advised Motown/EMI that the singer had signed a contract confirming British dates from 10 to 26 June 1981 inclusive and that rehearsals would commence on 4 June for six days at London's Rainbow Theatre before the tour's opening night at the Victoria Apollo. The memorandum also suggested that a further single be lifted from 'In Our Lifetime' to coincide with the dates and that the album be re-promoted. Now based in Ostend, Marvin had no access to those people who were in his company in London, but should he, the memorandum stated, be in contact with any of his past entourage, particularly his 'manager' Felice, the contract was null and void.

Lady Edith Foxwell, like many of Gaye's true friends with his best interests at heart, was relieved and delighted when he finally escaped the clutches of his so-called entourage whom she believed needed him and not vice versa. However, she pointed out that if it had been left to the singer they would still be in his company. He wasn't sufficiently strong-willed to sever the tie himself – 'Marvin was such a happy-go-lucky, laid back sort of person, who didn't want any hassle. He was quite lazy in a way, he just let time take him.' Gaye's tour promoter Jeffrey Kruger agreed, and added that the hangers-on had clung to him like leeches and had bled him financially dry – '[They] used Marvin's generous nature to sustain their own nefarious drug habits, and instead of building up Marvin's confidence, encouraged him to drink and take uppers and worse when he was down in spirits. They would give him downers when he couldn't sleep so his system was riddled which, in turn, clouded his judgment and left him in a permanent stage of lethargy.' This was also confirmed by Graham Canter who noted further serious complications – 'They wanted to show off – "I'm a friend of his, I can get you near him" – and of course it spread. The word was open and rife that Marvin took cocaine and the drug dealers came to him via these so-called friends. Marvin would get hooked . . . and probably got credit. He'd then wait for some money, maybe from royalties, I don't know, to pay the dealers. And they would only have a limited amount of patience. It was a vicious circle and one he found difficult to get out of.'

Even Motown/EMI's publicity manager fell foul of Gaye's vicious circle when she was subjected to the wrath of a drug dealer's 'colleague' outside a Soho nightclub. It transpired that Gaye owed the dealer a considerable sum of money which the dealer now felt Motown should pay. After a heated conversation the manager convinced the 'colleague' that he would need to look elsewhere for the debt. Gaye later apologised to her.

Both Canter and Kruger were extremely fond of the singer and were at one point alarmed at his deterioration due to his increased drug intake, and the influence of his entourage. The situation was exemplified by Kruger to a British journalist – 'He was able to understand that he had no problems that couldn't be solved relatively easily. But then as the day wore on he went back into the clutches of his own mob.

They undid all the good previously drummed into Marvin by his friends – like his attorney Curtis Shaw, his mother, his aunt, Mrs Price and even Berry Gordy, Mike Roshkind and Lee Young Jnr, all of Motown – who were always in Marvin's corner if only he was prepared to take the guidance and advice offered to him.'

Meanwhile, confident that Gaye would honour the promoters' touring contract, Motown/EMI's publicity and promotion got underway, to ensure the pending dates elevated the singer back to his former star status. The work was for nothing. A week after the tickets went on sale, the tour was cancelled! The excuse given this time was that Gaye's American band was unrehearsed and would not be ready for the opening night. Kruger explained the real reason – 'The tour was cancelled because I threatened to take legal action to prevent it from taking place. I am perfectly agreeable for Marvin to work in Britain 'he is too big a talent to lay dormant. However, a contract is a contract and must be honoured. As far as I'm concerned, Marvin has two alternatives; to tour with my company or with another company but with my prior agreement as to terms and conditions. I do have Marvin's best interests at heart, and believe that he is not always completely aware of what is involved in certain contracts presented to him.'

In typical fashion Marvin had committed himself without giving any consideration to his legally binding situation with the Kruger Organisation. He was not business-minded and never would be, and often sought advice from his close friend Lady Edith Foxwell, who helped when she could while admitting — 'I wasn't really interested in that side of his life. When he talked about it to me I'd say, "Why are you asking me, I'm hopeless too." I used to say it was like the blind leading the blind. I wasn't a business woman and he wasn't a business man, that's probably why we got on!'

However, Jeffrey Kruger wasn't an unreasonable man and was prepared to renegotiate with other promoters on Gaye's behalf, knowing that he needed to work to earn money. Marvin returned to London from Ostend in an attempt to rectify the situation between the two interested parties; he was irritated that contractual obligations were preventing him from returning to the stage to reclaim his 'Love Man' crown. He needed to convince his public that he was worthy of the title and a string of cancelled dates did not help his endeavours. However, agreement could not be reached with Outlaw/Kiltorch/IMCP, and the tour remained cancelled. Quite possibly these tours had been negotiated in good faith by Freddy Cousaert based on information Marvin had given him, which presumably did not include his legal obligations to the Kruger Organisation.

What happened next? Another British tour was announced for June 1981 by Concorde Management! This time though, Jeffrey Kruger resolved his differences with Gaye and his company released this press statement – 'Following several weeks of intense negotiations to settle outstanding contractual obligations, a mutually agreeable settlement has been reached by Freddy Cousaert [and] Jeffrey Kruger, who has promoted the previous two Gaye European tours. Under the terms of the settlement Marvin Gaye has paid an undisclosed sum to Kruger in consideration of which Marvin is now free of any former contractual options with the Kruger Concert Organisation.' Kruger had had the option of the singer's European services until 1983 but, by this settlement he was free to self-promote his own tours in future. Satisfied with the result of the negotiations Gaye returned to Ostend to rehearse for his forthcoming tour.

Unfortunately, with two false starts the public took little notice of Concorde's published dates – which began on 13 June at Bristol's Hippodrome Theatre, followed by London's Apollo Theatre on 16, 17 and 18 June, and others in Manchester, Ipswich, Bradford,

Birmingham, Southport, among others, through to the end of the month – until fly-posting had begun and the relevant theatres displayed the dates. In time, the tour was sold out.

Around this time Janis and daughter Nona flew to Ostend for a reconciliation with Gaye even though it was widely reported they were in the throes of divorce. Arguments persisted so Janis and Nona returned to Los Angeles taking Bubby with them. Gaye told author David Ritz – 'I let her have her son back, but I almost changed my mind. That woman and I can't spend a day together without drawing blood. I keep asking myself why. It doesn't matter. She left me alone, utterly and completely alone. Without Bubby I had no one.'

Motown/EMI lifted 'A Heavy Love Affair' from the 'In My Lifetime' album for release as a single in May (a month after its American outing where it failed to reach the pop chart but managed to become a top seventy R&B hit) even though Gaye refused to feature the song in his show. However, he borrowed the title to call his string of dates 'A Heavy Love Affair Tour 1981', where his support act this time was the established but hitless UK Players. Peter Harding's Harpo Publicity provided the tour's merchandise which included T-shirts showing diagrams of couples copulating following Gaye's original design. It was usual at this time for an artist's record company to be advertised, however discreetly, on a touring artist's merchandise. Motown/EMI flatly refused to allow its logo to be featured within the design and confined its advertising to the tour programme!

Marvin's brother Frankie flew to Britain to work on the tour, while Gil Askey was the musical arranger and, once again, Gordon Banks the musical director. Lady Edith Foxwell was also involved in the tour, encouraging Gaye to stick to his itinerary while also calming volatile situations – 'Marvin was rather shaky in the beginning. When I say shaky, I mean he had trouble with the wife and problems with his band. He had this strange man in charge and I didn't like him very much. He was staying in a terrible place, the other people connected with the tour wouldn't stay there because they said it was full of dead bugs! But once on stage Marvin had a certain magic, a huge personality.' While Foxwell supported Marvin, Frankie assisted her in a situation she would rather have avoided. She broke her elbow and Frankie took her to hospital. In spite of the painful circumstances of that visit Foxwell smiled when she remembered it – 'Frankie looks so much like Marvin and nobody took any notice of me at all because he was taking all the attention! I don't think Frankie ever let on he wasn't Marvin, although I think he attempted to at one point but nobody would believe him. It was terribly funny . . . we had a good laugh, both with Marvin and Frankie.'

On a muggy, stormy 17 June 1981 evening, during Marvin Gaye's performance at the Apollo Theatre when his audience was at fever pitch, Stevie Wonder strolled on stage to sing 'I Heard It Through The Grapevine' with him. A music critic reported that Gaye's whole performance was low-key – 'Marvin was relaxed in what turned out to be an informal show. Neither was it a night for new material – an hour and a half of old favourites, a handful of medleys and long, thoughtful pauses between songs. The highlights were his new versions of "What's Going On", "Inner City Blues" and "Distant Lover". It's still a thrill to attend a Marvin Gaye concert because he really is that bit special.' This particular performance was indeed Marvin at his finest, even though his act had changed little since the 1980 tour. The reason for this was questionable although it's likely he couldn't be bothered to spend time preparing a new show. To a large extent he remained a novelty to the British public and could have probably got away with the same show for at least a further two years even though he insisted on singing old favourites with re-arranged music, taken at a different pace from the original recordings.

Now living in Ostend, Gaye could see London from the outside, from a different perspective, and believed he knew the city and its inhabitants sufficiently to offer comment. He told friends the city had held a certain freedom he had not known in America, and the British way of life gradually became second nature to him. The class system, however, puzzled yet interested his inquisitive mind because he felt it was government motivated, as he told a British journalist – 'It's subtle in England but all governments have their individual systems of government. I have no great aversion to it . . . America doesn't have a class system. On the contrary, the bottom line in America is how much money you have, rather than who you are, or what your roots are and where you've come from. That doesn't seem to be important, so long as you have it.' In Britain, he believed, people were more concerned with their breeding and background rather than the size of their bank balance – 'The problem with that though is that no matter how affluent one may become, if his credentials are not impeccable, it appears that [he] cannot crack social circles.' Presumably he was intimating at his own situation, how he had been accepted into

British society because of who he was and not because of what he owned. Much of this was due to Lady Edith Foxwell – 'I introduced him to my friends like Lord Linley. Marvin wasn't in awe at these introductions. Why should he be? He was a great artist.'

Studying Britain, his second home, from across the North Sea in Belgium, Gaye was reminded of a conversation he had had – 'Apparently, if I'm going to receive the most positive energy from the universe I will get it while I'm in England. I have enjoyed some of the greatest success in terms of friendship and gifts of love, and I love the English because they're tolerant and very humane and they have lots of love for people.'

Marvin was, on more than one occasion, able to return the love shown to him, and one such incident was only revealed after his death. During 1981 Chris May, editor of *Black Music* magazine, became involved with the singer. May was also suffering from the delusion that cocaine was the answer to his every problem, as he wrote – 'I'm sure I'm not giving any secrets away when I say Marvin was then locked in the same blind alley. As it happened, we were both acquiring supplies of the drug from the same person and, whilst I wouldn't say I got to know Marvin well, I did see quite a lot of him. One day our mutual friend's luck ran out, he was busted and held on remand. He wasn't really a dealer, more a musician down on his luck who needed to pay the bills.' The musician contacted the editor to ask whether Marvin would give him a character reference for his court appearance. May thought it highly unlikely that he would want to become involved – 'Then to my surprise, Marvin immediately agreed to supply a letter. He told me, "I know what it's like to be up against it and I know what it's like to need friends." When our mutual friend's case came to court, Marvin's letter was submitted, and though the sentence was still eighteen months, it may have had some effect. And that wasn't the end of Marvin's interest in the matter either. He rang me on several occasions, asking how our friend was, and wrote a number of cheering, supportive letters to him in prison.'

Obviously Gaye had taken a reckless risk in writing the letters which again confirmed to the authorities that he too was a taker of the drug. However, he pushed that aside to help a friend in trouble. He knew only too well the feeling of being dependent on cocaine; probably this was the only part of his life he had come to terms with. It was a habit he knew would require a lot of willpower to break and if successful would drastically alter his lifestyle. When he was asked if the last two years were a period he was proud of, he said he honestly didn't know – 'I think it would take a greater being than myself to give an intelligible response. However, I feel that everything will work out just fine, but who knows? The only thing I can say at this point is that I feel positive and energetic. I know that if I were living in the States at the moment I wouldn't be feeling as positive as I am right now.' However, his positive outlook cracked when critics began comparing his old work with the new, a point that annoyed him intensely because he felt it was an unfair observation. 'The past is the past, the future is the future, and the present is now. I happen to be a very current-minded individual and the originality that I strive for is interwoven with my desire to be with-it in an original way. So I feel I cannot compare the new with the previous work.' He offered the following example – 'When I did "Let's Get It On" – the world seemed to be going through a sexual revolution. Now things are different, these are times for thought and times to prepare for the end of things as I see them. To compare things at different ends of the time scale is wrong. It's a misuse of power and it's too confining.' The world he referred to wasn't destined to change because within two years he resurrected his sexual revolution to retrieve his superstar status!

Meanwhile with the British tour over and most of his promotion work with Motown/EMI now more or less running to plan a curious incident occurred when Les Spaine, head of promotion, was due to accompany Gaye to Manchester to record a television appearance. While Spaine and Gaye waited for their plane at London's Heathrow, the singer excused himself to go to the toilet. He never returned! Spaine later discovered to his amusement that Marvin had climbed through the toilet window, jumped into a taxi and returned to his London base! Gaye later explained his actions to journalist Stephanie Calman – 'I didn't feel like going to Manchester! To admit such a thing would be unheard of for other artists. They'd cover it up I'm sure. They would never leave it so unexplained, but I am. Yes, I did it and I'll probably do it again. Although I'm not going to lay the blame on anyone and in this case my action was a reaction due to a negative action by somebody else. I don't fuck around. Sometimes though I give my word to do something in a general way just to see whether people are bullshitters, and if I find out that people are bullshitters, then I feel I have a right not to keep my word if they don't care.'

Once again, it was unclear to whom he was referring, but what was clear was that he had changed his mind about cooperating with Motown/EMI. The company had complied with Gaye's every whim, no matter how trivial, but now it sadly realised the love affair was over.

# 12. | Sexual Healing

*Yesterday was the birthplace of today.*

(Marvin Gaye)

*There were a few negative thoughts about signing him.*

(Larkin Arnold)

*I've heard many people say 'if one of my children ever raised their hand to me, I'd kill him'.*

(Kim Weston)

*I haven't made it to the top because I've got so much more to do.*

(Marvin Gaye)

In April 1981, twenty years and one month after the release of his first official single 'Let Your Conscience Be Your Guide' in May 1961, Marvin Gaye followed Diana Ross's move and left Motown. The announcement was made as his signature dried on a recording contract with CBS. Unlike Diana Ross whose record sales were often doctored, Gaye's had been erratic but on the whole regular, particularly when the three highspots – 'What's Going On', 'Let's Get It On' and 'I Want You' – genuinely sold millions, and when he left Motown he had recorded and released sixteen re-saleable solo albums, excluding compilations and 'Live' issues, while solo Ross left a catalogue of thirteen.

Signing with CBS arose when Gaye's determination to be freed of his Motown contract could not be swayed. Initially he was unsure which company to approach, fear of rejection plagued him, but knew he wanted to sign with another major operation so cautiously approached CBS. If he was rejected he would have no choice but to lower his standards by signing to a smaller, possibly independent label who, he hoped, would pay heavily for the privilege. It went without saying that Gaye needed a substantial advance to pay for his release from Motown, his IRS debts, future recording sessions and so on.

And to this end, he instructed his lawyer to first open negotiations with Berry Gordy, and depending on that outcome, tackle the other debtors afterwards. Gordy surprisingly agreed to release the singer pending agreement on financial issues as his recording contract still had time to run. It's fair to say at this point that the Motown boss appeared to want the best for Gaye, probably acknowledging there was no way he could sway his decision. As well as being one of his company's recording artists, Gaye had, of course, been a member of the Gordy family and, at one time a close, well-respected friend. So, after Diana Ross's departure, Gordy experienced another personal loss. Gaye: 'I've had my differences with Berry Gordy and now he's not my favourite person in the world. But one thing I or anyone else cannot take away from him is the very simple fact that it was him who made the dream come true for a lot of people including me. Berry Gordy has survived in one of the toughest businesses around and to do that takes a lot of balls, a lot of work, and a lot of risks. Believe me, he's given out a lot of shit in his time but he's had to take a whole lot himself. Nobody, particularly a cocky black guy fresh from the assembly lines in Detroit, gets to make it that big without making a few enemies and taking a few cuts. Deep down in my guts, I admire the man immensely. He'll be remembered a damn sight longer than any Motown artist.'

As Marvin Gaye closed the door on Berry Gordy he opened another on Larkin Arnold, whom he was to admire and respect in much the same way as he had the Motown boss. Like Gordy the new influence oversaw Gaye's career from the day his signature appeared on the recording contract, although when CBS first considered adding Gaye to its artist roster, Arnold had a hard job convincing the board of directors the move was a wise one, bearing in mind the singer's past reputation. Arnold: 'There were a few negative thoughts about signing him. He hadn't had a hit in seven years for example. People said he was old, music had passed him by and he wasn't mentally stable. It's true to say a lot of people were surprised at my signing him and I don't know if anyone else would have taken a chance on him. I respected Marvin so much, and he meant so much to black people and so much to the music business generally.' He also believed in Gaye's talent despite having negative arguments with him also – 'Marvin actually gave me a lot of reasons why there were so many conflicts, and it took a little bit of persuading CBS. But I was told, if you're willing to take the risk – a two and a half million dollar risk – well, I put my career on the line.' Gaye agreed – 'I think CBS took a bit of a chance on me because my sales had fallen off for the last four or so albums.'

Prior to joining CBS as a lawyer and vice-president, Larkin Arnold was involved in signing acts like Maze and Natalie Cole to Capitol Records in America. He first met Marvin Gaye at a social event during 1972. Arnold: 'Being in the music business in Los Angeles I came into contact with many people, and I knew most of the artists there. Marvin and I had an ongoing relationship since that meeting but we weren't on intimate terms then. I also knew Stevie Wonder and Smokey Robinson and I'd seen him with them socially from time to time.'

During Gaye's contract negotiations rumours were rife that he was burned out; cocaine abuse had left a shell of a man, incapable of working again. People gloated that he had left London a broken man; a physical and mental wreck, an incurable junkie. However, in typical fashion, Gaye bounced back to prove the rumour mongers wrong, and for the first time in a long while was enthusiastic about recording again. Nonetheless, Arnold travelled to Ostend, Belgium, to see for himself, and to discuss the recording agreement and their future working relationship – 'Marvin was having extreme difficulties, not so much with Motown but with his internal revenue problems. They filed against his future earnings, so that meant any money he generated would go to them. Things were difficult for him. We spent many hours talking about his life and shared tales on many things. In fact, there's not too much to do in Belgium except talk, especially where Marvin was. So we sat, talked and drank, mostly in Ostend in his small apartment looking out on the North Sea.'

Naturally, one of the most important factors to be discussed and finalised was the satisfactory financial reimbursement to be made to Berry Gordy which, Arnold envisaged, would be a lengthy process. But no. Arnold: 'Berry Gordy was great and totally respected Marvin's wishes. They finalised things between them and subsequently there was no problem between CBS and Motown. We reached a very amicable relationship.' It was thought that Motown received a small (?) percentage from Gaye's future CBS sales until the debt was cleared. However, this arrangement was never confirmed. What was confirmed was that Motown could not market Marvin's product for a specified period, enabling CBS a clear run with his new material. Gaye: 'I'm sure Motown has a tremendous back catalogue of unreleased material. Some of it is good. No, actually, I don't think any of it is any good.' Agreement was then reached with the IRS regarding Gaye's unpaid taxes, whereby he could pay off his debts by instalments.

So, with his financial dilemmas settled thanks to the expertise of others, Marvin Gaye only had to concentrate on his career, something nobody else could do for him.

With the contract now signed Marvin applied his mind to returning to the studios, but this in itself posed a problem. Arnold: '[He] hardly had any songs written before we signed him. He had a few sketches of songs, a few ideas and melodies but nothing was completed. He'd got no lyrics either, just a couple of concepts. So, he consulted me on the songs to be used, and I'd send him tapes of American music that was doing well. We'd confer regularly on this.'

Gaye was quick to acknowledge Larkin Arnold's assistance, particularly in choosing the repertoire for his new album – '[He] made several thousand trips to Belgium to check out material and decide which songs we should use for the album. I think he's a darn good decider because I wouldn't have put the songs in that he chose. In fact, none of them, because as an artist you want to release songs you feel strongly about. But in my case, these feelings may not reflect commerciality because as an artist I don't think commercially. I think artistically.'

While Gaye was working in the studios, in America his mentor from the Sixties, Harvey Fuqua, had contacted Curtis Shaw. After hearing about Gaye's London escapades, he was worried about his friend and felt he needed help. Also Fuqua expressed an interest in working with him again. However, it seemed unlikely Gaye would agree to this because he had actually made some headway with his music, and was now used to working alone in the studio. Wasn't creative freedom something he had fought for at Motown? However, when he heard of Fuqua's interest, he welcomed the idea of a re-collaboration, particularly as he was, he said, struggling for inspiration at the time.

Marvin Gaye's next work was vital to his continuing career – the make-or-break album – and this fact naturally made him extremely anxious. Once again he lacked confidence, needing someone his equal to bounce ideas off and Harvey Fuqua was the answer. Larkin Arnold thought the liaison was an excellent idea – 'Besides, he was able to take my place as a companion. And he was also someone Marvin trusted. Before this I had spent a lot of time in Belgium. In fact, from our initial meeting up to the first album I'd spent eighteen months or so with Marvin on and off, and I had other things to do, so I couldn't really spend all my time there with him.'

The gentle giant, Harvey Fuqua, possessed a calm and patient temperament, whereas his protégé was prone to have a volatile temper and periods of laziness and moodiness. It was the reuniting of musical minds, but also a battle of the wits.

Graham Canter believed that without Harvey's help at this time CBS would have had a long wait for any finished music – 'Gaye was on the brink of re-launching a potentially new and brilliant career and he couldn't make it alone. Harvey was the obvious choice. But then knowing Marvin he would have had one or two great albums, then would have sacked Harvey. But for now he really needed him.' Fuqua: 'Marvin called me and said, "I'm in Belgium and I'm having problems. Come over." I said, "Sure, love to." So I jumped on a plane and went over. It was in June [1982]. CBS said, "Look we want the album. He's been working on the album since December and he should have had the album out in March. But we know his reputation and nobody wants to deal with him. But you're his friend and so on." I said, "Well, he's not like that. He's a great guy. He's my friend . . . I can get him to finish [the album]."'

Travelling from Ostend to Studio Katy in Ohaine took up much of Marvin Gaye's time. The weather was bitterly cold and often the roads were impassable. Gaye: 'That's about two hundred miles a day and it was snowing quite a lot. That was a bit of a problem, so the album took four to five months to do.' He also experienced problems with musicians – 'We tried at first to use European musicians but I couldn't quite get the feeling I wanted. I think I could have gotten it if I had had the time but I didn't. I was also under a lot of emotional and economic pressures and other things which I'd rather not go into.' Subsequently, he abandoned the idea of using any musicians and plumped for synthesisers – 'It took a bit of doing but it was interesting and my musicianship has improved as well.'

When Harvey Fuqua arrived in Belgium he hadn't been aware that Gaye's visa had expired, forcing him to live in Paris for a time, before moving to Munich, Germany, where he recorded at the Arco Studios. Fuqua decided to stay in Brussels and told radio personality Stuart Grundy – 'It got to be a hassle because he was calling me. Every night I was in the studios, he'd say, "Oh, you know the third beat on the fourth bar on track forty-six, I put a turkish bell in there. Put that there, mix that." I got sick of being on the phone with him for four hours every night. So I told him, "I'm gonna mix it, I'll see you when you're here. If you don't like it then fine." He said, "It's critical. This is my album. I'm coming back. It just doesn't sound right." I said, "OK, fine. I'll re-mix the stuff in the States."'

True to his word, Fuqua took the album's tapes – mostly vocals – and worked almost non-stop in the Devonshire Studios, Los Angeles, trying to make up for Gaye's lost time, and endeavouring to keep within CBS's deadline. Fuqua: 'Marvin came back to the States in early September and went through all the re-mixing, the whole bit. And then he wound up liking all the mixes we did in Brussels!'

When the album was completed Gaye took the unprecedented step of giving Larkin Arnold total artistic control over his finished work which, among other things, meant he could choose the singles. The reason for this, Gaye said, was simple – 'Since Larkin and CBS had been so marvellous to me I decided to give [it to them].'

The record company lost no time in notifying its overseas branches of the pending album including its London office in Soho Square, where Graham Betts headed up Marvin's publicity campaign, working with product manager Steve Ripley and A&R chief Hugh Attwooll. Betts: 'When Marvin's album was delivered here it was a red letter day for many of us. Despite his reputation and some of his [inferior] recorded work for Motown, there were those of us who looked forward to hearing the new material, and working closely with him. I can't say I was afraid of his reputation because it occurred to me that having been given a second chance – in the nicest possible way – by CBS that he would want to do his utmost to please the company, which is pretty much the way it turned out in the end.'

In October 1982 'Sexual Healing' was chosen as the first single and his CBS debut. The track was lifted from his forthcoming 'Midnight Love' album, so titled by his manager Marilyn Freeman, who had been introduced to Gaye by Harvey Fuqua. It became the fastest-selling black single for many years, topping the American R&B charts for ten weeks, the first single to achieve this since 'I Can't Stop Loving You' by Ray Charles during 1962. 'Sexual Healing' also crossed over and soared to number three in the pop charts in January 1983, selling a million copies, following its British success three months earlier when it peaked at number four.

'Sexual Healing' was simplicity itself; no complicated chords, just an easy flowing melody against a mid-tempo rhythm with lyrics that spoke for themselves. Music critic Justin Lubbock summed up everyone's feelings when he wrote – 'The single is endorsed by some really sharp hand claps and a nice combination of soft, melodic electric piano and tight chopping, semi-acoustic guitar. Over the top of this classy backdrop, Marvin shows that his voice has lost none of its presence and sensuality; in fact he sounds as good today as he always has . . . Quite simply Marvin's debut release for CBS is one of the best records released this year – if not the best.' Larkin Arnold: 'When I first heard "Sexual Healing" I knew I hadn't made a mistake. I was delighted . . . and relieved. Marvin had not let anyone down.' Graham Betts: '"Sexual Healing" was without doubt a revelation. It was better than I had expected it to be, a return to his golden era.' Marvin Gaye: 'I started praying to God that it would be a hit. Coming from one record company to another, to have it come out and bomb would have been really bad for me. It would have been the kiss of death for me in the record industry I honestly do believe.'

Naturally CBS had hoped to secure the top of the charts on both sides of the Atlantic but in Britain in particular, the competition was intense. Paul McCartney duetted with Stevie Wonder on 'Ebony And Ivory' to grab the top, with Dexys Midnight Runners, Survivor and Bucks Fizz threatening to replace them. Radio airplay was a sensitive area because of the single's content so CBS took the precaution of putting parenthesis around 'Sexual' thereby indicating the record title to be 'Healing'. The move was effective because the single received maximum exposure. CBS's marketing and promotion was exhaustive – fly-posting, T-shirts and buttons proclaiming 'I Need Sexual Healing'. The comments the wearer received left nothing to the imagination!

What was needed to push the single from the top fifty into the top ten was a video which could be screened in nightclubs and on television. Gaye agreed and arrangements were made for him to fly from Ostend to London where it would be filmed in the London nightclub Xenon. Harvey Fuqua flew to London prior to the singer to work on the video's story-board due to include sequences of a scantily dressed nurse administering her 'sexual healing' to an ailing patient. However Gaye failed to arrive, not through any temperamental attitude but because his mother was suffering from a serious kidney complaint and had undergone an emergency operation at the Cedars Sinai Medical Centre, Los Angeles. It's thought that

Marvin's father didn't visit his wife in hospital; he had returned to preach in Washington, leaving his family behind at the Gramercy Place house, Los Angeles. For some reason, Gaye didn't stay in his parents' home but opted to stay with Marilyn Freeman in her Los Angeles apartment.

In time the singer would treat Freeman in the same offhand manner as he had Freddy Cousaert with whom he had argued over financial and mismanagement matters. Meanwhile Graham Betts was unsure that Freeman would be able to work with Gaye – 'At first I thought Marilyn was just the latest in a long line of people claiming to be Marvin's manager and I wouldn't have been surprised if she'd been unable to organise anything. She never once let me down on anything that had been organised. I think she did a good job in managing Marvin.'

When plans to film the 'Sexual Healing' video in London were aborted, presumably it was Freeman who arranged for one to be hastily filmed in Carlo's and Charlie's, a Los Angeles nightclub, where Gaye performed the song. Unfortunately by the time the film – Gaye's only video – reached London the single had dropped in the charts. It was the singer's last serious stab at the top spot.

Gaye: 'I know the single went to number one in many places, and I know there would have been a time when that fact would have made me overjoyed from an egotistical point of view. But that's not enough anymore. I'm overjoyed because I see the single and the album as a means to an end. It's a means of getting proper exposure and with the proper exposure I can deliver my proper message.' Many would be forgiven for thinking that the message was sex yet again, and when asked about this he smiled – 'I believe that I've been quoted more than any other artist on this subject. I cannot recall having had one interview without the topic being raised at some time or another. I guess people must look at me and wonder why I'm always on about sex.' Even when living in Ostend, away from the temptations of London, he said it was still as easy for him to become involved with women. This had alarmed him – 'I want to be free from this so, in a way, that's why I'm staying in Ostend. It makes my will stronger, not that there's not a large number of attractive women here, because there is. If I could become a priest or monk, and a good one, I would feel then that I had become free from women.'

With celibacy on his mind, he also felt he should change his stage act because – 'A lot of my act is sensual for those who want to join in. I feel there's something for everyone when I get on stage, but the ladies feel I have this joy in them. People say I am a sex symbol. Well, that's OK . . . but I don't believe it!'

Although Marvin Gaye was the credited composer of 'Sexual Healing', author David Ritz claimed he had in fact written the lyrics after travelling to Ostend in April 1982 to interview the singer and was played the song's backing tape. Gaye reputedly stole Ritz's lyrics and recorded them, promising him an equal share in the royalties, mechanical payments and so on. Ritz also contended that Odell Brown, one of Gaye's musicians, wrote the music, not Gaye. Odell is credited on the 'Midnight Love' album artwork as composing the song with Gaye, while Ritz is credited at the end of 'A Special Thank You' listing with 'David Ritz whose brilliant literary mind created the title "Sexual Healing".'

A year after his visit to Ostend David Ritz sued Marvin for $15 million in damages before the California Superior Court for allegedly failing to credit him as lyricist of the song. CBS was listed as co-defendant. In July 1983 *Billboard* reported that Ritz's suit claimed that 'on numerous occasions [after the lyrics were written] defendant Gaye acknowledged that said song would be a success and that plaintiff [Ritz] was responsible for it.' The magazine further reported that the suit also disclosed that during October 1982 CBS Records expressed interest in signing Ritz as a songwriter but that Gaye had 'interfered with and intimidated defendant CBS' into withdrawing its offer and that 'Gaye will continue to interfere with plaintiffs prospective business advantage'.

In his book *Divided Soul* Ritz wrote that Marvin had actually urged him to become a full-time songwriter. But – 'Unfortunately our musical collaboration spelled the end of our friendship. Once the tune was a hit and Marvin found himself back in America, we fought over credit and money.' However, before Gaye died the two men renewed their friendship and presumably the court case was dropped.*

'Midnight Love' was released in November 1982 and Marvin Gaye's public expected his genius to shine through after the abysmal 'In Our Lifetime'. Nobody was disappointed this time, the album was superbly conceived; a happy collection of songs which certainly re-affirmed his creative talent.

---

* In 1990 when Motown were considering including 'Sexual Healing' on 'The Marvin Gaye Collection' the songwriting credits included David Ritz.

A fast moving, multi-tracked 'Midnight Lady' opened the release to relay Gaye's thoughts on a visit to a nightclub where he (naturally) became enamoured by a 'freaky' dancer. The frantic beat was accentuated by his drum and bongo playing similar to that used by Surfaris on their 'Wipe Out' single. One could have been forgiven for noticing the similarity between this song and Rick James' hard funk work. 'Rockin' After Midnight' followed the same belting pace, where a raunchier-vocalled singer trotted through a song that had little to do with dancing! Multi-vocalled tracking overtook the pro-fusion of brass and guitar as Marvin detailed the ways of loving a woman. The 'Sexual Healing' mood returned with 'Til Tomorrow' where, after a sensually spoken introduction, intensely thoughtful lyrics of his passionate love blended perfectly with the beautiful, seductive musical backdrop highlighted by Bobby Stern's sax solo. The uncomplicated, relaxing 'Turn On Some Music' opened side two, followed by an unusual inclusion, 'Third World Girl', a slice of lightweight pop/reggae, originally earmarked as a single. It was thought that Gaye had been inspired by Stevie Wonder's 'Masterblaster (Jammin')' to produce this much-loved track. The remaining songs were 'Sexual Healing, 'Joy' and 'My Love Is Waiting'.

Only four musicians were credited on the album's artwork – Gordon Banks, James Gadson, Bobby Stern and Joel Perskin – while Gaye played a wide variety of instruments on most of the tracks including synthesisers, drums and Fender Rhodes.

The record's dark and moody front sleeve showed a half-smiling, smug-looking singer pictured against a city skyline where on the right-hand side, partly hidden in a building, a small clock showed midnight. The back cover featured the same skyline but much darker where, this time, the clock showed either five o'clock or eleven/twelve twentyfive. Below this the obligatory track listing and credits were printed, including a list of those involved in the album. Marvin thanked Harvey Fuqua (also acknowledged as executive producer), Judge Mednick, his bankruptcy judge; his manager, Marilyn Freeman, and his children Marvin Jnr, Nona and Frankie. And for the first time in several years, the songs' lyrics were printed in their entirety on the album's loose inner sheet.

If 'Midnight Love' had flopped Gaye told *NME* that he would probably have thought seriously about retirement – 'I would have felt my time was over. I'm a timing specialist and I would have seen that as an indication that I was through. But with the album's success I've been given a great indication that I've still got it, and it gives me more energy and desire to strive for greatness, wherever or whatever that greatness must be. [The album] belongs to the world now. It's not mine anymore. It was only mine before I released it. And once it's gone, like a mother bird who pushes her baby out of the nest, I give it up . . . At this point in time it looks like being more commercial than my last five albums, which haven't exactly been blockbusters. I am very happy to be with CBS and they helped me through a difficult period. I like to make people happy who have been nice to me.'

His happiness spread into promotion because for the first time in his recent past Gaye willingly cooperated with CBS in promoting the album. Graham Betts: 'I can honestly say Marvin did every interview that was organised. Not only that, he always did his best to ensure that the journalist got his story. Of course, there was a vast difference between the kind of interview he did at the beginning of his CBS career when "Midnight Love" had first hit one million sales in the US so his spirits were good, and those near the end when he was struggling again.'

The last interview Betts arranged for the singer was during his American tour – 'There seemed to be no end to the people claiming to represent Marvin, armed guards around him and so on. The interview was a disaster, with Marvin either losing control or losing his temper with the interview ending abruptly.'

However, while 'Midnight Love' continued to sell, Gaye attended CBS meetings including the company's sales conference where he played a selection of unfinished work, including the erotically offensive track 'Masochistic Beauty' which was not suitable for release until drastically rewritten. Nonetheless Gaye felt it was suitable for American release because that record-buying public had supported 'Sexual Healing' so easily. Gaye: 'They like to get down to the meat of the situation, for lack of a better expression . . . They tend to want what they want, when they want it. There's none of the foreplay that there is in Paris. When I was in France it took me forever to take a lady to bed, because I had to foreplay for two days. But I found it interesting, and sort of worthwhile because the intensity of the orgasm made it all worth it. In America everything is hurry, hurry, hurry . . . It's the same with concerts. Who has time for all that old stuff? Let's get to the new stuff, right, quick, so we can really get off, now.'

At this time Marvin remembered his Motown career and spoke warmly of the time he spent with the company. Seemingly his vehemence had disappeared as he acknowledged the fine work he had recorded there and the tolerance shown to him with that work. He even noted the talent of certain Motown colleagues whom he had worked with — 'I think Smokey Robinson, Norman Whitfield, Holland, Dozier and Holland, Johnny Bristol and of course Harvey Fuqua should have been better appreciated. And all the fine producers at Motown. But I'm not with Motown anymore, but I dug it – in fact, I still dig Motown. I love the songs I did for them, nostalgically speaking. I hope the work will be remembered.'

As 'Midnight Love' peaked in the American charts at number seven (no 10 in the UK) CBS threw a party in Gaye's honour during December 1982 at Carlo's And Charlie's on Sunset Boulevard. *NME* journalist Gavin Martin attended and reported that although the party wasn't due to start until six in the evening, limousines bearing music industry executives, artists and Gaye's family including his first wife Anna, Marvin III and Harvey Fuqua, arrived at five, whereupon the art was to convince the armed guards at the reception that you had an invitation. Gaye's twenty years of hits were played over the nightclub's sophisticated sound system while a screen at the back of the club played the video of 'Sexual Healing' almost constantly. Martin wrote: 'It's a good way to generate excitement, after all it's been ages since Marvin made one of these in-person appearances and people are just dying to see what he looks like. So you sit there sipping expensive cocktails, feeling relaxed, rich, soaking up that smooth LA record business cool. Around eight with everyone keyed and oiled for the entrance, Marvin arrives – through the back door, of course. [He] looks incredible. He's wearing a suave pinstripe suit, there's no sign of sag or paunch and that old charisma still glows around him.'

Once the introductions were completed a representative from the Los Angeles City Fathers read a citation from the mayor to which Gaye responded with a short speech of thanks. Martin: 'I catch his reflection in one of the mirrored walls and he's chewing madly. His eyes are closed and his head is raised towards the roof. It's as if he's waiting for a big hand to come through the ceiling and take him away. Speaking in a low, soft voice, the words drift away and tears well up in his eyes. "Thanks to my Maker . . . those who made it all possible." Well, it wasn't what you expected from a guy who has just been lauded as one of the greatest recording artists of our time, but then everyone knew Marvin was a little strange, so they smile and the party starts to get back into its swing.'

During the evening Larkin Arnold presented the singer with two gold discs and one silver disc and to show his gratitude Gaye sang an a cappella version of 'The Lord's Prayer' despite admitting he hadn't sung since recording 'Midnight Love'. Martin: 'And standing there alone in this flashy LA nightclub he lets all the old fire and fervour come pouring out. It's marvellous, sincere, soul-wrenching emotion transcending the setting and all the mumbo jumbo that preceded it. Welcome to the biz Marvin, it's sure good to have you back.'

Two days following the lavish reception Martin and his photographer Peter Anderson were invited to Marilyn Freeman's apartment for a pre-planned photo session. Martin: 'When Marvin finally arrives he's like one of the walking dead, his eyes hidden from the world behind a pair of mirrored shades. He shakes hands and manages a cardboard smile. The party that started two days ago was continued right through until now. I asked him how he feels. "Not too good," he replied, disappearing into the bedroom. He calls for Marilyn and she returns to tell us that there'll be no pictures or questions this morning.'

Gavin Martin's report suggests that no matter how intent the singer was on pleasing CBS by making himself accessible for promotion work, cocaine was once again dominating his life, and whatever hopes his new employers had of him overcoming his habit had been shattered during the early stages of their relationship. The clean living in Belgium had presumably done little to sway Gaye's reliance on the drug; subsequently CBS employees were faced with the same problem as Motown/EMI's staff some months earlier, although many refused to become drawn into this side of his life. Graham Betts: 'Thankfully, I didn't get involved in Marvin's private life. There was an employee of CBS who did, running off to Jamaica to pick up drugs for him. She now works for Julio Iglesias.'

'My Love Is Waiting' was the second British single to be lifted from 'Midnight Love', and it reached the top forty. Originally CBS had earmarked a song titled 'Sanctified Pussy' as the follow-up to 'Sexual Healing' but it was dropped because its lyrics were considered offensive to women and at that time Gaye had no intention of toning them down. (A revised version of the song would be issued after Gaye's death as a single in 1985.) 'Til Tomorrow' was lifted as an American single but it failed to register in the pop chart and crawled into the R&B top forty. So, another track 'Joy' was issued in 1983 and that bombed. None of the songs matched the success of 'Sexual Healing' much to Gaye's disappointment. A *Blues & Soul* reporter summed up the situation – 'Despite the unquestionable quality of "Midnight Love" it can never be considered to be overflowing with potential singles apart from the two ["Sexual Healing" and "My Love Is Waiting"] that have already been released. Quite simply "Joy", this mid-tempo number, is an album track that should have remained as such. That's not to say it's a bad track, far from it, but it does lack the commerciality necessary for a single.'

Prior to the release of 'Joy', Marvin Gaye's father returned from Washington D.C. to Los Angeles to live once again at the family residence. In his father's absence, as well as staying with Marilyn Freeman, Marvin divided his time between his sister Zeola's home and Gramercy Place. With father and son living under the same roof clashes reputedly began, arguments flared, Gaye making it clear he wanted his father to move out again.

However, on a happier note and still prior to the release of 'Joy' Marvin peaked professionally. For the first time in his career, despite numerous nominations and losing to George Benson, Otis Redding, Stevie Wonder (three times), Sam & Dave and Lou Rawls (twice) he won two Grammy Awards for 'Sexual Healing'! He collected the awards from Rick James and Grace Jones for the 'Best Instrumental Performance' and 'Best Male Vocal' during the twenty-fifth annual awards ceremony held at the Shrine Auditorium, Los Angeles, on 23 February 1983. Gaye: 'I've sat at the Grammies so many years now hoping I'd win an award and Lou Rawls has won them all from me. I don't think I'm bitter about that. But the last time he won an award he gave me such a smile . . . I told my wife I was gonna tackle him, go on stage and grab it, and cause a big stink at the Grammies. But she didn't think that was too wise an idea. So I didn't.'

At the awards ceremony Marvin performed 'Sexual Healing' live which was a mistake; his performance indicated a lack of rehearsal. However the audience in the auditorium and before the television sets at home didn't care – Marvin Gaye had returned and his talent had finally been honoured. His acceptance speech was drawn out, quietly delivered as he nervously stood behind the podium — 'Thank you very kindly ladies and gentlemen. I'm not very much for speeches. I'm not much of a public speaker, I always say that. I've waited a very long time, twenty some years to win an award such as this. Thank you to my family, my friends, my children who are out there, Bubba and Nona. Can you stand up, Bubba and Nona, and say "hello Dad" quickly? We can't take a lot of time, we've gotta go. There they are. Love you baby. My mom. I love everybody. Thank God. I love you. Stay with us. We're gonna try to give you more. I love you.' The audience response was deafening.

After the ceremony he told journalists that winning the Grammies was a means to an end which would benefit both him and his public – 'If you know the history of my recording career you'll know that I don't follow in my own footsteps nicely . . . I'm actually very happy with the success of the single and with the album too . . . and my ego is extremely gratified. I've had a few big hit records in my time and I think a man of my age should be able to take it in his stride.'

Another ceremony he took in his stride was singing the American national anthem at the NBA's (National Basketball Association) All Star Game. It was a glorious moment; spectators and players alike were hypnotised by Marvin's crystal-clear voice as it soared into the warm air. Nelson George reported the occasion in *Billboard* magazine – 'Striding to mid-court in a dapper white suit and shades, Gaye turned our stiff "Star Spangled Banner" into a warm, jazzy platform for his impeccable phrasing.' Gaye: 'It was difficult to sing because it was written for an operatic type of voice. A soul singer isn't exactly comfortable singing it but nor is any other ethnic person really. So I think in a country full of ethnic nationalities, we should sing in accordance with what is most comfortable . . . I can't sing it white . . . I have to sing it so it moves me. Since I am a soul singer, I must sing it my way, and I can't see singing it their way.' Berry Gordy: 'He "Marvin Gaye-ised" the anthem.' The song was released after Gaye's death on the 1988 album 'A Musical Testament 1964–1984'.

In 1983 Gaye's former record company boss, Berry Gordy, was to be honoured by his artists in a five-hour Gala entitled 'Motown 25: Yesterday, Today, Forever' presented on stage at the Pasadena Civic Auditorium, Los Angeles, with the ticket proceeds going to the National Association for Sickle Cell Diseases. This Gala held on 25 March 1983 was the climax to Motown's Twenty-Fifth Anniversary celebrations. Once more the timing was off, a year early this time because the Gala's executive producer and Motown's vice-president Suzanne de Passe had to set a date when all the participating artists would be available. Only Lionel Richie was absent – he was visiting Japan – so his segment was seen on film.

Naturally Diana Ross was one of the first artists to be approached. She was initially reluctant to perform because she did not want to upset her RCA Records' bosses, and her relationship with Berry Gordy was strained, almost to the point of non-communication. Eventually though she was persuaded to appear which was just as well because Motown's publicity machine had already cranked into operation suggesting she would be the special attraction. After all, a Motown reunion without her, Marvin Gaye and indeed Michael Jackson – who had stipulated he would only appear if he could lipsynch his CBS single 'Billie Jean', reluctantly agreed by Berry Gordy – was unimaginable. Once Ross had consented to appear, Cindy Birdsong and Mary Wilson had to be encouraged to perform with her. Sources indicate Birdsong was willing but Wilson might refuse because she was involved in another court case against Berry Gordy worth several millions of dollars regarding ownership of the name 'The Supremes'. Wilson agreed to appear.

Past and present artists returned with style and love to honour Berry Gordy on 'Motown 25: Yesterday, Today, Forever'. Irrespective of hit record status, the chosen few re-lived Motown's historical memories even though many were allocated only a few minutes stage time to do so. Smokey Robinson who appeared as a member of The Miracles and as a duettist, was master of ceremonies with comedian Richard Pryor, and before the close of the Gala his expertise was pushed to the limit. Stevie Wonder's performance captivated the audience while the Four Tops and The Temptations (minus Eddie Kendricks but including Glenn Leonard) traded hits during a joint act that saw the groups battling with vocals and dance routines.

In complete contrast to this energised show, Marvin Gaye, dressed in a white/cream suit, hypnotised the audience with a smooth, sophisticated performance that regrettably only spanned one song, his finest for Motown, 'What's Going On'. In a cool, reflective mood he sat alone at the piano, his eyes half-closed, his manner commanding but relaxed, his voice slightly slurred to sleepily recall the roots of black music against the soft strains of the song's opening verse – 'Maybe today is the result of yesterday spent in wooden churches, singing the praises of our Maker in joyous harmony and love. Part of it has to be the songs we sang, working under the blazing sun, to help pass the hard times. Yesterday was also Bessie Smith, New Orleans and gospel choirs, folk songs, Bojangles. Yesterday was the birthplace of today. Today is twenty-five years of climbing and building, and opening doors and breaking old rules. Today is also love songs, and guy-and-girl songs, and songs of protest and anger, songs of gentleness and songs of wounds left unattended for far too long, songs to march to, to fly to, to make love to. It's music pure and simple and soulful, and if you insist, full of promise and deter-mination, unity and humanity; today is the birthplace of forever.'

As the music became louder, Gaye left the piano, microphone in hand, his voice soaring like a dove in flight. It was an emotional return and the perfect tribute to Gordy who had originally resisted releasing the song in 1971 and who, when he did, saw his company expand musically and his bank balance grow. Berry Gordy: 'I know for Marvin, the loving reception he got from that audience came at a time in his life when he really needed that kind of support. And for us to see and hear him perform his most important song "What's Going On" in that setting is a moment none of us will ever forget. I never realised that that would be the last time I would ever see Marvin doing his thing.'

Other participating stars included Martha Reeves, Mary Wells, Jnr Walker, the Commodores, and The Jacksons (including Jermaine and Michael) with a stunning performance, as was Michael's solo spot. Motown's younger generation was represented by DeBarge and High Inergy, while the company's writers and producers were introduced on film and on stage, although little credit was given to the musicians who, after all, were responsible for the 'Motown Sound' that launched a million sales. No credit was given either to the wealth of acts who laid the foundation for the company's success, and it was inexcusable for the Gala not to include on stage The Marvelettes (who gave Gordy his first American number one single with 'Please Mr Postman'), Barrett Strong (whose 'Money (That's What I Want)' was Gordy's first big seller) and Marv Johnson (Gordy's first artist, among other things). The list of missing hitmakers was longer than the participating artists, a point quickly picked up by British fans.

Nonetheless the Gala was spectacular entertainment but not, needless to say, without upset, and perhaps that should now be put into perspective based on further research. For a change Marvin Gaye wasn't at fault, but an artist he viewed as a competitor at Motown.

The first incident occurred during British singer Adam Ant's performance when he sang The Supremes' chart topper 'Where Did Our Love Go'. For no apparent reason Diana Ross appeared on stage beside him for an unrehearsed dance routine. A visibly shocked Ant somehow overcame the intrusion to finish the song and leave the stage. Ross's intervention surprised the audience and stunned her fellow artists because it was planned for her to enter the auditorium from an aisle singing 'Ain't No Mountain High Enough' before introducing Mary Wilson and Cindy Birdsong on stage.

Diana Ross then returned to the stage to present a mediocre performance of the Gaye/Terrell evergreen, indicating to certain members of the audience that all was not well. Motown's shining star was dimming, the magic that existed between her and her audience was negligible. To be fair she was suffering from a heavy cold but being the true professional probably decided she could not disappoint her fellow artists, particularly Cindy Birdsong and Mary Wilson. Prior to introducing her singing partners, Diana Ross, possibly in an attempt to save the all-important finale, embarked upon a faltering speech aimed at Berry Gordy who was sitting some way from the stage – 'It's a strange thing, but Berry has always felt he's never been really appreciated . . . It's not about the people who leave Motown that's important, it's about the people who came back and tonight everybody came back.' Throughout her speech Gordy, looking confused and apprehensive, glared at the singer, a moment in time as memories flashed between them. Then, for some reason, Ross raised her arm high in the air demonstrating what appeared to be a Black Power fist clench. Gordy likewise raised his hand, little emotion on his face. Meanwhile, Wilson and Birdsong waited patiently in the wings for their cue . . .

It was originally planned for the trio to remember the hits with a Supremes' medley, the audience would expect it, before singing 'Someday We'll Be Together', their last single as a group, even though Wilson and Birdsong's vocals were not featured on the 1969 release. The medley was cancelled because reputedly Diana Ross had arrived too late to rehearse it, therefore to all intents and purposes there was no stage act. What audiences witnessed was a tacky tribute to the world's one-time greatest female group and which appeared to include public hostility between Ross and Wilson. Thankfully the incident was edited from the television show and subsequent commercial video.

Mary Wilson wrote in her autobiography — 'The applause died down as the opening notes of "Someday We'll Be Together" filled the room. "Mary, Cindy," Diana said as she looked to the wings. Cindy entered from stage right to more applause. After Cindy reached

Diana's side, I sauntered out from stage left, doing my slowest Detroit strut, just like we used to do in the Projects. The crowd roared. When Diana looked at me, she stopped singing. She hadn't reached the bridge of the song, so I couldn't understand why she stopped.' Actually Wilson thought Ross had forgotten the lyrics so took over, believing the move would jog Diana's memory, enabling her to take over the lead once again. It didn't. Instead she reintroduced her singing partners – 'This is Cindy Birdsong, *that's* Mary Wilson.' The latter remark was aggressively spoken and didn't go unnoticed by the audience or the viewing public, thus possibly confirming the animosity existing between the two singers and the fondness Ross felt for Birdsong.

As if this open display wasn't sufficiently embarrassing for the audience, the unthinkable happened! Ross walked towards the stage front, followed by her two partners (Wilson: 'Before the show I'd told Cindy to follow my every move. We'd had no rehearsal and there was no telling what could happen'), when she pushed Mary several feet away from her. It appeared to be an unprovoked action and momentarily stunned Wilson. The audience was aghast. Nelson George reported in *Where Did Our Love Go?* – 'Ross was wild-eyed and way off-key . . . It was an amazing moment of public revelation for someone who had worked so hard at controlling her image, and no one who was there will forget it.' Obviously the trio had lost the impetus of the performance and if allowed to continue the treasured legacy surrounding The Supremes would have been lost forever. Mary Wilson: 'I knew people were anxious to see a cat-fight. That Diana had so foolishly given them that satisfaction hurt me deeply.'

Quick-thinking Suzanne de Passe pushed Smokey Robinson back on to the stage. Only he could retrieve the damage, while Ross asked Berry Gordy to join them on stage. Viewers saw a reluctant Motown boss, dressed in a creased brown satin suit, saunter down the steps to the stage. He was hugged and kissed by artist after artist in a open display of emotion while others, hampered by the shortage of microphones, attempted to keep the finale intact. Marvin Gaye, now wearing a bright red jacket and sunglasses, hugged his former boss, publicly cementing the respect they have for each other, despite past conflicts. With the last strains of 'Someday We'll Be Together', Diana Ross's concert highlight 'Reach Out And Touch (Somebody's Hand)' began, bringing unison to the stage. Then once again Ross did the unexpected. It was reported that she left the cluster of performers to stand several feet above the stage at the orchestra's level. The only possible reason behind this was to ensure she was the focal point! When the song finished and an American magazine photographer wanted a group shot, she hastily returned to the stage.

A heavily edited 'Motown 25' was televised on 16 May 1983 and commanded the highest viewing figure in American television's history, winning an Emmy award for the Most Outstanding Variety Programme. The night the television special was screened Marvin Gaye was celebrating his own success, that of selling out several consecutive dates at Radio City Music Hall.

Now more or less settled into an American way of life again, Marvin Gaye naturally wanted to spend more time with his mother, now recovered from her kidney operation. He said he intended to stay in America until he had fulfilled his commitments to CBS and that included thinking seriously about another album to follow 'Midnight Love'. It seems he didn't intend to work with Harvey Fuqua again as he had approached Barry White (Gaye: 'Barry is a great talent, and I think I could do justice to his music') and/or Leon Sylvers to produce it. Gaye: 'I could do a very nice album with the incredible musicians in Los Angeles or in New York. If I do decide to use synthesisers again, which I quite enjoyed doing because when I play my own music, I think another dimension of me comes out and that's my soul . . . I not only have my voice but I have my music so I'll probably play more again on the next album. Anyway, I haven't decided yet if it'll be with live musicians or with synthesisers again.'

Also at this time he wasn't sure whether he would again give CBS's Larkin Arnold creative control because he now felt it was a redundant title in the long run, and, as had been proven in the past, it could not guarantee hit records. Gaye: 'If the record companies give you artistic control, the disc jockeys will play [about] with your records – so what is it, what is artistic control? I think it's total fallacy, because no artist really has artistic control, we're all subject to the power of the media. And that's very strong.'

While he contemplated his next recordings his colleague Bobby Womack, whose own life was steeped in tragedy, asked Gaye to contribute to his own next album 'Poet II' due to be released on the Beverly Glen label. (Motown had secured a licensing deal to release Womack's album, and its predecessor 'Poet I' in all countries excluding North America and Canada.) Gaye was honoured. Womack: '[Marvin said,] "Oh man that's fantastic!" The next day it was like he never said it. "Did I talk to you yesterday? No, I didn't talk to you yesterday. No, no, no Bobby you got this thing wrong. Look let me get back to you." And he never called back, never returned my calls. That was his trip.'

CBS meanwhile were anxious to maintain Marvin Gaye's high profile and with no new album on the way, insisted he should milk the current one and tour America. Gaye immediately rejected the idea but after accepting the fact he needed money, conceded to the record company's request. A month after participating in 'Motown 25' the forty-four-year-old singer began his first, and much belated, American tour which included dates in Nebraska, Oklahoma, Missouri, Ohio, Atlanta and Dallas. He opened the three-month trek on 18 April 1983 in San Diego where, according to reports, he attempted to reclaim his 'love man' crown, but all he achieved was an unfortunate display of sexy routines. A *Los Angeles Times* critic wrote – 'It . . . seemed peculiar that someone who has struggled so publicly to assert his artistic independence would surrender so completely to the most clichéd sex symbol stereotypes.'

On the other hand *Melody Maker*'s David Frick reviewed the New York performance – 'He strode out confidently on stage looking like nothing less than the grand admiral of soul. A sharp white dress-coat with epaulettes of authority contrasting with the stylish cut of his black military slacks. On his head sat a black yachtsman's sports cap. With a crew of more than twenty musicians, including three percussionists and a string section, at his command, Marvin Gaye launched his "Good Ship R&B" with an Indian war-whoop and a slice of suggestive bump-and-grind funk that sent the packed opening night into a swoon. He turned "Inner City Blues", from his classic R&B protest album "What's Going On" into a dark sexual shuffle, digging hard into the song with a voice cracked with pain and anger. "Rockin' After Midnight" – missed the futuristic intimacy of his one man soul and synth rendition on record. But here he turned the song into a party anthem with white gospel heat. But when he was on – slipping from a sexy black cat moan to a feverish howl in the finale "Sexual Healing", lighting up the stage with his incandescent readings of his old duet hits with Tammi Terrell, Mary Wells and Kim Weston – he left no doubt that he is still the coolest ruler of them all. Long may he wail!'

When the American tour ended in August 1983 (if he had the staying power and/or could be encouraged to honour all the dates), and after a brief break, Gaye intended to embark upon a European tour. He told *Blues & Soul*'s John Abbey that in spite of his aversion to performing, returning to the stage was an exciting challenge to him so long as his act was engineered not to exhaust him. Gaye: 'I'll still want to do an entertaining and lengthy show, but it's all a question of timing and pacing myself so that I can get my breaks.' Ideally, he'd prefer to perform a lengthy show every second night instead of a series of one-nighters – 'And that's what I think my fans would want. I've never been one to do a forty-minute show, anyway. Mind you, I'm in my forties now and I probably don't have as much energy as I used to have.' This statement, he said, reminded him of a story he was once told about an elderly man, which he relayed to Abbey – 'He said that he may not be as good as he once was, but that he's as good once as he ever was!'

Of the European shows' content Gaye said – 'I shall probably do a medley of the old hits, not in their entirety though. If I were to do all of my material, I don't know when I'd get the chance to rest. But hopefully we'll incorporate the songs that people want to hear . . . I'll do a different show in Europe because they don't want to hear all those old songs in America. So here [America], we'll just go out and concentrate on the tunes from the new album, and add a couple of goodies. That'll probably be enough.' Other countries would be added to the tour once the European trek had got underway – 'I understand [I've been] number one in New Zealand which is quite incredible. And I'm doing well in Finland, which is marvellous to me because I've always wanted to go to Finland. I'm terribly interested in those sauna baths and the cold dips afterwards. And the uninhibited-ness of the Finnish people. Perhaps I could lose a bit of my American inhibitedness!'

John Abbey: 'A bit more!'

Gaye: 'Yes, a bit more. It would allow me not to wear a towel because the family jewels have always been subject to close scrutiny in America – so I've always wanted to cover them up! Anyway, I do want to tour and I want to tour the whole world this time.'

Abbey: 'Are you looking forward to doing it back on stage?'

Gaye: 'Doing it on stage, eh? I've never actually done it on stage!'

Abbey: 'I was referring to the music basically, although your answer makes for a better question!'

Gaye: 'It would be one hell of an act!'

The proposed European tour did not take place because the American stint was beset with problems, despite the presence and support of a loyal backing group and entourage including his musical director Gordon Banks. The two major problems were Gaye's intensified cocaine intake – sources reveal he was eating the drug at one point – which resulted in the second problem, that of his life being in danger. It wasn't ascertained whether the death threats he said he received were genuine or not, but they were to him.

His paranoia about dying led to him refusing to take medication prescribed for a throat ailment because after one treatment he claimed it made him feel ill. It also led to him insisting that his immediate staff carry guns and follow him everywhere he went, including surrounding the stage and standing guard outside his hotel rooms. As his behaviour became more erratic and disturbing, his performances suffered, and he even resorted to an undignified act for an artist of his calibre and a man of his years – he 'exposed' himself on stage, or that was how it appeared to the audience. Smokey Robinson (who had tried contacting him at this time to no avail) wrote in his autobiography – 'There was talk that . . . Marvin was so coked out he was dropping his pants during the shows.' Kim Weston: '. . . I heard he had a very bad time because of his cocaine . . . and by the time [of the tour] he was already gone.' *NME* reported – 'By all accounts the shows were not a success. Gaye openly played up to his image by repeatedly blowing his nose in front of the audience, a direct reference to the use of cocaine.'

When Marvin Gaye came off stage he was exhausted, his weakened condition startled his entourage who believed him to be a very ill man. But still he continued. It took until June, after almost two months on the road, for him to finally collapse and be rushed to a Florida hospital suffering from exhaustion, dehydration and a suspected lung infection. Drug abuse was once again suspected. It took Gaye a week to recover sufficiently to return to the stage and complete the tour. Gordon Banks later told *Rolling Stone* magazine — 'The tour brought so many problems, it was ridiculous. People were pushing him to do world tours, Vegas, to do more than he could. They didn't care about him. He was a forty-four-year-old man and he was out of shape. He would do two shows in a row and do another show the next night after travelling. And he stayed up. Just like the Rockwell song, he was scared to go to sleep 'cause 'somebody's watching him'. (Rockwell [Berry and Raynoma Gordy's son Kerry] recorded the 'Somebody's Watching Me' single in December 1983 where the lyrics were inspired by the singer's experiences with a 'peeping tom', among other unsavoury things.)

None too soon the America tour was over, whereupon plans to

embark on a European tour after a short rest were cancelled as Gaye returned to the bosom of his family in Gramercy Place, Los Angeles. His mother, Alberta, told author David Ritz – 'I never saw Marvin in such a bad shape. He was exhausted. He should have checked into hospital. Every time I mentioned it, though, he said that if anyone came to get him, he'd scream and yell and bite them. I told him, it would be help. But Marvin was too stubborn . . . the people around him should have forced him to go, but they did whatever he wanted. That's the way it had always been.'

Marvin Gaye *was* a sick man, only with love and constant attention could he recover sufficiently to think about his career, particularly his next album. Thankfully, he had several instrumental tracks prepared which only required his vocals, and CBS hoped a possible single would emerge to keep his public interested until positive news of an album could be announced. By staying at home in the company of his family Marvin finally accepted what his true friends had told him for years – that cocaine was responsible for his personality change. And this personality change included his growing paranoia and his various obsessions, like being shot by a killer waiting in the shadows. However, in this instance the singer was unwittingly right . . .

He knew he had no choice; he made his mind up to leave cocaine alone, to cleanse his system and return to the recording studios with a fresh, vital, energetic mind. What happened? His drug-taking friends tracked him down, his resistance was low and the temptation overpowering. As fast as his mother and members of his family threw 'his friends' from the house, they returned under different guises. Within a short time Gaye's habit had returned with vengeance, and he spent much time lost in a drug haze locked in his bedroom. A friend told *Rolling Stone* magazine's Michael Goldberg – 'He was a crazy mother. He would sit with his back to the wall with a pistol and wouldn't let anyone near him. And then, all of a sudden, maybe for three or four hours, he would come down and be the other Marvin.'

A close relative further told Goldberg that the singer was convinced everybody hated him – 'He was talking to the fairies, ready to check out. In a suicide state of mind.' This statement prompted Goldberg to add – 'Less than three weeks before his murder, Gaye had announced to a group of family and friends that he was going to take his own life.' Said a friend: 'They were sitting around the house, and he pulled a gun out and said, "I'm going through with it." And he put the gun to his head. Three people rushed at him all at once and took the gun away from him.' Graham Canter: 'Yes, I think he had a suicidal wish at the back of his mind. At the times he had that wish he was antagonistic towards himself. Unless people rang up and showed they loved him, he felt he was being neglected. It's a horrible thing to say but I think he would have done it; certainly he wouldn't have made old bones.'

While many visiting colleagues believed Gaye was mentally disturbed, or at the very worst, possessed by the Devil itself, others believed it was all an act. They knew he enjoyed shocking people, the more they reacted the more he gave the impression he was unbalanced and evil. However, as regards his women visitors there was no doubt he was unbalanced because some suffered violently at his hand. Alberta Gay confided her anguish to Ritz – 'Yes, there were these women around who he treated terribly. An English woman and a Japanese girl. He lost control and hit them. My son, my poor son, turned into a monster.'

The women weren't identified. However Gaye did have a British girlfriend, Deborah Derrick, whom he'd met during his exile in London when she was still married. She had contacted him again in America where they became lovers. On 5 April 1984 twenty-two-year-old Derrick, a photographer's assistant, told the *Daily Star* and *The Sun* newspapers that she had been Gaye's live-in British girlfriend in his sumptuous home and that 'shortly before his death I lost his child through a miscarriage and we were both terribly upset . . . he had set his heart on a baby son.'

Regarding Gaye's violence, The *Los Angeles Herald* quoted police spokesman Sergio Diaz – 'At 8 p.m. on Jan 28 [1984] Gaye apparently phoned a girlfriend and asked her to come to the house. When she arrived, she became involved in an argument, possibly over alleged infidelity, when Gaye struck her with a closed hand, then threw her down and slapped her.'

There was, of course, another important factor to be taken into account: that of Marvin Gaye and his father living under the same roof. Smokey Robinson: 'Many people felt the two of them were on a collision course from the day Marvin was born.' Other sources believed it was a powder keg waiting to be lit and a variety of reasons were blamed. Both threatened each other with physical harm which research has revealed reminded Marvin of his childhood and his father's beatings. Marvin's sister Jeanne told Ritz – 'In the past Father had made it clear that if Marvin were to strike him, he'd murder him.' Kim Weston: 'The generation that we were raised in, I've heard many people say, "If one of my children ever raised their hand to me I'd kill him." And I think Marvin's father would probably fit into that category.'

Unfortunately, while the two men lived in this atmosphere, the wife and mother was locked in the middle, a situation she would later find herself in under the most tragic of circumstances.

Ironically, during or around this time Marvin Gaye actually conducted the occasional press interview. One began in a surprisingly light-hearted fashion, when he was asked how he had managed to stay at the top of his profession. He laughed – 'I really have no idea. Because if there's any artist out there in the history of this business who has ever done more to wreck his career, I would like to find him!' He even made light of his recurring business dilemmas which happened – 'not because I'm temperamental, arrogant or egotistical, although I am all those things, because my temperament, arrogance and ego are all because of my principles, but because I am too highly principled where my art is concerned. I am the artist. If the records are good enough, people will buy them. That's my philosophy. So, I ran into a bit of a problem. I became a temperamental asshole, but I don't regret it because I love me. I love being what I am.'

His temperament had not changed through the years but he pointed out now there was a difference – 'I want to fully realise my potential this time. I've procrastinated long enough with my talent. I think I am multi-talented and I think I have talents that have not been exhibited – mainly because I didn't see any reason to do so at the time. But now I would like to see all the facets of my talent recognised so I'm more than willing to engage myself in that type of work so that I can seriously pursue these goals.'

What of his future as a singer, composer and producer? Firstly, he intended to embark upon the European world tour as originally planned after the American trek, which he estimated would take at least a year to complete. He then intended to slip slowly from the spotlight to plough his creative energies into recording himself, his brother Frankie and other acts, because the satisfaction he had enjoyed working with The Originals in 1969 was a project he had never repeated and had longed to do.

His future in the music business itself would only encompass another eight or nine years, he wouldn't have the inspiration and stamina to continue after that, and anything not achieved in that time would remain undone – 'I've targeted my retirement for around fifty, fifty-one years, although I'll never totally retire from music. I'll only retire from the stage, from personal appearances. I won't have to worry about magazine interviews, or why somebody is saying some nasty things about me or trying to step on me. Or saying I'm attempting to become something or go someplace. Wherever that is, God only knows.

'I don't like to think of myself in terms of having made it to the top, because it's only a backward step after that. I haven't made it to the top because I've got so much more to do . . .'

# 13. | It's Madness

*Let's put it this way, I didn't dislike [Marvin].*

(Marvin Gay Snr)

*If the paramedics had gone in at the right time they could have saved Marvin's life.*

(Lady Edith Foxwell)

*It was hard to come to terms with such a tragedy.*

(Frankie Gay)

*I would like to be remembered as one of, if not the greatest artist, to have walked on the face of the earth.*

(Marvin Gaye)

It was 1 April 1984, April Fool's Day, when the television screens flickered to show pictures of a body shrouded in blue being pushed by a policeman from a house to a nearby ambulance. The mournful voice of an American reporter told the world that Marvin Gaye was dead.

The details of the tragedy were sketchy and misleading at first; comments regarding a family argument, gun fire, father shooting son were precariously spoken until the harrowing report in its full horror was pieced together for the digestion of a disbelieving public.

The following sequence of events leading to the death of Marvin Gaye has been reconstructed from extensive research in America and Britain, including interviews, police evidence and lengthy press reports particularly from the *Los Angeles Herald Examiner*.

Between 8 and 8.30 a.m. on Sunday, 1 April 1984 – the day before Marvin Gaye's forty-fifth birthday and in a two-storey, green-and-white Victorian house situated on the 2100 block of Gramercy Place in the Crenshaw district of Los Angeles, Alberta Gay was having a conversation with her son in an upstairs bedroom. Her husband was in a downstairs room searching for some insurance documents which should have been posted, or which had arrived in the post. His search had been fruitless, so he called upstairs for his wife's assistance. Lt Robert Martin, who headed the police investigation for the Los Angeles Police Department – 'A screaming match with his wife ensued. [Gay Snr] started yelling. He was yelling at his wife to help him find it. She didn't want to, and Marvin said, "Don't yell, come up here." He said, "I don't have to." It went back and forth.'

Eventually Gay Snr joined his wife and son, who was reputedly dressed in his maroon dressing-gown in the pocket of which was a gun. Upon his arrival Marvin told his father he resented the tone he used to ask for his wife's assistance ('You can't talk to my mother that way') and an altercation began between the two men. When that subsided Marvin demanded his father should return downstairs, leaving them alone. He refused to budge, a pushing match ensued in the bedroom before moving to the hall outside. Alberta Gay tried desperately to calm the situation, trying to physically part the two men. When she succeeded, her husband marched off downstairs, leaving her and Marvin to return to the bedroom. Within minutes Gay Snr returned carrying a .38 calibre handgun.

The *Los Angeles Herald Examiner*'s report differed – '[Gay Snr] went looking for his wife to ask her where to find one of the couple's insurance policies. Hearing her voice, he entered a guest bedroom which was being used by Marvin. "I saw her sittin' on the side of the bed, and Marvin was in bed," Gay recalled. He said he told his wife he'd come back later, but Marvin lashed out at him. "Why not tell her now?" Gay quoted his son as saying. Gay said he turned and headed back to his bedroom, and that his son followed him. "He took me from the back and he grabbed me and he slung me to the floor and he started beating me, kicking me. He knocked me on the bed, and when I fell my hand happened to feel the little gun under the pillow. Marvin was the very one that put that [gun] under my pillow four months ago. When he came home, he was always paranoid that someone was going to kill him . . . that's one of the reasons why he gave me the little gun – for protection."'

Marvin Gaye's father aimed the gun at his son, and in his wife's presence, fired a single shot. The bullet hit Marvin near the heart. A second shot quickly followed. The bullet hit Marvin's left shoulder.

Lt Robert Martin: 'My best guess is that that [the first shot] was the fatal round . . . Father fired the shot, Marvin slumped off the bed onto the floor, in a kind of sitting position, with his head back on the bed. Father took a couple steps forward and fired another shot at almost point-blank range, then left. He didn't say anything.'

Gay Snr walked slowly from the bedroom, downstairs, out into the garden where he threw the gun into some nearby bushes before sitting impassively on the front porch.

Upstairs Marvin Gaye lay dying in a pool of blood while his screaming mother raced downstairs through the garden to her son Frankie's house next door. It then appeared she returned to her son while Frankie phoned for the police and paramedics. He too then rushed to Marvin, while a crowd of neighbours, friends and bloodthirsty curious gathered outside the gates of the front garden where Gay Snr still sat.

It was believed mother and son were alone in the house at the time of the shooting, although in May 1984 *Rolling Stone* magazine reported several sources claim – ' . . . that there were others in the house at the time of the shooting. In the pandemonium that ensued, friends and other family members scattered; drugs and drug paraphernalia were reportedly disposed of. When the mother started hollering "Marvin got shot", everybody ran out.' Another source indicated that these friends had in fact arrived for Marvin's birthday party the following day and were witness to the shooting. The police later discounted this on the grounds of no evidence.

When the police and paramedics arrived the scene was inevitably one of confusion and chaos. Lady Edith Foxwell: 'Everybody was completely panicky. The father was downstairs sitting outside on the steps doing nothing, gazing into space. The gun was missing, and the paramedics refused to go inside the house thinking they'd be shot as well.'

However, more alarming and distressing are the absurd, tragic circumstances which followed because Marvin Gaye *need not* have died! He could still be alive today. Foxwell: 'If the paramedics had gone in at the right time they could have saved Marvin's life. The father had shot Marvin and did something with the gun, but [the police] couldn't find it. Marvin was bleeding profusely. Frankie couldn't find the bullet holes to stop the blood flowing. These were Frankie's words to me. He couldn't find where the hole was – he told me he couldn't find it.'

Foxwell paused, caught her breath, before whispering – '[The paramedics] wouldn't go in until the gun was found, and it took half an hour to find the gun . . . they had to look for the gun and that took them half an hour! Marvin would still be alive today. That's exactly what Frankie himself told me, and you can verify that with him. I was given all the details by Frankie. He wouldn't lie. They got Marvin into the ambulance but he was already dead. He'd lost too much blood.'

His body was rushed to the California Hospital Medical Center where he was admitted at approximately 12.52 p.m. with a reported 'traumatic cardio pulmonary arrest and a gunshot wound to the chest.'

Marvin Gaye was pronounced dead at 1.01 p.m. on a warm Los Angeles afternoon on 1 April 1984. If the circumstances surrounding his death had been different he could have survived the shooting . . .

Lady Edith Foxwell's statement regarding Marvin's death appears for the first time in print. It will undoubtedly cause distress to Gaye's devoted public who, until now, perhaps were not aware of all the circumstances surrounding his death. Nonetheless Lady Edith Foxwell's interview was granted with this book in mind.

Smokey Robinson: 'I was on my way home from the golf course and I had stopped at a gas station with my radio on. This bulletin came on, they interrupted the programme I was listening to and said the singer Marvin Gaye was fatally shot and was admitted to some hospital . . . I thought it was a joke, that somebody was just saying something, and I couldn't believe that had been said. So immediately I got out of my car and went to the phone booth. I started to make some calls to find out what had happened. I reached Anna and she told me he was dead and that his father had shot him over an argument that they'd had. It was such a shocking thing to be confronted with.'

Police interviewed members of the Gay family and neighbours before arresting seventy-year-old Marvin Gay Snr. He was taken to Parker Central jail where he was booked on suspicion of murder without bail. Gay pleaded self-defence – 'Marvin struck me and his eyes were glazing. He was like a man possessed. I managed to get free of him and grab a gun I kept in case of burglars. I had no choice but to shoot him.' According to reports, Marvin Gaye was unarmed; he did not remove the gun from his dressing-gown pocket. If indeed a gun was actually there. At the recommendation of Deputy District Attorney, Robert Schirn, Gay was later charged with murder because 'there was sufficient time to reflect between the two shots that hit the singer in the chest and killed him. The killing was committed with malice and premeditation, which constitutes murder rather than a heat-and-passion manslaughter.'

Lt Robert Martin: 'There's been bad blood between father and son for some time although we don't know the extent of it.' He added that there was no significant issue at all behind the shooting because the content of the insurance letter was immaterial.

Marvin Gay Snr stood before the Los Angeles court on 4 April 1984 on the charge of murder when a police spokesman said – 'There was only one witness to the shooting and that was the Reverend Gay's wife. She has given a different account to that of her husband. We don't believe this was a shooting in self-defence. Also at this time there is no evidence to support Mr Gay's claim that Marvin had been high on drugs.'

Following the court appearance Gordon Banks told *Rolling Stone* magazine — 'I wish it were out in the open what his [Gay Snr] mental state really is because he's never really been through a lot. He's been through a lot of easy times really. He didn't have to do nothing all his life. He didn't have the responsibilities Marvin had. So, you know, his attitude was just as cocky as Marvin's sometimes. It's like teacher and student. Clever people.'

The *Los Angeles Herald Examiner* printed two of several contradictions regarding the shooting. Firstly – 'While Gay admitted that he did in fact shoot his son, he did so, he said, from a distance of approximately twenty feet. Alberta Gay told the police the shots were fired from nearly point-blank range.' Secondly – 'Gay said his son came after him, threw him to the floor and beat him severely. Alberta Gay told police that her husband went after their son. And while the younger Gaye threw his father to the floor, he did not appear to have been beaten, police said.'

Lt Robert Martin later confirmed – 'Gay had some bruises on his shoulders and leg . . . There was no indication of bruises on his head, nothing like he'd been punched out or that kind of stuff . . . [He] had apparently been injured by somebody. We can only assume it was his son.'

An autopsy on Marvin's body was held at 2 p.m. on the day after the shooting at the Los Angeles County Coroner's office by Dr Joe Choi. When the British music paper *NME* contacted the Office for the results of the autopsy – whether Gaye died from gunshot wounds or a cardio pulmonary arrest – the Coroner's spokesman William E. Gold said – 'Of course it is pretty obvious what the cause of death was. He was shot. But you're asking a medical question and I won't be able to answer that until we've fully examined the body. The cardio pulmonary phrase came from the hospital but we'll probably go with gunshot wounds.'

Routine toxicological tests for drugs and other substances were carried out on the body as a matter of course, and the results indicated evidence of cocaine, confirming the singer had taken the drug for some time. An anonymous police source told the *Herald Examiner* – 'There's already a little bit of evidence that suggests that he'd [Gaye] been using cocaine lately. Apparently, the left nostril was rather destroyed. Also, one of his pinky fingernails was extremely long. Those two things suggest that he was still in that [drug] culture.'

The official cause of death was given as gunshot wounds to the chest.

Marvin Gaye's funeral was held on Thursday, 5 April, at Los Angeles Forest Lawn Cemetery. His body was dressed in a military-style white uniform as it lay in a silver coffin. It was an outfit Marvin had worn on his last American tour. The jacket was decorated in white braid and the collar was white ermine. Wreaths from friends and artists including Diana Ross (a huge display of white lilies with a white sash) were placed at the foot of the coffin. After Alberta Gay had touched her son's face and gently kissed him, the coffin lid was closed.

The funeral service, which began with a tape of the late singer's version of the American national anthem, was conducted by Bishop Rawlings, a long-standing friend of Marvin's father. Five hundred people attended including his immediate family – his first wife Anna, and their son Marvin III; his second wife Janis and their children Bubby and Nona; his brothers Frankie and Michael (half brother) and his sisters Zeola and Jeanne. Industry figures and artists included Martha Reeves, Harvey Fuqua, Berry Gordy, Norman Whitfield, Brian and Eddie Holland, Larkin Arnold, Quincy Jones, Dick Gregory, Stevie Wonder and Smokey Robinson.

Following a reading of the Twenty-Third Psalm, several spoke. Stevie Wonder (who later swore that he would never play another April Fool's joke) was one – 'Marvin was the person who encouraged me that the music I had within me I must feel free to let out.' He then sang 'Lighting Up The Candle', a song inspired by Gaye's death. Smokey Robinson told the congregation that Marvin was now 'somewhere else where nobody can hurt him from now on. And we should all remember him for the good times and the good things and understand that he is resting. He needed a rest.' Larkin Arnold:

'Marvin was not a hypocrite. He lived his life with his collar open.' Comedian Dick Gregory was the only speaker to make reference to Gay Snr – 'I wish he was sitting here somewhere. I'd tell him how much I love him.' Martha Reeves: '[Marvin is] not here, but he'll never die with me. His music will always live on, his spirit will always be present.'

At the end of the service Gaye's body was cremated, and a thirty-five-piece band played 'What's Going On' while the mourners filed out of church. The next day his three children and his first wife scattered his ashes at sea.

Marvin's father did not attend the funeral, he was in the Los Angeles County Men's prison. He made a further appearance in Municipal Court, where participants were searched by bailiffs using hand-held metal detectors because it was thought Marvin Gaye fans would seek revenge, when he told Judge Michael Tynan – 'I fear and respect God, I regret what happened. I didn't mean to do it.' Gay's lawyer Philip Schreiber requested the court to order his client to undergo psychiatric tests to determine, among other things, his competency to stand trial. Tynan granted the request, and entered a plea of innocence until the results were known. Bail was set, said to be either $10,000 or $100,000 although Gay was not eligible during the psychiatric examinations.

Following this court appearance, where Gay wore crumpled yellow pyjamas, his family hired new defence lawyers Arnold Gold and Michael Schiff to represent him when the results of the tests were made available by court psychiatrist Dr Ronald Markman. Deputy District Attorney Ralph Ayala: 'If Gay is found incapable of understanding the charges against him, and if the district attorney's office doesn't challenge the finding Gay would be periodically examined to determine if he is mentally able to stand trial.' The *Herald Examiner* further reported – 'David Guthman, the deputy district attorney in charge of the psychiatric section, said last week that he thought the district attorney's office would challenge a non-competency finding. Guthman explained that Gay appeared to be "lucid" and seemed to know what he was doing when he allegedly shot his son. According to Al Albergate, a spokesman for the district attorney's office, the issue of Gay's competency to stand trial is unrelated to the question of his sanity at the time he allegedly shot his son. Consequently even though Gay could be found mentally capable of standing trial, he still could plead insanity as a defence.'

Despite appearing unsure and subdued in court, journalists reported that Gay Snr had no objection to meeting them in his prison cell where, wearing a dark blue prison-issued jumpsuit he stressed – 'I didn't mean to do it. I do know I did fire the gun. I was just trying to keep him off me. I want the world to know it wasn't presumptuous on my part.' He then related his version of the tragedy, that Marvin had pushed him down on the bed whereupon he felt the gun hidden under the pillow – 'I thought it was loaded with blanks or BBs . . . I didn't know any bullets was in the gun . . . I finally got to my feet and he lets me have one right in the side. I laid there and tried to get my poor self together, and he stomped out of my room into the hallway. Ma was crying, trying to tell him to stop.'

Gay Snr was also adamant that Marvin had been twenty feet away when he turned on him again, threatening, 'Oh, you want some more do you?' Gay: 'I pulled the trigger. The first one didn't seem to bother him. He put his hand up to his face like he'd been hit with a blank. And then I fired again. I was backing up toward my room. I was going to go in there and lock the door. This time I heard him say "oh" and I saw him go down. I didn't know whether the injury was real or put on or what. Ma comes in, she says, "Marvin's bleeding." I went down the hall and looked. "Babe," I said, "call the paramedics." Now I am wondering what was in the gun, and the paramedics came and took him away. I still didn't know how bad it was.' When told by detectives that his son was dead, Gay said he didn't believe them. 'Oh God of Mercy, it shocked me. I just went to pieces.'

During these prison interviews Gay insisted time and again that his son had been taking cocaine heavily – 'I heard him sniffing all the time. He turned into something like a beast-like person.' When asked if he loved his son Gay replied – 'Let's put it this way – I didn't dislike him.'

Marvin Gaye in death also presented problems because apart from unpaid alimony for both his wives estimated at $200,000 and a tax bill estimated $1,200,000, he reputedly owed a total of approximately $950,000 to Marilyn Freeman, Harvey Fuqua and Ron Russom (a promoter). Also Gaye did not leave a will, therefore his estate – said to be in the region of $1 million – was handled by his eldest son. And an assault and battery suit filed against him by an unnamed forty-eight-year-old woman on 18 February 1984 was made public for the first time. *NME* reported – '[She] hadn't filed the charge earlier because she was afraid of being hurt again. Her wounds were not described but she had seen a doctor following the incident.' When the *Los Angeles Daily News* carried the story it reported the charge was filed on 20 March after Gaye had allegedly attacked her with 'bodily force' at 8 p.m. on 20 January.

Marvin Gaye's death had the same impact on the music industry and record buyers as Marilyn Monroe's equally tragic demise on 5 August 1962 had on the movie industry and cinema patrons. But this time instead of flocking to see her films, the public rushed to buy his music as exemplified by Motown/USA's Miller London Jnr who told the *Hollywood Reporter* – 'We've been getting a tremendous amount of calls from distributors, retailers and consumers. Because Marvin was with us for so many years the bulk of available product is on Motown. One of our depots ordered two thousand pieces on one selection in a morning and then, right away, they ordered another four thousand five hundred.' The MCA Records Group, Motown's record distributor, agreed the sales increase was dramatic – 'particularly in the two days after his murder. It's incredible that this happened so fast.' MCA's George Collier said that the New York office alone sold more than four thousand unsolicited records and 'record shops that don't sell black music primarily were ordering Marvin's product. All the TV coverage brought back into everyone's mind just who Marvin Gaye was. On the radio stations "I Heard It Through The Grapevine" is like the national anthem. Everything he's done is on the air. Every R&B radio station in the country is doing a special or a tribute to Marvin Gaye.'

Michael Tearson from WMMR Philadelphia was one of many DJs who reported on Gaye's death – 'I couldn't be glib. I felt cheated. I spoke from the heart. I took Marvin's songs very personally as a youngster and I knew to a certain extent I was educating my audience, so I dedicated the first hour of my show to him.' Not every listener however appreciated Tearson's motive – 'One guy phoned and asked me "what's this Marvin Gaye shit? I thought you played rock and roll?" But that's the lay of the land in 1984.' Over in Los Angeles, KRLA operations director Penny Biondi recalled the last time she interviewed Gaye – 'He was very tired when we talked. He was about to perform at the Greek and his defences were down.' Unfortunately, because of the nature of the interview much of it wasn't broadcast.

On television, the popular, established black entertainment programme *Soul Train* featured its own tribute on 21 April 1984. The programme included the late singer happily answering questions put to him by members of the audience and performing five songs. Don Cornelius, the programme's executive producer – 'The tribute was one of the most memorable episodes in the show's history. No additional sponsors or rate increases were solicited for this special broadcast because our compensation lies in the potential for the maximum number of Americans to see Marvin Gaye at his best and at the peak of his career.'

British radio too remembered Marvin Gaye, particularly the pirate stations scattered at secret locations across the country, while national radio DJ Paul Gambaccini repeated on air his 1976 interviews with Gaye – 'He had the distinction of being Motown's first successful male soloist and he also expanded the parameters of black music with albums like "What's Going On". He had a superb voice that was capable of many moods – playful, mournful, passionate – and all of them convincing. Marvin talked about dying a number of times during the interviews. It was as though he was willing for his death to occur at any time. He was a very troubled man in later years.'

Otis Williams: '. . . The press portrayed him as a tormented genius on his way back, but it was only half true. As long as I'd known Marvin, he always seemed to be haunted; a beautiful man, a genius, but truly tortured.'

Also in Britain record shops reported a considerable demand for all Gaye's work but neither CBS nor Motown made any effort to exploit his catalogue after his death. Demand was particularly high for a compilation album 'Greatest Hits' released by the television promotion company Telstar late in 1983. And what was advertised on prime time television on the very evening Marvin died? Telstar's 'Greatest Hits' album! Sean O'Brien, the company's managing director – 'We were supposed to be screening the Michael Jackson album. It was very unfortunate that we messed them up.' As *No 1* magazine pointed out – 'Unfortunate, but a highly profitable boob!' Needless to say the album became a best-seller peaking at number thirteen in the charts. When Telstar's rights to the album expired Motown/BMG re-released it minus the CBS tracks.

While the majority of record shops were grateful for the additional trade few advertised his demise. However, not all were respectful as exemplified by a north London outlet which filled its front window with Marvin's work, and on his 'Live! At The London Palladium' album affixed a note reading 'Sorry, we mean dead!'

Fans, friends, the media and business acquaintances joined recording artists to pay tribute to Marvin Gaye. His work had inspired so many fellow artists and young acts, while his music was listened to by millions more. Motown artists were among the first to remember his magic including The Temptations who dedicated their 'Truly For You' album to him — 'Thanks for such wonderful music memories and happy times from "Mama Luchi" in '59 with The Moonglows to "Sexual Healing" of '83. From the Motown Revue shows of the '60s to "Motown 25" of '83. Marvin Gaye you were truly one of a kind and it goes without saying that we love you.'

Smokey Robinson: 'One of my greatest pleasures was to work in the studio with Marvin, singing one of my songs. He was a producer's and songwriter's dream. You simply had to show him the song once or twice, and he proceeded to "Marvin Gaye-ise" it, which also turned out great.' Robinson later dedicated his 'Essar' (Smokey Robinson) album to his friend, Emgee, Jermaine Jackson: 'Marvin has left a big void in my life. He influenced the way I work and it's this influence that has kept me going. When I was younger we used to play basket ball together and I'd also see him in the studios working away. I really admired him so much.'

Valerie Simpson: 'I always felt his career was exceptional early on and he became even more brilliant when he went into "What's Going On". His music will be even bigger in his demise, but I would rather have the man. Marvin and Tammi were also such a powerful magnum, and now they've both gone. It takes a lot of thinking about, doesn't it? And quite honestly, the fact that both of them have gone is something I still can't believe, it just doesn't seem fair.'

Anna Gordy Gaye: 'I knew when I heard [about Marvin's death] that it was God's will. I thought about the fact that, oddly and ironically, the very person who helped bring him into this world . . . God had the same person take him out of this world. There is probably something there.'

Janis Gaye: 'He was a good father, very close to the kids when he was able to spend time with them. He would go through periods when he didn't really want to sing. He would sing for himself at home, or he would sing for us. But as far as recording or entertaining he just didn't want to. He'd rather spend time with the kids in the yard, in the pool, or just doing daddy kind of things. These were the times that they cherish I'm sure and I think about them quite often myself,'

Harvey Fuqua: 'In my opinion Marvin was the most well-rounded singer I have ever known, from R&B to gospel to classical. He was awesome. I am grateful for having had the opportunity to have worked with him.' Mickey Stevenson: 'To me he was more than just a musician, singer and artist, he was a friend who was concerned about others, and he expressed that concern the only way he knew how – through his music.' Brian Holland: 'The music industry is replete with persons possessing good voices, and in some respects, unique sounds. It is most unusual, however, for those qualities to be forged into an unerring intuition. When it does occur, that is a rare artistry. Such was Marvin Gaye.'

Dave Godin: 'Part of Marvin's real charm was, if he liked you, letting you see the chinks in the armour of his public persona. He was caught up many times between how he should act, and how he really felt. The two did not always coincide . . . Marvin was trying to find a meaning and purpose in life: his need for love and affection was inordinate, but he also gave these things in equal measure. To many people he was something of an enigma, but this was to be expected. Marvin knew that nobody had all the answers to life's mysteries and in any case he wasn't that greedy. He just wanted to know a bit more than was generally on offer.'

Jeffrey Kruger: 'For all his personal troubles, Marvin will be remembered for the countless years of pleasure via his outstanding ability to combine a lyric and melody and write the great songs he did. He'll be sadly missed.'

Graham Betts: 'My first reaction was one of shock. Although we were aware of his problems we had not believed them to be that bad. Very few CBS personnel seemed to be similarly affected. I suppose you had to have worked with the man or really admired the music to have felt the sense of loss. I don't mean that in a derogatory way.'

Certain artists took their tributes one step further by recording their feelings. Gaye's colleague Edwin Starr released one of the first singles in May 1984 titled 'Marvin: From A Friend To A Friend'. Such tribute singles are often treated indifferently and suspiciously by the public as they tend to be considered as tragedy cash-ins. Not so Starr's single. Edwin: 'My main concern was that the tribute said what I wanted to say without any over-the-top embellishments and that the kids in the street accepted it for what it was meant to be . . . I am extremely proud of this record, and I feel I could walk into Marvin's mother's house and play it to her with no qualms whatsoever. I was very shocked and stunned at the news of his death. I had known him on a very personal and intimate basis for years.'

'Marvin: From A Friend To A Friend' written by DJ Mick Collins within hours of Gaye's death, was first offered to the late Steve Walsh for his Total Control Records operation. Walsh was unsure of the best way to present the song so passed on it. Edwin Starr had no such doubts – 'The minute I heard it I knew that I had to record it myself. It said everything that I felt about the tragedy and the man, and the decision was made there and then. I changed only a few words here and there, and used the basic eight track, and simply bounced it up to a twenty-four-track recording. I could have started from scratch but Mick's demo had such honesty and feeling that I considered it would be wrong to ignore it. I was never worried at the lack of total professionalism in the concept. In fact, I don't suppose I'd have been interested in the project had it been written by a Lionel Richie or a Stevie Wonder.'

Nonetheless – someone else was interested in a Lionel Richie composition – Diana Ross. Bearing in mind how Marvin Gaye had seen her as a competitor at Motown and the clashes that occurred while recording the 'Diana & Marvin' album, it seemed to the public a strange move for her to make. The song, 'Missing You', was the perfect loving tribute, containing all the heartfelt emotions expected from Richie's pen complemented by Ross's wistful vocals against a moody, low-key arrangement. Diana Ross said the song was born from a conversation she had had with Smokey Robinson – 'We were talking about how we were missing Marvin and what he meant to us as well as to music. Then Lionel and I got to talking about how we need to tell people that we love them while they're still alive. Lionel used all this to write that beautiful and special song.'

The single soared into the American top ten (no 1 R&B) and bombed in Britain, surprisingly for a Lionel Richie ballad, and for a single accompanied by one of the most thoughtfully compiled promotional videos. Ross decided to take second place on the film to devote most of the viewing time to sequences of two other Motown casualties, Florence Ballard and Paul Williams; her own late mother, and extensive footage of Marvin. It transpired that the video was played more than the single despite Ross's record company Capitol's extensive re-promotion activities.

A year later Lionel Richie's ex-group the Commodores paid their respects to Gaye with 'Nightshift' which became an international hit, the group's first since losing Richie. While black singer Billy Paul, best known for his hits like 'Me & Mrs Jones' (1973) and 'Bring The

Family Back' (1979) recorded 'Sexual Therapy' also in 1985 based on 'Sexual Healing'. Paul: 'Marvin and I were very close and I wanted "Sexual Therapy" to be taken as a tribute to his great talent. I must admit I expected some flack but I have received nothing but praise so far.' And prior to the end of 1985, Washington-born Frankie Kelly released 'Ain't That The Truth' an ersatz of 'What's Going On'. Since this time, cover versions of Marvin Gaye's work have been released regularly and of course his own recordings have been re-released and repackaged.

On 2 May 1984 Marvin Gay Snr's lawyers Arnold Gold and Michael Schiff disclosed in court that he was suffering from a tumour located on the pituitary gland. The small gland which produces several hormones and assists in the growth of young people, is attached to the base of the brain. The tumour which had gone undetected prior to the psychiatric tests was the size of a walnut. Gay's lawyers also divulged that Frankie Gay's wife Irene had discovered her father-in-law's diary – 'Mrs Gay just found his diaries from 1969 and on every day on the pages he complained about headaches.' She said she had no knowledge of Gay Snr taking medication or of consulting a doctor.

Also on 2 May 1984 Gay's lawyers requested a continuance in order to ascertain 'a pre-surgery evaluation, probable surgery and a follow-up [psychological] re-evaluation.' *NME* reported that Gold had told the Presiding Superior Court Judge Michael Pirosh that the tumour 'may have caused the behaviour leading to the shooting' and that its size and nature [benign or malignant] hadn't as yet been determined. He claimed it was 'absolutely necessary that the tumour be removed lest it render Gay blind – or perhaps even kill him – within months.'

Dr Ronald Markman, the court-appointed psychiatrist, disclosed in a two-page letter that on 16 April last Gay was 'confused and somewhat disorientated', but that on 27 April when he had conducted his second and last evaluation Gay was mentally fit to stand trial. His report also mentioned Gay's 'past history of alcolohism', his senility and that a growing tumour would worsen his condition. In conclusion his report urged that an '. . . evaluation of the cranial mass precede any further criminal proceedings.'

Meanwhile the Deputy Probation Officer Alexander Peace also prepared a report for submission to the court. The *Los Angeles Daily News* reported – 'Gay's wife, Alberta, told the probation department that her husband suffered from memory lapses and had been "drinking for years". She also said that Gay often became argumentative, accused her of "carrying on with other men" and refused her access to their combined finances that were compiled from the sale of their Washington D.C. home.'

At 8.24 a.m. on 16 May 1984 two neurosurgeons operated on Gay Snr in the Los Angeles County University of California Medical Centre. The operation took two hours and a walnut-sized benign tumour was removed from his pituitary gland. After surgery Gay was in a good and stable condition, spent two days in the neurosurgical intensive care unit and a further week in hospital. One of the surgeons, Dr Martin H. Weiss, said that since 1968 he had performed this operation over six hundred times and that 'it would be extremely rare for such a tumour to cause behavioural symptoms in a patient.'

Six months following Marvin Gaye's killing, his father pleaded no contest to voluntary manslaughter. His lawyer Michael Schiff said the charge was reduced from first-degree murder on a plea bargain and that he felt the judge could be persuaded not to send his client to prison. Schiff: 'This is better for the family and himself. We have been assured there is no opposition to this, including the mother and the investigating officer. I look for a wise and compassionate decision.' If Gay Snr were proven guilty of the crime he could have faced a prison sentence of no less than thirteen years including enhancement for use of the gun. Many British fans believed he deserved this sentence; certainly he did not appear to have shown his son any compassion.

On 2 November 1984, after approximately eighty days imprisonment, Marvin Gay Snr stood in court for the last time. The Los Angeles Superior Court Judge Gordon Ringer imposed a six-year suspended sentence and a five-year probation period for voluntary manslaughter. The original murder charges were dropped. If Gay complied with the terms of his probation which included further psychiatric counselling he would not return to prison.

Judge Ringer said that imposing prison time would amount to a 'death sentence' and put the blame for the killing squarely on the victim. Ringer: 'This is one of those tragic cases in which a young life was snuffed out. But . . . the young man who died, although tragically, provoked this incident. It was his own fault.'

Deputy District Attorney Dona Bracke: 'I believe the sentence was the most equitable in this situation. This was definitely not a case of self-defence. I believe it fell somewhere between second degree murder and voluntary manslaughter. But there would be no purpose served by sending him to prison now. He's an old man, and he was physically, mentally and emotionally deteriorating every time he came to court. He basically kind of sentenced himself. It doesn't appear he has very much to live for,'

Frankie Gay: 'When Marvin died the pressures on me were enormous. The whole incident was a shattering experience, for the father I love so deeply had shot the brother who had done so much for me. It was hard to come to terms with such a tragedy.'

Prior to the court's decision, in June 1984 and after nearly fifty years of marriage, Alberta Gay instigated divorce proceedings citing 1 April 1984, the day her beloved son died, as the official separation date.

Gay Snr: 'I'm paying the price . . . it's killing me. I loved my son.'

Meanwhile Marvin Gaye's record company CBS began exploring avenues in which to recoup some of the reported $2.5 million paid for the singer's signature. Larkin Arnold remembered the unfinished tracks Gaye's mother held and some unfinished songs recorded for an aborted Motown album. He retrieved these and asked Harvey Fuqua and Gordon Banks to work on them by adding synthesisers, bass, percussion, drums and additional vocals to bring them up to release standard. The result was 'Dream Of A Lifetime' released in June 1985. Arnold: '[The album] is made up of different elements – some of it is scandalous, some is very sad. There are religious overtones and some very funny material in there. Some tracks are prophetic, some philosophical. And all these are ingredients of Marvin Gaye, the man.'

The three Motown songs were 'Symphony' (which Gaye wrote with Smokey Robinson), 'It's Madness' and the album's title (written by solo Gaye). The latter track was originally titled 'I Thank God For My Wonderful Life' which Marvin intended to record on Sammy Davis Jnr in the Seventies for release on his Ecology label. 'Symphony', 'Life's Opera' (written by Gaye and Ivy Hunter) and 'Dream Of A Lifetime' were linked conceptually and hinted at the singer's death. Gospel vocals covered the song in a religious coating before it climaxed with the unlisted 'The Lord's Prayer'. It was Larkin Arnold's idea to include the prayer – 'It's part of a whole concept of that section. It shows the difference between the devilment in Marvin and his religious upbringing – the son of a preacher – and the conflict between the two during his life . . . I had to end the album with "Dream Of A Lifetime" because of the lyrics. It was a heart breaking time for me doing it, yet when I heard this track I felt a little better because that song sums up Marvin's life. He was a good friend and I felt an extremely deep loss when he died.'

'Savage In The Sack' (originally written by Gaye under the title 'Dem Niggers Are Savage In The Sack') and 'Masochistic Beauty' (which Gaye co-wrote with Gordon Banks) were considered lyrically offensive although in both they were practically indecipherable. Arnold: 'He was always somewhat controversial with his material because he was a man of many facets and if Marvin was alive he'd explain the reasoning behind it more clearly than I, although I must confess it still took me a little while to get into the songs.' Nonetheless, CBS took the precaution of over-stickering the front album sleeve with a warning that both these tracks could be considered offensive and were unsuitable for radio play.

A month prior to the album's release, 'Sanctified Lady' (previously written by Gaye and Gordon Banks as 'Sanctified Pussy') was lifted as the first single to peak outside the pop 100 (no 2 R&B), while becoming a British number fifty-one. Justin Lubbock: 'This is unmistakenly Marvin Gaye in a Marvin Gaye mood. Behind his inimitable vocalising lies a tight, tricky mid-tempo rhythm that features prominent drums and percussion, simple bass-line and the minimum of keyboard support. The melody is also very simple in appearance but the more you become exposed to it the more infectious it becomes. The music lives on!'

'Sanctified Lady' was followed by another album track 'It's Madness' in August 1985 and as a bonus selling point CBS included a thirty x forty-inch poster with the twelve inch version and a limited pressing of attractive picture discs. Lubbock: 'The man may be gone but the legend lives on, and will continue to do so thanks to songs like this. "It's Madness" is vintage Marvin – beautiful melody, striking lyrics, lush production and an awesome amount of soulfulness all contained of rare quality.' The single bombed in Britain and struggled to number fifty-five in the American R&B chart. Marvin's penned 'Ain't It Funny (How Things Turn Around)' completed the album. Larkin Arnold: 'I tried as much as possible in the selection to come up with something that painted a picture of him; the person I knew. There were deep conflicts, combined with a tremendous sense of humanity and a deep sensitivity.'

The front sleeve of 'Dream Of A Lifetime' showed a casually dressed, smiling singer while Arnold's sleeve notes dominated the back. The record's inner bag was covered in photographs of Gaye in various moods. Graham Betts: 'The album might well have been better had Marvin been able to finish it. But there again, had he lived he might well have put something completely different out.'

In spite of extensive marketing campaigns neither 'Dream Of A Lifetime' nor the two singles reached CBS's expectations (the album reached number forty-six in the UK charts). The failure remained a mystery but did not deter the company from planning a second posthumous release, the promised love album. Aptly titled 'Romantically Yours' it was issued in November 1985 and once again contained material owned by CBS and Motown. Larkin Arnold was responsible for the compilation where the tracks were reworked by him, Harvey Fuqua and Gordon Banks. It wasn't a commercially slanted release by any means, more a middle-of-the-road collection, with not a 'Sexual Healing' or offensive lyric in sight!

Side one contained Marvin's much-loved Bobby Scott productions of the standard compositions 'Why Did You Choose Me?', 'The Shadow Of Your Smile' and 'I Won't Cry Anymore', while Hal Davis and Marc Gordon produced 'More', 'Maria' and 'Fly Me To The Moon (In Other Words)'. Gaye wrote and produced four tracks on side two – 'Just Like', Walkin' In The Rain', 'I Live For You' and 'Stranger In My Life', while the final song 'Happy Go Lucky' was written by Eddie Holland and Norman Whitfield, who also produced it. The whole album was relaxed and easy going, and proved beyond doubt that this type of music was Gaye's forte. It's a pity he wasn't able to pursue this avenue further while at Motown instead of churning out banal pop songs which did little to compliment his then innate untapped talent.

The music's mood was reflected in the album's artwork where the front cover featured the singer looking seductively suave in a dark dinner jacket, a red silk handkerchief lopping in the top pocket, black bow tie and white shirt. The photo was taken by Sam Emerson presumably at the Grammy Awards ceremony in 1983. The back cover only contained the track listing.

Graham Betts: 'I don't think Marvin's CBS material quite matched his Motown material simply because there wasn't enough of it. I very much doubt that CBS have anything left . . . During Marvin's time with the company I thought that he was well on the way to achieving the kind of heights he had reached with Motown . . . I had hoped this would have been the start of a tremendous relationship. Instead, it merely signalled the end.'

'If 'Romantically Yours' remains Marvin Gaye's last CBS album, he ended his career in much the same manner as he began it – with a middle-of-the-road release containing the songs he loved so much.*

While CBS were endeavouring to recoup its financial advances with these two albums Motown did not openly promote Gaye's material although, of course, much of his work was available on catalogue and sold steadily. However, two years after his death the British offshoot (now a subsidiary of BMG after leaving EMI in 1981) broke its silence by re-releasing his 1969 chart topper 'I Heard It Through The Grapevine' to cash in on a successful jeans television advertisement. The re-release became a number eight in the UK charts in April 1986.

A month prior to this success and in America, Motown released the 'Motown Remembers Marvin Gaye' compilation. The March 1986 release was aimed at collectors because it contained twelve original unreleased tracks recorded during the Sixties and early Seventies. All the songs were incomplete so Hal Davis added musical overdubs, vocals and his inimitable expertise to ensure the results were commercially viable. The album's only single ('I Heard It Through The Grapevine' was added to the British release only due to its recent success) was the 1971 recorded 'The World Is Rated X', a masterpiece of a song. Hal Davis: 'I remember how elated Marvin was the night he recorded "The World Is Rated X". He got in the car with me to share his enthusiasm, excitement and joy that we were working together again.' The unusual mid-tempo song was updated by electronic improvisation and aggressive backing vocals including Motown's solo songstress Monalisa Young with Jessica Smith and Josef Powell, who was also the vocal arranger. The full orchestration turned an ordinary track into a chart contender. Unfortunately, the single bombed through lack of promotion. Holland, Dozier and Holland's 'Lonely Lover' was an ersatz of 'Put Yourself In My Place', typical of the trio and certainly on a par with their other 1965 releases. A rousing 1964 solo Smokey Robinson composition 'Just Like A Man' was a welcome addition to this compilation, where a

---

* It appears that CBS Records planned a fourth album entitled 'Vulnerable' which included the tracks 'She Needs Me', 'Funny', 'This Will Make You Laugh', and 'I Wish I Didn't Love You So'. All were produced by Gaye. To date the album remains unreleased.

gravel-voiced Gaye complemented the foot-tapping track. Marvin's penned 'I'm Going Home' was lyrically simple, somewhat repetitive, but amply padded with additional vocals, while Howard Lemon's 'No Greater Lover' revealed the true erstwhile nature of Gaye's soul in a tense gospel anthem. A prodigious choir transformed the song into a glorious few musical moments. Ashford & Simpson's 'Dark Side Of The World' – probably using the same backing track as Diana Ross's version – offered a distinctive pounding beat à la Van McCoy and an easy-voiced singer. A 'Pride And Joy' soundalike was included under the title 'Loving And Affection' which Gaye co-wrote, thus indicating how certain songs' riffs and melodies were used time and again. The five remaining tracks, in much the same vein as the other pop-slanted songs were: 'I'm In Love With You' written by Clarence Paul and Morris Broadnax, dating back to 1967; 'That's The Way It Goes', a 1965 Mickey Stevenson and Hank Cosby track; 'I Gotta Have Your Lovin'', written by Berry Gordy and recorded in 1964; 'Baby I'm Glad That Things Worked Out So Well', penned in 1966 by Smokey Robinson, Warren Moore and Marv Tarplin; and the gem in collectors' eyes, an out-take from the 'Take Two' album – 'Baby (Don't You Leave Me)' written by Clarence Paul and featuring Kim Weston as duettist.

This release helped to bridge the gaps in Gaye's recording career and, it was hoped, would signify the start of further searches being made for his unreleased product by its executive producer Brenda M. Boyce. The record's front sleeve featured the dapper pose of the singer first used on the back-cover of 'In Our Lifetime'. However, this time the picture was clearer, and the handkerchief flopping from his top jacket pocket was trimmed, indicating either air-brushing or a direct transfer from the negative. The back cover was crammed with tributes from fellow artists and colleagues.

In May 1988 Motown released its second posthumous album 'A Musical Testament 1964-1984'. It comprised twenty-one tracks over two albums and acted as a timely reminder of Marvin's lesser-exposed, sensitive songs. Some were specially sequenced together – the previously unreleased 'The Star Spangled Banner' and 'Save The Children' were good examples of this. Several singles from 1964 to 1966 were included like 'Try It Baby', 'Baby Don't You Do It' and the tracks previously unreleased until 1986: 'Loving And Affection' and 'Lonely Lover'. Other tracks were lifted from his million-selling projects – 'Right On', 'Wholly Holy' from 'What's Going On'; 'If I

Should Die Tonight', 'Just To Keep You Satisfied' from 'Let's Get It On'; 'After The Dance' from 'I Want You'; 'Life Is A Gamble' from 'Trouble Man'; and 'When Did You Stop Loving Me, When Did I Stop Loving You', and 'Anger' from 'Here, My Dear'.

The album was divided into four sections (one side, one section) as follows: 'Crossroads', 'A Parting Of The Ways', 'A Witness To Love' and 'Introspection'. The front sleeve was unattractive in dull colours, showing a grey-faced Gaye dressed in a checked shirt, his shadow behind him, while the back featured a handful of small coloured shots depicting various stages of his career, the track listing and Ed Townsend's sleeve notes which included – 'In this LP you'll hear a part of Marvin's soul that I had the privilege of sharing on many occasions, sometimes late at night, sitting alone in the studio, riding in a car, or walking in the wide open deserts of Arizona, where he and I ventured on a couple of occasions . . . He was indeed an artist whose imagination and feelings were deep and extreme . . . Aside from his impressive talent, the most cooperative, humble, punctual, professional and loving artist I've ever recorded was Marvin Gaye, contrary to public belief! . . . This should be profoundly clear when you listen to the wide range of material contained in this album . . . You could probably save yourself a trip to your analyst by simply playing this LP, and listening . . . with your heart . . . with your body . . . with your mind and soul.'

This was the first Marvin Gaye compilation for over two years and was, to date, the last to be issued by Motown although several albums have been reissued and/or re-released in compact disc form. While his public await Motown's next move, their film subsidiary has released the commercial video *Motown Presents Marvin Gaye* during 1989. The hour-long film was hosted by Smokey Robinson – 'How sweet Marvin was and how stubborn he could be . . . compassionate, exciting was his music. Marvin Gaye was one of our greatest artists and was my friend for a quarter of a century.' The video was a brief insight into his career and included contributions from Anna and Berry Gordy, Valerie Simpson and Nickolas Ashford who sang from the studio where Marvin Gaye and Tammi Terrell had recorded, Janis Gaye and Alberta Gay among others. Snatches of the Belgian television programme *Marvin Gaye – Transit Ostend*, record promotional films, television appearances including his Grammy acceptance speech and an on-stage appearance with Gladys Knight and the Pips to sing 'I Heard It Through The Grapevine', and

Marvin's own interviews, were shown over a background of his music.

Taken as a whole Marvin Gaye's British single success was broken down as follows. His only chart topper was 'I Heard It Through The Grapevine' in February 1969 and according to the seventh edition of Guinness' *British Hit Singles* he enjoyed twenty-four hits including his duets with Mary Wells, Kim Weston, Tammi Terrell and Diana Ross, re-issues and re-entries.

'Sexual Healing' was his second biggest seller, peaking at number four during October 1982, followed by two number five hits – 'Too Busy Thinking About My Baby' in July 1969 and 'You Are Everything' (with Diana Ross) in March 1974. 'Got To Give It Up' was a number seven entrant in May 1977 and 'I Heard It Through The Grapevine' (re-issue) became a number eight hit during April 1986. 'The Onion Song' (with Tammi Terrell) reached number nine in November 1969, as did his solo 'Abraham, Martin And John' in May 1970. Gaye's remaining releases failed to reach the top ten listings.

According to the same publication Marvin Gaye spent 101 weeks on the British charts up to December 1988 as a solo artist; sixty-one weeks with Tammi Terrell, twenty with Diana Ross, eleven with Kim Weston, and five with Stevie Wonder, Smokey Robinson and Diana Ross, and one with Mary Wells.

He enjoyed eight hit solo albums from March 1968 with his 'Greatest Hits' until June 1985 with 'Dream Of A Lifetime'. Only one album reached the top ten – 'Midnight Love' in November 1982 – the remainder reached the top sixty. His 'Greatest Hits' compilation with Tammi Terrell peaked at number sixty in August 1970, while 'Diana & Marvin' soared to number six in January 1974 upon its first outing, and number seventy-eight when re-issued during 1981. In 1988 Telestar released the 'Love Songs' album which featured solo tracks by Gaye and Smokey Robinson. It reached number sixty-nine in the November. According to Guinness' *Book of British Hit Albums* Gaye spent a total of 151 weeks on the album charts; ninety-three as a solo act, forty-five weeks with Diana Ross, nine with Smokey Robinson, and four with Tammi Terrell. These figures do not include various artist compilations.

In America and according to *Billboard* magazine, Marvin Gaye's recorded achievements were better, with fifty-five chart entries from 1962 until April 1984, including his duets. Forty singles reached the top forty listings; eighteen reached the top ten including three number one hits – 'I Heard It Through The Grapevine', 'Let's Get It On' and 'Got To Give It Up'. His first chart topper actually held the top spot for seven weeks and until 1981 was Motown's longest running number one single when 'Endless Love' by Diana Ross and Lionel Richie beat the record by two weeks. 'Sexual Healing' was Gaye's biggest hit on the R&B chart; it stayed at the top for ten weeks during 1982.

Marvin Gaye's albums took longer to chart in the American top ten. The first was 'What's Going On' in 1971 when it reached number six, whereupon he was recognised as a cross-over artist for the first time. 'Let's Get It On' followed where, in October 1973, it peaked at number two to remain his highest charting pop album.

Marvin Gaye had no equal; he was one of the true artists of our time, someone who refused to toe the line to live by his own standards. On stage he could be the ultimate demigod who wooed his audience with a gentle seductive manner few of his contemporaries possessed. Behind the spotlight, he coped with a personal life of his own design where the only permanent casualty was himself. He tried to be a devoted parent and loving husband, and in many ways he succeeded; but when he failed the bottom fell from his world, to interfere withz and influence his professional life. Indeed many personal dilemmas inspired his finest work – his brother Frankie's experiences in Vietnam resulted in 'What's Going On'; his love for Janis Hunter became 'Let's Get It On' and his divorce from Anna Gordy, 'Here, My Dear'.

Gaye's twenty-three years as a professional solo artist began with an explosive contradiction of public demand and self-satisfaction until the two merged in the Seventies, halfway through his career. The concluding part of his career became his most innovative, exciting and satisfying; he was given freedom of expression and subsequently recorded his finest work.

There are many questions that remain unanswered about Marvin's life but as he was unable to answer them to his own satisfaction, what chance do others have? In death too, questions cry out to be answered. Many British fans in particular remain saddened and confused at the lenient sentence handed to his father in view of the evidence placed before the court, believing he was shown more mercy by a judge than his own son received when faced with a gun barrel. Whether or not Marvin Gaye provoked the altercation that killed him is irrelevant; the volatile situation should have been controlled by the elder. Perhaps Marvin would have felt differently, maybe his feelings would have been more generous, taking the tragedy in his stride, accepting it as his destiny.

Gaye's close friends and family felt he was tired of living; he had fulfilled most of his ambitions, and the strain of life itself was too heavy a burden for him to carry easily. One wonders if these beliefs are indeed true, bearing in mind he intended to tour the world again before devoting his life to his precious music, by recording himself and others. On a personal level he longed to see his children grow up and possibly follow his profession, while finding a way to settle into a stable relationship which he could nurture and enjoy for the remainder of his life.

With his life so suddenly snatched from him, Marvin Gaye had no time to prepare for a dignified departure. However, shortly before his death he did write his own epitaph which, under the circumstances, is the most fitting finale to his extraordinary life: 'I would like to be remembered as one of, if not the greatest, artist to have walked the face of the earth. I would like to be remembered as one of the twelve music disciples, and as a man who was aware and conscious of his environment, and as a person who was full of sensuality, erotic, profound. A person who has depth, feeling and concern for the needs of others. A man who tried to create music, a whole individual . . . I thank God for my wonderful life.'

# Discography

*American Seven-inch Singles*

The discography is listed in record number order and does not include 12" singles and re-issues. Singles released prior to the Tamla and Motown discography feature Marvin Gaye as a group member. Certain singles are duets and Gaye's singing partners are identified in brackets.

Abbreviations:
u/n = unnumbered
promo = promotional release, not commercially available
NR = not released
instru = instrumental
− = information unknown

| Record No | Record Title | Release Date |
|---|---|---|
| RED ROBIN | | |
| | *The Rainbows:* | 1955 |
| 134 | Mary Lee | |
| | Evening | |
| PILGRIM | | |
| 711 | Shirley | 1956 |
| | Stay | |
| OKEH | | |
| | *The Marquees:* | 1957 |
| 7095 | Baby You're My Only One | |
| | Billy's Heartache | |
| | (recorded by Billy Stewart) | |
| 7096 | Wyatt Earp | 1957 |
| | Little School Girl | |

## CHESS

|  | ***Harvey and the Moonglows:*** |  |
|---|---|---|
| 1725 | Twelve Months Of The Year | 1958 |
|  | Don't Be Afraid Of Love |  |
|  | (recorded by Harvey Fuqua) |  |
| 1739 | Mama Loochie | 1958 |
|  | Unemployment |  |
| 1749 | Blue Skies | 1959 |
|  | Ooch Ouch Stop |  |
|  | (recorded by Harvey Fuqua) |  |
| 1770 | Beatnik | 1959 |
|  | Junior |  |
|  | (recorded by The Moonglows) |  |
| – | Almost Grown | 1959 |
|  | Back In The USA |  |
|  | (recorded by Chuck Berry) |  |
| – | Chained To My Rocking Chair | 1959 |
|  | (recorded by Etta James) |  |

## TAMLA (T)

| u/n | (I'm Afraid) The Masquerade Is Over | 1960/61 |
|---|---|---|
|  | Witchcraft (promo) |  |
| 54041 | Let Your Conscience Be Your Guide | 5.1961 |
|  | Never Let You Go (Sha-Lu-Bop) |  |
| 54055 | Mister Sandman | 1.1962 |
|  | I'm Yours, You're Mine |  |
| 54063 | Soldier's Plea | 5.1962 |
|  | Taking My Time |  |
| 54068 | Stubborn Kind Of Fellow | 7.1962 |
|  | It Hurt Me Too |  |
| 54075 | Hitch Hike | 12.1962 |
|  | Hello There Angel |  |
| 54079 | Pride And Joy | 4.1963 |
|  | One Of These Days |  |
| 54087 | Can I Get A Witness | 9.1963 |
|  | I'm Crazy 'Bout My Baby |  |
| 54093 | You're A Wonderful One | 2.1964 |
|  | When I'm Alone I Cry |  |

## MOTOWN (M)

| 1057 | Once Upon A Time | 4.1964 |
|---|---|---|
|  | What's The Matter With You Baby |  |

|       | (with Mary Wells) |         |
|-------|-------------------|---------|
| 54095 | Try It Baby | 5.1964 |
|       | If My Heart Could Sing | |
| 54101 | Baby Don't You Do It | 9.1964 |
|       | Walk On The Wild Side | |
| 54104 | What Good Am I Without You | 10.1964 |
|       | I Want You 'Round | |
|       | (with Kim Weston) | |
| 54107 | How Sweet It Is (To Be Loved By You) | 11.1964 |
|       | Forever | |
| 54112 | I'll Be Doggone | 2.1965 |
|       | You've Been A Long Time Coming | |
| 54117 | Pretty Little Baby | 6.1965 |
|       | Now That You've Won Me | |
| 54122 | Ain't That Peculiar | 9.1965 |
|       | She's Got To Be Real | |
| 54129 | One More Heartache | 1.1966 |
|       | When I Had Your Love | |
| 54132 | Take This Heart Of Mine | 5.1966 |
|       | Need Your Lovin' (Want You Back) | |
| u/n   | The Teen Beat Song | 1966 |
|       | Loraine Alterman Interviews | |
| 54138 | Little Darling (I Need You) | 7.1966 |
|       | Hey Diddle Diddle | |
| 54141 | It Takes Two | 12.1966 |
|       | It's Got To Be A Miracle (This Thing Called Love) | |
|       | (with Kim Weston) | |
| 54149 | Ain't No Mountain High Enough | 4.1967 |
|       | Give A Little Love | |
|       | (with Tammi Terrell) | |
| 54153 | Your Unchanging Love | 6.1967 |
|       | I'll Take Care Of You | |
| 54156 | Your Precious Love | 8.1967 |
|       | Hold Me, Oh My Darling | |
|       | (with Tammi Terrell) | |
| 54160 | You | 12.1967 |
|       | Change What You Can | |
| 54161 | If I Could Build My Whole World Around You | 11.1967 |

|            | If This World Were Mine            |         |
|            | (with Tammi Terrell)               |         |
| 54163      | Ain't Nothing Like the Real Thing  | 3.1968  |
|            | Little Ole Boy, Little Ole Girl    |         |
|            | (with Tammi Terrell)               |         |
| 54169      | You're All I Need To Get By        | 7.1968  |
|            | Two Can Have A Party               |         |
|            | (with Tammi Terrell)               |         |
| 54170      | Chained                            | 8.1968  |
|            | At Last (I Found A Love)           |         |
| 54173      | Keep On Lovin' Me Honey            | 9.1968  |
|            | You Ain't Livin' Till You're Lovin'|         |
|            | (with Tammi Terrell)               |         |

MOTOWN (M)

| 1128       | His Eye Is On The Sparrow          | 9.1968  |
|            | Just A Closer Walk With Thee       |         |
|            | (B-side recorded by Gladys Knight  |         |
|            |    and the Pips)                   |         |
| 54176      | I Heard It Through The Grapevine   | 10.1968 |
|            | You're What's Happening (In The    |         |
|            |    World Today)                    |         |
| 54179      | Good Lovin' Ain't Easy To Come By  | 1.1969  |
|            | Satisfied Feelin'                  |         |
|            | (with Tammi Terrell)               |         |
| 54181      | Too Busy Thinking About My Baby    | 4.1969  |
|            | Wherever I Lay My Hat (That's My Home) | |
| 54185      | That's The Way Love Is             | 8.1969  |
|            | Gonna Keep On Trying Til I Win Your Love | |
| 54187      | What You Gave Me                   | 11.1969 |
|            | How You Gonna Keep It (After You Get It) | |
|            | (with Tammi Terrell)               |         |
| 54190      | How Can I Forget?                  | 12.1969 |
|            | Gonna Give Her All The Love I've Got | |
| 54192      | The Onion Song                     | 3.1970  |
|            | California Soul                    |         |
|            | (with Tammi Terrell)               |         |
| 54195      | The End Of Our Road                | 5.1970  |
|            | Me And My Lonely Room              |         |
| 54201      | What's Going On                    | 1.1971  |
|            | God Is Love                        |         |

| 54207 | Mercy Mercy Me (The Ecology) | 6.1971 |
| | Sad Tomorrows | |
| 54209 | Inner City Blues (Make Me Wanna Holler) | 9.1971 |
| | Wholy Holy | |
| 54221 | You're The Man Part 1 | 4.1972 |
| | You're The Man Part 2 | |
| 54228 | Trouble Man | 11.1972 |
| | Don't Mess With Mister 'T' | |
| 54229 | I Want To Come Home For Christmas | NR |
| | Christmas In The City | |
| 54234 | Let's Get It On | 6.1973 |
| | I Wish It Would Rain | |

MOTOWN (M)

| 1280 | You're A Special Part Of Me | 9.1973 |
| | I'm Falling In Love With You | |
| | (with Diana Ross) | |
| 54241 | Come Get To This | 10.1973 |
| | Distant Lover | |
| 54244 | You Sure Love To Ball | 1.1974 |
| | Just To Keep You Satisfied | |

MOTOWN (M)

| 1269 | My Mistake (Was To Love You) | 1.1974 |
| | Include Me In Your Life | |
| | (with Diana Ross) | |

MOTOWN (M)

| 1296 | Don't Knock My Love | 6.1974 |
| | Just Say, Just Say | |
| | (with Diana Ross) | |
| 54253 | Distant Lover (live version) | 9.1974 |
| | Trouble Man (live version) | |
| 54264 | 1 Want You (vocal) | 4.1976 |
| | I Want You (instru.) | |
| 54273 | After The Dance | 7.1976 |
| | Feel All My Love Inside | |
| 54280 | Got To Give It Up (Part 1) | 3.1977 |
| | Got To Give It Up (Part 2) | |

MOTOWN (M)

| 1455 | Pops, We Love You | 12.1978 |
| | (With Diana Ross, | |
| | Smokey Robinson, Stevie Wonder) | |

|          |                                         |          |
|----------|-----------------------------------------|----------|
|          | Pops, We Love You (instru.)             |          |
| 54298    | A Funky Space Reincarnation (Part 1)    | 1.1979   |
|          | A Funky Space Reincarnation (Part 2)    |          |
| 54300    | Anger                                   | NR       |
|          | Time To Get It Together                 |          |
| 54305    | Ego Tripping Out                        | 9.1979   |
|          | Ego Tripping Out (instru.)              |          |
| 54322    | Praise                                  | 2.1981   |
|          | Funk Me                                 |          |
| 54326    | Heavy Love Affair                       | 4.1981   |
|          | Far Cry                                 |          |

COLUMBIA

|          |                                          |          |
|----------|------------------------------------------|----------|
| 03302    | Sexual Healing (vocal)                   | 10.1982  |
|          | Sexual Healing (instru.)                 |          |
| –        | Turn On Some Music                        | –        |
|          | Star Spangled Banner                     |          |
| 03589    | 'Til Tomorrow                            | 2.1983   |
|          | Rockin' After Midnight                   |          |
| 03935    | Joy                                      | 5.1983   |
| –        | –                                        | –        |
| 04861    | Sanctified Lady (vocal)                  | 3.1985   |
|          | Sanctified Lady (instru.)                |          |
| 05442    | Ain't It Funny (How Things               | 6.1985   |
|          | Turn Around)                             |          |
|          | It's Madness                             |          |
| 05791    | Just Like                                | –        |
|          | More                                     |          |

MOTOWN

(New numbering system introduced to replace individual labels; records now identified by the suffix)

|          |                                          |          |
|----------|------------------------------------------|----------|
| 1836T    | The World Is Rated X                     | 5.1986   |
|          | No Greater Love                          |          |
| 2083     | My Last Chance                           | 10.1990  |
|          | Once Upon A Time                         |          |
|          | (with Mary Wells)                        |          |

## American Extended Play Singles (EP)

TAMLA (TM)

| | | |
|---|---|---|
| 60252 | ***Greatest Hits*** | 1965 |
| | Can I Get A Witness/ | |
| | You're A Wonderful One/Stubborn | |
| | Kind Of Fellow/I'm Crazy 'Bout My Baby/ | |
| | Pride And Joy/Hitch Hike | |
| 60266 | ***Moods of Marvin Gaye*** | 1966 |
| | I'll Be Doggone/Little Darling | |
| | (I Need You)/Take This Heart | |
| | Of Mine/Hey Diddle Diddle/ | |
| | One More Heartache/Ain't | |
| | That Peculiar | |

## American Albums

This discography is printed in record number order and does not include re-issues or various artist compilations. The majority of the albums listed are now available on both compact disc and cassette. The listings include tracks, writers, producers, record numbers and release dates. Certain albums are duets and Gaye's singing partners are identified in brackets. All information is taken from original album sleeves.

### The Soulful Moods of Marvin Gaye
TAMLA 221
Released 6.1961

| *Tracks* | *Writers* |
|---|---|
| (I'm Afraid) The Masquerade Is Over | H. Magidson/A. Wrubel |
| My Funny Valentine | R. Rodgers/L. Hart |
| Witchcraft | C. Colena/C. Leigh |
| Easy Living | L. Robin/R. Rainger |
| How Deep Is The Ocean | I. Berlin |
| Love For Sale | C. Porter |
| Always | I. Berlin |
| How High The Moon | M. Lewis/N. Hamilton |
| Let Your Conscience Be Your Guide | B. Gordy |
| Never Let You Go (Sha-Lu-Bop) | A. Gaye/H. Fuqua |
| You Don't Know What Love Is | D. Raye/J. De Paul |

Produced by Berry Gordy

*That Stubborn Kinda' Fellow*
239
Released 1.1963

| *Tracks* | *Writers* |
| --- | --- |
| Stubborn Kind Of Fellow | M. Gaye/W. Stevenson/ B. Gordy |
| Pride And Joy | M. Gaye/W. Stevenson/ N. Whitfield |
| Hitch Hike | C. Paul/M. Gaye/ W. Stevenson |
| Got To Get My Hands On Some Lovin' | M. Gaye/W. Stevenson |
| Wherever I Lay My Hat (That's My Home) | N Whitfield/B. Strong/ M. Gaye |
| Soldier's Plea | W. Stevenson/F. J. Hale/ G. Gordy |
| It Hurt Me Too | M. Gaye/M. Knight/ W. Stevenson |
| Taking My Time | W. Stevenson/A. Gordy |
| Hello There Angel | A. Gordy/W. Stevenson |
| I'm Yours, You're Mine | W. Stevenson/A. Gordy |

Produced by William 'Mickey' Stevenson


*Recorded Live! On Stage*
242
Released 9.1963

| *Tracks* | *Writers* |
| --- | --- |
| Stubborn Kind Of Fellow | M. Gaye/W. Stevenson/ B. Gordy |
| One Of These Days | W. Stevenson |
| Mo Jo Hanna | Paul/Paul/Hale |
| The Days Of Wine And Roses | Mancini/Mercer |
| Pride And Joy | N. Whitfield/M. Gaye/ W. Stevenson |
| Hitch Hike | C. Paul/M. Gaye/ W. Stevenson |
| Get My Hands On Some Lovin' | M. Gaye/W. Stevenson |
| You Are My Sunshine | Davis/Mitchell |

Produced by William 'Mickey' Stevenson

***Together*** (with Mary Wells)
MOTOWN 613
Released 4.1964

| Tracks | Writers |
|---|---|
| Once Upon A Time | C. Paul/ D. Hamilton |
| Deed I Do | Rose/Hirsch |
| Until I Met You | Wolf/Greene |
| Together | Desylva/Brown/Henderson |
| (I Love You) For Sentimental Reasons | Best/Watson |
| The Late Late Show | Berlin/Alfred |
| After The Lights Go Down Low | Lovett/White |
| Squeeze Me | Jacobs/Pleis |
| What's The Matter With You Baby | C. Paul/W. Stevenson |
| You Came A Long Way From St. Louis | Russell/Brooks |

Produced by William 'Mickey' Stevenson except 'Once Upon A Time' produced by Clarence Paul

**Greatest Hits**
TAMLA 252
Released 4.1964

| Tracks | Writers | Producers |
|---|---|---|
| Can I Get A Witness | E. Holland/L. Dozier/ B. Holland | B. Holland/ L. Dozier |
| You're A Wonderful One | E. Holland/L. Dozier/ B. Holland | B. Holland/ L. Dozier |
| Stubborn Kind Of Fellow | M. Gaye/W. Stevenson/ B. Gordy | W. Stevenson |
| I'm Crazy 'Bout My Baby | W. Stevenson | W. Stevenson |
| Pride And Joy | N. Whitfield/M. Gaye/ W. Stevenson | W. Stevenson |
| Hitch Hike | C. Paul/M. Gaye/ W. Stevenson | W. Stevenson |
| Aster Sandman | P. Ballard | W. Stevenson |
| Hello There Angel | W. Stevenson/A. Gordy | W. Stevenson |
| One Of These Days | W. Stevenson | W. Stevenson |
| I'm Yours, You're Mine | W. Stevenson/A. Gordy | W. Stevenson |
| Taking My Time | W. Stevenson/A. Gordy | W. Stevenson |

| It Hurt Me Too | M. Gaye/W. Stevenson/ | W. Stevenson |
| | M. Knight | |


### *When I'm Alone I Cry*
251
Released 6.1964

| *Tracks* | *Writers* |
| --- | --- |
| You've Changed | Fischer/Carey |
| I Was Telling Her About You | George/Charlap |
| I Wonder | Gant/Leveen |
| I'll Be Around | A. Wilder |
| Because Of You | Hammerstein/Wilkinson |
| I Don't Know Why | F. E. Alhert |
| I've Grown Accustomed To Her Face | Loewe/Lerner |
| When Your Lover Has Gone | E. A. Swan |
| When I'm Alone I Cry | Vandenberg/Broadnax/Foreman |
| If My Heart Could Sing | Vandenberg/Broadnax |

Produced by William 'Mickey' Stevenson/Clarence Paul


### *Hello Broadway*
259
Released 11.1964

| *Tracks* | *Writers* |
| --- | --- |
| Hello Broadway | Miller/O'Malley |
| People | Merrill/Stone |
| The Party's Over | Comben/Green/Styne |
| On The Street Where You Live | Lerner/Loewe |
| What Kind Of Fool Am I | Bricusse/Newley |
| My Kind Of Town | Cahn/Van Heusen |
| The Days Of Wine And Roses | Mercer/Mancini |
| This Is The Life | Strouse/Adams |
| My Way | Miller/Jacques |
| Hello Dolly | J. Herman |
| Walk On The Wild Side | David/Bernstein |

Produced by Hal Davis/Marc Cordon

*How Sweet it is to be Loved by You*
258
Released 1.1965

| Tracks | Writers | Producers |
|---|---|---|
| You're A Wonderful One | E. Holland/L. Dozier/ B. Holland | B. Holland/ L. Dozier |
| How Sweet It Is (To Be Loved By You) | E. Holland/L. Dozier/ B. Holland | B. Holland/ L. Dozier |
| Try It Baby | B. Gordy | B. Gordy |
| Baby Don't You Do It | E. Holland/L. Dozier/ B. Holland | B. Holland/ L. Dozier |
| Need Your Lovin' (Want You Back) | C. Paul/M. Gaye | C. Paul |
| One Of These Days | W. Stevenson | W. Stevenson |
| No Good Without You | W. Stevenson | W. Stevenson |
| Stepping Closer to Your Heart | H. Fuqua/M. Gaye | H. Fuqua/ M. Gaye |
| Need Somebody | W. Stevenson/ I. J. Hunter | W. Stevenson |
| Me And My Lonely Room | N. Whitfield/B. Strong | N. Whitfield |
| Now That You've Won Me | W. Robinson | W. Robinson |
| Forever | L. Dozier/F. Gorman/ B. Holland | B. Holland/ L. Dozier |

*A Tribute To The Great Nat King Cole*
261
Released 11.1965

| Tracks | Writers |
|---|---|
| Nature Boy | Ahbez |
| Ramblin' Rose | N. Sherman/J. Sherman |
| Too Young | Dee/Lippman |
| Pretend | Douglas/Parman/Lavere |
| Straighten Up And Fly Right | Mills/N. K. Cole |
| Mona Lisa | Livingston/Evans |
| Unforgettable | Gordon |
| To The Ends Of The Earth | N. Sherman/J. Sherman |
| Sweet Lorraine | Parish/Burwell |
| It's Only A Paper Moon | Rose/Harburg/Arien |

| Send For Me | Jones |
| Calypso Blues | George/N. K. Cole |

Produced by Hal Davis/Marc Gordon/Harvey Fuqua

*Moods Of Marvin Gaye*
266
Released 5.1966

| *Tracks* | *Writers* |
| --- | --- |
| I'll Be Doggone | W. Robinson/W. Moore/ M. Tarplin |
| Little Darling (I Need You) | E. Holland/L. Dozier/ B. Holland |
| Take This Heart Of Mine | W. Moore/W. Robinson/ M. Tarplin |
| Hey Diddle Diddle | H. Fuqua/M. Gaye/J. Bristol |
| One More Heartache | W. Robinson/M. Tarplin/ W. Moore/R. White/R. Rogers |
| Ain't That Peculiar | W. Robinson/M. Tarplin/ W. Moore/R. Rogers |
| Night Life | Nelson/Buskirk/Brieland |
| You've Been A Long Time Coming | E. Holland/L. Dozier/ B. Holland |
| Your Unchanging Love | E. Holland/L. Dozier/ B. Holland |
| You're The One For Me | S. Wonder/C. Paul/ M. Broadnax |
| I Worry 'Bout You | Mapp |
| One For My Baby (And One More For The Road) | Arlen |

Produced by Berry Gordy

*Take Two* (with Kim Weston)
270
Released 8.1966

| *Tracks* | *Writers* |
| --- | --- |
| It Takes Two | W. Stevenson/S. Moy |

| | |
|---|---|
| I Love You, Yes I Do | S. Nix/H. Clever |
| Baby I Need Your Loving | E. Holland/L. Dozier/ |
| | B. Holland |
| It's Got To Be A Miracle (This Thing | S. Moy/V. Bullock/ |
| Called Love) | W. Stevenson |
| Baby Say Yes | W. Stevenson/K. Weston |
| What Good Am I Without You | A. Higdon/W. Stevenson |
| Till There Was You | M. Wilson |
| Love Fell On Me | S. Moy/W. Stevenson |
| Secret Love | P. Webster/S. Fain |
| I Want You 'Round | W. Stevenson/W. Robinson |
| Heaven Sent You I Know | W. Stevenson/H. Cosby/ |
| | V. Bullock |
| When We're Together | V. Bullock/S. Moy |
| Produced by William 'Mickey' Stevenson | |

*Greatest Hits Volume 2*
278
Released 6.1967
*Tracks*
How Sweet It Is (To Be Loved By You)
One More Heartache
Your Unchanging Love
I'll Be Doggone
Little Darling (I Need You)
Pretty Little Baby*
Ain't That Peculiar
Baby Don't You Do It
Try It Baby
Take This Heart Of Mine
Hey Diddle Diddle
Forever
All tracks previously released except* written by C. Paul/M. Gaye/
D. Hamilton and produced by Clarence Paul.

***United*** (with Tammi Terrell)
277
Released 8.1967

| *Tracks* | *Writers* |
| --- | --- |
| Ain't No Mountain High Enough | N. Ashford/V. Simpson |
| You Got What It Takes | B. Gordy/G. Gordy/R. Davis |
| If I Could Build My Whole World Around You | J. Bristol/V. Bullock/H. Fuqua |
| Semethin' Stupid | C. Carson Parks |
| Your Precious Love | N. Ashford/V. Simpson |
| Hold Me Oh My Darling | H. Fuqua |
| Two Can Have A Party | H. Fuqua/T. Kemp/J. Bristol |
| Little Ole Boy, Little Ole Girl | H. Fuqua/E. James/B. Benton |
| If This World Were Mine | M. Gaye |
| Sad Wedding | J. Bristol/ R. Beavers |
| Give A Little Love | J. Bristol/H. Fuqua/C. Wilson |
| Oh How I'd Miss You | H. Davis/F. Wilson/V. Wilson |

Produced by Harvey Fuqua/
    Johnny Bristol

***You're All I Need*** (with Tammi Terrell)
284
Released 8.1968

| *Tracks* | *Writers* |
| --- | --- |
| Ain't Nothing Like The Real Thing | N. Ashford/V. Simpson |
| Keep On Lovin' Me Honey | N. Ashford/V. Simpson |
| You're All I Need To Get By | N. Ashford/V. Simpson |
| Baby Don'tcha Worry | J. Beavers/J. Bristol |
| You Ain't Livin' Till You're Lovin' | N. Ashford/V. Simpson |
| Give In, You just Can't Win | H. Fuqua/J. Bristol |
| When Love Comes Knocking At My Heart | G. Knight/V. Bullock |
| Come On And See Me | H. Fuqua/J. Bristol |
| I Can't Help But Love You | H. Fuqua/J. Bristol |
| That's How It Is (Since You've Been Gone) | R. Gordy/T. Kemp/ M. Gaye |
| I'll Never Stop Loving You Baby | H. Fuqua/J. Bristol/ V. Bullock |

Memory Chest                         H. Fuqua/J. Bristol/
                                     B.Verdi/M. Bainius
                                     H. Fuqua/J. Bristol
Produced by Nickolas Ashford/Valerie Simpson/Harvey Fuqua/Johnny
Bristol


*I Heard It Through The Grapevine/In The Groove*
285
Released 8.1968

| *Tracks* | *Writers* | *Producers* |
| --- | --- | --- |
| You | J. Goga/I. Hunter/ J. Bowen | I. Hunter |
| Tear It On Down | N. Ashford/V. Simpson | N. Ashford/ V. Simpson |
| Chained | F. Wilson | F. Wilson |
| I Heard It Through The Grapevine | N. Whitfield/ B. Strong | N. Whitfield |
| At Last (I Found A Love) | A. Gaye/E. Stover/ M. Gaye | H. Fuqua/ J. Bristol |
| Some Kind Of Wonderful | C. King/G. Goffin | M. Gentile |
| Loving You Is Sweeter Than Ever | I. Hunter/S. Wonder | I. Hunter |
| Change What You Can | M. Gaye/E. Stover/ A. Gaye | H. Fuqua/ J. Bristol |
| It's Love I Need | I. Hunter/S. Bowden | I. Hunter |
| Every Now And Then | E. Holland/F. Wilson | F. Wilson |
| You're What's Happening (In The World Today) | A. Story/G. Gordy/ R. Gordy | G. Gordy |
| There Goes My Baby | B. Nelson/L. Patterson/ G. Treadwell | M. Gentile |

*MPG*
292
Released 5.1969

| Tracks | Writers | Producers |
| --- | --- | --- |
| Too Busy Thinking About My Baby | N. Whitfield/B. Strong/ J. Bradford | N. Whitfield |
| This Magic Moment | D. Pomus/M. Shuman | M. Gentile |
| That's The Way Love Is | N. Whitfield/B. Strong | N. Whitfield |
| The End Of Our Road | N. Whitfield/B. Strong/ R. Penzabene | N. Whitfield |
| Seek And You Shall Find | W. Stevenson/I. Hunter | W. Stevenson |
| Memories | A. Story/L. Brown/ A. Gaye/G. Gordy | G. Gordy |
| Only A Lonely Man Would Know | I. Hunter/B. Verdi | I. Hunter |
| It's A Bitter Pill To Swallow | W. Robinson/W. Moore | W. Robinson/ W. Moore |
| More Than A Heart Can Stand | W. Stevenson/I. Hunter | W. Stevenson/ I. Hunter |
| Try My True Love | H. Cosby/J. Dean/ S. Wonder | H. Cosby |
| I Got To Get To California | I. Hunter/S. De Mell | I. Hunter |
| It Don't Take Much To Keep Me | E. Holland/L. Dozier/ B. Holland | E. Holland/ L. Dozier/ B. Holland |

*Marvin Gaye And His Girls*
293
Released 5.1969
*Tracks*
Once Upon A Time*
What's The Matter With You Baby*
It's Got To Be A Miracle (This Thing Called Love) †
It Takes Two †
Your Precious Love ††
Good Lovin' Ain't Easy To Come By ††
You're All I Need To Get By †
You Ain't Livin' Till You're Lovin' ††

What Good Am I Without You †
I Want You 'Round †
Deed I Do*
Together*
* with Mary Wells/† with Kim Weston/†† with Tammi Terrell
All tracks previously released


*Easy* (with Tammi Terrell)
294
Released 9.1969

| Tracks | Writers | Producers |
| --- | --- | --- |
| Good Lovin' Ain't Easy To Come By | N. Ashford/V. Simpson | N. Ashford/ V. Simpson |
| California Soul | N. Ashford/V. Simpson | N. Ashford/ V. Simpson |
| Love Woke Me Up This Morning | N. Ashford/V. Simpson | N. Ashford/ V. Simpson |
| This Poor Heart Of Mine | N. Ashford/V. Simpson | N. Ashford/ V. Simpson |
| I'm Your Puppet | S. Oldham/D. Penn | N. Ashford/ V. Simpson/ F. Wilson |
| The Onion Song | N. Ashford/V. Simpson | N. Ashford/ V. Simpson |
| What You Gave Me | N. Ashford/V. Simpson | N. Ashford/ V. Simpson |
| Baby I Need Your Loving | E. Holland/L. Dozier/ B. Holland | N. Ashford/ V. Simpson |
| I Can't Believe You Love Me | J. Bristol/H. Fuqua | J. Bristol/ H. Fuqua |
| How You Gonna Keep It (After You Get It) | N. Ashford/V. Simpson | N. Ashford/ V. Simpson |
| More, More, More | C. Wilson/W. Jackson/ H. Fuqua/J. Bristol | H. Fuqua/ J. Bristol |
| Satisfied Feelin' | N. Ashford/V. Simpson | N. Ashford/ V. Simpson |

*That's The Word Love Is*
299
*Released* 1.1970

| Tracks | Writers |
| --- | --- |
| Gonna Give Her All The Love I've Got | N. Whitfield/B. Strong |
| Yesterday | J. Lennon/P. McCartney |
| Groovin' | F. Cavaliere/E. Brigati |
| I Wish It Would Rain | N. Whitfield/B. Strong/ R. Penzabene |
| That's The Way Love Is | N. Whitfield/B. Strong |
| How Can I Forget? | N. Whitfield/B. Strong |
| Abraham, Martin And John | D. Holler |
| Gonna Keep On Tryin, Till I Win Your Love | N. Whitfield/B. Strong |
| No Time For Tears | E. Holland/N. Whitfield |
| Cloud Nine | N. Whitfield/B. Strong |
| Don't You Miss Me A Little Bit Baby | N. Whitfield/R. Penzabene/ B. Strong |
| So Long | N. Whitfield/R. Dean Taylor/E. Holland |

Produced by Norman Whitfield

*Greatest Hits* (with Tammi Terrell)
302
Released 5.1970
*Tracks*
Your Precious Love
Ain't No Mountain High Enough
You're All I Need To Get By
Ain't Nothing Like The Real Thing
Good Lovin' Ain't Easy To Come By
If This World Were Mine
The Onion Song
If I Could Build My Whole World Around You
Keep On Lovin' Me Honey
What You Gave Me

You Ain't Livin' Till You're Lovin'
Hold Me Oh My Darling
All tracks previously released


*Super Hits*
300
Released 9.1970
*Tracks*
I Heard It Through The Grapevine
Pride And Joy
The End Of Our Road
Ain't That Peculiar
Stubborn Kind Of Fellow
Can I Get A Witness
How Sweet It Is (To Be Loved By You)
That's The Way Love Is
Too Busy Thinking About My Baby
Chained
You're A Wonderful One
Try It Baby
I'll Be Doggone
Hitch Hike
You
Baby Don't You Do It
All tracks previously released


*What's Going On*
310
Released 5.1971

| *Tracks* | *Writers* |
|---|---|
| What's Going On | A. Cleveland/M. Gaye/ R. Benson |
| What's Happening Brother | J. Nyx/M. Gaye |
| Flyin' High (In The Friendly Sky) | M. Gaye/E. Stover/A. Gaye |
| Save The Children | A. Cleveland/M. Gaye/ R. Benson |

| God Is Love | M. Gaye/A. Gaye/E. Stover/ |
| | J. Nyx |
| Mercy Mercy Me (The Ecology) | M. Gaye |
| Right On | E. De Rouen/M. Gaye |
| Wholy Holy | R. Benson/A. Cleveland/ |
| | M. Gaye |
| Inner City Blues (Make Me Wanna Holler) | M. Gaye/J. Nyx |

Produced by Marvin Gaye

*Trouble Man*
322
Released 12.1972
*Tracks*
Main Theme From Trouble Man
'T' Plays It Cool
Poor Abbey Walsh
The Break-In (Police Shoot Big)
Cleo's Apartment
Trouble Man
Theme From Trouble Man
'T' Stands For Trouble
Main Theme From Trouble Man
Life Is A Gamble
Deep-In-It
Don't Mess With Mister 'T'
There Goes Mister 'T'
Written and produced by Marvin Gaye

### Let's Get It On
329
Released 8.1973

| Tracks | Writers | Producers |
|---|---|---|
| Let's Get It On | M. Gaye/E. Townsend | |
| Please Don't Stay (Once You Go Away) | M. Gaye/E. Townsend | M. Gaye/ E. Townsend |
| If I Should Die Tonight | M. Gaye/E. Townsend | |
| Keep Gettin' It On | M. Gaye/E. Townsend | |
| Come Get To This | M. Gaye | |
| Distant Lover | M. Gaye/G. Gordy Fuqua/S. Greene | |
| You Sure Love To Ball | M. Gaye | M. Gaye |
| Just To Keep You Satisfied | M. Gaye/A. Gaye/ E. Stover | |

### Diana & Marvin
MOTOWN 803
Released 10.1973

| Tracks | Writers | Producers |
|---|---|---|
| You Are Everything | L. Creed/T. Bell | H. Davis |
| Love Twins | M. McLeod/M. Bolton | H. Davis |
| Don't Knock My Love | W. Pickett/B. Shapiro | H. Davis |
| You're A Special Part Of Me | G. Wright/H. Johnson/ | B. Gordy |
| Pledging My Love | A. Porter/D. D. Robey/ F. Washington | B. Gaudio |
| Just Say, Just Say | N. Ashford/V. Simpson | N. Ashford/ V. Simpson |
| Stop, Look, Listen (To Your Heart) | T. Bell/L. Creed | H. Davis |
| I'm Falling In Love With You | M. Gordy | M. Davis/ M. Gordy |
| My Mistake (Was To Love You) | P. Sawyer/G. Jones | H. Davis |
| Include Me In Your Life | M. McLeod/ M. Bolton | H. Davis |

Executive producer:
  Berry Gordy

*Anthology*
MOTOWN 791
Released 4.1974
*Tracks*
Stubborn Kind Of Fellow
Hitch Hike
Pride And Joy
Once Upon A Time*
Can I Get A Witness
What's The Matter With You Baby*
You're A Wonderful One
Try It Baby
Baby Don't You Do It
What Good Am I Without You †
Forever
How Sweet It Is (To Be Loved By You)
It Takes Two †
I'll Be Doggone
Pretty Little Baby
Ain't That Peculiar
Ain't No Mountain High Enough ††
One More Heartache
Take This Heart Of Mine
Your Precious Love ††
Little Darling (I Need You)
Your Unchanging Love
If This World Were Mine ††
You
If I Could Build My Whole World Around You ††
Chained
Ain't Nothing Like The Real Thing ††
How Can I Forget?
Heaven Sent You, I Know †
I Heard It Through The Grapevine
Good Lovin' Ain't Easy To Come By ††
Too Busy Thinking About My Baby
That's The Way Love Is
You're All I Need To Get By ††
The End Of Our Road
What's Going On

Mercy Mercy Me (The Ecology)
Inner City Blues (Make Me Wanna Holler)
Save The Children
You're The Man (Part 1)
Trouble Man
Let's Get It On
Come Get To This
Distant Lover (live)
I Want You
Got To Give It Up
After The Dance
* with Mary Wells/† with Kim Weston/†† with Tammi Terrell
All tracks previously released


***Live!***
333
Released 6.1974
*Tracks*
The Beginning:
> Introduction
> Overture
> Trouble Man
> Inner City Blues (Make Me Wanna Holler)
> Distant Lover Jan
Fossil Medley:
> I'll Be Doggone
> Try It Baby
> Can I Get A Witness
> You're A Wonderful One
> Stubborn Kind Of Fellow
> How Sweet It Is (To Be Loved By You)
Now:
> Let's Get It On
> What's Going On
Executive producer: Ewart G. Abner
All tracks previously released except 'Jan' written by Marvin Gaye

*I Want You*
342
Released 3.1976

| *Tracks* | *Writers* |
| --- | --- |
| I Want You (vocal) | L. Ware/T. Boy Ross |
| Come Live With Me Angel | L. Ware/J. Hilliard |
| After The Dance (instru.) | M. Gaye/L. Ware |
| Feel All My Love Inside | M. Gaye/L. Ware |
| I Wanna Be Where You Are | L. Ware/T. Boy Ross |
| I Want You (intro jam) | L. Ware/T. Boy Ross |
| All The Way Around | L. Ware/T. Boy Ross |
| Since I Had You | M. Gaye/L. Ware |
| Soon I'll Be Loving You Again | M. Gaye/L. Ware/ T. Boy Ross |
| | |
| I Want You (intro jam) | L. Ware/T. Boy Ross |
| After The Dance (vocal) | M. Gaye/L. Ware |

Produced by Leon Ware
Executive producers: Berry Gordy/Marvin Gaye

*Greatest Hits*
348
Released 9.1976
*Tracks*
Let's Get It On
I Want You (vocal)
How Sweet It Is (To Be Loved By You)
I Heard It Through The Grapevine
Mercy Mercy Me (The Ecology)
What's Going On
After The Dance
Can I Get A Witness
Trouble Man
Distant Lover (live)
All tracks previously released

*Live! At The London Palladium*
352
Released 3.1977
*Tracks*
Intro Theme
All The Way Around
Since I Had You
Come Get To This
Let's Get It On
Trouble Man
Medley I:
       Ain't That Peculiar
       You're A Wonderful One
       Stubborn Kind Of Fellow
       Pride And Joy
       Little Darling (I Need You)
       I Heard It Through The Grapevine
       Hitch Hike
       You
       Too Busy Thinking About My Baby
       How Sweet It Is (To Be Loved By You)
Medley II:
       Inner City Blues (Make Me Wanna Holler)
       God Is Love
       What's Going On
       Save The Children
Medley III:*
       You're All I Need To Get By
       Ain't Nothing Like The Real Thing
       Your Precious Love
       It Takes Two
       Ain't No Mountain High Enough
       Distant Lover
       Closing Theme
       Got To Give It Up †
All tracks previously released except † written by Marvin Gaye and produced by Art Stewart
* duets with Florence Lyles

***Here, My Dear***
364
Released 12.1978

| Tracks | Writers |
|---|---|
| Here, My Dear | M. Gaye |
| I Met A Little Girl | M. Gaye |
| When Did You Stop Loving Me, When Did I Stop Loving You | M. Gaye |
| Anger | M. Gaye/D. Ashby/ E. Townsend |
| Is That Enough | M. Gaye |
| Everybody Needs Love | M. Gaye/ E. Townsend |
| Time To Get It Together | M. Gaye |
| Sparrow | M. Gaye/E. Townsend |
| Anna's Song | M. Gaye |
| When Did You Stop Loving Me, When Did I Stop Loving You (instru.) | M. Gaye |
| A Funky Space Reincarnation | M. Gaye |
| You Can Leave, But It's Going To Cost You | M. Gaye |
| Falling In Love Again | M. Gaye |
| When Did You Stop Loving Me, When Did I Stop Loving You (reprise) | M. Gaye |

Produced by Marvin Gaye


***In Our Lifetime***
374
Released 1.1981
*Tracks*
Praise
Life Is For Learning
Love Party
Funk Me
Far Cry
Love Me Now Or Love Me Later
Heavy Love Affair
In Our Lifetime
Written and produced by Marvin Gaye

*Midnight Love*
COLUMBIA 38197
Released 11.1982

| *Tracks* | *Writers* |
| --- | --- |
| Midnight Love | M. Gaye |
| Sexual Healing | M. Gaye/O. Brown |
| Rockin' After Midnight | M. Gaye |
| 'Til Tomorrow | M. Gaye |
| Turn On Some Music | M. Gaye |
| Third World Girl | M. Gaye |
| Joy | M. Gaye |
| My Love Is Waiting | G. Banks |

Produced by Marvin Gaye


*Every Great Motown Hit of Marvin Gaye: 15 Spectacular Performances*
MOTOWN 6058M
Released 9.1983
*Tracks*
How Sweet It Is (To Be Loved By You)
Your Precious Love †
If I Could Build My Whole World Around You †
That's The Way Love Is
You're All I Need To Get By †
I Heard It Through The Grapevine
Too Busy Thinking About My Baby
What's Going On
Ain't Nothing Like The Real Thing
Inner City Blues (Make Me Wanna Holler)
Mercy Mercy Me (The Ecology)
Trouble Man
Let's Get It On
Distant Lover
Got To Give It Up (Part 1)
† with Tammi Terrell
All tracks previously released

*Compact Command Performances: 15 Greatest Hits*
MOTOWN 6069T
Released 2.1984
*Tracks*
How Sweet It Is (To Be Loved By You)
Ain't That Peculiar
I Heard It Through The Grapevine
You're All I Need To Get By
Your Precious Love *
Too Busy Thinking About My Baby
That's The Way Love Is
What's Going On
Mercy Mercy Me (The Ecology)
Inner City Blues (Make Me Wanna Holler)
Trouble Man
My Mistake (Was To Love You) †
Let's Get It On
1 Want You
Got To Give It Up †
* with Tammi Terrell/† with Diana Ross
All tracks previously released


*Dream Of A Lifetime*
COLUMBIA 39916
Released 6.1985

| *Tracks* | *Writers* |
| --- | --- |
| Sanctified Lady | M. Gaye/G. Banks |
| Savage In The Sack | M. Gaye |
| Masochistic Beauty | M. Gaye/G. Banks |
| It's Madness | M. Gaye |
| Ain't It Funny (How Things Turn Around) | M. Gaye |
| Symphony | M. Gaye/W. Robinson |
| Life's Opera | M. Gaye/I. Hunter |
| Dream Of A Lifetime | M. Gaye |

Produced by Marvin Gaye/Gordon Banks/Harvey Fuqua
Executive producer: Larkin Arnold

**Romantically Yours**
COLUMBIA 40208
Released 11.1985

| Tracks | Writers | Producers |
| --- | --- | --- |
| More | N. Newell/R. Ortolani/ N. Oliviero | H. Davis/ M. Gordon |
| Why Did I Choose You? | H. Martin/ M. Leonard | B. Scott |
| Maria | L. Bernstein/ S. Sondheim | H. Davis/ M. Gordon |
| The Shadow Of Your Smile | P. F. Webster/J. Mandel | B. Scott |
| Fly Me To The Moon (In Other Words) | B. Howard | H. Davis/ M. Gordon |
| I Won't Cry Anymore | F. Wise/A. Frisch | B. Scott |
| Just Like | M. Gaye | M. Gaye |
| Walkin' In The Rain | M. Gaye | M. Gaye |
| I Live For You | M. Gaye | M. Gaye |
| Stranger In My Life | M. Gaye | M. Gaye |
| Happy Go Lucky | N. Whitfield/ E. Holland Jnr | N. Whitfield |

Compiled, assembled and remixed by Harvey Fuqua/Gordon Banks
Executive producer: Larkin Arnold

**Motown Remembers Marvin Gaye: Never Before Released Masters**
MOTOWN 6172T
Released 3.1986

| Tracks | Writers | Producers |
| --- | --- | --- |
| The World Is Rated X | M. McLeod/M. Bolton/ R. Gordy | H. Davis |
| Lonely Lover | E. Holland/L. Dozier/ B. Holland | B. Holland/ L. Dozier |
| Just Like A Man | W. Robinson | W. Robinson |
| I'm Going Home | M. Gaye | M. Gaye |
| No Greater Love | H. Lemon | H. Fuqua |
| Dark Side Of The World | N. Ashford/V. Simpson | N. Ashford/ V. Simpson |
| Loving And Affection | M. Gaye/C. Paul/ C. Grant | C. Paul |
| I'm In Love With You | C. Paul/M. Broadnax | C. Paul |

| That's The Way It Goes | W. Stevenson/H. Cosby | W. Stevenson/<br>H. Cosby/<br>I. Hunter |
|---|---|---|
| I Gotta Have Your Lovin' | B. Gordy | B. Gordy |
| Baby I'm Glad That Things Worked Out So Well | W. Robinson/W. Moore/ M. Tarplin | W. Robinson/<br>W. Moore |
| Baby (Don't You Leave Me)* | L. Brown/G. Gordy/ M. Reeves/L. Woodard | C. Paul |

*with Kim Weston

Executive producer: Brenda M. Boyce

*Compact Command Performances: Volume Two*
6201T
Released 9.1986
*Tracks*
Stubborn Kind Of Fellow
Hitch Hike
Pride And Joy
Can I Get A Witness
You're A Wonderful One
Try It Baby
Baby Don't You Do It
I'll Be Doggone
Pretty Little Baby
One More Heartache
Take This Heart Of Mine
Little Darling (I Need You)
Your Unchanging Love
You
Chained
How Can I Forget?
The End Of Our Road
Come Get To This
After The Dance
Distant Lover
All tracks previously released

*A Musical Testament 1964–1984*
6355ML2
Released 9.1988
*Tracks*
Crossroads:

> Right On
> After The Dance (instru.)
> Try It Baby
> I Heard It Through The Grapevine
> Loving And Affection
> A Parting Of The Ways
> Just To Keep You Satisfied
> When Did You Stop Loving Me, When Did I Stop Loving You
> Distant Lover (live)
> Anger

A Witness To Love:

> Baby Don't You Do It
> Little Darling (I Need You)
> Lonely Lover
> That's The Way Love Is
> Dark Side Of The World
> The End Of Our Road

Introspection:

> The Star Spangled Banner*
> Save The Children
> Wholy Holy
> His Eye Is On The Sparrow
> Life Is A Gamble
> If I Should Die Tonight

All tracks previously released except * taped live at the 1984 NBA All-Star Game, produced and arranged by Marvin Gaye


*The Marvin Gaye Collection*
MOTD4-6311
Released 1990
*Tracks*
Stubborn Kind Of Fellow
Hitch Hike

Pride And Joy
Can I Get A Witness
You're A Wonderful One
Try It Baby
How Sweet It Is (To Be Loved By You)
I'll Be Doggone
Ain't That Peculiar
1 Heard It Through The Grapevine
Too Busy Thinking About My Baby
That's The Way Love Is
What's Going On
Mercy, Mercy Me (The Ecology)
Inner City Blues (Make Me Wanna Holler)
Trouble Man
Let's Get It On
I Want You
Got To Give It Up
Sexual Healing
Once Upon A Time*
What's The Matter With You Baby *
It Takes Two †
Ain't No Mountain High Enough ††
Your Precious Love ††
If I Could Build My Whole World Around You ††
If This World Were Mine ††
Ain't Nothing Like The Real Thing ††
You're All I Need To Get By ††
You Are Everything §
You're A Special Part Of Me§
My Mistake (Was To Love You) §
Don't Knock My Love §
Pops, We Love You §§
Let Your Conscience Be Your Guide
Never Let You Go (Sha-Lu-Bop)
Sweeter As The Days Go By
Distant Lover (live)
Jan (live)
60s Medley including: Little Darling (I Need You), You, etc
Star Spangled Banner
I've Grown Accustomed To Her Face

Straighten Up And Fly Right
Too Young
Mona Lisa
It's Only A Paper Moon
What Kind Of Fool Am I
The Days Of Wine And Roses
Why Did I Choose You
The Shadow Of Your Smile
I Won't Cry Anymore
with * Mary Wells/† Kim Weston/†† Tamni Terrell/§ Diana Ross/
§§ Diana Ross, Stevie Wonder and Smokey Robinson
All tracks previously released

| Tracks | Writers | Producers |
| --- | --- | --- |
| I'm Yours, You're Mine* | A. Gaye/W. Stevenson | W. Stevenson |
| All I Got* | Al Gilberto/V. Montana | W. Stevenson |
| You Can Dance* | W. Stevenson | W. Stevenson |
| Rilleh †† | B.Page | H. Davis/<br>M. Gordon |
| So Good To Be Loved By You †† | G. Pipkin/C. Pipkin | H. Davis/<br>M. Gordon |
| Was It A Dream †† | S. Coslow/L. Spier/A. Britt | H. Davis/<br>M. Cordon |
| Steadies†† | B. Page | H. Davis/<br>M. Gordon |
| Exactly Like You † | D. Fields/J. McHugh | W. Stevenson |
| Teach Me Tonight † | S. Cahn/G. De Paul | W. Stevenson |
| Let's Do It (Let's Fall In Love) † | C. Porter | W. Stevenson |
| It's Me † | W. Stevenson | W. Stevenson |
| It's Party Time | W. Stevenson | W. Stevenson |
| The Christmas Song (Chestnuts Roasting On An Open Fire) – Live From The Apollo | M. Torme/R. Wells | W. Stevenson |
| Down And Under When You Limbo | N. Whitfield/B. Strong | W. Stevenson |
| My Girl | W. Robinson/R. White | M. Gentile |
| It's Not Unusual | G. Mills/L. Reed | M. Gentile |

| | | |
|---|---|---|
| Sunny | B. Hebb | M. Gentile |
| Sweet Thing | W. Stevenson/ I. J. Hunter | W. Stevenson |
| I Love You Secretly (aka My Last Chance) | M. Gaye | M. Gaye |
| I Want To Come Home For Christmas | M. Gaye/F. Hairston | M. Gaye |
| 5, 10, 15, 20 Years Of Love | W. Boyd/A. Powell | H. Davis |
| You're My Everything (aka I'd Give My Life For You) | M. Gaye | M. Gaye |
| Come Get To This (live) | M. Gaye | M. Gaye |
| Mack The Knife | B. Brecht/K. Weill | H. Davis/ M. Gordon |
| Hello Young Lovers | R. Rodgers/ O. Hammerstein | H. Davis/ M. Gordon |
| Happy Days Are Here Again | J. Yellin/M. Ager | H. Davis/ M. Gordon |
| She Needs Me | J. Emerson/ E. Montgomery | M. Gaye |
| Funny | L. Holoscener/ E. Scott | M. Gaye |
| This Will Make You Laugh | I. Higginbotham | M. Gaye |
| I Wish I Didn't Love You So | F. Loesser | M. Gaye |

with * Mary Wells/†† Kim Weston/†† Oma Page née Heard

All tracks previously unreleased

The above is the proposed track listing for Motown's four cassette and four Compact Disc release as at October 1990. It is not planned to release the 81 tracks on record.

## British Seven-inch Singles

Following a brief association with London-America and Fontana (1959–1962), Motown licensed its recordings to Oriole Records in September 1962 for one year. That label was replaced by Stateside in October 1963 which released product until March 1965 when EMI Records opened the Tamla Motown label to service the world outside North America and Canada. This licensing association lasted until October 1981 when Motown moved to RCA Records (now known as BMG) and to date that relationship remains.

During 1976 the Tamla Motown logo was replaced by a newly-designed Motown label. The TMG numbering system remained until 1985 when a European system was introduced to enable UK Motown releases to be included in BMG's central numbering system.

This discography, which differs in parts from the US listing, is printed in record number order and does not include 12" singles. Certain releases are duets and Gaye's singing partners are identified in brackets.

| Record No | Record Title | Release Date |
|---|---|---|
| ORIOLE (CBA) | | |
| 1803 | Stubborn Kind Of Fellow | 2.1963 |
| | It Hurt Me Too | |
| 1846 | Pride And Joy | 7.1963 |
| | One Of These Days | |
| | | |
| STATESIDE (SS) | | |
| 243 | Can I Get A Witness | 11.1963 |
| | I'm Crazy 'Bout My Baby | |
| 284 | You're A Wonderful One | 4.1964 |
| | When I'm Alone I Cry | |
| 316 | Once Upon A Time | 7.1964 |
| | What's The Matter With You Baby | |
| | (with Mary Wells) | |
| 326 | Try It Baby | 8.1964 |
| | If My Heart Could Sing | |
| 360 | How Sweet It Is (To Be Loved | 11.1964 |
| | By You) | |
| | Forever | |
| 363 | What Good Am I Without You | 12.1964 |
| | I Want You 'Round (with | |
| | Kim Weston) | |
| | | |
| TAMLA MOTOWN (TMG) | | |
| 510 | I'll Be Doggone | 4.1965 |
| | You've Been A Long Time Coming | |
| 524 | Pretty Little Baby | 8.1965 |

|   | I Can't Believe You Love Me (with Tammi Terrell) |   |
|---|---|---|
| 718 | That's The Way Love Is | 11.1969 |
|   | Gonna Keep On Tryin' 'Til I Win Your Love |   |
| 734 | Abraham, Martin And John | 4.1970 |
|   | How Can I Forget? |   |
| 775 | What's Going On | 5.1971 |
|   | God Is Love |   |
| 796 | Save The Children | 11.1971 |
|   | Little Darling (I Need You) |   |
| 802 | Mercy Mercy Me (The Ecology) | 2.1972 |
|   | Sad Tomorrows |   |
| 817 | Inner City Blues (Make Me Wanna Holler) | 5.1972 |
|   | Wholy Holy |   |
| 846 | Trouble Man | 3.1973 |
|   | Don't Mess With Mister 'T' |   |
| 868 | Let's Get It On | 8.1973 |
|   | I Wish It Would Rain |   |
| 879 | You're A Special Part Of Me | 11.1973 |
|   | I'm Falling In Love With You (with Diana Ross) |   |
| 882 | Come Get To This | 1.1974 |
|   | Distant Lover |   |
| 890 | You Are Everything | 3.1974 |
|   | Include Me In Your Life (with Diana Ross) |   |
| 906 | Stop, Look, Listen | 6.1974 |
|   | (To Your Heart) |   |
|   | Love Twins (with Diana Ross) |   |
| 920 | My Mistake (Was To Love You) | 10.1974 |
|   | Just Say, Just Say (with Diana Ross) |   |
| 923 | I Heard It Through The Grapevine | 11.1974 |
|   | Chained |   |
| 953 | Don't Knock My Love | 7.1975 |
|   | I'm Falling In Love With You (with Diana Ross) |   |
| 984 | What's Going On | 2.1983 |
|   | God Is Love |   |
| 987 | What's Going On | 11.1983 |
|   | I Heard It Through The Grapevine |   |
| 993 | The Onion Song | 4.1985 |
|   | You Ain't Livin' Till You're Lovin' |   |
|   | (with Tammi Terrell) |   |
| 998 | You Are Everything | 4.1985 |

|      | Stop, Look, Listen (To Your Heart) |         |
|      | (with Diana Ross)                  |         |
| 1026 | I Want You                         | 4.1976  |
|      | I Want You (instru.)               |         |
| 1035 | After The Dance                    | 8.1976  |
|      | Feel All My Love Inside            |         |
| 1045 | I'm Gonna Make You Love Me         | 9.1976  |
|      | (A-side recorded by Diana Ross     |         |
|      | and the Supremes and The Temptations) |      |
|      | I Heard It Through The Grapevine   |         |
| 1047 | You Are Everything (with Diana Ross) | 9.1976 |
|      | The Onion Song (with Tammi Terrell) |        |
| 1069 | Got To Give It Up (Part 1)         | 4.1977  |
|      | Got To Give it Up (Part 2)         |         |
| 1136 | Pops, We Love You (with Diana Ross, Smokey | 2.1979 |
|      | Robinson, Stevie Wonder)           |         |
|      | Pops, We Love You (instru.)        |         |
| 1138 | A Funky Space Reincarnation (Part 1) | 2.1979 |
|      | A Funky Space Reincarnation (Part 2) |       |
| 1165 | Ben (A-side recorded by Michael Jackson) | 2.1980 |
|      | Abraham, Martin And John           |         |
| 1168 | Ego Tripping Out                   | 11.1979 |
|      | Ego Tripping Out (instru.)         |         |
| 1225 | Praise                             | 3.1981  |
|      | Funk Me                            |         |
| 1232 | Heavy Love Affair                  | 5.1981  |
|      | Far Cry                            |         |

TAMLA MOTOWN (TM)

| 1381 | Got To Give It Up (Part 1)         | 4.1985  |
|      | How Sweet It Is (To Be Loved By You) |       |

CBS

| 2855 | Sexual Healing                     | 10.1982 |
|      | Sexual Healing (instru.)           |         |
| 3048 | My Love Is Waiting                 | 12.1982 |
|      | Rockin' After Midnight             |         |
| 32421 | Joy                               | 3.1983  |
|      | Turn On Some Music                 |         |

| 4894 | Sanctified Lady (vocal) | 4.1985 |
| | Sanctified Lady (instru.) | |
| 6462 | It's Madness | 8.1985 |
| | Ain't It Funny (How Things Turn Around) | |

## TAMLA MOTOWN (TM)

| 40701 | I Heard It Through The Grapevine | 4.1986 |
| | Can I Get A Witness | |

## MOTOWN EUROPEAN SERIES (ZB)

| 40757 | The World Is Rated X | 6.1986 |
| | Lonely Lover | |

## TAMLA MOTOWN EXTENDED PLAY SINGLES (EP)
### TME

| 2016 | *Marvin Gaye* | 4.1966 |
| | Ain't That Peculiar/Pretty Little | |
| | Baby/I'll Be Doggone/How Sweet It | |
| | Is (To Be Loved By You) | |
| 2019 | *Originals From Marvin Gaye* | 3.1967 |
| | Can I Get A Witness/Stubborn Kind | |
| | Of Fellow/Baby Don't You Do It/ | |
| | You're A Wonderful One/Hitch Hike/ | |
| | Pride And Joy | |

## MOTOWN CASSETTE SINGLES
### ZV

| 40702 | *Marvin Gaye* | 4.1986 |
| | I Heard It Through The Grapevine/ | |
| | That's The Way Love Is/Can I Get A | |
| | Witness/You're A Wonderful One | |

MOTOWN EPS ON CASSETTE (MOTOWN FLIP HITS)
CTME

| | | |
|---|---|---|
| 2041 | *Marvin Gaye* | NR |
| | I Heard It Through The Grapevine/ | |
| | Cot To Give It Up (Part 1)/Too Busy | |
| | Thinking About My Baby/Abraham, Martin | |
| | And John | |
| 2042 | *Marvin Gaye & Tammi Terrell* | NR |
| | You're All I Need To Get By/The | |
| | Onion Song/You Ain't Livin' Till | |
| | You're Lovin'/Good Lovin' Ain't | |
| | Easy To Come By | |

## British Albums

This discography, in release date order, contains record numbers, release date and titles only except where track listing differs to the American release. It does not include reissues, various artist compilations or albums licensed to other record companies. Certain albums are duets and Gaye's singing partners are identified in brackets. All information is taken from original album sleeves.

| Record No | Album Title | Release Date |
|---|---|---|
| STATESIDE | | |
| 10097 | *Together* (with Mary Wells) | 10.1964 |
| 10100 | *Marvin Gaye* | 11.1964 |

*Tracks*
You're A Wonderful One
Get My Hands On Some Lovin'
Takin' My Time
Soldier's Plea
Hello There Angel
I'm Crazy 'Bout My Baby
Try It Baby
I'm Yours, You're Mine
Mister Sandman
Hitch Hike
Wherever I Lay My Hat

Can I Get A Witness
All tracks previously released

## TAMLA MOTOWN (TML/STML)

| 11004 | *How Sweet It Is* | *3.1965* |
| 11015 | *Hello Broadway* | *9.1965* |
| 11022 | *A Tribute To The Great* | *2.1966* |
| | *Nat King Cole* | |
| 11033 | *Moods Of Marvin Gaye* | *10.1966* |
| 11049 | *Take Two* (with Kim Weston) | 5.1967 |
| 11062 | *United* (with Tammi Terrell) | 1.1968 |
| 11065 | *Greatest Hits* | 2.1968 |

*Tracks*
Your Unchanging Love
Take This Heart Of Mine
Try It Baby
Pride And Joy
Stubborn Kind Of Fellow
One More Heartache
You're A Wonderful One
Forever
Can I Get A Witness
Now That You've Won Me
Baby Don't You Do it
Little Darling (I Need You)
Ain't That Peculiar
Pretty Little Baby
I'll Be Doggone
How Sweet It Is (To Be Loved By You)
All tracks previously released

| 11084 | *You're All I Need* | 10.1968 |
| | (with Tammi Terrell) | |
| 11091 | *In The Groove* | 1.1969 |
| 11119 | *MPG* | 9.1969 |
| 11123 | *Marvin Gaye And His Girls* | 1.1970 |
| 11132 | *Easy* (with Tammi Terrell) | 1.1970 |

| 11136 | *That's The Way Love Is* | 4.1970 |
| 11153 | *Greatest Hits* (with Tammi Terrell) | 8.1970 |
| 11190 | *What's Going On* | 9.1971 |
| 11201 | *The Hits Of Marvin Gaye* | 2.1972 |

*Tracks*
I Heard It Through The Grapevine
Abraham, Martin And John
What's Going On
Inner City Blues (Make Me Wanna Holler)
That's The Way Love Is
How Sweet It Is (To Be Loved By You)
Mercy Mercy Me (The Ecology)
Too Busy Thinking About My Baby
You
Your Unchanging Love
Chained
How Can I Forget?
The End Of Our Road
Little Darling (I Need You)
All tracks previously released

| 11125 STMA | *Trouble Man* | 2.1973 |
| 8013 STMA | *Let's Get It On* | 9.1973 |
| 8015 STMA | *Diana & Marvin* | 12.1973 |
| 8018 TMSP | *Live!* | 7.1974 |
| 1128 | *Anthology* | 5.1974 |

*Tracks*
Stubborn Kind Of Fellow
Hitch Hike
Can I Get A Witness
Baby Don't You Do It
Pride And Joy
You're A Wonderful One
Try It Baby

How Sweet It Is (To Be Loved By You)
What's The Matter With You Baby *
I'll Be Doggone
Pretty Little Baby
Ain't That Peculiar
One More Heartache
Take This Heart Of Mine
Little Darling (I Need You)
It Takes Two †
Your Unchanging Love
You
You're All I Need To Get By ††
Chained
You Ain't Livin' Till You're Lovin' *
I Heard It Through The Grapevine
Too Busy Thinking About My Baby
Abraham, Martin And John
Save The Children
That's The Way Love Is
The Onion Song ††
What's Going On
You're A Special Part Of Me §
Mercy Mercy Me (The Ecology)
Inner City Blues (Make Me Wanna Holler)
Trouble Man
Let's Get It On
All tracks previously released
* with Mary Wells/† with Kim Weston/†† with Tammi Terrell/§ with
Diana Ross (The US 3-album 'Anthology' was UK released on a 2-CD set
in 4.1987 – ZD 72534)

| 12025 | *I Want You* | 4.1976 |
| 12042 | *The Best Of Marvin Gaye* | 9.1976 |

*Tracks*
I Heard It Through The Grapevine
Too Busy Thinking About My Baby
That's The Way Love Is
Abraham, Martin And John
What's Going On

Inner City Blues (Make Me Wanna Holler)
Mercy Mercy Me (The Ecology)
Let's Get It On
Come Get To This
You Sure Love To Ball
I Want You
After The Dance (vocal)
Come Live With Me Angel
Save The Children
All tracks previously released

| TMSP | | |
| 6006 | *Live! At The London Palladium* | 4.1977 |
| TMSP | | |
| 6008 | *Here, My Dear* | 12.1978 |
| STMR | | |
| 9004 | *The Early Years 1961–1964* | 10.1980 |

*Tracks*
Can I Get A Witness
I'm Crazy 'Bout My Baby
Pride And Joy
Got To Get My Hands On Some Lovin'
One Of These Days
You're A Wonderful One
Hitch Hike
Try It Baby
Stubborn Kind Of Fellow
I'm Yours, You're Mine
Never Let You Go (Sha-Lu-Bop)
Taking My Time
Wherever I Lay My Hat (That's My Home)
Let Your Conscience Be Your Guide
Mister Sandman
It Hurt Me Too
All tracks previously released

| 12149 | *In Our Lifetime* | 2.1981 |
| CBS | | |
| 85977 | *Midnight Love* | 11.1982 |

| 26239 | *Dream Of A Lifetime* | 6.1985 |
| 26783 | *Romantically Yours* | 11.1985 |

MOTOWN (ZL)

| 72463 | *Motown Remembers Marvin Gaye: Never Before Released Masters + I Heard It Through The Grapevine* | 5.1986 |
| 72639 (WD) | *A Musical Testament: 1964–1984* | 7.1988 |
| 72645 | *18 Greatest Hits* | 1.1989 |

*Tracks*
I Heard It Through The Grapevine
Let's Get It On
Too Busy Thinking About My Baby
How Sweet It Is (To Be Loved By You)
You're All I Need To Get By
Got To Give It Up (Part 1)
You Are Everything †
Can I Get A Witness
I'll Be Doggone
What's Going On
Abraham, Martin And John
It Takes Two ††
Stop, Look, Listen (To Your Heart) †
Chained
Trouble Man
You Ain't Livin' Till You're Lovin' ††
The Onion Song *
Wherever I Lay My Hat (That's My Home)
All tracks previously released
* with Tammi Terrell/† with Diana Ross/†† with Kim Weston

| 72422 | *Compact Command Performances* | 6.1989 |
| 72508 | *Compact Command Performances: Volume Two* | 8.1989 |
| (ZK/ZD) | | |
| 72725 | *The Marvin Gaye Collection* | 1990 |

# Bibliography

Benjaminson, Peter – *The Story of Motown*
Davis, Sharon – *Motown: The History*
George, Nelson – *Where Did Our Love Go*
Hirshey, Gerri – *Nowhere to Run*
Ritz, David – *Divided Soul*
Robinson, Smokey – *Inside My Life*
Taraborrelli, J. Randy – *The Life And Career Of Diana Ross*
Williams, Otis – *Temptations*
Wilson, Mary – *Dreamgirl: My Life As A Supreme*
Wilson, Randall – *Forever Faithful*

All chart positions included in text are American unless otherwise stated. Information regarding UK and USA chart positions for all records were taken from Motown's in-house files, *Billboard's* charts, *Blues & Soul*, Guinness' *British Hit Singles Volume 7* (Paul Gambaccini/Tim Rice/Jo Rice), Honor Head's files, Joel Whitburn's *Top R&B Singles 1942–1988* and Jobete's in-house catalogue.

## PUBLICATIONS FEATURING INTERVIEWS INCLUDED

*Blues & Soul* – Bob Killbourn/David Nathan/John Abbey/Jeff Tarry/
Roger St Pierre/Justin Lubbock/Scott Taylor
*Black Music* – Chris May
*Echoes* – unknown
*NME* – Cliff White/Gavin Martin/Chris Salewicz
*Melody Maker* – Paolo Hewitt/David Frick
*Sounds* – unknown
*The Sunday Times* Magazine – unknown
*The Daily Mirror* – unknown
*The Sun* – unknown
*The Daily Star* – unknown
*Billboard* – Nelson George
*Record World* – unknown

*Crawdaddy* – Paul Bernstein
*Soul* – unknown
*Ebony* – unknown
*Rolling Stone* – Tim Cahill/Michael Goldberg
*Goldmine* – Wayne Jancik
*San Francisco Chronicle* – unknown
The Detroit *Courier* – unknown
*The Los Angeles Times* – unknown
*The Washington Post* – Tom Zito
*The* Los Angeles *Herald* – unknown
The Los Angeles *Daily News* – unknown

ALBUM SLEEVE NOTES (previously uncredited)

Dream of A life
Motown Remembers Marvin Gaye

FILM/RADIO FEATURING INTERVIEWS INCLUDED

Marvin Gaye – Transit Ostend
Motown Remembers Marvin Gaye
A Soul Divided – Stuart Grundy
The Marvin Gaye Story – Tony Blackburn

AUTHOR'S INTERVIEWS AND CONVERSATIONS
INCLUDED

Larkin Arnold
Nickolas Ashford
Rose Banks
Bertha Barbee-Fairhurst
Norma Barbee-McNeil
Graham Betts
Graham Canter
Carolyn Crawford
Lady Edith Foxwell
Marvin Gaye
Carolyn Gill
Mildred Gill-Arbour
Dave Godin

Brenda Holloway-Davis
Marv Johnson
Lynda Lawrence
Ian Levine
Scherrie Payne
Barbara Randolph
Martha Reeves
Valerie Simpson
Eddie Singleton
Dusty Springfield
Edwin Starr
Syreeta
Jean Terrell
Gill Trodd
Mary Wells
Kim Weston
Mary Wilson

## PICTURE ACKNOWLEDGEMENTS

*Blues & Soul*
Motown/EMI Records
Pete Scotney Collection
Jeff Tarry Collection
Peter Vernon
Wiltshire Music
Justin Thomas

# Index